The Dutch Wars of I╷

In *The Dutch Wars of Independence*, Marjolein 't Hart assesses the success of the Dutch in establishing their independence through their eighty years' struggle with Spain – one of the most remarkable achievements of the sixteenth and seventeenth centuries. Other rebellions troubled the major powers of this epoch, but none resulted in the establishment of an independent, republican state. This book:

- tells the story of the Eighty Years War and its aftermath, including the three Anglo-Dutch wars and the Guerre de Hollande (1570–1680)
- explores the interrelationship between war, the economy and society, explaining how the Dutch turned their wars into commercial successes
- illustrates how war could trigger and sustain innovation in the economic field and in state formation as the new ways of organization of Dutch military institutions favoured a high degree of commercialized warfare
- shows how other state rulers tried to copy the Dutch method of commercialized warfare, in particular adopting the protection of capital accumulation. As such, the book reveals one of the less known pillars of European state formation (and of capitalism).

The volume investigates thoroughly the economic profitability of warfare in the early modern period and shows how smaller, commercialized states could sustain the prolonged war violence common to that period. It moves beyond traditional explanations of Dutch success in warfare with a focus on geography, religion and diplomacy, while presenting an up-to-date overview and interpretation of the Dutch Revolt, the Anglo-Dutch wars and the Guerre de Hollande.

Marjolein 't Hart is head of research at the Huygens Institute for the History of the Netherlands (Royal Netherlands Academy of Arts and Sciences) in The Hague and professor of the History of State Formation at VU University Amsterdam. She has published extensively on the early modern history of the Netherlands (from a comparative perspective), including books on warfare and state formation (1993) and financial history (1997).

MODERN WARS IN PERSPECTIVE
General Editors: H.M. Scott and B.W. Collins

This ambitious series offers wide-ranging studies of specific wars, and distinct phases of warfare, from the close of the Middle Ages to the present day. It aims to advance the current integration of military history into the academic mainstream. To that end, the books are not merely traditional campaign narratives, but examine the causes, course and consequences of major conflicts, in their full international political, social and ideological contexts.

Also in the series:

The Dutch Wars of Independence

Warfare and Commerce in the Netherlands 1570–1680

Marjolein 't Hart

Routledge
Taylor & Francis Group

LONDON AND NEW YORK

First published 2014
by Routledge
2 Park Square, Milton Park, Abingdon, Oxon OX14 4RN

and by Routledge
711 Third Avenue, New York, NY 10017

Routledge is an imprint of the Taylor & Francis Group, an informa business

© 2014 Marjolein 't Hart

British Library Cataloguing in Publication Data
A catalogue record for this book is available from the British Library

Library of Congress Cataloging in Publication Data
Marjolein 't Hart.
The Dutch wars of independence : warfare and commerce in the Netherlands 1570–1680 / Marjolein 't Hart.
pages cm. – (Modern wars in perspective)
Includes bibliographical references and index.
1. Netherlands–History–Eighty Years' War, 1568-1648. 2. Netherlands–History–Eighty Years' War, 1568-1648–Economic aspects. I. Title.
DH186.5.H37 2014
949.2'03–dc23
2013033353

ISBN: 978-0-415-73422-6 (hbk)
ISBN: 978-0-582-20967-1 (pbk)
ISBN: 978-1-315-81707-1 (ebk)

Typeset in Sabon
by Taylor and Francis Books

To Karel Davids
for his loving companionship in life and history

Contents

List of tables

List of figures

Timeline of major events

1549	Unification of the Low Countries under Habsburg Emperor Charles V
1555	Abdication of Charles V; King Philip II of Spain becomes ruler of the Low Countries
1566	Iconoclast revolts
1567	Duke of Alva becomes governor-general of the Low Countries
1568	Unsuccessful invasion by William of Orange of the Low Countries; Battle of Heiligerlee; beginning of the Eighty Years War
1572	Capture of Brill and Flushing; meeting of the rebellious provincial states of Holland; William of Orange becomes stadholder
1573	Alva replaced by Requesens as governor-general
1576	Mutiny of Spanish soldiers; 'Spanish Fury' in Antwerp; Pacification of Ghent
1578	Amsterdam joins rebellious provinces; Farnese, later Duke of Parma, becomes governor-general of the Low Countries
1579	Union of Arras (Spanish Netherlands) and Union of Utrecht (rebellious north)
1584	Death of William of Orange
1585	Maurice becomes stadholder; Antwerp taken by the Spanish; arrival of Leicester as governor-general of the rebellious provinces
1586	Van Oldenbarnevelt becomes grand pensionary
1587	Departure of Leicester
1588	Establishment of the Dutch Republic
1596	Archdukes Isabella and Albert become governors-general of the Spanish Netherlands
1598	Philip III becomes King of Spain
1602	Formation of East India Company
1602–4	Siege of Ostend
1604	Spinola becomes commander-in-chief of the Army of Flanders
1609–21	'Twelve Years Truce' between Spain and the northern Netherlands
1609–14	Dutch military involvement in the War of the Jülich Succession
1618–19	Political conflict between Maurice and Van Oldenbarnevelt; Van Oldenbarnevelt executed

1621	Philip IV becomes King of Spain
1625	Death of Maurice; Frederick Henry becomes stadholder
1629	Siege of 's-Hertogenbosch
1633	Cardinal-Infante Ferdinand appointed governor-general of the Spanish Netherlands
1635–59	Franco-Spanish War
1647	Death of Frederick Henry; William II becomes stadholder
1648	Peace of Münster; end of Eighty Years War; formal recognition of the independence of the Dutch Republic
1650	William II's offensive against Amsterdam; death of William II
1651	Beginning of First Stadholderless Period
1652–4	First Anglo-Dutch War
1653	John de Witt becomes grand pensionary
1657–61	Dutch-Portuguese War
1658–60	Danish-Swedish War; involvement of the Dutch Republic in the fighting around the Baltic
1665–7	Second Anglo-Dutch War
1666–7	Dutch-Münster War
1672–4	Third Anglo-Dutch War; wars with Münster and Cologne
1672–8	War with France
1672	Death of John de Witt; William III becomes stadholder
1688	Glorious Revolution; William III and Mary become king and queen of England, Ireland and Scotland
1795	French invasion; end of the Dutch Republic

Map 0.1 Map of the Dutch Republic around 1650

NORTH SEA

GRONINGEN

Groningen

FRIESLAND

DRENTHE

OVERIJSSEL

Hoorn

Enkhuizen

Kampen

ZUIDER ZEE

Zwolle

Purmerend

Haarlem

Amsterdam

Deventer

Leiden

UTRECHT

HOLLAND

The Hague

Delft

Utrecht

Waal

GELDERLAND

Gouda

Rotterdam

Dordrecht

Nijmegen

ZEELAND

Breda

s'Hertogenbosch

Veere

Tilburg

GENERALITY LANDS

Middleburg

Bergen-op-Zoom

Vlissingen

Maas

Rhine

Maastricht

0   50 mls

0   80 kms

Introduction

The Dutch Revolt, the Military Revolution and the global context

> Of all the World they [the Dutch] are the people that thrive and grow rich by
> Warre, which is the Worlds ruine, and their support.[1]

The success of the Dutch in establishing their independence through their eighty
years' struggle with Spain was one of the most remarkable achievements of the
sixteenth and seventeenth centuries. Other rebellions troubled major powers of
this epoch, but none resulted in the establishment of an independent, republican
state. Other early modern rebels seized power, but none managed to retain it
with a federal, urban-based system of government. Other European wars
interlinked with increasing globalization, but none promoted international
capitalist structures so vigorously. And while virtually the whole of Europe was
racked by conflicts, none yielded so much long-lasting profit to the belligerents
as the Eighty Years War did for the Dutch.

Most early modern wars brought physical destruction and financial ruin to
the belligerents, irrespective of whether they were on the winning or losing side.
The Dutch Wars of Independence, however, coincided with a true Golden Age.
The economy boomed, immigrants arrived in flocks, numerous entrepreneurs
started and extended their businesses, overseas trading posts and colonies were
established, and the arts and sciences flourished. The paradox of such an
exceptional profitable war did not escape the attention of contemporaries. The
famous Amsterdam burgomaster Pieter Corneliszoon Hooft remarked:
'Whereas it generally is the nature of war to ruin land and people, these countries have been noticeably improved thereby';[2] the English author Owen Feltham noticed: 'War which is the worlds ruin, and ravins upon the beauty of all,
is to them [the Dutch] Prosperity and Ditation';[3] and the Council of State of the
United Provinces observed:

> War is ruinous for other countries, but it did strengthen the United Provinces
> in its trade, riches, and power, it did improve its territories and cities, and
> those funds extracted from the common people seemed to return by other
> ways again, like the waters which are transported by the rivers into the sea
> and which are returned by nature to its resources in a way unknown to us.[4]

On the side of the other belligerent, the Council of State of the Spanish Netherlands observed in the last decade of the sixteenth century:

> For several years now the Dutch have waged war on us outside their own territories; ... it is remarkable how they carry out warfare for such a long time at no costs, even enriching their country, exhausting the treasuries and condition of his Majesty and ruining all the provinces.[5]

Although the war was expensive for the northern Netherlands, this book argues that the economic benefits of the Dutch Wars of Independence depended upon an early example of successful commercialization of warfare, exemplified above all by the province of Holland. To secure long-lasting profits from war exploits, an independent territorial state was indispensable, a state geared towards the furthering of trade and industry, a state also providing sufficient protection against hostile incursions from outside and securing the property of the well-to-do burghers, irrespective of their ethnic backgrounds or religious beliefs. Such a state was only accommodated through strong military institutions which supported large numbers of soldiers. In the early modern period, the presence of troops usually brought distress and insecurity to the population, not least through attacks on civilians and army mutinies that affected living circumstances and property rights in a negative spiral, yet Dutch armed forces proved an exception in this regard. That is the reason this book revives a crucial but largely forgotten aspect of Michael Roberts' Military Revolution thesis: discipline. Dutch soldiers behaved in a disciplined way because the army demonstrated a strong professionalizing ethos and because it was paid on time. Instead of causing destruction, the substantial expenditure on warfare (soldiers' pay, naval establishments, fortifications and interest payments on loans) could thus stimulate economic demand. The economic benefits of warfare in the northern Netherlands went far beyond the most obvious windfall of the war: colonial trade. Naturally, the Golden Age was not caused by the war. Yet war was endemic in early modern Europe, and the question is how warfare was able to contribute to Dutch economic growth. Above all this book hopes to reveal the 'unknown ways', in the words of the Dutch Council of State quoted above, in which much of the voluminous military expenditure was pumped back into Dutch economy and society and thus furthered the Dutch Golden Age and, in its turn, the global expansion of Western Europe.

Interpretations of the Dutch Revolt

The interpretation of this book deviates from the standard stories of the Dutch Wars of Independence that stress either conservative or modernizing tendencies, establish either statist or revolutionary achievements – with either the bourgeoisie or the Calvinists in the vanguard – and accentuate either the civil war disturbances or the more regularized struggle to achieve national independence.[6] What started out in the 1560s as a scattered revolt against Spanish and local oligarchic rule connected to a wish for greater tolerance in religion, reduced taxation and the defence of local privileges, furthered by class struggles instigated by increased economic distress, turned into a civil war by the early 1570s, with a particular strong Calvinist minority. The conflict evolved subsequently into a more moderate movement with increasingly national traits a decade or so later, involving increasingly a number of larger provinces and resulting eventually in an independent federal state dominated by a powerful merchant class.[7] Widespread popular unrest destabilized the regime mainly in the later 1560s, yet declined thereafter; resistance against Alva's tenth penny furthered the revolutionary cause but became a hollow theme as soon as the rebel regime imposed far higher taxes; while the role of Calvinist ideology in mobilizing opposition was undoubtedly strong, religious discontent faded, though it was to remain a permanent factor in the conflict.[8] In my view the Dutch Revolt was multifaceted; never did 'the rebels' constitute a homogeneous entity: some revolted for a religious cause, others for more freedom or more power; some for a restoration of their family's authority, while others just wanted to get rid of the Spanish troops. In fact, 'the rebels' harboured many a contradictory strategy.

The naming of the war varies too, with historians who study the earlier decades – stopping in 1609 or even before – preferring 'Dutch Revolt', while works that include the last phases of the war tend to speak of 'the Eighty Years War'. The title adopted for this study, 'The Dutch Wars of Independence', recognizes the distinctive stages of the conflict: urban revolt, provincial revolt, civil war, struggle for national independence, international power struggles and economic warfare, up to 1648. For a while the term Eighty Years War was viewed as rather old-fashioned, but it has been revived by a recent internationalist perspective looking, for example, at the struggle from the viewpoint of the Spanish opponent or discerning similarities and links with the French Wars of Religion and the Thirty Years War, or stressing the global character of the fighting.[9] Indeed, the Eighty Years War involved numerous states. Apart from the Low Countries and Spain, England and France were also heavily involved (sending subsidies, troops, governors and even a potential ruler); numerous German princes were personally involved, such as Frederick V, the former king of Bohemia and Elector Palatine;[10] manpower was supplied by German and Italian territories; the links between the two Habsburg realms were all too obvious; and last but certainly not least, the struggle extended to the Far East and other overseas areas.

This book will use the terms Dutch Revolt, Eighty Years War and the Dutch Wars of Independence interchangeably, dependent upon the scope of the argument. Now and then I will label the Dutch troops 'rebels', but only in the first decades; from the 1580s warfare attained a more regular character. The starting date of my investigation is around 1572, when the Provincial States of Holland assumed sovereign powers and raised troops of their own. Although peace was signed in 1648, the terminal date of my study is around 1680, after the Treaty of Nijmegen removed the direct military threat of France. This permits a full examination of the Franco-Dutch War of 1672–78, when the independence of the northern Netherlands was again at risk. Ending thirty years after 1648 also allows me to investigate possible longer-lasting social and economic consequences of the Dutch Wars of Independence and examine the impact and consequences of the first three Anglo-Dutch wars as well.[11]

The Military Revolution, its societal impact and global repercussions

In studying the interrelation between war, economy and society this book profits enormously from the fact that military history has lost its isolation during the last decades. Scholars have increasingly investigated the links between state power and military elites, the lot of the common soldier and the economic bases of army operations such as provisioning and taxation.[12] Throughout the early modern period powerful states experienced usually limited difficulties in *raising* troops; *keeping* those men under arms proved much more exacting as few rulers had the disposal of adequate and reliable mechanisms to provision and fund them.[13]

This book also links up with the old but still on-going debate regarding the thesis of the Military Revolution. In my view this debate has remained strongly military and statist, with most participants focusing on the timing of tactical developments, the size of armies and the consequences of new fortifications. What is largely overlooked or neglected is Michael Roberts' initial stress on the societal consequences of the late sixteenth century military developments.[14] This study will show that the Dutch military, fiscal and political reforms of the late sixteenth century *collectively* constituted an outstanding development in military history, with far-reaching economic and societal consequences for the northern Netherlands.

Above all, the reforms of Maurice of Nassau in the 1590s gave the Dutch Republic substantial military staying power, which served its struggle against Spanish rule but entailed global ramifications as well. Scholars have emphasized that the consequences of the advanced military developments did not halt at the North Sea coast but pertained also to the 'Rise of the West', not least because of significant improvements in naval warfare.[15] The role of European military institutions in gaining world-wide dominance was not as straightforward as is usually assumed, however.[16] It was not so much the possession of firearms or the application of tactical measures that in the end proved decisive for the colonizing Europeans; much more important was the societal context of military power, their practical experience and logistics of training, organization and supply, combined with the economic capacity to maintain their pressure. The majority of the non-European armies remained essentially aggregations of individual warriors who were able to fend off most hostile attacks up to the nineteenth century. But it was the enduring presence of the Europeans that constituted the problem. European fortresses could be captured by other Europeans, yet they rarely fell to native sieges.[17] In the course of decades and even centuries it was their long-lasting military presence that allowed Europeans to intervene and reap the fruits when indigenous powers suffered from (temporary) internal weaknesses or crises.

Scholars from the school of world systems regard global wars – that is, wars between contenders for power on the global scale – crucial for the redefinition of world economic relations. In this line of thought the Dutch Wars for Independence ranked among those rare global wars that overturned an existing pattern of relations; the Dutch Republic emerged victorious and surpassed the former world leader (Spain, which also ruled Portugal) in both military and economic respects.[18] What was remarkable about the United Provinces was their staying power, so vital for stable and profitable national and international capitalist connections, despite and even most probably (as this book will show) also due to warfare. Although this was not a unique phenomenon for Italian city-states like Genoa and Florence, it was for territorial states. Scholars have observed in Venice some kind of 'military Keynesianism' through which military expenses boosted the income of the citizens, allowing for increased taxation, enabling in turn even higher spending and thus advancing the power of the city-state still further.[19]

Although the conducive economic effects for warfare have been established for the Venetian case, no such study exists as yet for the Dutch Republic. Michiel de Jong investigated the profits in the armaments industry, yet virtually all other scholars focused on the negative consequences of war, such as privateering and trade bans.[20] In 1975 Geoffrey Parker enumerated the substantial losses at sea and on land and concluded that the costs of the Revolt weighed more than the gains, for both Spain and the Netherlands. Expanding on Parker's analysis Wilfried Brulez estimated the net war costs roughly at 13 per cent of the trade and 16 per cent of the Low Countries' industrial production, in both north and south.[21] Yet such calculations use the economy of the 1560s as standard, excluding possible wartime shifts in production and the appearance of new economic openings because of the war. The most recent estimates of the development of Dutch GNP suggest that growth rates accelerated between 1570 and 1650, to stagnate thereafter. What is more, the substantial rise of government from around 5 per cent to 10 per cent in the later sixteenth century, mainly because of the extension of the army and navy, did not seem to hamper growth rates – perhaps even the contrary.[22] On the whole, though, historians are remarkably silent on the subject of possible beneficial wartime effects on the Dutch economy.[23]

Warfare, territorial state formation and capital accumulation

But how was wartime economic growth possible in view of the fact that wars usually carried disastrous consequences for the belligerents?[24] Few European states had developed the instruments to extract the necessary resources from society without hurting the economy; even fewer managed to have war gains counterbalance the war costs.[25] Sheer territorial size was important in this respect, as it furthered diversity and permitted imperial rulers to tap resources from various groups or regions, but for small states (like the Dutch Republic) no such options existed. For them it was not so much the size of armies that mattered but rather how warfare stimulated the economy and, in its turn, how economic growth supported warfare. That cycle provided the real basis of Dutch endurance: the organization of their military institutions favoured a high degree of commercialized warfare, stimulated their trade and furthered new capitalist networks. In other words: the Dutch knew how to make money out of organized violence, with continuing profits in the longer term.[26]

In most of Europe, warfare served above all the territorial aspirations of European rulers. In general, monarchs attempted to strengthen their prestige and enlarge their lands. The logic of accumulating territorial power surely did not always stand in the way of merchants and entrepreneurs; the extension of such state power enabled among other things more stable opportunities and improved protection along trade routes. The larger the empire the more secure the trade with communities further away; a larger territory permitted merchants to extend their long-distance networks. The rise of Antwerp, profiting from the widening trade networks of the Spanish Habsburg Empire, provides a convincing example of such benefits; also the trade accrued by Amsterdam during the rule of Charles V thanks to the peace with other territories.[27] However, such advantages often faded during long-lasting wars since any accumulated private funds were desperately needed to pay the soldiers. More often than not, no institutions existed to protect the merchants and entrepreneurs from burdensome taxation, defaulting repayments on government loans, injurious debasements of the currency, or outright exactions by territorial rulers. The decline of Antwerp because of recurrent state bankrupcies (the Spanish Habsburgs failed in 1557, 1575, 1596, 1607, 1627 and 1647), which ruined numerous banking houses, illustrates the dilemma for all early modern capitalists.

During wartime, capital funds needed a safe environment to ensure a steady development in the longer term. Merchants developed familial, ethnic or religious networks to reduce the risks but this was often not sufficient to counterbalance the demands of 'voracious' rulers.[28] Before the seventeenth century only a handful of self-governing cities, mainly in the north of Italy, managed to create dependable conditions for the 'logic' of capital accumulation for *all* the inhabitants on their territory. The Dutch Republic was the first *territorial* state that provided comparable services for capital owners.[29] In return for reasonable and predictable taxes the traders and entrepreneurs in Holland received adequate territorial protection with all its advantages *plus* unequalled financial services *plus* a colonial trade network. The Bank of Amsterdam created a stable unit of account (the bank guilder) that provided – among other things – useful currency for trade, the navy protected the major trade routes, advanced litigation procedures regulated all sorts of smaller and larger transactions, and the Amsterdam Bourse provided information regarding the major international trade routes. These services lowered transaction costs and helped to safeguard the value of accumulated funds.[30] Only in the eighteenth century did a number of other European governments begin to recognize the advantages of stimulating both 'logics' – not just the one that extended territorial power but also the one that served capital accumulation of domestic capitalists. Britain was the first to copy the Dutch successfully in this respect.[31]

Up to that time most European wars were predominantly capital destructive – with the remarkable exception for the Dutch in the Eighty Years War. This undoubtedly facilitated the rise of the northern Netherlands as the core of the new capitalist world-system and strengthened the shift of economic gravity within Europe from the Mediterranean to the Atlantic coastal economies of the north-west.[32] The twin results of the Dutch Wars of Independence, *national independence* and *efficient state formation*, were thus crucial for the rapid economic maturation in the northern Netherlands. Any continuation within the Habsburg imperial system would have forestalled that development by several decades or even centuries. The example of Antwerp demonstrated the injurious effects of warfare dominated by monarchical territorial ambitions: the state bankruptcies disrupted the confidence in capitalist property rights and numerous Antwerp-based entrepreneurs preferred to move their networks to Dutch cities like Amsterdam, Middelburg and Rotterdam.

About this book

A recent synthesis of the history of the seventeenth-century Netherlands concluded that 'The republic of 1650 was still reaping the fruits of a wartime economy,' not least because 'the interaction between military exploits and economic development contributed to the favourable outcome of war.'[33] To gain insights into the how of that interaction, this book divides its argument into eight chapters. Chapter 1 provides a general overview of the most important military and political developments between *c*.1570 and *c*.1680 and analyses the different strategies of the belligerents; it offers the historical context of the subsequent chapters. Chapter 2 follows in explaining how the Dutch managed to establish a comparatively professionalized force at an early stage, a *conditio sine qua non* for all further developments. Above all, the reorganization of the military by Orange deserves substantial credit. The implications of the Maurician reforms in tactics are dealt with in Chapter 3; the formation of military discipline is regarded as the outstanding phenomenon, with far-reaching consequences for society and economy, not least because that discipline permitted the Dutch to enjoy their economic earnings within a situation of relative stability at home. How the reforms, involving numerous fortifications and garrisons, affected the urban populace is discussed in Chapter 4. Here the first clear advantageous signs of warfare are discerned, since a substantial part of the war expenditure was pumped back into the towns. However, warfare also had its dark side in the Netherlands, above all for the countryside, which I explore in Chapter 5; a partial transfer of wealth from the peasantry to the towns was the result. This points to a crucial finding of this book: the war seems to have been particularly favourable for the trading communities in the province of Holland, but was less positive for the inland provinces and sometimes quite detrimental for the agrarian population. Chapter 6 discusses the costs and beneficial effects of maritime warfare. While the costs turn out much lower than is assumed in prevailing historiography, the degree of naval protection along trade routes is shown to have been impressive, from which above all local merchant communities profited. The new power at sea supported colonial companies that explored new ways of capital accumulation. Chapter 7, then, establishes the substantial advantages in Dutch war finance, with a tax and loan flexibility unequalled in early modern Europe; its redistributive effects further stimulated economic demand, above all in the province of Holland. The last chapter discusses the crucial links between warfare and the economy in the northern Netherlands, notably the enormous profitability of the Republic's arms trade and how the (new) economic opportunities accrued in particular to Holland to the detriment of other provinces. Throughout the book my aim is to put the military experiences and repercussions in a comparative perspective. The Conclusion will discuss the interrelation of war and economy in the context of early modern Europe and stress the specific conditions that permitted the rise of the Dutch Golden Age during the Dutch Wars of Independence.

My research has profited enormously from the recent studies that emanated from the NWO-research programme 'War and Society during the Golden Age' of the University of Amsterdam (2001–6); this book also aims to bring their findings into a new synthesis.[34] Erik Swart's book on the professionalization of the Dutch army in its first decades proved of enormous help for Chapters 2 and 3; Peter de Cauwer's study on the 's-Hertogenbosch Siege of 1629 yielded significant insights for Chapters 3 and 4; Griet Vermeesch' work on two garrison towns was indispensable for the writing of Chapters 4 and 7; Olaf van Nimwegen's study on the States' army provided a wonderful context for Chapters 2 and 3; and last but certainly not least, Leo Adriaenssen's book on the Brabant experiences of war furnished excellent material for Chapters 5 and 8. In addition I profited from other recent work of Dutch scholars, above all Michiel de Jong's book on the Dutch arms trade and Paul Holthuis' study on Deventer during the war; the results of the project *Gewestelijke Financiën* under the leadership of Wantje Fritschy allowed for new financial reconstructions; and Ronald de Graaf's general study on the Eighty Years War also yielded new knowledge regarding the local effects of war.[35] The studies by Pepijn Brandon, Thomas Goossens and Jeff-Fynn Paul from the VNC-project 'Networks of State and Capital' gave further insights that permitted a strengthening of my argument.[36] Columbia University offered an extremely hospitable environment that stimulated me to write the book.[37] Friends and colleagues read parts of the manuscript and were kind enough to suggest improvements; I am grateful to Leo Adriaenssen, Herman Amersfoort, Dan Bogart, Pepijn Brandon, Adriaan de Kraker, Jeff Fynn-Paul, Wantje Fritschy, Oscar Gelderblom, Thomas Goossens, Martha Howell, Joost Jonker, Paul Knevel, Emmanuel Kreike, Deirdre McCloskey, Maarten Prak, Natalie Scholtz, Erik Swart, Bas van Bavel, Petra van Dam, Joris van den Tol, Roelof van Gelder, Henk van Nierop, Milja van Tielhof and Griet Vermeesch. I owe special thanks to Hamish Scott for his enormous encouragement during the writing process and his meticulous improvements to language and style. I devote my book to Karel Davids, for his loving companionship in life and history.

Notes

1 Anon., *Dutch Drawn to Life*, p. 42 [orig. 1664].
2 Quoted by Geyl, *Revolt*, p. 233.
3 Feltham, *Brief Character*, p. 84 [orig. 1652]. Ditation = enrichment.
4 Dutch Council of State on 1637, quoted by Aitzema, *Historie of verhael*, II, p. 427. The term United Provinces, northern Netherlands and the Dutch Republic all signify more or less the territory north of the major rivers Meuse and Rhine; in this book 'Low Countries' is used for the southern and northern Netherlands together.
5 Quoted by Swart, *Krijgsvolk*, pp. 171–2.
6 General overviews of the different interpretations include Van Nierop, 'Troon', pp. 205–23; 't Hart, 'Dutch Revolt'; Noordegraaf, 'Economie en Opstand'. For works on the Dutch Revolt with reference to sociological theories, see Nadel, 'Logic', Ellemers, 'Revolt', and Schöffer, 'Dutch Revolt'. Marxist interpretations include Kuttner, *Hungerjahr*; Griffiths, 'Revolutionary character'; Tilly, *European Revolutions*, p. 66; Brandon, 'Marxism and the Dutch miracle'; for an overview see Van der Linden, 'Marx und Engels' and Ingenthron, 'Einleitung', pp. 16–104. On modernizing tendencies, see Zagorin, *Rebels and Rulers*, II, p. 80; on civil war aspects: Van Nierop, *Noorderkwartier*.
7 The term 'national' is an anachronism, yet the idea connotes territorial sovereignty, and this was the case for the Dutch Republic. 'State' is likewise a problematic term, yet the following chapters will show that the bureaucracy of the Provincial States of Holland and the government by the Dutch States General were quite efficient and state-like. See also 't Hart, *Making*.
8 The number of Calvinists was very small, though; Van Gelder, *Revolutionnaire reformatie*, p. 22; Koenigsberger, 'Organization', p. 343; Woltjer, *Tussen vrijheidsstrijd*, p. 55; Boogman, 'Overgang'; Van Nierop, *Verraad*, pp. 156–7. On the tenth penny: Grapperhaus, *Alva*.
9 Pollmann, 'Internationalisering'; on the weaknesses of the Catholic communities: Pollmann, 'Countering'; stressing the position of the opponent: Parker, *Dutch Revolt* and also De Cauwer, *Tranen*; pointing to the global character of the war: Thompson, *War and Society*, III, p. 262.
10 Groenveld, *Winterkoning*.
11 In addition, my choice of the time period is guided by the available studies that arose out of the NWO programme 'War and Society during the Golden Age', which includes studies that partly extended to 1680; see also footnote 3.
12 Duindam, 'Geschiedschrijving', pp. 455–6; Ulrich, 'Militärgeschichte';Wilson, 'German history', pp. 423–7; Vermeir, *In staat*; Rowlands, *Dynastic State*; Kroener and Pröve, *Krieg*; Kroener, 'Soldat'; Lynn, *Feeding Mars*; Nimwegen, *Subsistentie*; Bonney, *Economic Systems*.
13 Parrott, 'Strategy', p. 245.
14 Though Roberts saw this as primarily proceeding from a strengthened state. For a handy introduction regarding the debate: Rogers, 'Military Revolutions'; Black, *European Warfare*, pp. 3–11; see also Drake, *Problematics*, p. 260; Murray and Knox, 'Thinking about revolutions', p. 13.
15 Parker, *Military revolution*, p. 4; Black, 'Military revolution?', p. 104; Kyriazis, 'Seapower', p. 100. I focus on the military aspects and do not discuss other factors that furthered European dominance, such as the role of epidemic diseases and environmental conditions; see Wolf, *Europe*; Diamond, *Guns*; McNeill, *Plague*; Richards, *Unending Frontier*.

16 Cipolla, *Guns*, pp. 138, 144–5; Thompson, 'Military superiority thesis'; Lorge, *War*, p. 172.

17 Black, 'Military revolution?', pp. 108–10; Black, *European Warfare*, pp. 28, 237; Howard, 'Tools', p. 240; Chase, *Firearms*, p. 200; Roy, 'Hybrid military establishment', pp. 215–17; Hoffman, 'Prices', p. 51; Parker, *Military Revolution*, pp. 120, 130–1, 136. Parker notes that the East Asian peoples were only subdued after 1800, when the industrial revolution produced extremely efficient killing machines.

18 Modelski, 'Long Cycle', pp. 214–35; Thompson, *Global War*; Rasler and Thompson, *War and State Making*; Davids and Lucassen, *Miracle Mirrored*; Prak, *Dutch Republic*.

19 Arrighi, *Long Twentieth Century*, p. 38; Lane, *Profits*. Lane, 'Family partnerships', describes how the merchants did not need to worry about long-run overhead costs of a merchant fleet as they could rent the vessels from the Arsenal. The term Keynesianism refers mainly to economic growth led by demand, not to the impact of warfare; Keynes himself was opposed to military expenditure, which he regarded as inherently unproductive. See also Coulomb and Fontanel, 'Disarmamanent', p. 198; Bernstein and Wilson, 'New Perspectives', p. 4; Engel, 'Not yet a garrison state', p. 176.

20 De Jong, *Staat*; Israel, *Dutch Primacy*, p. 124; Snapper, *Oorlogsinvloeden*. The findings of these studies are discussed in the following chapters.

21 Parker, *Spain*, pp. 178 ff. (an extended version of the 1975 article); Brulez, 'Gewicht', p. 403. See also Stradling, 'Spanish Dunkirkers', p. 557. To calculate the possible gains and losses of the war falls beyond the scope of this book. Instead, it tries to unravel how commercialization of warfare actually worked in the case of the Dutch Republic.

22 Van Zanden, 'Economic growth', p. 270. The proportion of government in GDP declined sharply after 1650, back to around 5 per cent again; see Van Zanden and Van Leeuwen, 'Persistent', p. 123. One of the innovative aspects of the approach by Van Zanden and Van Leeuwen is that they include the economic effects of the employment in government in their calculations, thus also the army and the navy.

23 See for example the standard work of De Vries and Van der Woude, *First Modern Economy*. In another work Van der Woude noted remarkable economic benefits of the Münster Peace settlement, thus *after* the war; see Van der Woude, 'Vrede', p. 104. In an earlier publication De Vries points to the important notion that wars tend to dislocate economic activities rather than influencing them; De Vries, *Economy of Europe*, p. 22.

24 On the endemic warfare: Jones, *European Miracle*; on its disastrous consequences: Vries, 'Governing growth'; cf. also the thesis of imperial overstretch: Kennedy, *Rise*.

25 Vries, 'Governing growth', p. 82.

26 McNeill, *Pursuit of Power*, p. 69 uses the term commercialization of organized warfare in relation to mercenaries. This book will show that true commercialization went beyond the – often short-term – profits of mercenaries.

27 Van der Wee, *Growth*, pp. 340, 348. Among other things Charles V also introduced legislation that improved contract negotiability and reduced the risks in trading.

28 Greif, *Institutions*; Blockmans, 'Voracious states'.

29 Arrighi, *Long Twentieth Century*, p. 135. Next to the 'logic' of territorial power, a mechanism among major rulers that tends to accumulate control over territories, Arrighi discerns a 'logic' within capitalist structures in which capital furthers accumulation of capital.

30 Lesger, *Handel*; Neal, 'How it all began', pp. 120–2. These insights link up with the recent trend in economic history, following Douglass North, to stress the role of institutions in economic development, not least the lowering of transaction costs. North, *Structure and Change*; Van Zanden and Van Riel, *Strictures*; Glete, *War and the State*.

31 Arrighi, *Long Twentieth Century*, pp. 45–6; Wilson, *England's Apprenticeship*; Sombart, *Krieg und Kapitalismus*, p. 33.
32 Wallerstein, *Modern World System*, II, p. 37; Braudel, *Civilisation*, III: chapter 3; Chase-Dunn, *Global Formation*, p. 166; Arrighi, *Long Twentieth Century*, pp. 127 ff.
33 Frijhoff and Spies, *Hard-Won Unity*, p. 18. Unfortunately, the authors do not expand further into the background of that interaction.
34 Dossier 360-51-000; participants: Henk van Nierop, Herman Amersfoort, Olaf van Nimwegen, Erik Swart, Peter de Cauwer, Griet Vermeesch, Leo Adriaenssen, and the author of this book.
35 Swart, *Krijgsvolk*; De Cauwer, *Tranen*; Vermeesch, *Oorlog*; Van Nimwegen, *Deser landen crijghsvolck*; Adriaenssen, *Staatsvormend geweld*; De Jong, *Staat*; Holthuis, *Frontierstad*; De Graaf, *Oorlog*. Tracy's recent *Founding Republic* provided numerous new details regarding the first decades of the Republic. I also want to thank the participants of the conference in Rijswijk (2005) on War and the Golden Age: The Netherlands in comparative perspective, *c*.1550–1700; of the Conference of the Economic History Association in Toronto 2005; of the Amsterdam University History staff seminars; of the seminars at the Amsterdam Centre for the Study of the Golden Age; and of the Social and Economic History seminars in the History department at Utrecht University.
36 'Netwerken van Staat en Kapitaal: Oorlog, Militaire Instituties en Ondernemers in de Nederlanden (*c*.1670–*c*.1795)', VNC Dossier 205-53-234; Brandon, *Masters of War*; Goossens, *Staat, leger*; Fynn-Paul (ed.), *War, Entrepreneurs*.
37 With thanks to the subsidy from NWO, Dossier 365-51-016.

1 Military events

From the Dutch Revolt to 'la Guerre de Hollande', c.1570–c.1680

We are destroyers of citadels but builders of free cities.[1]

The war that became known as the Dutch Revolt or the Eighty Years War started as a series of minor revolts in the Low Countries against the lawful overlord, Philip II King of Spain. The movement gained ground as towns and whole provinces allied themselves to the rebels and by the 1580s the Dutch Republic was firmly institutionalized. The military confrontation proved to be extended, lasting many decades – not least because the terrain, by nature already intersected with waters and marshy grounds, was additionally dotted with numerous fortresses and strongly fortified towns. Any military operation in this area was doomed to lose momentum before long; in a couple of months defenders (from either side) were able to regain their strength. That the terrain was stronger than man was shown on numerous occasions: during the Spanish advances of 1573 and 1629 in the north and the Dutch campaigns of 1568 and 1635 in the south, and again in 1672 when the French invasion was forced to stop short at Holland's provincial borders. Not only the terrain but also the capacities of the belligerents caused the Dutch Wars of Independence to last so long. The Spanish monarchy drew enormous resources from its imperial base, while the Dutch had the advantage of outstanding logistics as part of their war finances and a burgeoning economy. What follows is an overview of the most significant political and military developments, concluded by a summary of the contrasting strategies of the belligerents. The chapter also provides essential context for the other chapters of this book.

The Dutch Revolt and the struggle for survival, 1570s to 1580s

Being one of the wealthiest and most urbanized regions of Europe, the Low Countries cherished their 'liberties and privileges' under Spanish-Habsburg rule. Emperor Charles V had just united the 17 provinces in 1549 (see Figure 1.1). The relationship between the overlord and his subjects was one of fluctuating loyalty and criticism. After the abdication of Charles V, criticism directed against his son Philip II intensified. Like all other major upheavals, the Dutch

1 Friesland
2 Groningen
3 Overijssel with Drenthe
4 Holland
5 Utrecht
6 Gelderland
7 Zeeland
8 Brabant
9 Flanders
10 Mechelen
11 Limburg
12 Luxembourg
13 Artois
14 Doornik
15 Hainault
16 Namur
17 Cambrésis

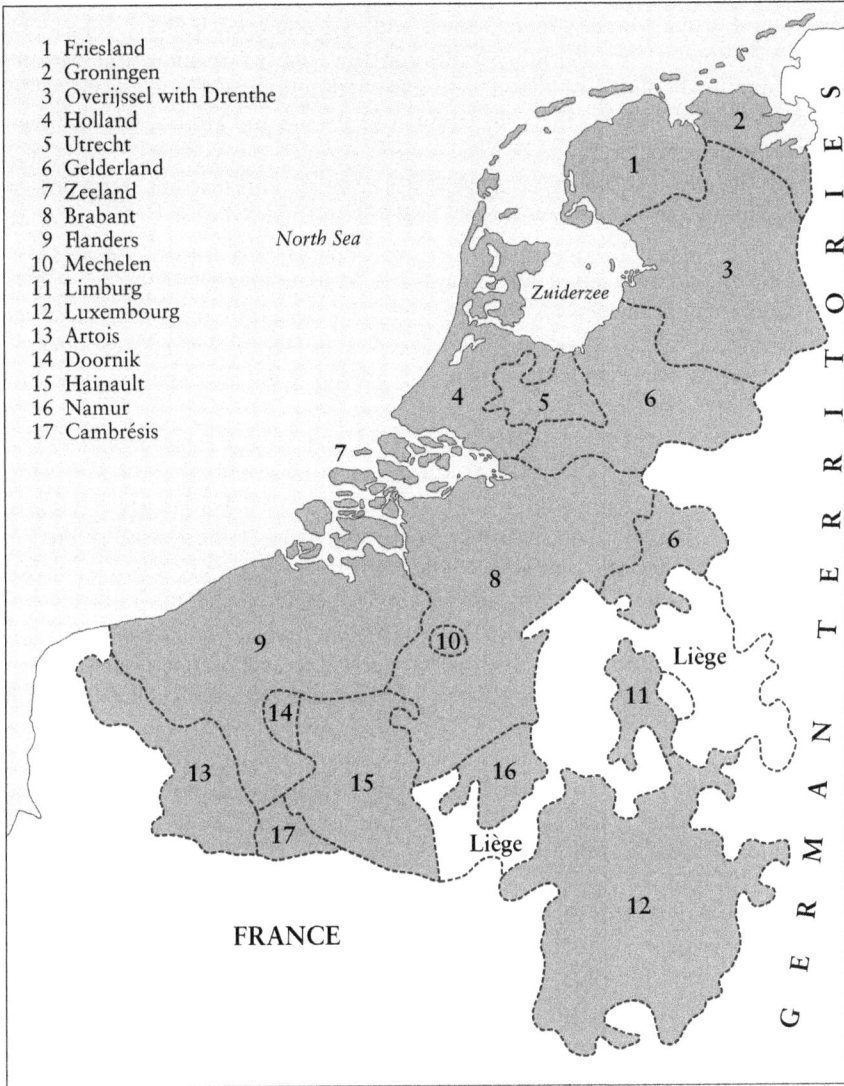

Figure 1.1 Map of the Low Countries around 1550

Revolt was caused by a mix of unstable conditions and highly varied discontent that involved several layers of society at the same time. After repeated large-scale open-air Calvinist sermons and iconoclast outbursts had threatened Catholic rule, the Spanish king sent the Duke of Alva in 1567 as the new governor-general to restore order. Alva was convinced that his work of pacification would be a matter of just a couple of months, not least because of the numerous factional divisions in the Low Countries, but also because the Spanish troops were at that time Europe's largest, best trained and best equipped military force.[2] The duke was known for his ruthless attitude towards his enemies and within a short time his 'Council of Blood' had over a thousand of the regime's 'adversaries' executed, among others the counts of Egmond and Hoorn, who belonged to the highest nobility.[3]

From the start Alva's expert troops were unruly and insolent, regarding all inhabitants of the Low Countries as heretics and harassing the citizens of the towns in which they were quartered.[4] In response, the much weaker Dutch rebel forces adopted 'small war' tactics. A band of lesser nobles and adventurers who called themselves *Watergeuzen* (Sea Beggars) engaged in raids and privateering along the coast, while the *Bosgeuzen* (Wood Beggars) conducted a bitter, low-intensity guerrilla campaign, predominantly in the Flanders and Brabant countryside.[5]

William of Orange, who – unlike Egmond and Hoorn – had not wished to rely on a possible reconciliation with the Spanish government, had taken refuge at his parental estate in Germany and refused to appear before Alva's punitive court. Before long all other potential political leaders of the resistance died on the scaffold or were taken prisoner, which left him as the only major nobleman able to take up arms. However, his attempt to invade the Low Countries with an army in 1568 misfired when Alva successfully applied the strategy of simply wearing out his opponent's troops. That same year, in the far north-east, the first battle of the Eighty Years War took place at the small village of Heiligerlee, to the east of Groningen, between the armies of the Count of Aremberg for Spain and Count Louis of Nassau, Orange's brother. The confrontation ended in a victory for Louis, and at the Ems estuary the Sea Beggars defeated a Dutch royalist fleet. Yet these victories were soon followed by a series of defeats for the rebels, and for a couple of years the outlook for the Beggars was extremely bleak.[6]

On the first of April 1572 prospects suddenly changed with the capture of the small town of Brill, a small fishing town on the west coast, by the Sea Beggars. Shortly after, Flushing (in Zeeland) and Enkhuizen (in the north of Holland) rose in revolt too. These three ports assured a strategic position for the rebels on Holland's major overseas trade routes. Within a couple of months other towns joined the Revolt, some pushed by rioting of the populace and restive militias, others because of shifting alliances or a coup within the urban government, while yet others were conquered by Beggars or forced to join because their trade routes had been effectively blocked by the rebels. Economic distress, caused by among other things flooding and high prices in preceding years, and sheer hatred for the Spanish soldiers added to the tension.[7] Orange once more assembled an army. The capture of Mons (capital of Hainault) by Louis of Nassau and the involvement of Huguenot forces distracted Alva's troops southwards and enabled a major re-alignment of the revolutionary forces in the north in 1572.

This permitted the famous gathering of the States of the Province of Holland on 19 July 1572, assembled in a truly revolutionary meeting in the old town of

Dordrecht.[8] Previously the provincial delegates had met only on the request of the Spanish governor-general, mainly to discuss tax levies and loans, yet now they asserted sovereign powers over their territory. Refusing a royal summons to appear at The Hague, the delegates in Dordrecht also decided to proclaim William of Orange as their new stadholder (in Dutch *stadhouder*, literally place-keeper, the representative of the lawful sovereign) instead of the Count of Bossu, appointed by the governor-general. The assembly also furnished Orange a sound territorial-political base and the means to pursue his armed resistance, supported by the loans and tax revenues of the province. This backing rendered Orange's military operations of 1572 far more important than those of 1568, even though his aim to gain a stronghold in the south (Mons) failed again. Without the Dordrecht meeting the Dutch Revolt would have simply comprised a mixture of local rebellions, piracy, religious strife, and civil war with which the superior Spanish forces, aided by the typically factious nature of urban and provincial government in the Low Countries, might well have coped. Yet the revolt of the townspeople of Holland in the spring of 1572 and the subsequent convention of the independent States-Provincial in the summer created a focal point of resistance against Spain (see Figure 1.2). Of the major Holland towns only Amsterdam remained loyal to the king, at least for another six years. After the province's leading city joined the rebel cause, the independent staying power of Holland assured the continuation of rebel war efforts throughout the Dutch Wars of Independence.[9]

As soon as Alva recaptured Mons in September the struggle turned rapidly in favour of the Spanish. Mechelen was seized and its inhabitants massacred, followed by the equally brutal treatment of Zutphen and then Naarden. All three were intended to serve as examples of how Alva would reward a decision to support Orange. Haarlem was besieged next, yet by then the Spanish raids had clearly lost their momentum. The town eventually capitulated but only after a siege that lasted six long months and contributed to Spanish military exhaustion. During the following siege at Alkmaar the troops even refused to assault the town because they had not been paid. Meanwhile the Dutch towns strengthened their defences and warfare increasingly became a protracted phenomenon. One of Alva's commanders, Chiapino Vitelli, had already warned in 1572:

> That by reason of the Sea and Rivers, Merchandise did very much abound there; as also monies and victuals: and that every Town there was so strong by Nature, that allow but a little time to Industry, every Pass would require an Army to overcome it, and every Siege almost an Age to finish it.[10]

This view was corroborated in a letter from Alva himself to the Spanish king in 1573:

> You cannot conceive the great number of troops that is required to invest a position in this country. There is no place, great or small, not even the most wretched village that has not a water-filled ditch that requires bridging for its passage.[11]

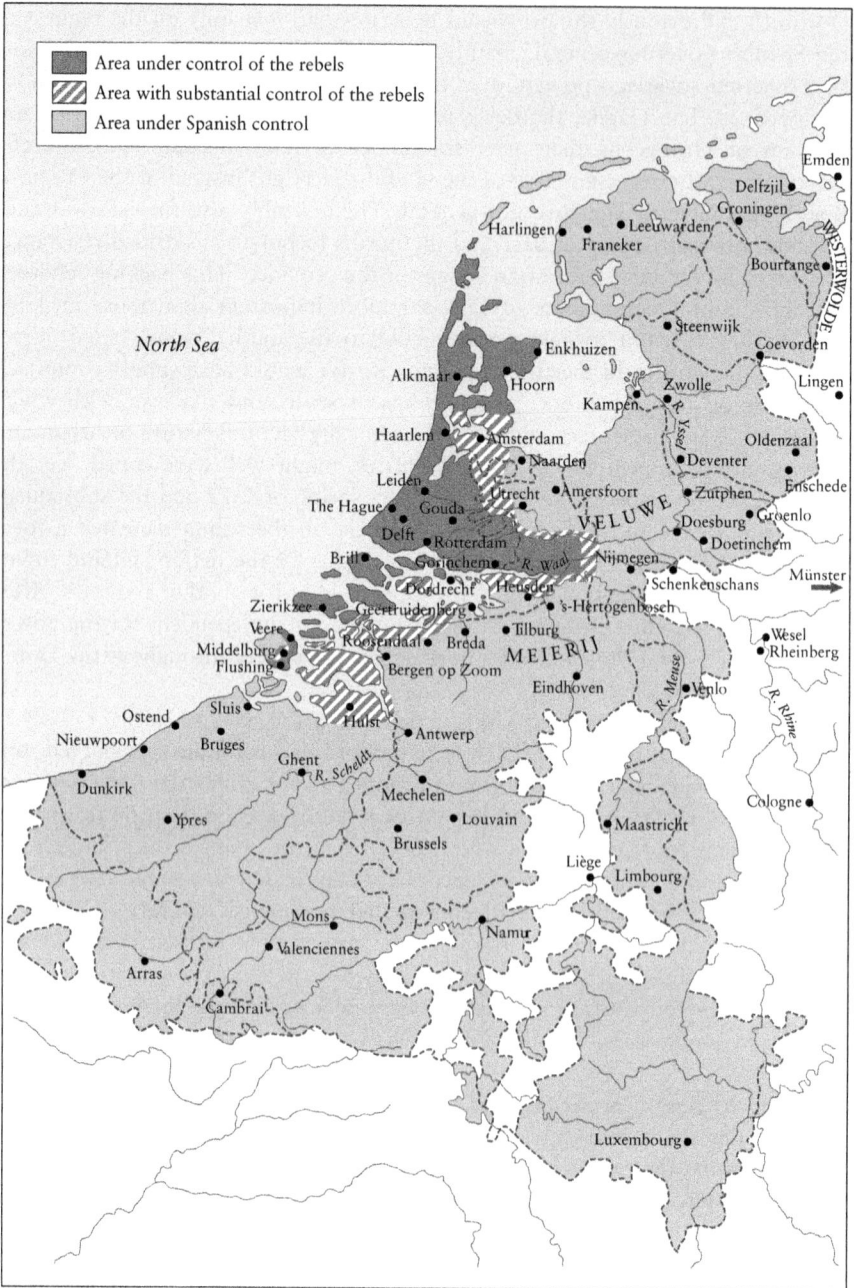

Figure 1.2 Map showing the spread of the Dutch Revolt in the autumn of 1572, with the location of places mentioned later in the text

Alva was replaced as governor-general by Requesens in 1573. This time no fewer than 86,000 troops were put into action; they must have consituted the largest army of sixteenth-century Christendom. Madrid was convinced of the urgency of the situation: the new governor-general was allowed to spend no less than ten million guilders a year. Yet despite his enormous assets Requesens also realized that

> There would be no time or money enough in the world to reduce by force the twenty-four towns that have rebelled in Holland, if we are to spend as long in reducing each one of them as we have taken similar ones so far.[12]

Indeed, Leiden was besieged twice in vain; mutinies and desertions depleted the strength of the Spanish troops by one third between December 1573 and January 1575. Even so the Dutch encountered enormous difficulties in expelling the Spanish from the territory of Holland. The rebel forces could prevent the Army of Flanders from advancing but not drive it out. In 1575 The Spanish achieved a deep penetration into the rebels' core region with the taking of the small towns of Buren, Oudewater, Schoonhoven and Krimpen aan de Lek, but from then on their position deteriorated. The fact that powerful Amsterdam remained loyal to the king up to 1578 was of remarkably little importance, since the major entrepôt did not control any significant part of Holland's countryside. In addition, the town's trade languished because of the rebel blockades. In Zeeland the fall of Zierikzee in 1576 constituted a temporary success for the Spanish; when the soldiers mutinied directly afterwards, the military power of the Army of Flanders collapsed.[13]

The difficulties the Spanish encountered in their efforts to subjugate the Hollanders had little to do with advanced fortification works in the style of the *trace italienne*, as has been suggested by some scholars; these were only completed in subsequent decades.[14] More important was Madrid's setting of imperial priorities; time and again the Army of Flanders failed to receive sufficient funds because Spain's military involvements elsewhere (against the Ottomans, the French, and in northern Italy) took precedence.[15] But the sheer number of Dutch-held towns, above all in Holland and Zeeland, was also important. In the eastern Netherlands the area was difficult to traverse because of extended moorland in Groningen, Drenthe and Overijssel. The Yssel river tended to be shallow and could be crossed rather easily, yet a string of fortified towns, fortresses and redoubts prevented an uncomplicated passage. Likewise along the two major rivers, the Rhine and the Meuse, fortifications strengthened the Dutch lines of defence. Orange, the commander of the Holland troops, deployed his forces with tactical defence in mind, aiming at the exhaustion of the enemy, and took full advantage of the terrain by carrying out strategic inundations.[16]

By 1576 the Holland 'garden' was relatively secured and, after Amsterdam was pressed by blockades to join the Revolt, war was kept out of Holland's core region; the major battlegrounds moved towards the Yssel river area in the east and the districts to the south of the Rhine and Meuse. By the later 1570s the military confrontations gained a more conventional character with the increased authority of provincial and Union institutions. After 1576 the Revolt thus gradually shifted from a rebellion into a struggle for territorial independence.[17]

Meanwhile the war effort had strained Spanish finances and in 1575 Philip II declared the state bankrupt; all payments were halted. The sudden death of Requesens left a power vacuum and the Army of Flanders fell into disarray. Mutinous soldiers drifted about, carrying out outrages – principally the infamous Sack of Antwerp, which killed thousands and set whole neighbourhoods alight. The widespread atrocities and disorder prompted the signing of the Pacification of Ghent in 1576. For the time being the political adversaries decided to cooperate and a restructured States-General, representing several of the most powerful provinces of the Low Countries, called for a restoration of domestic order.[18]

The States-General assumed sovereign powers following the 1576 Pacification treaty and raised an army of their own. Philip II's success in winning over towns by reconciliation, however, eroded Dutch willingness to maintain a closed front against the Spanish. Orange was eventually appointed as general commander of the troops. He was one of the few Dutch leaders who continued to think in terms of the wider conflict, but discontent with his strategy increased as each major town demanded priority in the deployment of forces to deal with their particular problems, such as the suppression of mutineers in their neighbourhood. Differences between Catholic and Calvinist factions also came to a head again.[19] In early 1579, the Union of Arras (nowadays in the north of France) rallied the Catholic regions and towns under the king's leadership and was followed by the signing of the Union of Utrecht, in which mainly northern provinces and towns agreed to cooperate more closely under the leadership of the States-General (see Figure 1.3).

This division radicalized the struggle, and in due course the divisions between north and south were solidified by the successes of the new military leader in the south: Alexander Farnese (who became Duke of Parma in 1586). Major renewed financial injections from Spain accompanied his campaigns and within only 12 years his troops (numbering a staggering 80,000) reconquered no fewer than 83 towns, mainly located in the southern Netherlands.[20] Parma started to restore obedience to the king in the provinces bordering France. The capture of Dunkirk and Nieuwpoort followed, thus re-establishing footholds on the sea; in Dunkirk he immediately installed an admiralty board for the *Armada de Flandes* that was set to attack Dutch fisheries and overseas trade.[21] Then Parma went on to capture a series of major southern towns – Brussels, Mechelen, Bruges, Ypres and Ghent – employing his field army effectively and cleverly contriving river blockades. His impressive range of successes was crowned by the recapturing of Antwerp in 1585. In the north too significant territories were lost to the Spanish, notably the towns of Groningen and Oldenzaal, since Georges of Lalaing, stadholder of the provinces of Friesland, Groningen, Drenthe and Overijssel, switched sides from the Union of Utrecht to the Union

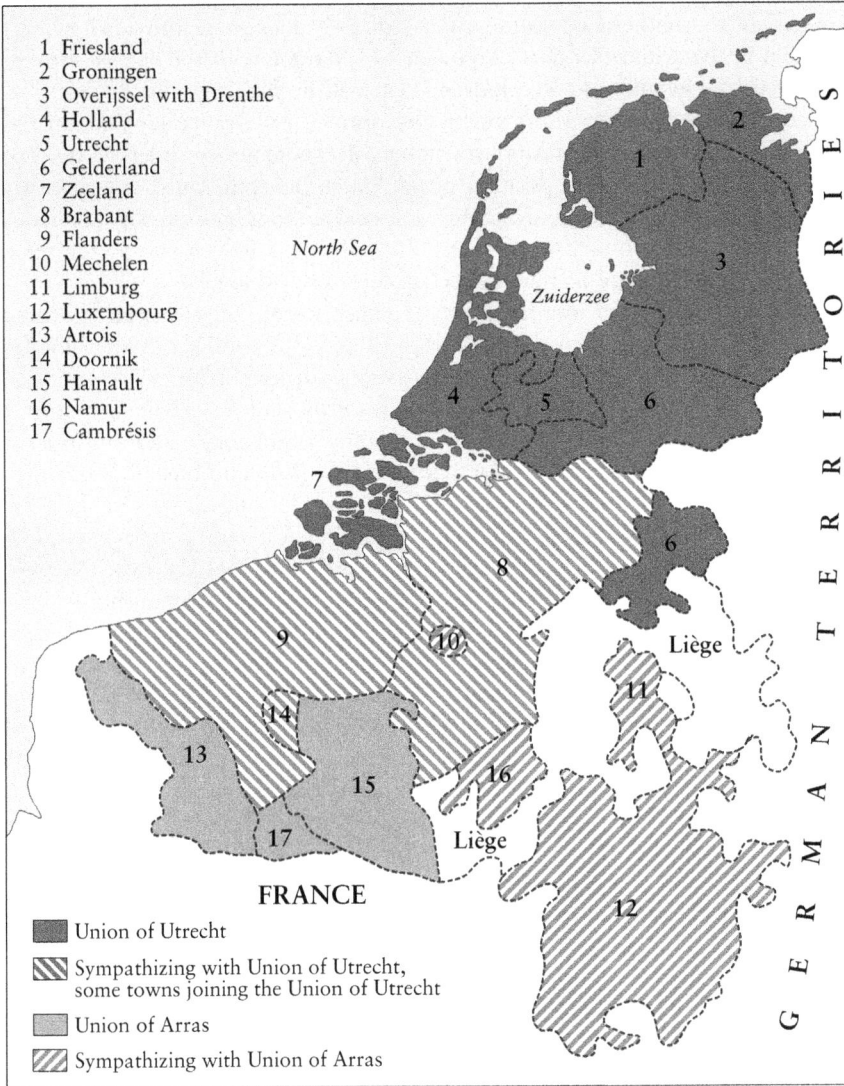

1 Friesland
2 Groningen
3 Overijssel with Drenthe
4 Holland
5 Utrecht
6 Gelderland
7 Zeeland
8 Brabant
9 Flanders
10 Mechelen
11 Limburg
12 Luxembourg
13 Artois
14 Doornik
15 Hainault
16 Namur
17 Cambrésis

North Sea

Zuiderzee

Liège

Liège

FRANCE

GERMAN TERRITORIES

■ Union of Utrecht

◫ Sympathizing with Union of Utrecht, some towns joining the Union of Utrecht

▢ Union of Arras

▨ Sympathizing with Union of Arras

Figure 1.3 Map of the Low Countries in 1579, showing the division in the Union of Arras and the Union of Utrecht

of Arras. His successor Francesco Verdugo managed to conquer the towns of Steenwijk and Coevorden, while the Overijssel town of Zutphen was taken by surprise by his fellow commander Taxis.

The States' army, in the field since 1576, proved no match for the much more centralized and efficient Spanish. Initially the Dutch army encountered enormous financial difficulties because Holland and Zeeland were reluctant to contribute to southern operations; most of the funds were provided by war-stricken Brabant and Flanders. Arguments over trade with the enemy, strongly favoured by Holland and Zeeland and opposed by Flanders and Brabant, further weakened joint efforts. General disapproval of Orange's pliant attitude towards the French duc d'Anjou, a potential candidate for ruler of the Low Countries, jeopardized the position of the States-General; Anjou's unsuccessful coup against Antwerp in January 1583 damaged Orange enormously. Soldiers in the French-Dutch military force destined to relieve Eindhoven bluntly refused to obey Laval, the general of the cavalry appointed by Anjou.[22]

In 1584 Orange was murdered by a Spanish agent. This was an enormous loss to the States as it deprived the Dutch of a skilful politician, one of the few who had been able to counter particularistic tendencies in the meetings of the Provincial States of Holland and mediate between radical Calvinists and more moderate factions. The troops lost their supreme commander, and this loss was also significant. In the far north Orange's nephew William Louis of Nassau was appointed stadholder for Friesland; Holland and Zeeland chose Orange's son, Maurice of Nassau, the following year. The fall of Antwerp in 1585 implied the disappearance of a solid financial base, and on top of that the major town of Nijmegen, in the eastern Netherlands, decided to re-join the Spanish.

Thus, by the middle of the 1580s the prospects for the rebels had again become poor. Parma's reconquest of the cities of Flanders and Brabant was almost complete, apart from Sluis, Ostend and Bergen op Zoom. The attempts to secure foreign support for the United Provinces came to nothing as neither Henry III of France nor Elizabeth I of England wanted to become directly involved at this point. The queen was prepared to send her favourite, the Earl of Leicester, with 7,000 troops. The period of Leicester's command (1585–7) has rightly been labelled a formative period for the Dutch Revolt. A political crisis arose because the earl could not and would not cope with the well-established political culture of towns' bargaining, which led to the conscious choice of a republican state model over (centralized) monarchy.[23] Van Oldenbarnevelt, appointed grand pensionary of the Provincial States of Holland (a position comparable to prime minister nowadays) in 1586, was to lead the opposition to Leicester's centralizing policies. The points of conflict were many and varied, but particular difficulties were caused by Leicester's attempt to impose a ban on all trade with the Spanish Netherlands, while his hard-line Calvinist stance gave rise to much discontent. He resented the rather tolerant policy of the Dutch urban oligarchs and chose Utrecht, not a Holland town, as his government's residence after Utrecht's town council was purged with the support of the Calvinist militia.[24]

Leicester's political base weakened as his army failed to relieve Sluis in Flanders from a Spanish siege in the summer of 1587. The town was lost to Parma's forces. In addition an English garrison in Overijssel defected to the enemy.[25] Leicester tried to stir up opposition against the urban councils in Holland but his strategy failed and he departed for England, leaving the military forces in great confusion. Among others the English in the Geertruidenberg garrison in Holland mutinied and eventually defected to the Spanish. It was some consolation then that the English and Dutch navies defeated the famous Spanish Armada in 1588; this significantly undermined the prestige of Philip II and brought Parma's successes to a halt. After that year, the Dutch were able to begin a counter-offensive.

Respite and consolidation in the 1590s

After his impressive series of successes in the 1580s, Parma began to besiege Bergen op Zoom in Brabant, but prospects suddenly changed when the death of King Henry III (1589) resulted in a political crisis over the succession in France that lured Spanish forces away from the northern Netherlands. The Dutch were now allowed some respite, which they exploited to the full. The first 20 years of the Revolt, the 1570s and 1580s, can truly be characterized as a struggle for survival, but the 1590s brought expansion and consolidation. This permitted the Dutch military leaders to improve their army's organization and experiment with new tactics. Ironically, the loss of almost all the southern territories (including the rich provinces of Flanders and Brabant) in the 1580s had strengthened the strategic position of the United Netherlands, now a more compact territory with good interior lines of communication, in particular the Rhine and Waal rivers. Furthermore, the loss of Antwerp and Brussels contributed to the province of Holland's domination of the Union of Utrecht, particularly after the departure of Leicester. Despite the fact that the Dutch Republic was a federation, the sheer financial might of Holland (which provided almost 60 per cent of the war funds) enabled unofficial centralized tendencies in the field of finance and logistics, cleverly advanced above all by the Pensionary Van Oldenbarnevelt. Throughout the Dutch Revolt Holland's strength enabled it to overcome some of the worst particularistic inclinations. The position of the young Maurice of Nassau was significantly strengthened in 1590 and 1591 when he obtained the post of stadholder for the provinces of Utrecht, Gelderland and Overijssel alongside his stadholdership of Holland and Zeeland. In the north his cousin William Louis was stadholder for Friesland (the stadholderships for Groningen and Drenthe were added in 1594 and 1596), and the cooperation between the two was excellent. The elderly William Louis acted periodically as Maurice's mentor in tactics and strategy.

In March 1590 Spanish-controlled Breda was taken by surprise, yet such easy successes were not to be expected in the short term. Their High Mightinesses, as the delegates in the States-General were called, were determined to strengthen the army. In 1591 Maurice had control over a field army consisting of 9,000 infantry and 1,500 cavalry – still much less than the Spanish forces, but these were partly occupied in France. Maurice started his counter-offensive in the east, linking up with the forces of William Louis, and after sieges lasting only a couple of days the Yssel towns of Zutphen and Deventer both capitulated. In the north Groningen still proved too strong, but Delfzijl (crucial for Groningen's trade, thus permitting an effective rebel blockade of the city) fell to the States. Then the Dutch managed to recapture Hulst in the south and the major city of Nijmegen in the east. The latter surrendered unexpectedly rapidly because of disagreements between the citizens and the garrison.[26]

Overall, 1591 had been an enormously successful year for the Dutch and established Maurice's reputation as a great military leader. But all the sieges so far had required relatively little effort; the military operations of 1592 met with much more resistance. The siege of the Overijssel town of Steenwijk was bloody and long-lasting and the taking of Coevorden in Drenthe was likewise hazardous, but both resulted in Dutch gains. In December 1592 Parma died, which further weakened the Spanish position. The siege of Geertruidenberg in 1593 resulted in a triumph for the Dutch: now all of Holland was free of Spanish soldiers and this operation in particular showed Maurice's outstanding military skills. William Louis called this success: 'a signal victory that skilful direction and patient labour are more potent in warfare than brute force'.[27]

In the following year, 1594, the major town of Groningen in the north was at stake. The siege lasted two months and the town capitulated mainly because the citizens wished to join the rebels, preferring Protestant rule to economic decline resulting from trade blockades. In 1595 the new French king Henry IV declared war on Spain and an alliance was concluded in which the Dutch supported the French with subsidies. But an attempt to relieve Cambrai from the Spanish failed and in the eastern Netherlands Maurice and William Louis were unable to strengthen their positions. 1596 was another year of disappointments for the Dutch. In Brussels a new governor had arrived, Archduke Albert, bringing with him more than 8,000 highly trained and motivated Spanish and Italian soldiers.[28] The new military commander showed enormous determination: first he captured Calais and then directly went on to besiege Hulst. Maurice's troops were outnumbered (Elizabeth I had recalled her 2,200 English soldiers) and he could not prevent the capitulation of Hulst to the Spanish.

This defeat spurred the States-General to vote for a significant enlargement of the field army to 10,000–12,000 troops. A spectacular victory by the Dutch followed at Turnhout (1597, in Brabant), where the Spanish were taken by surprise, not least due to the clever manoeuvring of the English forces under the command of Sir Francis Vere. Then the Spanish took Amiens (Picardy, France), the town that had been used by the French king to store quantities of artillery and ammunition. All French troops were now involved in trying to regain this town. While the Archduke's troops remained committed at Amiens, Maurice and William Louis managed to take Rheinberg, an important fortress on the Rhine that controlled trade on the river, followed by the successful capture of a number of other places in the east: Meurs, Groenlo, Bredevoort, Enschede, Oldenzaal, Ootmarsum and Lingen.[29]

Now the Dutch position in the eastern Netherlands was secured and the Republic controlled a more consolidated territorial area: the 'garden' was closed.[30] This had been exactly the strategic aim of the States' military leaders; William Louis had declared in 1589 that one need not to concentrate on Flanders or Brabant but besiege all towns on the rivers, such as Deventer or Zutphen on the Yssel, Nijmegen on the Waal, Grave, Venlo or Roermond on the Meuse, or Groningen. First one, then the next. ... As soon as all river towns are captured, the smaller inland towns are to follow, because they will lose their roots and nourishment and will easily fall into our hands. ... In this way the Garden of the United Netherlands is enlarged and strengthened and can be defended thereafter with fewer difficulties and concerns.[31]

Stalemate and truce, 1600–1621

By the later 1590s, with the consolidation of Dutch territory, the character of warfare changed: the frontiers were more compact and thus more defensible. What was at stake now for the Dutch was to retain what had been gained, because the Spanish were unlikely to accept the independence of the northern Netherlands. The coronation of Philip III (1598–1621) brought a new ruler anxious to get his name in the history books, and the French had agreed to a peace treaty with Spain at Vervins (1598) after they recaptured Amiens. With renewed vigour the Spanish commander Mendoza recaptured the Rheinberg fortress, invaded the province of Gelderland and seized the town of Doetinchem. Then the Spanish besieged Zaltbommel (on the Waal river), but Maurice was able to keep a supply line open by means of a ship-bridge and Mendoza was forced to retreat. The latter's forces were soon undermined by mutinies and William Louis was in a position to reconquer Doetinchem.

Van Oldenbarnevelt then decided to shift the struggle from Gelderland to the south, aiming to capture the important port of Dunkirk, whose privateers were so harmful for the trade and fisheries of Holland and Zeeland. Maurice viewed this strategy less favourably because he rated the chance of success low. The enterprise resulted in the well-known battle of Nieuwpoort in 1600. The field armies were of approximately equal size because the Spanish mutinies had ceased just in time. The men from the Army of Flanders were more experienced, while the States' troops were more disciplined. They also received significant support from the broadsides fired by Dutch vessels at sea. Ultimately what decided the battle was the retreat of some States' companies, which caused the rapid but rather chaotic advance of the Spanish forces in pursuit of the Dutch, after which the *tercios* were fiercely attacked by the Dutch cavalry held in reserve, leading to an important victory for the Republic's army. The main aim of the campaign, though, the capture of Dunkirk, could not be achieved, and the weakened States' troops sailed home from Ostend.[32]

Since Ostend was the last Dutch stronghold in the southern Netherlands, this small town (with a population of 3,000 and a garrison of 4,500 under the leadership of the English commander Vere) became in 1602 the main target of the Spanish forces. The fortress was extremely difficult to capture as supplies and reinforcements were continually provided by sea. Maurice tried to distract the Spanish from the Ostend siege by luring them into battle; he recaptured the

Rheinberg fortress and then laid siege to 's-Hertogenbosch. But he lacked sufficient troops to encircle the latter town and the Spanish carefully avoided an open fight. A minor Dutch triumph was the capture of the Brabant town of Grave on the Meuse river, which succeeded thanks to the mutiny of the 1,000-strong Spanish garrison, but thereafter the States' army was exhausted and needed time to recover.

The problem was that both sides increased their number of troops, but both armies remained too small to achieve a decisive outcome in enemy territory. The States' army was twice as strong as in the preceding decade, numbering 24,000 in 1602, but in the south the Spanish had the advantage of the interior lines of communication, and moved their troops easily from one part of the country to the other. An army of 16,000–17,000 was sufficient to maintain the Dutch position in the north, but an army of 24,000 could never dislodge the Spanish from their strongholds in the south. Besieged Ostend could thus not be relieved. The Italian political theorist Giovanni Botero wrote in 1605:

> [Nowadays] war is dragged out for as long as possible, and the object is not to smash but to tire, not to defeat but to wear down the enemy. This form of warfare is entirely dependent upon money.

The Spanish minister observed that same year: 'Whoever is left with the last escudo will win.'[33] Indeed, the new fortifications, increasingly modelled after the *trace italienne*, were all but ubiquitous, and resulted in a war with crippling financial consequences: henceforth extended sieges were to be expected, as defenders were able to hold out behind their new-style fortifications. The strategic impasse between the Dutch and the Spanish thus carried on.

Meanwhile the siege of Ostend continued, achieving epic proportions because of its duration. The arrival of a new commander for the Spanish troops, Spínola, started to make a difference. With his entrepreneurial outlook – he was from a Genoese banking family, with no military experience at all – he was not afraid to 'use' his troops in risky and brutal undertakings, exploiting his men to the full before they deserted or died. He also secured loans (totalling no less than five million florins!) which ensured the troops were paid. Above all, Spínola proved an expert engineer, quickly absorbing the lessons in siege warfare of Parma and others.[34] His heroic and bloody offensive of 1604 ended in a victory for the Spanish and drove the Dutch from the southern Netherlands altogether. A minor consolation for the States was the capture of Sluis.

Next year the war moved to the north-eastern border as Spínola attacked the Dutch at Oldenzaal, Lingen and the Gelderland towns of Wachtendonk, Lochem and Groenlo. His entrepreneurial attitude resulted in rapid Spanish victories. Disagreement among the United Provinces and financial difficulties hindered the States' troops. Maurice's attempts to relieve Rheinberg from Spínola's siege and take Wesel in Gelderland ended in failure. But financial problems also affected Spínola's forces, and the Spanish mutinies allowed Maurice to recapture Lochem. With both sides exhausted by the fighting, the option for a truce arose. In 1607 the Dutch fleet mustered a victory over the Spanish at Gibraltar and the Spanish crown had to issue another decree of bankruptcy.[35] A ceasefire came about in the same year and a treaty was signed in 1609, to last for 12 years (the Twelve Years Truce). The Truce applied to Europe: in the Far East, the Americas and the Caribbean fighting was to continue.

The Truce permitted vigorous Dutch economic expansion, above all in the Far East, and a reorganization of the troops, which were kept in shape thanks to military involvement in the nearby Jülich crisis. In Holland itself a conflict arose between Van Oldenbarnevelt and Maurice regarding the command of the troops, a struggle that became entangled with a religious divide within Calvinism between the more tolerant Arminians (headed by Van Oldenbarnevelt) and the more orthodox Counter-Remonstrants, with whom Maurice identified. Eventually Van Oldenbarnevelt was accused of high treason and put to death in 1619. The political crisis weakened the coherence in the Dutch body politic, resulting among other things in the marginalization of the wealthy Arminian faction and a reluctance by the new, less experienced urban councillors to raise taxation. This was highly problematic because new taxes were needed to contract new troops: the Truce was about to expire.

Frederick Henry's counter-offensive and the renewed stalemate, 1620s to 1640s

As soon as the Truce ended, the Spanish were determined to get rid of the pacification policy that was generally thought of as humiliating. Spínola launched a major offensive in the south, taking Jülich and besieging Bergen op Zoom in 1622, one of the Republic's strongest fortresses. The attempt failed, but more because of the town's links to water than the strength of the States' forces. The Dutch army was weakened by problems in its high command; William Louis had died in 1620 and Maurice fell ill, unable to prevent the Spanish capture of Breda in 1625, which was a significant blow to Dutch prestige. Even so, Breda was of much less strategic value than Bergen op Zoom and the town was taken only with great Spanish losses.[36] After this rather disappointing success – and also because of his involvement in the Thirty Years War – the new Spanish king, Philip IV (1621–5), decided to shift to a more defensive war; he favoured the more moderate Hendrik van den Bergh (a nephew of Maurice) over Spínola as military commander. His strategy was to bring the Dutch down through economic warfare, with trade blockades and Dunkirk privateers preying on Dutch shipping.

While the Spanish were moving from direct to indirect warfare tactics, a new counter-offensive was launched in the north. Frederick Henry, the younger brother of Maurice (who died in 1625), was appointed as stadholder in five provinces and as the central commander of the Dutch forces.[37] Oldenzaal was reconquered in 1626, Groenlo in 1627, and in 1628 the Dutch admiral Piet Heyn took the Spanish silver fleet in the Bay of Matanzas (near Cuba), which directly damaged the loans that had been contracted to finance the Spanish troops. In

1630 the Dutch West India Company captured Pernambuco on the coast of Brazil. But the Spanish did not step up their military involvement against the Dutch; instead, the king decided to interfere in the crisis over the Mantuan succession that diverted funds and troops from the borders of the United Provinces.

Unlike his brother, who had done so only occasionally, Frederick Henry consulted a military council with the chief officers on a regular basis, in addition to the *Secreet Besogne*, a council for the army in the field made up of eight to ten deputies of the States-General. Both these institutions shortened the communication lines within the high command and thus enhanced the stadholder's speed of decision-making. By contrast, the commanders in the Army of Flanders had to wait for instructions from Brussels, which in the later 1620s was racked by factional rivalries – for example, between Hainault and Artois. Van den Bergh's military council, for example, was poorly informed and riven with internal competition.[38]

The start of the 's-Hertogenbosch siege in 1629 thus caught the Spanish at an extremely awkward moment. Army leadership was weakened by the departure of Spínola and disagreements between different aristocratic factions over command and military strategies, resulting in an inability to organize a relief army on time.[39] In an attempt to divert Frederick Henry from taking 's-Hertogenbosch, a Spanish army invaded Gelderland, supported by troops of the Emperor Ferdinand II (1619–37), an opportunity directly related to the German Thirty Years War that raged nearby.[40] But even when Montecuccoli captured Amersfoort Frederick Henry stayed put. The invasion was short-lived as the Dutch colonel Van Gent took Wesel by surprise, which deprived the Spanish-Austrian troops of essential provisions, and Montecuccoli was forced to retreat. 's-Hertogenbosch fell to the Republic's forces in September, and although of limited strategic value to the Dutch, for the Spanish the victory constituted a major loss of face.

However, the siege had cost the Dutch an enormous amount of money – some 18 to 19 million guilders – which led to renewed demands for a peace settlement. Although talks began at Roosendaal, the Dutch and Spanish soon disagreed on the conditions and the opportunity ebbed away. In 1631 halfhearted Dutch war preparations for the invasion of Flanders led to nothing. On the other hand, the Spanish hardly advanced either. A frustrated general of the Flanders army stated in 1631: 'If we want to cross a river with all our main army, they cross another with theirs. If we lay siege to one place, they lay siege to another of ours.'[41] The war in the Low Countries was eternalizing itself and a decisive outcome seemed more remote than ever.

The next year Frederick Henry successfully besieged Maastricht, then Limbourg and Orsoy (next to Rheinberg). In 1633 the Dutch captured the strategic Rheinberg fortress, which relieved the Rhine trade and the territories in Gelderland and Overijssel that paid war taxes to the Spanish. The Dutch army had grown enormously since 1628, amounting – at least on paper – to some 90,000 in 1633. But Frederick Henry's invasion of Brabant lacked the military resources to be sustained. Financial support started to crumble, the problem being weakened support from Holland, whose wealthy Remonstrant/Arminian factions had favoured war in the hope that Dunkirk's privateers, the cause of so much hardship to Dutch shipping, would be eliminated. Yet the conquest of Dunkirk seemed remote as the Spanish defence of Flanders appeared insurmountable. In the early 1630s the relationship between Frederick Henry and powerful Amsterdam grew increasingly tense.

Into this stalemate new opportunities presented with the Dutch–French alliance of 1635. In the spring of that year the Franco-Spanish war (1635–59) broke out, which diverted Spanish troops to the French front. During the first battle at Huy (Liège) the French vastly outnumbered the Spanish (29,000 against 9,000) and achieved an impressive victory. The next target was Brussels, but the good fortune of the alliance soon waned as the strength of the French was sapped by poor pay.[42] The Dutch took the small Brabant town of Tienen, yet they were once again forced to retreat. The Spanish (now under the command of the new governor, Cardinal-Infante Ferdinand of Austria) took Diest (Brabant) and then the fortress of Schenkenschans in Cleves, but in early 1636 Frederick Henry recaptured Schenkenschans after an exhausting siege.

In the following years the Spanish brought huge armies into the field and maintained a constant threat on the Republic's southern and eastern borders. In order to win over the support of the Amsterdam financiers Frederick Henry aimed to attack Dunkirk from the sea. But contrary winds delayed the departure of the squadron and, while Dunkirk was strengthened, Frederick Henry besieged Breda in 1637, which was gained from the Spanish after a lengthy siege. On the other military front, the Cardinal-Infante captured Venlo and Roermond in the south-east, cutting the lines of communication between Maastricht and the United Provinces and preventing future attacks on the Spanish Netherlands from the east. In 1638 the Dutch field marshal, Count William of Nassau-Siegen attempted to besiege Antwerp, but his troops suffered a decisive defeat at nearby Kallo. All plans to capture this Brabant metropolis led thus to nothing once again. In the meantime the French sent another army, but lack of money and provisions drove numerous French soldiers to desert and their plan to capture Saint-Omer (Artois) failed.

For several years Frederick Henry had tried unsuccessfully to invade the Spanish Netherlands. At sea warfare raged and disrupted the Dutch shipping routes. It was some solace that the Dutch won the battle at Downs in 1639, the last major confrontation with the Spanish at sea, during which Admiral Tromp applied for the first time line-tactics, with war vessels sailing in a line and firing broadsides. Happily, not only the Dutch but also the Spanish king faced enormous financial difficulties and political setbacks – such as the revolt of Catalonia and Portugal's 1640 attempt to restore independence after six decades of government from Madrid.

Offensives and counter-offensives thus alternated one side to the other. One important reason for stalemate in the later 1630s and 1640s was the size of the armies. Not only lack of funds but also operational problems – above all provisioning and the supply of bread (see Chapter 3) – imposed limits: field armies rarely exceeded 25,000 men (the other troops were needed for garrisons). Gains were thus only possible through surprise moves, in trying to reach a town and beginning the siege before the other army could start the relief. For offensive purposes a field army of 25,000 was barely sufficient given the usual reductions during a campaign due to desertion and disease. Above all Antwerp, with its strong natural defences of the rivers Scheldt, Leie, Dijle and Demer, required many more troops because two armies were needed, one on the Flemish side and another on the Brabant side, amounting in all to forces of at least 30,000 to 35,000.[43]

War thus dragged on, with losses and gains on both sides, but gradually the Spanish position deteriorated. In 1641 Frederick Henry finally secured a victory again in taking Gennep (Limburg), while the French captured four towns in the south. Spain suffered a further devastating defeat by France at the battle of Rocroi (1643, in the Champagne region), which constituted above all a psychological blow. The Dutch military focus shifted temporarily to the Baltic, where the war (1643–5) between Denmark and Sweden threatened the imposition of high Sound tolls. Dutch warships were sent and secured the trading position of the Netherlanders. Between 1644 and 1645 Frederick Henry captured Sas van Gent and Hulst while the French advanced in Artois. 1646 saw the final unsuccessful attempt to recapture Antwerp, but of much more importance was the fact that the French conquered Dunkirk and thus eliminated the damaging privateering enterprises there. Dutch shippers could finally sigh with relief.

In 1647 Frederick Henry died; his son William II took over his position as stadholder. In the meantime peace talks had resumed, but rumours of a possible marriage between young Louis XIV and the Spanish infanta Maria Theresa, with the Spanish Netherlands as a possible dowry, aroused enormous distrust in the Dutch Republic. Such an alliance would threaten the whole balancing act against the Spanish Habsburgs, giving the Netherlands a dangerous southern neighbour. Obviously the chief strategy of the Republic (safeguarding Dutch sovereignty) conflicted with that of France (destroying the power of the Spanish Habsburgs or, if they could not be beaten, joining them).[44] The Dutch had gained little from the Dutch–French coalition of 1635: only Breda, Gennep, Sas van Gent and Hulst, against French wins of Landrecies, Arras, Thionville, Gravelines, Béthune, Lillers, Saint-Venant, Kortrijk, Sint-Winoksbergen, Fort Mardyck, Veurne and Dunkirk. Such thoughts postponed any peace deliberations. In the end, no French–Spanish marriage came about (at this point) and war between Spain and France continued until 1659.

Independence, the stadholderless period and the wars with England and Münster

The peace of Münster in 1648 recognized the United Provinces as an independent, sovereign state; the treaty stipulated the continuation of the closure of the Scheldt; and Dutch conquests in Flanders, Brabant and the colonies were confirmed, to the humiliation of the Spanish. However, debate over a reduction in the size of the army culminated in a serious domestic political crisis. The young stadholder William II (1647–50) observed with dismay the plans of – above all – the Provincial States of Holland to reduce the size of the army to only 39,000 men. In an attempt to force Amsterdam to join him, he planned a secret attack on the town with the stadholder of Friesland, William Frederick. Amsterdam was blockaded for four days; then the town government conceded and removed a number of oligarchic families from office – among them the Bickers, who had traditionally opposed the stadholder's policies. But the victory was a hollow one and even the landward provinces criticized William II's actions. A contemporary wrote from Zutphen that 'his Excellency had impaired the rights of the States of Holland, and … most youngsters here also think His Excellency has acted incorrectly'.[45] Just a couple of months later William II died of smallpox. Mary Stuart, his wife and an English princess, bore him a son (the later William III) eight days afterwards. This situation permitted the anti-Orange faction to reign supreme and no new stadholder was appointed in five provinces: Holland, Zeeland, Utrecht, Gelderland and Overijssel. In the north Groningen chose to appoint William Frederick, the stadholder of Friesland.

Peace was not of long duration and war soon began again, this time with England. The First Anglo-Dutch War (1652–4) turned into a disaster for the Republic. England had invested significantly in the construction of a great number of men-of-war that proved superior to the more traditional Dutch armed merchantmen. At the Peace of Westminster (1654) the Dutch had to accept the Act of Navigation, which excluded their merchants from all commerce with England and its colonies. But already during the war the new grand pensionary, John de Witt, launched a new shipbuilding programme, and by the Second Anglo-Dutch War (1665–7) the Dutch fleet proved able to withstand the English naval power in Europe.[46]

The Dutch also intervened in the Second Northern War (1655–60), sending a fleet to the Baltic to contain the spread of Swedish power and ensure an open Sound, and stationed troops in the garrison of Copenhagen and also at Danzig to protect the position of Dutch merchants there. Furthermore, the States' troops were maintained along the eastern border in German territories, in the garrisons of Emden, Leerort, Dijlerschans, Emmerik, Rees, Wesel, Büderich, Rheinberg, Orsoy and Meurs. This nearby Dutch presence was much to the chagrin of the ambitious and powerful Prince-Bishop of Münster, Christoph Bernard von Galen. His attempts to subdue the autonomy of his own town of Münster failed after the urban authorities called in the help of the Dutch military.[47]

Despite all these military commitments, the number of Dutch troops was further reduced, even though von Galen remained a threat on the eastern border. He did manage in the end to establish an absolutist rule in the town of Münster, and then he invaded East Frisia in 1664, where he captured the Dijlerschans fortress. The Dutch mobilized an army and troops under the leadership of William Frederick restored the Republic's presence in the fortress.

News about England's colonial gains and ambitions contributed to the out-break of the Second Anglo-Dutch War in 1665. The sea battle at Lowestoft constituted a victory for the English, not least because of the failing leadership of Dutch Admiral Van Wassenaer-Obdam. On top of that, 20,000 Münster troops, partly financed by England, invaded the eastern provinces of the Republic and captured a series of towns, including Doetinchem, Oldenzaal and Almelo. The Dutch army under Johan Maurice of Nassau-Siegen remained at the Yssel frontier to prevent an attack on the Yssel towns, while the Münster army moved north in a strategy to establish a direct link with the English at the coast. French troops came north to support the Dutch position on the Yssel, but their counter-attack almost came to nothing as funds to feed the soldiers were lacking. Diplomatic intervention on behalf of the Dutch by the Great Elector of Brandenburg, Frederick William (1640–88), resulted in the retreat of von Galen, who was in dire financial difficulties when funds promised by the English dried up. The Prince-Bishop thus accepted the peace conditions rapidly. At sea the Dutch Admiral Michiel de Ruyter successfully defeated the English in a four-day battle, but the English then gained the upper hand in a two-day battle. The war ended when the Dutch, in a daring raid, sailed up the Thames to Chatham in 1667 and inflicted serious damage on English ships based there.[48]

That year a new danger arose when French troops overran the Spanish Netherlands with 50,000 troops in the War of Devolution (1667–8).[49] For the Dutch the direct threat this represented was avoided by creating a Triple Alli-ance with England and Sweden, which forced Louis XIV to accept a more moderate peace than might otherwise have been achieved. Nevertheless, the French gains from this War of Devolution were considerable: Armentières, Charleroi, Ath, Sint-Winoksbergen, Veurne, Doornik, Douai, Kortrijk, Oude-naarde, Lille and Alost (significant stretches of Hainault, French Flanders and the southern part of Flanders). Louis XIV continued to strengthen his position and allied with Charles II of England, thereby undermining the restrictions that the Triple Alliance had imposed. The French invasion of Lorraine in 1670 led to increased uneasiness in the Netherlands. The States' army was rapidly rein-forced and the threat of war prompted the appointment of William III, William II's son, as Captain-General in February 1672.

1672: the Year of Disaster and its aftermath

In April and May 1672, France, England, Münster and Cologne declared war on the Republic. Again, exactly as in the War of Devolution, the French struck fast. The Dutch garrisons of Wesel, Rheinberg, Orsoy, Büderich, Rees and Emmerik (all located along the eastern border of Gelderland) were overrun and forced to surrender. At the same time the armies of von Galen (Münster) and Henry Maximilian of Bavaria (Archbishop-Elector of Cologne) took Lingen and invaded the Netherlands, capturing – among other towns – Deventer, Kampen, Zwolle and Steenwijk. France marched into Gelderland, besieged Schenkenschans (which fell almost immediately) and then took Arnhem; four days later the Holland town of Naarden was taken by surprise, and Utrecht was occupied too. Hasty deliberate flooding of the region along the Holland-Utrecht border stopped the enemy troops from advancing into Holland's heartlands.

Within a period of only three weeks the Republic was threatened with destruction. Since they stood no chance of stopping the French from advancing, the Dutch focused on getting their forces organized behind the inundation lines and improving the defences of Holland. Coevorden was taken by von Galen, who continued to advance to Groningen, but the States did not send a relief force as they expected the 4,000 to 5,000 soldiers in the garrison would be sufficient to withstand the attack. Indeed, the Münster forces of 24,000 men melted away because of financial difficulties and Groningen resisted the siege, inflicting heavy losses on the attackers.[50]

The Dutch were unexpectedly granted some respite as troops of the German emperor and the Brandenburg-Prussian Great Elector rallied to the support of the Republic, threatening to invade France from the east. The French commander Condé was sent with 18,000 troops to Alsace, while Turenne advanced with 20,000 to the eastern Rhine. Although a considerable number of French troops remained behind in the Netherlands, no direct attack was feared for the time being, and William III (soon named stadholder) could start the organization of a counter-offensive. The political balance within Holland had changed rapidly with the resignation of John de Witt (he was murdered by an angry mob two weeks later, together with his brother Cornelis). In numerous town councils Orangists replaced the former adherents of De Witt. This was less an advantage for the new stadholder than is commonly thought: the new councillors proved reluctant to vote for additional taxation.

> Everywhere and in all matters an enormous disorder prevails ... the regents being for the most part new and inexperienced administrators who do not know how to steer the ship,

wrote a correspondent from The Hague in November 1672.[51] This made the levying of new resources for war extremely difficult.

At the same time William assumed overall military command; unlike Frederick Henry, who had operated with a war council, the Prince planned the campaigns himself, with a few close advisors. The field deputies of the States-General ceased to have any powers; the Council of State was reduced to an executive body carrying out the stadholder's orders. This went against every tradition of the Republic and its politics, but because of the war any opposition was silenced.[52]

While the Imperial and Brandenburg troops put pressure on the territories in the east recently occupied by Münster and Cologne, William's counter-offensive did not directly result in victories, although the attempt to chase out the French from the small Holland town of Woerden (near Utrecht) served to revive Dutch morale. Continuing financial difficulties prevented a proper defence of a number of villages and towns against French attacks along the Holland-Utrecht waterline defence, however. Only at the end of the year was a small Dutch success achieved, when Coevorden was recaptured from Münster in a surprise attack.

1673 was a year of mixed fortunes for both sides. France directed its efforts at Maastricht with an army of 40,000. Louis XIV hoped that the capture of this town would make the Dutch accept peace, after which he could concentrate on attacking the Spanish Netherlands. Maastricht was indeed captured by French forces, but William managed to recapture Naarden. One drawback for the Dutch was the departure of the Brandenburg-Prussian Great Elector from the war when he accepted the French peace conditions after his territories in Westphalia had been occupied. Instead of Brandenburg-Prussia, the Dutch gained Spain as a new coalition partner. France occupied Trier in an attack against the emperor, but the allied forces besieged Bonn, the capital of Cologne, which fell into their hands. Now Cologne and also Münster withdrew from the war and enemy troops left Overijssel, Gelderland and Utrecht, although France still kept the garrisons at Grave and Maastricht.

In the meantime, fighting also continued at sea; De Ruyter defeated a superior French-English fleet at Schooneveld, at the mouth of the Westerschelde, but the threat of coastal invasion remained. In August the battle of Kijkduin ended in another Dutch victory under De Ruyter, despite his smaller fleet, mainly because of poor cooperation between the English and French. Undoubtedly the victories of the Dutch navy in 1672/3 proved of crucial importance for the Republic.[53] England's financial difficulties soared, not least because the 'Stop of the Exchequer' (a repudiation of state debts, 1672) damaged financial markets. After the king's brother, the later James II, married the Catholic Maria d'Este, parliament refused to support the war and England sought peace with the Dutch.

This left only France as an enemy, but the French monarchy commanded huge armies and superior logistics. By 1674 the Dutch army amounted to around 30,000 men, to which Spanish and Imperial troops could be added to make up a total of some 70,000, but foreign support diminished and in 1676 the allied forces stood at 56,000 troops, 36,000 of whom were Dutch. The Spanish commander Villa Hermosa needed 26,000 to defend the garrisons in the southern Netherlands, leaving 30,000 for William's siege of Maastricht. Yet his army was completely outnumbered by the French, who came to relieve the town with 40,000 to 45,000, and the siege failed.[54] Meanwhile, Condé strengthened the French position along the Meuse, while ill-discipline on the part of the Imperial troops and poor central command among the allies further weakened the position of the Dutch. The battle of Seneffe, near Charleroi (Hainault), proceeded in a chaotic way, resulting in enormous losses on both sides. In contrast to the army leaders of the Eighty Years War, William III (1672–1702) was somewhat reckless and had no experience of leading an army in battle.[55] The Dutch attempt to besiege Oudenaarden failed due to lack of cooperation between the Dutch and imperial forces. In addition, Spain proved a weak ally, as it increasingly needed Dutch support to finance its garrisons; the French invasion of Catalonia and the revolt in Sicily further diverted Spanish attention and resources.[56] But finally the siege of Grave ended in a clear success for William. French pressure on the Republic's territory grew less relentless and the war was henceforth fought only on the territory of the Spanish Netherlands.

In 1675 the French had taken Dinant (Namur), Huy (Liège) and Limbourg (Limburg), but their troops mutinied at Trier, which resulted in the loss of this town again. Following Vauban's advice, Louis XIV revised his strategic aims and became willing to give up towns too far into enemy territory, instead strengthening the frontier with Condé-sur-l'Escaut, Valenciennes, Bouchain and Cambrai and consolidating the grip on Hainault. In the last years of the war the French raised an enormous field army, with 60,000 troops, and captured a new series of towns in the southern Netherlands. William's attempt to besiege Maastricht and his attack on the French at Mont-Cassel both ended in failure, not least because of his poor leadership and glaring tactical mistakes. His siege of Charleroi also came to nothing, but on the diplomatic front the promise of marriage to Mary Stuart, the niece of Charles II, opened up new opportunities.

The defeat at Mont-Cassel and the failure of the Charleroi siege had convinced many in the Republic that the French could not be driven out of their recent acquisitions. Although the organization of the Dutch troops had improved (see Chapter 2), the French were simply too numerous. In addition, France had conquered Ghent and Ypres and peace (Nijmegen, 1678/9) was quickly signed. The settlement resulted in France adding a significant number of towns to its territory – including Ypres and Valenciennes – but Ghent was yielded to the Spanish and Maastricht to the Dutch. Louis XIV made territorial gains elsewhere, with the important acquisition of the Franche Comté from Spain, thereby rounding out France's eastern frontier.

Conclusion: the different strategies of the belligerents

The French-Dutch War (1672–8/9) showed the enormous difference in strategy between the Dutch and the other belligerents. France strove towards the position of most powerful state on the continent and the dynastic concerns of the king dominated. The English fought their wars for the power and profit of the crown and the merchant community, trying to get more of what the Dutch had and claiming sovereignty over the seas through the impositions of their navigation acts. Prestige and reputation were also crucial for the Spanish kings, who aspired to hegemonic power. Philip II could not afford to permit the secession of the Netherlands, even if the cost of preventing Dutch independence resulted in bankruptcy.[57] The territorial ambitions of Dutch leaders were, by contrast, modest. Apart from achieving independence and recognition as a sovereign state, their main aims were defence and protection; even in their colonial enterprise it was the expansion of trade and increase of prosperity that prevailed, rather than territorial gains.[58]

'Maintenance and increase of prosperity', however, was a strategy that only became dominant after the 1590s. The beginning of the Dutch Revolt had been characterized by small-scale warfare on the part of groupings with often conflicting interests; the civil war that broke out after 1572 highlighted the enormous divisions within the Netherlands. The army of the States-General, in existence since 1576, could not stop the counter-offensive led by Parma, but a professional army was gradually created in the north. After *c.*1580 the military followed increasingly conventional rules and after 1600 frontiers did not change fundamentally: each side kept the other more or less in check. The signing of a ceasefire in 1607 was simply an expression of mutual exhaustion, and during the 1630s and 1640s military stalemate prevailed again.

Sieges dominated the Eighty Years War, but battles were more important than suggested by the established historiography. Numerous sieges were accompanied by smaller-scale battles – for example, between besieging and relieving troops. These were also regarded by contemporaries as major opportunities for glory or defeat, even though they were rarely decisive. The defending side tended to avoid battle, preferring to exhaust the enemy troops rather than confront them. Often such battles saw one side caught by surprise, as for example at Gembloux (1578, Namur) when the States' troops were attacked while marching, or at Ingelmunster (1580, Flanders) when the States' commander La Noue did not even have time to put on his military gear.[59]

The Dutch state was in fact little more than a military alliance during its earlier decades, but the decentralized political system allowed coordination and natural leadership by the Provincial States of Holland and in particular by their stadholder and grand pensionary. Zeeland periodically urged a more offensive strategy, as did many in the landward provinces, but the war – sustained above all by Holland's economy – continued to stimulate concord and unity in the provinces riven by particularist tendencies.[60] It was Holland's unofficial leadership in a decentralized setting that dictated the dominant strategy of defence. Its commercial gains would always be greatest while Europe's more powerful monarchies were kept in balance: hence Dutch diplomatic efforts to create alliances and coalitions to prevent any one power becoming preponderant.

1672 was a true year of disaster, with several states joining in an attack on the Republic. The resilience of the Netherlands during the fighting which followed was impressive, not least thanks to the territorial circumstances which permitted strategic use of flooding. But the problem was obvious. Huge states like Habsburg Spain and France could always, if they wished, field major armies. It was the good fortune of the Dutch that these same states had significant difficulty in maintaining these troops, feeding, arming and paying them, and avoid mutinies: time and again the military threat faded because enemy troops deserted or were short of provisions. The solution of the Dutch was simple: their military forces must be more professional than those of their opponents. And that is what they achieved. During the sixteenth century the Dutch created a highly professionalized army: it was the only way to fulfil the strategic aims of the Republic – defence and protection with forces that were often much smaller than those fielded by their opponents. How the Dutch accomplished this is the subject of the next chapter.

Notes

1 Provincial States of Friesland in 1577, quoted by Arnade, *Beggars*, p. 165.
2 Parker, *Army*, p. 92. I use the term 'Spanish army' interchangeably for the 'Army of Flanders'.
3 Arnade, *Beggars*, p. 168.
4 Parker, *Dutch Revolt*, p. 104; Van Deursen, 'Holland's experience', pp. 24–7.
5 Van Loo, 'For freedom', p. 174.
6 Tracy, *Founding*, p. 79; Van Vliet, 'Foundation', p. 166.
7 Rooze-Stouthamer, *Opmaat*, pp. 101ff., 225.
8 't Hart, 'The Dutch Revolt', pp. 19–24; Woltjer, *Tussen vrijheidsstrijd*, p. 54.
9 See Chapter 7 for an explanation of Holland's political and financial staying power.
10 Quoted by Bentivoglio, *Compleat History*, p. 82. Vitelli added that by sea France, Germany, and England could always send new forces to the rebels.
11 Letter of Alva to Philip II, dated 30 August 1573, quoted by Caldecott-Baird, *Expedition*, p. 38.
12 Quoted by Parker, *Army*, p. 114; on Requesens' assets: ibid., p. 94 – in comparison: more than three times the revenue of England at that time.
13 Vermeesch, *Oorlog*, pp. 45–6; Swart, *Krijgsvolk*, pp. 157–8; De Graaf, *Oorlog*, p.177. Buren, Schoonhoven, Oudewater and Krimpen aan de Lek are situated on Holland's eastern frontier.
14 See also Chapter 4.
15 Parker, *Spain*, p. 50; Elliott, *Richelieu and Olivares*, p. 95; Thompson, *War and Government*, p. 69.
16 Swart, *Krijgsvolk*, pp. 145, 159–60.
17 't Hart, 'The Dutch Revolt', p. 31; Tracy, *Founding*, p. 148.
18 Schulten, 'Ontstaan', pp. 26–7; Van Peteghem, 'Vlaanderen', pp. 341, 351.
19 Parker, *Dutch Revolt*, p. 179; Schulten, 'Ontstaan', p. 34; Swart, *Krijgsvolk*, p. 162; Nolan, *Sir John Norreys*, p. 39.
20 Parrott, *Business of War*, p. 89. Parker, *Army*, pp. 7, 204: his earliest victories were spurred on by funds that had become available now the hostilities with the Turks had ended and in addition the Spanish Americas yielded 19 million ducats in the 1580s compared to only 12 million in the 1570s. However, already by 1583 financial shortages dominated Spanish policies again. Tracy, *Founding*, pp. 223–4: present-day Belgium has been created for a great part by Parma during 1579–91.
21 Stradling, *Armada*, pp. 7ff.; Van Vliet, 'Foundation', p. 168. Despite the enormous losses of ships on the Dutch side, the latter could not be defeated by sea. A Spanish official wrote in 1601: 'If we bring out 100 ships they bring out 400, and if more, more; and they are always happy to lose ten of their ships if they can sink one of ours'; see Parker, *Army*, p. xxxii.
22 Swart, *Krijgsvolk*, pp. 48–51; Nolan, *Sir John Norreys*, pp. 56, 59.
23 Israel, *Dutch Republic*, p. 221; see also Tracy, *Founding*, pp. 229, 277, 297. On the power of bargaining towns, see Tilly, *Coercion, Capital*, p. 47.
24 Oosterhoff, *Leicester*, p. 92ff.
25 Nolan, *Sir John Norreys*, p. 100; Oosterhoff, *Leicester*, pp. 145, 176, 183.
26 Van Nimwegen, *Deser landen crijghsvolck*, pp.134–6; Van Deursen, *Maurits*, p. 123.
27 Quoted by Duffy, *Siege Warfare*, p. 84.
28 Parker, *Dutch Revolt*, p. 231; Duerloo, *Dynasty and Piety*, p. 88ff.
29 Fissel, *English Warfare*, p. 173; Duffy, *Siege Warfare*, p. 113; Van Nimwegen, *Deser landen crijghsvolck*, pp. 142–3. Meurs garrison was located on the Rhine, near

Wesel; Bredevoort, Enschede and Oldenzaal are situated in the eastern part of Overijssel; Groenlo is in the east of Gelderland.

30 Fruin, *Tien jaren*, p. 349.
31 Quoted by De Graaf, *Oorlog*, p. 314.
32 Van Nimwegen, *Deser landen crijghsvolck*, pp. 145–6; Duerloo, *Dynasty and Piety*, p. 119.
33 Both quotes in Parker, *Army*, p. 14.
34 Duffy, *Siege Warfare*, p. 84; Parker, *Army*, pp. 102, 212; Parrott, *Business of War*, p. 93.
35 Parker, *Army*, p. 213; Van Vliet, 'Foundation', p. 170.
36 De Cauwer, *Tranen*, pp. 29–30.
37 Frederick Henry also became stadholder for Groningen and Drenthe in 1640.
38 De Cauwer, *Tranen*, pp. 52, 93, 106–7, 280–1; Vermeir, *In staat*, p. 33; Gonzalez de
   Léon, *Road to Rocroi*, pp. 217–18, 243. Parrott, *Richelieu's Army*, p. 504: such a
   military council was rare in France, as the bringing together of powerful *grands*
   constituted a danger for the government.
39 De Cauwer, *Tranen*, pp. 10, 28, 48–9.
40 Wilson, *Thirty Years War*, p. 437.
41 Parker, *Army*, p. 17.
42 Parrott, *Richelieu's Army*, pp. 114–17; in fact, the French had overstretched their
   resources in the 1635 campaign and by the end of the year it was clear that they
   failed to achieve anything.
43 Vermeir, *In staat*, p. 147: the Spanish army numbered only 16,000–18,000 in the later
   1630s; Van Nimwegen, *Deser landen crijghsvolck*, pp. 107–8. Between 1635 and 1646
   the strategy was focused on Antwerp. But this town was extremely difficult to
   besiege, demanding a circumvallation of 40 kilometres – on the Brabant side, 20,000
   to 22,000 troops were needed, and on the Flemish side, 8,000 to 10,000, thus 30,000
   troops in all, with communication for both sides over bridges that were liable to be
   destroyed by the enemy (see also Chapter 3).
44 Sonnino, *Mazarin's Quest*, pp. 110, 114.
45 Quoted by Van Nimwegen, *Deser landen crijghsvolck*, p. 255.
46 Jones, *Anglo-Dutch Wars*, pp. 64–81.
47 Between 1665 and 1678 Von Galen raised substantial forces for France, Spain, Denmark and the German Empire as a true military entrepreneur: Tallett, *War and
   Society*, p. 79.
48 Rommelse, *Second Anglo-Dutch War*, pp. 180–1.
49 Sonnino, *Louis XIV*, *passim*, on the continuous and increasing war threat from
   France; Lynn, 'Tactical evolution', p. 177.
50 Van Nimwegen, *Deser landen crijghsvolck*, p. 370.
51 Quoted by ibid., p. 298.
52 Troost, *William III*, pp. 105–6.
53 Diekerhoff, *Oorlogsvloot*, p. 98; Israel, *Dutch Primacy*, p. 300. Kijkduin: a village on
   the North Sea coast, south of The Hague.
54 Van Nimwegen, *Deser landen crijghsvolck*, p. 317.
55 Ibid., p. 276.
56 Rooms, *Organisatie*, pp. 47–8.
57 Sonnino, *Louis XIV*, p. 49; Tallett, *War and Society*, pp. 17–20; Oosterhoff, *Leicester*, p. 194; Manning, *Apprenticeship*, pp. 5, 31; Howard, *War*, p. 47; Parker, *Grand
   Strategy*, p. 296; Parker, *Spain*, p. 51; Duerloo, *Dynasty and Piety*, p. 525.
58 Glete, *War and the State*, p. 108; Price, 'State', p. 184; Jones, *Anglo Dutch Wars*, pp.
   11–12; Schulten, 'Ontstaan', p. 40; Manning, *Apprenticeship*, p. 92: Maurice was
   always very careful and avoided battle; in addition, it was difficult to find new
   recruits.
59 Swart, *Krijgsvolk*, p. 166; Schulten, 'Ontstaan', p. 37.
60 Frijhoff and Spies, *Hard-won Unity*, p. 139.

2 The making of a professional army

> So I trotted off and joined the Dutch army. Although the pay was good, their war was too boring for my taste – we were kept like monks and supposed to have the chastity of nuns.[1]

With these words Olivier, a soldier friend of Von Grimmelshausen's famous Simplicius Simplicissimus, referred to his stay in the Dutch army in the 1620s. Such a well-controlled army was obviously a rare phenomenon in early seventeenth-century Europe. Plunder and mutiny were familiar all over the continent, due above all to the impact of the increasingly large, uncontrolled armies of the sixteenth and seventeenth centuries.[2]

Michael Roberts observed that, since the sixteenth century, 'the state was concerned to make its military monopoly absolute. It declared its hostility to irregular and private armies'.[3] The fifteenth century had shown the dangers of *condottieri* dominating in Italian states.[4] Wars grew undoubtedly bigger and more complex thereafter, but they did not stimulate state formation everywhere. Historians of France, for example, nowadays tend to emphasize the negative consequences of the seventeenth-century growth of armies for existing state institutions. John Lynn even called the seventeenth-century army 'a monster' that the French monarchy was unable to control.[5] What prevented the complete downfall of France was its network of *clientèles* and the role of patronage; when one network failed another could come to the rescue of the state. An increased patrimonial possession of state offices through the system of venality was the result, at the expense of central authority.[6]

A professional force that monopolized the execution of violence while being subordinated to civilian society was obviously indispensable for successful state formation. The continued existence of the companies and with it the creation of a standing army were requirements for such professionalism; only such permanence permitted the development of an experienced military force. Yet in the sixteenth century standing armies were few. Most governments simply did not have the means to 'put all their military eggs into the single basket of a military force';[7] in England a standing army was avoided until the later seventeenth century because of the threat it might pose to civil society. In France units were often disbanded after each campaign, which had the effect that the soldiers had little experience and were consequently at a disadvantage against the forces of true standing armies like those of Habsburg Spain.[8] Even the Army of Flanders under Olivares suffered from the fact that the high command was not given permanent positions: appointments usually lasted for a single campaign.[9]

In the later sixteenth century the Dutch Republic was one of the few states that kept a standing army in the field. By the late 1580s and early 1590s the troops had evolved from a loose band of individual guerrilla fighters into a highly disciplined corps of 'common soldiers' in which proficiency and obedience were valued over prowess or courage. This was a significant achievement, which has been ascribed by most historians solely to the reforms of Maurice of Nassau. His famous Articles of War of 1590 are said to have transformed soldiers from independent warriors into a reliable and efficient war machine.[10] Yet it is questionable whether such a young commander (he had just turned 18 on his appointment as stadholder in 1586) could have made all the difference, even if he received help from his cousin William Louis. Recent evidence shows that Maurice's father William of Orange should receive much more credit in this regard, as will be explained below.

Within two decades then, after the ground had been prepared by Orange, the 'monopoly of violence' in the Netherlands was in the hands of a well-trained standing army under firm civilian control. Dutch troops were quite advanced in professionalization if measured in terms of the following characteristics: a strong, common identity that belonged to their trade; a formal hierarchy; permanent status as soldiers; a formal system of pay; expertise acquired by means of instruction; efficiency in applying this expertise; and a mindset that belonged particularly to the military.[11]

Yet military professionalization in early modern Europe was always held back by the continuing existence of semi-private arrangements. This was, after all, the 'Age of Brokerage', in the words of Charles Tilly, in which middlemen took care of specific state tasks.[12] Captains were usually paid a lump sum by agents of the state, and from that lump sum they had to pay their soldiers and provide them with arms and clothing. Captains' commissions thus always entailed business-like considerations.[13] State commissioners had little control over the spending by the captains, let alone over the actual number of soldiers in the company. Fewer soldiers in the company than its paper strength indicated meant a welcome profit for a captain but might constitute a serious hazard on the battlefield. This semi-private system was not so much a problem while the Republic's rivals suffered the same drawbacks, but it became notably troublesome in the later seventeenth century when substandard soldier numbers weakened Dutch efforts to keep the much more numerous French at bay.

This chapter discusses how civilian control over the military was extended due to several crucial measures introduced by Orange and Maurice. Their reforms furthered peaceful co-existence between citizens and soldiers. Troops lost their traditional corporative institutions and the authority of the officers was strengthened, embedded in a uniform system of justice. Improved rules of appointment were added, alongside regulations concerning the treatment of wounded soldiers and a pay system eased by urban loans. Yet not all improvements lasted after the signing of the Peace of Westphalia. Only the renewed military threat caused a further strengthening of professionalization under William III.

From Beggars and landsknechts to professional standing army

Upon his appointment as stadholder of Holland in 1572, one of the first tasks of William of Orange was to incorporate the unruly 'Beggar' forces into the regular army. Officers of the Beggars who refused to comply were removed. Orange even discharged Lumey because of ill discipline, despite the fact that this officer had captured Brill, the event that led to the revolt of the Holland towns in 1572.[14] At sea the Beggar forces remained of vital importance for rather longer, but following their contribution to the relief of Alkmaar and Leiden in 1574 Orange had them merged with the newly established navy of Holland (see Chapter 6).

Reducing the burden of the soldiery upon the population was essential for Orange's strategy. Glaring examples of misconduct by Beggar troops alienated popular support; numerous Holland regents even pondered a negotiated return to the authority of Philip II. Towns were reluctant to admit soldiers within their walls when misdeeds by members of the garrison were left unpunished. In Leiden, for example, six soldiers raped a girl; in addition the garrison menaced town council meetings. Citizens were threatening to flee or take up arms against the troops.[15] Grievances regarding marauding, above all during the extremely unruly time period of August 1573, added to the discontent and the unwillingness to vote for new taxes. The population in fact strongly disliked all soldiers, Spanish and Dutch alike. In the Provincial States of Holland the towns controlled no fewer than 18 of the 19 votes. In order to obtain the support of the voting towns, not least with regard to new taxes that might pay for the army, Orange had no choice but to take such complaints seriously.[16]

The task was a knotty one as exposure to danger gave soldiers a distinctive moral pretext, different from society's norms: in war killing was not murder and the taking of booty not theft. Blurred boundaries of right and wrong rendered extortion, torture or rape justified when instrumental to achieve soldiers' ends – above all when lack of pay had broken their contract requiring obedience. It is not true that criminals and other marginalized individuals dominated the military.[17] These men joined the army too, but most soldiers came from the ranks of apprentices, journeymen, farmers' sons and farm labourers.[18] Yet they changed, as Francisco de Valdés, a Spanish general commanding several garrisons in Brabant, remarked in 1589: 'The day a man picks up his pike to become a soldier, he stops being a Christian.'[19] The new social identification and the behaviour that went with it were emphasized by nicknames such as Bloedhont (bloodhound), Lucifer, Jonckbedorven ('early rotten'), Magere Hein (grim reaper) or simply Neus (Nose); such names signalled the belonging to very particular norms.[20]

To reduce the Beggars' influence Orange raised new troops, mostly from Dutch and German territories.[21] One drawback of these men was their 'landsknecht' tradition. The individual skills of landsknechts might be outstanding but their disciplinary reputation was poor. The French soldier and chronicler Brantôme characterized them in the following way in the late sixteenth century:

> I have heard great captains say that such manner of *landsknechts* are worthless in a besieged place, because they have a strong tendency to mutiny if they do not have everything they need. They are spendthrift, ungovernable, destructive, and dissipated.[22]

Contemporaries said that Spanish soldiers mutinied after the battle, the German landsknechts before the battle.[23]

Discipline could only be improved with difficulty. Landsknechts might be hired by any government or warlord, but the army command had little to say about the appointment of junior officers. Each month the soldiers elected their own sergeants and officers for quartering and provisioning (two *Webels*, a furier or *Foerier*, and a *Führer* or *Voerder*). In case of grievances the landsknechts chose representatives (*Ambossaten* or *Amissaten*) to discuss their objections with the commanders. The soldiers were usually organized in *rotten* (squads) of ten with a *rotmeester* (squad-master), also popularly elected. The inner cohesion of the squad was strong; its members supported each other finding food or when wounded. They regarded their pay appropriate for 'ordinary' service only; for battles and assaults extra money was demanded, frequently in advance.[24]

Needless to say such practices rendered the imposition of a formal hierarchy and central command structure difficult.[25] In 1573 Orange began by having corporals appointed from above, by the captains, who were to replace the landsknecht squad masters. Similar regulations followed for sergeants and quartermasters. The position of *Voerder* (guide to troops' quarters) was abolished altogether.[26] While the number of landsknecht officers had varied and been subject to negotiation, the size of the standard infantry staff was fixed by Orange at 13. These measures established a more hierarchical structure of command and made Dutch forces both better disciplined and more effective.

His next step was to reduce the size of the large landsknecht company. Between 1574 and 1577 companies with 150 men instead of 300 or more became standard. Orange's reforms were in all probability inspired by French, or rather Huguenot, army patterns. Huguenots – linked to Orange in various ways – probably taught him recent innovations in the tactical use of firearms during the French Wars of Religion. Their military units were rather small with a comparatively high ratio of officers to soldiers, and no landsknecht-like corporations existed.[27] Orange's new companies were likewise reduced and a larger number of men armed with firearms, permitting more flexible operations which suited the warfare in the Netherlands extremely well. Elsewhere at that time – such as in the Army of Flanders – units of landsknechts were significantly larger and consisted predominantly of pikemen.[28]

The comparatively high proportion of officers to soldiers improved control over the conduct of the rank and file. Orange's basic company structure remained virtually unaltered in the decades to come. Infantry companies of the Dutch army – regardless of the actual number of men (companies of 100 became standard shortly afterwards) – contained three higher officers (captain, lieutenant and ensign), two sergeants, four corporals, two drummers, a company clerk and a barber-surgeon. The standard cavalry company consisted of eight officers: captain, lieutenant, cornet, quartermaster, two trumpeters, company clerk and farrier.[29] Sergeants and quartermasters had specific tasks regarding the maintenance of discipline, supported by corporals who were answerable for their section (one-third or one-quarter) of the soldiers. The latter also trained new recruits. The writer or clerk had to be an honest man with some means of his own, taking care of the registration of soldiers' pay and keeping account of their actual number. The drummers not only had to be able to drum but were also expected to speak a couple of foreign languages, as they could be sent out to ransom soldiers taken hostage by the enemy. All these lower officers were appointed by the captains. The higher officers (captains, lieutenants, cornets and ensigns) received their commissions from the higher army command or the paymasters.[30]

Orange also introduced standardized military trials of jurisdiction. In mercenary units discipline had been enforced communally rather than hierarchically. Landsknecht trials had typically taken place in a ring with all soldiers present, the accused being represented by the *Voerder* or *Führer*.[31] In such settings disciplinary measures were difficult to enforce as officers and soldiers tended to stick together. Between 1573 and 1576 military courts presided over by the captains replaced landsknecht jurisdiction; no representatives of the accused were permitted to be present. In addition, each garrison town received a sergeant major who looked after discipline. Orange named provosts who had the power to apprehend soldiers who misbehaved and punish them on the spot. Henceforth even the stealing of an egg was severely punished, all under the rubric laid down by Orange's explicit orders.[32]

The abolition of the private jurisdiction of the landsknechts ensured that captains exerted full juridical powers over their men. In case captains failed to exercise these, in particular with respect to mutinous soldiers, the States-General had appointed an 'auditor' and a 'capitaine de justice' in 1576 and the field marshall stood at the head of the military juridical system. When the latter died Maurice took over his juridical capacities and replaced the auditor and the *capitaine de justice* by a court-martial with a regular seat in The Hague. This step increased the influence of civilians on military jurisdiction.[33]

Civilians also increased their judicial powers vis-à-vis the military at lower levels. In garrisons a sergeant major supervised all matters of discipline, but legally educated civilians joined him as military auditors. In 1600 the military auditors received an elaborate instruction to act as public prosecutors, advisors and secretaries for the garrison courts-martial. The military provosts acted as a kind of police force for the military auditors and were also responsible for the execution of the verdicts. The significance of the role played by civilians was remarkable and stadholders saw to it that the rules were obeyed. The level of interference by civil authorities was extremely high. For instance, when three farmer's children lost their lives as a result of some stupid act by soldiers from the Zutphen garrison, a public outcry arose in which the Zutphen government sued the garrison governor, Van Dorth.[34] By comparison, in almost all other early modern armies prosecutors came from the military ranks.[35]

Under Orange's direction the Articles of War were also changed, with the creation of additional disciplinary regulations. Most important was the fact that the Articles were no longer a kind of contract between soldiers and their paymasters but a set of duties for soldiers imposed from above. The Articles no longer addressed the soldiers as 'you' ('U' or 'Ghy'); instead the requirements were stated in the abstract third person. All references to landsknecht traditions disappeared (the ring, the *Ambossaten*), along with mention of the *Schlacht-monat* (battle month), which stated that a new pay month was to begin after each battle. Earlier in the century a soldier usually took service for three months, but the Articles now made no reference to the duration of the contract, which was assumed to be indefinite. Soldiers now signed on for life; even elderly soldiers remained in the army, performing guard duties or looking after the training of new recruits.[36] This permanency constituted a significant marker of professionalization, alongside the obligatory requirements of obedience and discipline imposed from above.

In the established historiography, Maurice is usually credited with the famous Articles of War of 1590, although some authors point to Leicester as the *auctor intellectualis*.[37] Yet when the wording is examined, it becomes obvious that this evolved from Orange's original set of 1574 (for Holland's army, with 34 clauses) and his improved version of 1578 (for the States' army, increased to 48). Leicester copied them and added some new items, totalling 55, in 1585. In 1590, under Maurice, there were no fewer than 82 Articles. The last set remained in use until 1799 with only a minor revision in 1705.[38]

The permanent contract, introduced by Orange's Articles, became a real permanency after 1588 when Dutch troops were no longer disbanded after the campaigns but remained in service year after year, permitting the emergence of a true standing army with increasingly professional characteristics. The troops might be labelled mercenaries, but the institutional setting was thoroughly state-controlled.[39] In times of emergency additional mercenaries in the pay of the United Provinces were contracted. The number of truly independent military entrepreneurs – commanders with their own armies, typical of the Thirty Years War – was always limited. Under pressure from the Spanish counter-offensive of the early 1620s the Dutch contracted the celebrated military entrepreneurs, Count Ernst of Mansfeld and the Duke Christian of Brunswick, for a period of two years. Civilians feared their reputation: the troops under Christian (nick-name 'the Mad Duke') had allegedly killed 5,000 peasants on their way to Brabant.[40] Indeed, they proved extremely difficult to control and as soon as possible their high mightinesses tried to get rid of these mercenaries again.

Apart from these mercenaries the regular Dutch forces always contained a significant proportion of soldiers from other countries, both Protestant and Catholic. English companies were valued highly, by Orange as well as his sons, for their long military experience. Numerous French and German soldiers took up service too.[41] The mix of nationalities occasionally hampered the command structure since soldiers hesitated to obey a colonel who belonged to a country other than their captain's.[42] Rivalries between the different nationalities also caused disturbances in army camps, usually related to drinking and gambling. In 1600 a gambling dispute involved as many as five or six hundred French, German and Frisian soldiers, of whom at least six were killed. Guards were placed between the different camps and after 1603 such fights seemed to have disappeared altogether.[43]

Pay, mustering, medical care and prisoners of war

The Articles of War and improved juridical institutions were unable to solve all these problems on their own because the main cause of ill-discipline was lack of pay. This too was addressed at a very early stage of the military struggle with Spain. A major advance under Orange was more frequent payments, with the introduction of weekly 'loans' or instalments instead of monthly payments.[44] New taxes voted in by the Provincial States in the 1570s provided the bulk of these funds (see Chapter 7); the towns advanced soldiers' pay in the form of loans; the sums were deducted later from the towns' tax contribution to the province. This solved most difficulties with troops in the garrisons; the payment of the field army remained more problematic. Orange also raised soldiers' pay to eight guilders per month, up from the five guilders that had been the standard rate since the early sixteenth century.[45]

This initiative was too optimistic, however, in view of available resources. A solution was to increase the length of the pay month, first from 30 to 32 days in 1574 and then to 42 days in 1576. Soldiers in the Geertuidenberg garrison mutinied in protest.[46] Yet the cuts were necessary in view of the ever-rising expenses. In 1588 the States-General decided to lengthen the pay month even further to 48 days, effectively restoring the standard rate from before the Revolt: eight guilders per 48 days is equal to five guilders per 30 days. That such measures did not meet with much more widespread resistance can be explained by the regularity of pay: Dutch soldiers did not earn more than their counterparts elsewhere but they received their money reliably and in a steady pattern, which was far from the case in other armies. The regularity of pay also underpinned cohesion in an army where over half of the troops came from outside the Republic.[47]

In addition, Dutch soldiers could often considerably supplement their income by digging. Maurice was by no means the first commander to impel them to pick up a shovel, as some historians want to have it.[48] Such tasks were not uncommon in most contemporary armies of the Spanish and German princes, and Orange had also ordered his soldiers to dig ditches for siege works.[49] The construction of defence works for their own quarters did not carry additional remuneration, but for fortifications and during sieges Dutch soldiers received additional payments ranging from eight *stuivers* a day in 1575 to 15 guilders per month in the 1580s. Compared to their eight guilder per month wage, this was quite substantial. The Frisian stadholder William Louis declared in 1589 that soldiers needed to be paid well in this respect because otherwise they would feel too humiliated to take up the spade. In the seventeenth century the standard rate stood at ten *stuivers* a day, twice as much as their ordinary earnings.[50]

Improvements in the mustering of troops was another of Orange's concerns in order to ensure the support of the towns and provinces. Paymasters always wished to know the exact numbers of soldiers, but deception was widespread and could be inventive – for example, when dummy soldiers were hired to make the company appear at full strength. The problem was that captains managed their companies as private enterprises: receiving pay for soldiers who had deserted represented significant additional income.[51] Mustering was complicated as the troops suffered from considerable 'natural' wastage and renewal. For example, the regiment of governor Sonoy of 1583 (12 companies, 1,450 men) was almost completely renewed within a couple of years. The reasons for the soldiers' disappearance varied: the largest group had left with a passport for furlough or pension; next came desertion; and a minority had died in action from wounds or diseases.[52]

The muster masters appointed by Orange in 1572 consisted of people of noble birth with military experience in order to give the mustering additional authority and weight. But the urban authorities valued ability and trustworthiness more than noble status; over time status became less important and men from a less exalted background were chosen. In addition, the citizens of the Provincial States of Holland demanded the right to supervise the mustering. As a rule, two representatives of the urban government attended. To combat fraud a controller-general of mustering was appointed to whom the muster masters had to report, and in the later 1580s muster masters were deliberately assigned separate districts so they could grow acquainted with 'their' troops. The frequency of the musters (usually every four months) depended on the availability of money, as soldiers could receive any outstanding pay there and then and sometimes provisions and ammunition as well. Alongside this financial control mechanism, muster masters also mediated between army and citizens and reported any misconduct to the authorities.[53]

The increasingly detailed regulations for the muster masters were a particular mark of professionalization. In 1578 their instructions contained 18 articles, but this total had increased to 31 by 1586 and 38 by 1590. The 1572 muster rolls listed the soldiers by their nicknames, such as 'Droncken Jan' from Amsterdam, 'Bonte Krae' from Stavoren and 'Slampamper' from Eindhoven. But such nicknames came to be avoided because they permitted deserters to hide their identity when taking service in another company. By 1578 the instructions specified that a soldier's Christian name had to be listed first, next to a possible nickname, and profession and place of origin had to be noted down as well; by 1582 height and physical appearance had to be added, and by 1586 (approximate) age, colour of hair and beard, and parents' names, too. In the 1590s the mustering administration specified all these personal details, together with place of birth; nicknames were now prohibited.[54]

This elaborate documentary evidence regarding the identity of the soldiers was also to be found in the muster rolls of other early modern armies but generally only by the seventeenth century.[55] Although by no means all fraud was abolished, around 1590 contemporaries noted that a captain in another army could earn more money from their single company than a States' colonel with ten companies: an estimate which underlined the extent to which malpractice had been reduced in the Dutch army. It was nevertheless advantageous to be a captain in the Dutch forces because pay was much more regular than in most other armies and captains lost less money having to arrange private loans for their soldiers to keep them going.[56]

Further requirements for the system of mustering were introduced following the standardization of weaponry in 1596 (see Chapter 3). After 1599 soldiers had not only to be present but also armed according to the latest standards. Fines – for example, half a guilder for a pikeman with no proper helmet and ten guilders for a cuirassier with no packhorse – kept the troops in good condition.[57] In 1627 there was further standardization with the regulation that captains had to buy the weaponry for their troops from Dutch military depots.[58]

The treatment of sick or wounded soldiers constituted a permanent problem for all early modern armies. The ordinary barber-surgeons were not particularly well qualified and the care provided tended to be rudimentary. Once again, however, the Dutch army provided rather better medical services than were to be found in many early modern forces. A master surgeon for the States' army had been appointed in 1588 to supervise the company surgeons, but grave cases always had to be transferred to urban hospitals.[59] In the southern Netherlands Parma had a field hospital installed, together with a permanent military hospital in Mechelen in 1585. These institutions are heralded in the literature as 'admirable medical care', but in fact only elite Spanish and Italian soldiers were treated there, and only because towns refused to admit them to their own hospitals. All other sick and wounded from the Army of Flanders still had to be transported to local hospitals, exactly as in the northern Netherlands.[60]

Treatment for wounded and sick soldiers was possible in the established town hospitals upon individual request. In 1574 Orange developed an arrangement with Rotterdam's hospital to provide standard medical care for soldiers, but with the shift of warfare to the south this was discontinued after 1577. In 1586 a new solution was introduced: sharing the burden of care between the Holland towns – from 70 beds in Amsterdam to five beds in the small towns of Woerden, Naarden, Muiden and Purmerend. Amsterdam even built a permanent military hospital, just one year after the one in Mechelen. The costs were deducted from the financial contribution of the province to the States-General and the service seemed to have functioned well; even other provinces sent their wounded and sick soldiers to Holland.[61]

The medical services were extended in the years to come. Maurice introduced a field apothecary in 1603. Under Frederick Henry military hospitals existed not only in Holland but also in Zwolle, Amersfoort, Arnhem, Utrecht and Breda. A study of hospitalized soldiers in Zwolle during 1621–47 showed that about four-fifths of them recovered, an unusually high proportion of casualties at this time. The English visitor John Evelyn admired the Amsterdam soldiers' hospital, which he described in 1666 'for state order & accommodations one of the worthiest things that I thinke the world can show of that nature'.[62]

One novelty was the reciprocal agreements concerning prisoners of war, following an initiative by the Spanish.[63] Capturing soldiers and then asking for ransoms was found to yield a fine additional income, but the negotiations always demanded a lot of time and energy, above all when high-ranking commanders were imprisoned. As much as 10,000 guilders were paid in 1595 for Ernst Casimir, Orange's nephew and the future Frisian stadholder. The Spanish commander Mendoza (himself a victim of capture and ransom) proposed a regulation for the exchange of their respective prisoners of war. This understanding came into practice in 1602, the first of its kind in history.[64] The ordinance specified the amount to be paid for each prisoner of war: thus, lieutenants, cornets and ensigns 60 guilders, their captains 600 guilders, and so forth, and compensation for the daily expenses of food and shelter was not to exceed ten *stuivers* a day for an ordinary soldier and for the officers one guilder. Soldiers' wives and children under the age of 12 were not to be taken prisoner. Under the same regulation, all attacks on women and children were prohibited. At sea a separate system of prisoners' exchange came into being in 1626, this time following an initiative by the States.[65] Such regulations speeded up the transactions and reduced the costs that had to be paid relating to hostages' living expenses.

Officers and men

Civilian control over the army was strong, as earlier demonstrated in relation to military jurisdiction, regulation of pay and mustering of troops. With regard to the appointment of officers, the role of civilians was likewise prominent. After Leicester had left in 1587 the provinces established themselves firmly in the forefront as paymasters of the troops and thus also responsible for the appointment of senior officers, from the rank of ensign up to colonel. The power of the Council of State was reduced; troops were only to be raised after explicit approval by the provinces in the States-General. Henceforth the Council exercised only an administrative oversight where Dutch forces were concerned, under guidelines laid down by the States-General, and the higher officers were appointed in a process dominated by the stadholder and the provincial governments. The lower officers (sergeants and corporals) received their commissions from the captains, as during Orange's time.[66]

One disadvantage of such regulations was that officers who enjoyed good relations with the provincial government but who were not necessarily experienced in military matters were often selected. In 1618 Maurice, William Louis and Frederick Henry drew up a decree that enhanced furthered professionalization.[67] For the ranks of captain and above all candidates should have served a minimum for at least four years in the States' army; for lieutenants, ensigns and cornets three years' service was required. Captains were chosen from a list of five candidates, compiled in consultation with the provincial government but obligatorily including the current lieutenant and the current ensign/cornet of the company. For the positions of lieutenants and ensigns/cornets, the captain was to make a list of suitable candidates, from which the provincial paymasters were to select three; in the case of a lieutenant's position the current ensign/cornet was always added as the fourth candidate. The stadholder picked the officers from these lists, giving prominence to the individuals' past military records. In the case of equally suitable candidates from both native and foreign backgrounds, the Dutch were to be given the advantage. In addition, all captains, lieutenants and corporals of the cavalry too old or injured to serve were to be discharged with a pension, permitting more able officers to take their place. In the infantry such rules were unnecessary as elderly or disabled officers could still perform duties in garrisons; the cavalry involved much more active service, however, with many hours on horseback during convoys or raids in the countryside. And although forbidden since the very beginning of Orange's command, the 'Ordre' of 1618 stipulated once again that the position of captain or other officer rank must never be bought or sold.[68]

This was another step towards a more professional army, and it was exemplified by the career of Johan Maurice, Count of Nassau-Siegen. Having started in 1618 as a pikeman in the guard of William Louis, Maurice followed Frederick Henry to the Palatinate as a cavalryman in 1620 and became ensign shortly thereafter. In 1624 he was commissioned as captain of a company, becoming lieutenant-colonel in 1626, colonel in 1629, and ending up as field marshal of the Dutch army. Johan Maurice was a descendant of one of Orange's brothers, Jan IV of Nassau. In 1625 no fewer than 25 other descendants of Jan IV served in the Dutch army, almost all as officers.[69]

The hierarchical chain of command, the functional assignments to more experienced officers subject to formal regulations and the increased powers of the military authorities exercised in tandem with the Provincial States of Holland together made the States' troops a model army of the time. Since the 1590s war had increasingly become 'not an act of uncontrolled violence, but rather the orderly application of force, directed by a competent and legitimate authority, in the interest of the state', exactly as the famous scholar Lipsius had recommended.[70]

Yet at the same time there remained a number of significant shortcomings. The absence of commanding officers, sometimes even during field operations, was endemic. It was all but impossible to dismiss officers guilty of fraud, insubordination or military incompetence, as any dismissal of a commanding officer would almost certainly lead to the disintegration of the company concerned.[71]

Furthermore, though posts were not sold openly, captains were able to require 'gifts' from their successors. Regulations regarding the prohibition of the sale of military offices had to be amplified in 1628 and again in 1637.[72]

Another problem was the high attrition rate in the number of troops. Maurice estimated that after a campaign of three or four months one-quarter to one-third of the men were lost due to desertion, disease or death. Such high 'wastage' rates were normal in early modern Europe. In the cavalry, the desertion of soldiers was much less of a problem, but the need to find good, strong horses to replace the animals crippled or killed restricted the availability of the horsemen. In the second half of the seventeenth century a cavalry horse cost 120 to 130 guilders, twice the annual pay for an infantryman.[73]

An additional drawback affecting operational efficiency was that not all soldiers were acquainted with their senior commanders; neither did they always know their comrades in arms. Under Maurice, troops were divided in wintertime between the garrisons; he decided the composition of the regiments for the subsequent campaign and often redistributed soldiers to new units. The pressure of the Spanish counter-offensive of the early 1620s produced a change in this practice. The first permanent infantry regiment dated from 1623, when the troops were dissolved in wintertime but returned to the same units the following spring.[74] Throughout the later decades of the Eighty Years War the continuing war threat kept regimental organization intact and encouraged regular exercise and drill, further enhancing professionalization. However, that was to change once peace was signed in 1648.

Decreasing professionalization after 1648

The Peace of Münster resulted in a significant reduction in the size of the States' army. More important than the simple reduction was the fact that numerous experienced senior officers were discharged – although many continued to receive a pension, they were not expected to resume active service. The result was that the coherent regimental experience that had proved such an important source of success under Frederick Henry disappeared completely. The decision of the Provincial States of Holland to retain only 30,000 men – barely sufficient for defensive purposes – after 1648 can be explained by the fact that the real war threat came from the sea, not over land. Capable Grand Pensionary John de Witt devoted much time and energy to reconstructing the navy, which justly earned him the title Saviour of the United Provinces (see Chapter 6). But during that same period the army languished.

With no stadholder after William II's early and unexpected death in 1650, the central army command lacked guidance and clarity. Only a stadholder exerted sufficient weight to convince the provincial authorities to take appropriate measures – and spend considerable sums for that purpose. The commissioning of new officers grew increasingly lax: the requirement of a minimum number of years' previous military experience was no longer maintained. Appointments depended more and more on favouritism as the provincial deputies and councillors took turns to advance their relatives and friends; new captains were young and inexperienced; drill and exercise were grossly neglected; junior officers no longer showed respect for the army command; weaponry was worn out, and in the cavalry, the horses were poorly trained. A dispute regarding the hierarchy of command dragged on for years.[75]

In 1658 the Provincial States of Holland ordered a series of improvements and decided to reinforce the decree of 1618 on appointments, emphasizing the requirement of a minimum period of military service. There was a new rule concerning the minimum age: 19 for a cavalry captain, 17 for captains of the infantry and all lieutenants, cornets and ensigns. Sergeants, low in rank but of immense importance with regard to drill and discipline, needed to have four years' military experience before appointment; in addition they were required to pass a practical examination. Governors and commanders of garrisons had to see to it that the soldiers on sentry duty were exercised every two to three days, the companies as a whole at least once a month, and the regiments every two to three months.

These rules did not change the situation overnight, but within a couple of years the cavalry (2,000 men) was found to be in good condition and excellently armed. The infantry (26,000 men), however, took much longer to overhaul. In the 1660s the threat of war with England and the mounting crisis in Münster postponed reforms because the army needed to be expanded so rapidly. To support the captains the Council of State decided to raise the bounty for newly recruited foot soldiers from five to 15 guilders. But the lack of central control was then keenly felt, since the provinces were slow to provide the necessary information. During the raids by the Münster troops the Council of State had not even an overview of the number of new men recruited.

The Münster invasion was luckily short-lived, but the poor performance of the field army prompted its commander-in-chief, Johan Maurice of Nassau-Siegen, to introduce reforms, further amplified by the Council of State in 1667. Previously existing permanent companies were now restored. Each regiment was to consist of 1,400 foot soldiers (14 companies) and 480 horsemen (six companies). Ideally, the troops were to remain in the same garrison during the winter, making possible weekly training with the whole regiment. The entire field army was to exercise once a year under the command of the generals, experimenting with various methods and orders of attack. Indeed, between April and June 1668 the field army exercised at Bergen op Zoom.[76]

Laxity returned, however, as soon as the threat of war appeared to evaporate with the Triple Alliance of 1668 with Sweden and England (see Chapter 1). The provinces decided to reduce the strength of the army from 69,000 to 33,000 men and the regiments were once again divided. Only at the end of 1671, when war with France seemed imminent, was paper strength tripled to 95,000, aided by an increased recruitment bounty for captains of 20 guilders per soldier, but in the war that followed the inexperienced recruits stood no chance against the much better organized and trained French forces. Even the officers lacked adequate experience. In May 1672 Colonel Diderik Stecke wrote to the Frisian stadholder:

> God give that our discipline may return to its former state. Your Excellency would not believe the disorder and disobedience I encounter among all the inexperienced young officers of my regiment.[77]

The situation was critical, but the sudden cooperation between the Provincial States of Holland and the young stadholder William III resulted in a number of far-reaching emergency reforms. Because a number of provinces had been overrun by the French and remained under occupation for an extended period of time, Holland now paid almost 70 per cent of all companies, giving this well-organized province a massive influence over practical arrangements. In July 1672 the 'Holland' troops were to directly receive one month's pay, which boosted morale and discipline. Furthermore, the Holland Provincial States promised the captains a compensation of seven and a half guilder for each soldier taken prisoner by the enemy. This speeded up the return of soldiers awaiting ransom and resulted in the rapid reappearance of some 20,000 troops. Before this restructuring captains had had to find the funds for ransoms from their own budget. In the reforms William cooperated closely with Johan Maurice, Field Marshal Count of Waldeck, and Gaspar Fagel, grand pensionary of Holland since August 1672.

Professionalism was furthered by new States' support for the captains. Because of the continual difficulty in finding new recruits, the Provincial States of Holland decided in 1673 to accept the reality of the situation and announced that all companies with a strength of at least 90 per cent were to receive pay for a full company. Captains were thus granted 10 per cent additional pay as a free subsidy. Some slippage below these limits was condoned, but the bonus disappeared in that case (they only received pay for soldiers present at mustering). Companies with less than three-quarters strength were heavily fined; if the numbers were not supplemented within a certain period of time, the captain faced dismissal. Furthermore, for the first time in the history of the Dutch army, captains received compensation for soldiers who died: 33 guilders for a foot soldier, increased to 41 guilders four years later. Deserters and those who died from their wounds remained the full responsibility of the captains. At first these regulations applied only to the troops in Holland's pay, but in 1674 they became standard practice across the entire army.[78]

In this way the captain remained a semi-private supplier and commander but the conditions allowed him to meet the demands of the government in a more professional way. The limitations and sanctions in case of non-fulfilment were clear. During the whole Eighty Years War, finding new recruits had always competed with a multitude of other tasks and burdens; now the bounty permitted him to keep up a necessary minimum. A permanent muster commissioner for the field army supplemented the increased discipline of the captains. The Count of Waldeck, field marshal and William's right-hand man during these years, obtained full authority to restructure the companies, discharging captains who performed poorly and transferring the troops to the companies of better officers.

The new regulations proved to be a great success. The gap between the strength on paper and in reality remained but now only around 14 to 15 per cent, whereas during the time of Maurice and Frederick Henry the gap had amounted to a quarter or even a third. The attrition that was usual during campaigns diminished considerably too, since the financial compensations encouraged the captains to continually search for new recruits. Six to eight weeks was sufficient to bring numbers up to their former strength.[79]

Within two years the Dutch army was significantly reinforced and morale and discipline restored. Although not all problems were solved,[80] as a whole the Dutch army had recuperated remarkably fast. After the Peace of Nijmegen of 1678 the army was again reduced in size (to 40,000), but this time the organization of regiments was retained. It marked another step towards a more professional army. Military experience was not lost and the commanders staged regular exercises – in the garrisons and in the field – to keep troops disciplined and trained. By 1681 the difference in infantry strength on paper and in practice had declined to a mere 13 per cent.[81] At the time of the invasion of England (1688) Dutch troops acted as a model force for the English: disciplined and professional. William III introduced several reforms to the English army based on Dutch practice, and during the Nine Years War Dutch soldiers again operated with great efficiency.[82]

Conclusion: civilian control over the army

Since the 1570s military professionalization and the emerging institutions of the state had reinforced each other in the United Provinces. It is important to note that many of Orange's reforms applied initially only to Holland's forces. It was Orange in tandem with the Holland provincial government who moved the army strongly towards greater professionalism, in which it was followed by a States-General increasingly dominated by Holland after the Union of Utrecht (1579). Additional measures introduced by Orange – and principally the introduction of regular payments for soldiers who were quartered on the inhabitants of the garrison towns (see Chapter 4) – reduced much of the tension and unrest between soldiers and citizens throughout the northern Netherlands, while also enhancing civilian control over the army.

Orange's determination to get rid of the landsknecht corporative structures provided an excellent base for the reforming achievements of his son Maurice. The reforms of the 1570s provided a basic disciplinary code, permanent soldiers' contracts, a stricter hierarchy of command, a uniform military jurisdiction, and the establishment of regular, fixed pay. With the disappearance of corporate landsknechts' companies a new, common soldiers' identity emerged. Orange had thus created an organization in which the ordinary soldier was 'a salaried employee of the state rather than an adventurer' and 'more amenable to programmatic training and discipline'.[83] With this professionalization the soldiers lost much of the individuality that had characterized the age of the landsknechts.

Like his father, Maurice was determined to improve discipline. Thanks to the increased capacity of the Dutch state in comparison with the early decades of the Revolt – including the ability to pay the troops on a more regular base, not only in the garrisons but also in the field – Maurice's reforms advanced to a higher, integrated level. Maurice also introduced standardization of weaponry and achieved a higher degree of discipline through regular drill (see next chapter), aided by improved financial institutions (Chapter 7). As a consequence, the danger of mutinies rapidly disappeared after 1590. An army exceptionally advanced in professionalism was the result; without this efficient use of Dutch forces the likelihood of surviving the threat from Spain would have been much less.

The reforms ensured that Dutch military organization was renowned throughout Europe. The pamphlet *Dutch drawn to life* remarked:

> The Souldiers commit no where fewer Insolencies upon the Burgers, fewer Robberies upon the Countrey, nor the Officers fewer deceits upon the Souldiers. And lastly, they provide well that their General shall have small means to invade their Liberties; for ... the Commanders are disposed by the States themselves, not by the General.[84]

The persistence of some typical early modern semi-private arrangements, however, limited Dutch military professionalism, as in all other armies of the time. The captains of the company remained crucial middlemen but were difficult to dismiss in cases of glaring mismanagement or fraud. During the Eighty Years War the continuing military threat enforced professional conduct, but that constraint was removed as soon as war ended in 1648. The march towards a fully professional army was only resumed under William III, who introduced a new set of regulations that encouraged captains to manage their companies in a more professional way.

Throughout, the functional relationship between regular pay, civilian control and military discipline was very clear. Civilian control of Dutch military forces constituted an enormous advance in state formation. This lesson was not lost upon contemporaries. During the English Revolution General Monck tried to end the involvement of the army in politics. He told his officers that 'nothing was more injurious to discipline than their meeting in council to discuss civil things'. He had been trained in the Dutch service, where, as he said, 'soldiers received and observed commands, but gave none'.[85]

The rise of professionalism reduced significantly the negative burden on society represented by mutinies or uncontrolled provisioning by bands of soldiers. In the southern Netherlands mutinies disappeared after the early 1600s, but underpaid soldiers continued to pillage in order to obtain a decent living for the remainder of the century.[86] That transition, from mutinous, pillaging soldiers to a disciplined force, was evolutionary in most European countries. In the Netherlands, though, it was a revolutionary transition, achieved within two decades. The years around 1590 constitute a clear break in this regard, first in

Holland and then in the other provinces of the Dutch Republic. By the standards of the time, the Dutch army quickly reached a high degree of professionalism. This was the framework that allowed the typical Maurician tactics and drill to flourish, which is the subject of the next chapter.

Notes

1 Von Grimmelshausen, *Simplicius Simplicissimus*, p. 354; also quoted by De Graaf, *Oorlog*, p. 569.
2 Jones, 'Military revolution', p. 154.
3 Roberts, 'Military revolution', p. 20.
4 McNeill, *Pursuit of Power*, p. 76.
5 Lynn, *Giant*, 184. The French army even applied the old feudal *ban* and *arrière-ban* again in 1635 and 1636 with *grands nobles* sustaining part of the financial burden of a regiment which strengthened the position of noble fief-holders: Parrott, *Richelieu's Army*, pp. 63, 229–30.
6 Rowlands, *Dynastic State*, pp. 210, 361; Potter, 'War Finance', p. 139. For comparable developments in Venice: Hale and Mallett, *Military Organization*, p. 493. Thompson, 'Money', pp. 290 signals a rise of feudalism in the countryside of Naples as a result of warfare.
7 Anderson, *War*, p. 26.
8 Parrott, *Richelieu's Army*, p. 353.
9 Vermeir, *In staat*, pp. 172, 185, 188–9, 311; González de Léon, *Road to Rocroi*, p. 243.
10 Roberts, 'Military Revolution', p. 14; Hahlweg, *Heeresreform*, p. 25; Parker, *Military Revolution*, pp. 18–23; Nickle, *Military Reforms*, p. 6.
11 These markers of military professionalization are listed by several authors in more or less the same composition: Swart, *Krijgsvolk*, pp. 21–2; Trim, 'Introduction', pp. 6–11; Abrahamsson, *Military Professionalization*, pp. 15, 19; Thompson, *War and Society*, III, p. 262; Manning, *Apprenticeship*, pp. 430ff.
12 Tilly, *Coercion, Capital*, p. 53; Fynn-Paul (ed.), *War, Entrepreneurs*.
13 Redlich, *German Military Enterpriser*, I, p. 41, II, p. 107; Jones, 'Military Revolution', pp. 151–2; Landers, *Field*, p. 382; Manning, *Apprenticeship*, pp. 23, 40; Rowlands, *Dynastic State*, pp. 156–7, 217. In the Dutch navy too, captains operated as private entrepreneurs; see Bruijn, 'Mercurius', p. 104; Diekerhoff, *Oorlogsvloot*, p. 68.
14 Swart, *Krijgsvolk*, p. 35.
15 Van Deursen, 'Holland's experience', pp. 26–7; Arnade, *Beggars*, p. 226.
16 Hibben, *Gouda*, pp. 80–3; On the impact of towns in Dutch state formation, 't Hart, 'Cities and statemaking'; 't Hart, 'Urban impact'.
17 Wijn, 'Military forces', p. 209: 'It is general knowledge that the armies were made up from the scum of the nations.'
18 Adriaenssen, *Staatsvormend geweld*, pp. 158, 163–4; Kroener, 'Soldat', pp. 115, 120. Occasionally women also joined the service, dressed as men – for instance Catharina Simons in the Deventer garrison, whose true identity was only revealed at her death; see Holthuis, *Frontierstad*, p. 90; see also Dekker and Van der Pol, *Tradition*, pp. 37, 48, 91, 100.
19 Quoted in Adriaenssen, *Staatsvormend geweld*, p.162.
20 Ibid., pp. 170, 178; De Swaan, 'Widening circles'.
21 During the Eighty Years War about half of the States' troops came from Dutch-controlled territories.
22 Quoted by Wood, *King's Army*, p. 112.
23 Gunn, Grummit, and Cools, *War, State, and Society*, p. 254; Rooze-Stouthamer, *Opmaat*, p. 202; Parrott, *Business of War*, pp. 60–1.

24 Swart, *Krijgsvolk*, pp. 72–4; Möller, *Regiment*, pp. 95–100; Millar, 'Landsknecht', p. 98; Burschel, *Söldner*, pp. 27ff., 319.

25 Tracy, *Founding*, p. 27: In 1554 Charles V had already ordered that appointments of officers from below was not permitted in view of the poor quality of persons elected and the unrest that accompanied such elections.

26 Around the turn of the seventeenth century the corporative system gradually faded out in most armies with German foot soldiers; Sikora, 'Söldner', p. 226. Even then several remnants remained among the German troops in the Army of Flanders: Rooms, *Organisatie*, pp. 85, 88.

27 Wood, *The King's Army*, pp. 88–90. French companies remained rather small in the seventeenth century; the average number of men per company even shrunk to 22, which resulted in a significant increase in overall military costs; see Parrott, *Richelieu's Army*, p. 56.

28 Swart, *Krijgsvolk*, pp. 75–7. Showalter, 'Caste', p. 427: the typical landsknecht regiment numbered 4,000 men divided into ten companies. The usual landsknecht company at that time numbered around 300–400 men: Parrott, *Business of War*, p. 54. The Spanish also reduced the size of their companies but less rapidly: Thompson, 'Money', p. 281. On the ratio of pikemen to musketeers, see Chapter 3.

29 For larger companies a piper was added; since 1599, a provost was also appointed (standard until 1668) to prevent, among others, the desertion of troops. Chaplains were not appointed at company level but received commission by regiment.

30 Van Nimwegen, *Deser landen crijghsvolck*, p. 24.

31 Parrott, *Business of War*, p. 66.

32 Swart, *Krijgsvolk*, pp. 36, 116–24, 132–6; Friesland and Groningen maintained several landsknecht jurisdictional elements up to the eighteenth century.

33 A new president was appointed, but Maurice remained the highest in the hierarchy as 'Gerichtsherr'; Swart, *Krijgsvolk*, pp. 128–31, 138. On the strict military jurisdiction of the Dutch compared to the English, see Manning, *Apprenticeship*, p. 59. Alva's system of military jurisdiction was comparable to the Dutch (the latter may even have copied certain elements from the Spanish), but the jurisdiction in the Army of Flanders broke down after Alva and in particular under Olivares; see González de Léon, *Road to Rocroi*, pp. 109, 117, 272–6. By comparison the French army jurisdiction was not a pyramid and did not have a single coordinating authority, but consisted of a series of different administrative hierarchies, which prevented an effective response of civilians to crimes by soldiers: Parrott, *Richelieu's Army*, pp. 390, 461, 528–31.

34 Vermeesch, *Oorlog*, pp. 103–4; the event occurred in 1650.

35 Vermeir, *In staat*, pp. 193–7: in the Army of Flanders the civilian courts tried to obtain more influence on military jurisdiction in the 1630s; the result was only a continuing bickering over competences.

36 Swart, *Krijgsvolk*, pp. 79–80. No such thing as a pension existed for elderly soldiers. Some of the men were really old, like the 80-year-old quartermaster of the cuirassiers of Floris II of Culemborg. They remained on the pay list: Van Nimwegen, *Deser landen crijghsvolck*, pp. 63–4. Redlich, *German Military Enterpriser*, I, p. 506, on the continuation of the *Schlachtmonat* system in the Swedish army of the 1630s. Parrott, *Business of War*, p. 90: contracts in the Army of Flanders increasingly became open-ended after the 1570s, as in the States' army. In Germany, the transition towards more 'abstract' Articles of War and contracts for life service took place in the first half of the seventeenth century: Burschel, *Söldner*, p. 133.

37 Hale, *War and Society*, p. 169; Nickle, *Military Reforms*, p. 70.

38 Swart, *Krijgsvolk*, pp. 41, 82, 86. Later on, Sweden and England copied the 1590 articles for their own troops.

39 Van Slingelandt, *Staatkundige Geschriften*, pp. 150, 158; see also Landers, *Field*, p. 306, on permanent troops.

40 Adriaenssen, *Staatsvormend Geweld*, p. 275. On Ernst von Mansfeld, see also Parrott, *Business of War*, pp. 106–7.

41 Fissel, *English Warfare*, p. 174; Nolan, *Sir John Norreys*, p. 62. Scots, Walloons, Swiss, and Swedish also served. Despite the presence of Catholic soldiers, only Protestant ministers were allowed in the army camps; Van Nimwegen, *Deser landen crijghsvolck*, p. 43. Soldiers from the Netherlands constituted roughly 50 per cent of the armed forces; Zwitzer, *Militie*, p. 45. Other countries likewise showed a comparable national diversity in their armies, for example the 17 different national groupings in the Bavarian regiment of 1644; Tallett, *War and Society*, p. 89.

42 On desertion: Parker, *Thirty Years War*, p. 180. On the rivalries: Nolan, *Sir John Norreys*, pp. 55, 60; Van Nimwegen, *Deser landen crijghsvolck*, 109; Van Deursen, *Maurits*, p. 34. Rivalries among nationalities also resulted in difficulties within the Spanish army and the Army of Flanders: White, 'Experience', p. 35; González de Léon, *Road to Rocroi*, pp. 102, 169.

43 Van Deursen, *Maurits*, p. 85; Van Nimwegen, *Deser landen crijghsvolck*, pp. 44–5.

44 Probably since 1573 already in some towns: Tracy, *Founding*, p. 114, but since 1574 widespread in Holland. See also Nolan, *Sir John Norreys*, p. 41. In France a weekly pay arrangement came about in 1629, but this seems to have been abandoned again and re-introduced only after the War of Devolution: Lynn, *Giant*, p. 154; Parrott, *Richelieu's Army*, p. 343; Rowlands, *Dynastic State*, p. 209.

45 Equal to the standard pay of landsknechts of four Rhenish guilders. A mason earned about 15 guilders in the 1570s and a labourer between five and nine guilders. Although the latter's pay could be higher, Dutch soldiers were paid the year round, labourers only when they had work. On the level of pay for soldiers in general which shows that soldiers stood at the lower end of the social ladder: Hale, *War and Society*, pp. 111–12.

46 De Graaf, *Oorlog*, p. 185; as a punishment five soldiers were hanged.

47 Swart, *Krijgsvolk*, pp. 77–8; Tracy, *Founding*, p. 233, notes that in companies under Holland pay the 1588 measure had already been introduced in 1583; the other States' companies followed in 1588. On the irregularity of pay of the Spanish soldiers: Hale, *War and Society*, p. 114; Parker, *Army*, pp. 133–4. Wilson, *Thirty Years War*, p. 145: the so-called 'Dutch month' was introduced in Austria, reducing the year to nine months by 1607; two months consisted of cloth to make uniforms. The Austrian measures merely prompted further mutinies, since the imperial soldiers already had huge pay arrears. By contrast the Dutch made it work because they at least honoured their promise to pay the reduced rates.

48 Nickle, *Military Reforms*, p. 175; McNeill, *Pursuit of Power*, p. 128.

49 On digging in other armies: Hale, *War and Society*, p. 71. But indeed, Spanish and Italian elite troops in the Army of Flanders and ordinary soldiers in the French army also regarded manual tasks as not part of their 'vie militaire', Wood, *King's Army*, p. 304.

50 De Graaf, *Oorlog*, p. 312; Swart, *Krijgsvolk*, pp. 83–4. One guilder is 20 *stuivers*.

51 On similar difficulties of mustering elsewhere: Hintze, *Staat und Verfassung*, p. 70; Corvisier, *Armies*, pp. 64–5; Vermeir, *In staat*, p. 199; Rooms, *Organisatie*, pp. 184–5. Parrott, *Richelieu's Army*, p. 359 and Nolan, *Sir John Norreys*, p. 106 note that such fraudulence of officers was actually regarded as a legitimate means to recover costs incurred. Payment per head was a solution against fraud and proposed time and again, but in most early modern armies payment remained by lump sum to the captain. See also Parrott, *Business of War*, pp. 295–6.

52 Swart, *Krijgsvolk*, p. 95.

53 Ibid., pp. 98–111: by the 1580s, the provincial muster masters were gradually replaced by those of the States-General, although occasionally individual provinces still exerted their power to demand a mustering. In France the Third Estate also demanded presence at mustering, but this was not allowed.

54 Ibid., pp. 102–4. It should be remarked that already in 1584 and 1586 hardly any nickname was noted down in the Dutch muster rolls. Nicknames remained common in the German territories, but they disappeared in the course of the Thirty Years War too.

55 Corvisier, *Armies*, p. 65: In comparison with the Dutch, muster instructions of the Germans and the French were much more limited.

56 Swart, *Krijgsvolk*, p. 114. On irregular payments in other armies, see also Parrott, *Business of War*, p. 162.

57 De Jong, *Staat*, p. 32; these sums were considerable in comparison with soldiers' pay. See also Manning, *Apprenticeship*, p. 59.

58 Van Nimwegen, *Deser landen krijgsvolk*, pp. 88–9.

59 Swart, *Krijgsvolk*, p. 186.

60 Ibid., p. 188; Parker, *Military Revolution*, p. 72. De Cauwer, *Tranen*, p. 183: on the failure to house all wounded soldiers of the Spanish army in 1629. On the poor medical care in France: Lynn, *Giant*, pp. 421–2, 432 and Parrott, *Richelieu's Army*, pp. 535–7. In Spain itself only one military hospital existed, in Pamplona; see White, 'Experience', p. 21. On the non-existence of medical care in the Thirty Years War, Pagès, *The Thirty Years War*, p. 179. Corvisier, *Armies*, p. 84: Queen Christina of Sweden erected the Krigmanshus, a military hospital, in Vodsterna in 1647.

61 The solution of 1586 was modelled after Orange's schemes, which had not been put into practice; Swart, *Krijgsvolk*, pp. 187–8, 198. Muiden is situated to the south-east of Amsterdam, Purmerend to the north of Amsterdam.

62 In connection with plans to erect a naval hospital at Chatham, quoted by Darley, *John Evelyn*, p. 198. Leuftink, *Geneeskunde*, p. 124 notes a gradual improvement in medical care for the sailors of the navy; he mentions a death rate of 12 per cent in the hospitals; on the Zwolle rates, De Graaf, *Oorlog*, p. 501. In 1603 Maurice had a field apothecary installed; De Graaf, *Oorlog*, p. 366.

63 The regularization of warfare also sometimes resulted in agreements between the troops not to shoot, such as in the siege of Breda in 1625, when States' soldiers threw tobacco and cheese towards the Spanish in the trenches and the others threw back bread. Vorsters, *Beleg*, p. 93.

64 Parker, *Army*, p. 144; Tallett, *War*, p. 130.

65 Van Vliet, *Vissers*, pp. 260–1; Van Nimwegen, *Deser landen crijghsvolck*, p. 64–6; Van Deursen, *Maurits*, p. 92; Van Deursen, 'Holland's experience', p. 37. Between France and Spain such a treaty came about first in 1639: Lynn, *Giant*, pp. 427–8. On children in the Thirty Years War, see Hahn, 'Kriegserfahrungen'.

66 All these measures pertained only to the officers in garrisons, since the officers of the field army (including captains and lower officers) were appointed by Maurice as captain general (= head of the army) and after him by Frederick Henry. Van Nimwegen, *Deser landen crijghsvolck*, p. 37.

67 The date: 1618 is significant as it points to a diminishing influence of the provinces' powers and a strengthening of the stadholders'. In this time period Van Old-enbarnevelt was imprisoned on the charge of treason (see Chapter 1). While the Dutch appointment system professionalized its army, in the Army of Flanders there was a departure from the strict rules imposed by Alva – for example, the requirements regarding merit and experience were no longer observed; see González de León, *Road to Rocroi*, pp. 72–80, 333–4.

68 Van Nimwegen, *Deser landen crijghsvolck*, pp. 38–9. All these regulations pertained to the Dutch companies; for the foreign companies in the Dutch army – the French, Scottish and English – the appointment of officers remained in the hands of the stadholders as captain-general. After the Peace of 1648, the Holland States-Provincial demanded the disbanding of 31 foreign companies, leaving only 'Dutch' troops whose officers' appointments were significantly in their control. A major side effect was the decrease in the influence of Stadholder William II, which explains in part his violent move towards Amsterdam (see Chapter 1).

69 Van Nimwegen, *Deser landen crijghsvolck*, pp. 36–7; Frijhoff and Spies, *Hard-won Unity*, p. 97; on the nobility in the Dutch army and their martial culture, Trim, 'Army', pp. 279ff.; Swart, 'Mythe van Maurits'.

70 Lipsius' *Politicorum Libri Six* (published 1589), a copy of which he presented to his sometime student Maurice, quoted by Rothenberg, 'Maurice', p. 35; see also Trim, 'Army', p. 270. Hierarchy of command existed in the French army, but there the problem was that some nobles still raised private armies: Lynn, *Giant*, pp. 285–6.

71 Van Nimwegen, *Deser landen crijghsvolck*, pp. 37–40. Absenteeism was particularly strong among the French officers; see Lynn, *Giant*, pp. 277–9; Parrott, *Richelieu's Army*, p. 363; Anderson, *War*, pp. 56–7; see also González de León, *Road to Rocroi*, p. 188, on the growing absenteeism in the Army of Flanders. In contrast to the Dutch, the French and the Spanish army commanders were less afraid to 'reduce' companies that failed, discharging officers and distributing the soldiers over other units, but this included the risk of soldiers leaving the army. Finding new recruits was always difficult in the Low Countries because of the high demand for labour in industry and trade.

72 The sale of offices was endemic in most armies of the time; see also Thompson, *War and Society*, IV, p. 25. In the French army sale of offices was widespread, but Lynn, *Giant*, pp. 268, 275, noted that during Louis XIV's reign a minimum of two years' service as a cadet (volunteer) was required before a company could be bought.

73 Van Nimwegen, *Deser landen crijghsvolck*, pp. 53–6, 62. Corvisier, *Armies*, p. 69: the Dutch recruitment method, according to which the recruit came under the orders of the army the moment he was signed on, was quite costly too. Comparable rates of attrition (one-third to one-quarter) also existed in the Spanish armies: De Cauwer, *Tranen*, p. 47; Parker, *Army*, p. 177; White, 'Experience', p. 5.

74 Wijn, 'Military forces', p. 213; the cavalry had permanent regiments from 1635 onwards. In comparison, in the French army regiments became permanent only under Louis XIV; Rowlands, *Dynastic state*, p. 99.

75 Valkenier, *'t Verwerd Europa*, p. 253; see also Van Nimwegen, *Deser landen crijghsvolck*, pp. 260–7.

76 Ibid., pp. 269–71.

77 Quoted by ibid., p. 273.

78 Ibid., pp. 280–5; Van Nimwegen 'Transformation', pp. 175–6. In comparison to the Dutch, the Spanish and French companies were much smaller in the second half of the seventeenth century (between 40 and 55): Rooms, *Organisatie*, p. 87; Lynn, *Giant*, p. 51.

79 Van Nimwegen, *Deser landen crijghsvolck*, pp. 281–4, 291.

80 Since William had nothing to say about the companies of Friesland, Drenthe and Groningen, their numbers remained on the low side; their garrisons also suffered considerably from absentee commanders. Ibid., pp. 286–7.

81 By comparison, the lapse in the French army (around 40 per cent in the 1630s, see Parrott, *Richelieu's Army*, p. 168) also dropped to between 10 and 20 per cent in the 1690s: Rowlands, *Dynastic State*, p. 171.

82 Manning, *Apprenticeship*, pp. 432, 438–9.

83 Feld, 'Middle-class society', p. 433.

84 Anon., *Dutch Drawn to Life*, pp. 121–2.

85 Clark, *English Provincial Society*, p. 75. One by one the armies of Europe conformed to this rule. Manning, *Apprenticeship*, p. 441 shows that in the course of the eighteenth century the British army became legally subordinated to civilian control.

86 Vermeir, *In staat*, p. 16.

3   The Dutch 'Schoole of War'

Drill, tactics and siege warfare

[The Maurician linear formations] were fundamental changes; and they were essential tactical in nature. But they entailed others *of much larger implication*. They entailed, for instance, a new standard in the training and discipline of the ordinary soldier. ... The army was no longer a brute mass, in the Swiss style, nor a collection of bellicose individuals, in feudal style; it was to be an articulated organism of which each part responded to the impulses from above.[1]

The professional framework of Dutch army organization and the way it was strongly embedded in urban society and under civilian control, as set out in the last chapter, constituted necessary conditions for the introduction of new tactics and regular drill. Although few historians deny the accomplishments of Maurice in the introduction of linear tactical formations,[2] the most important critical trend in the Military Revolution debate contends that these tactics had little practical impact because the Dutch-style methods were rarely applied – partly because of the relative absence of battles in warfare dominated by sieges. Jeremy Black put it succinctly: 'the Dutch did not sweep to victory over Spain after the adoption of the Nassau reforms'.[3] Other critics suggest that the principal ideas concerning discipline and drill were of Roman origin and that this heritage was neither reserved for Dutch military leaders alone nor intimately connected to the introduction of firearms. Military commanders all over Europe also read the classics and the formations of pikemen in the earlier sixteenth century likewise demanded regular training.[4]

These arguments are, up to a point, convincing and will be discussed more fully below. Yet the critics of Michael Roberts have overlooked one major point: *of much larger implication* (he wrote) was the fact that the new tactics entailed new standards of discipline and drill (see also quotation above). The importance of drill and discipline can hardly be denied. John Lynn observed that armies could grow only when manageable, and discipline-bred drill was thus of huge importance that soldiers would not turn against civilians.[5] This line of argument went back at least to Max Weber, who suggested that the introduction of regular drill constituted a fundamental development in the history of European warfare: 'Gunpowder and all the war techniques associated with it became significant only with the existence of discipline'.[6] Thanks to drill, not only did the rate of fire increase,[7] but troops were also more likely to remain in formation and obey their superiors: the 'rationally uniform' character of the 'obedience of a plurality of men' was crucial.[8] Drill as such was not new, but regular and standardized drill, implemented as part of a daily routine, was.[9] To what degree this was primarily an achievement of the Maurician reforms will be examined in this chapter.

The tactical reforms of Maurice did not take place in a void. They were accompanied by the changes in organization and funding described in the previous chapter, but also involved standardization of companies, standardization of weaponry, the application of ancient models to new tactical formations, the introduction of regular drill, and innovations in fortifications and siege warfare. It was this 'package' that for contemporaries made the army troops of Maurice and William Louis the 'Military Schools where most of the Youth of Europe did learn their Military Exercises'.[10] Reform-minded rulers looked at the Dutch military system for inspiration; numerous celebrated commanders had taken service in the army of Maurice and Frederick Henry, among others Frederick William, elector of Brandenburg-Prussia, and Turenne, later field marshal for Louis XIV.[11]

The central question of this chapter is to what extent these tactical reforms under Maurice constituted an outstanding, typically 'Dutch' development. The previous chapter has already pointed to significant Huguenot inspiration; a certain degree of interaction with the Army of Flanders must have occurred as well. The conclusions of recent research are discussed in relation to the following fields: the role of firearms, standardization, the countermarch, the drill that accompanied the countermarch, innovations in siege warfare and also the tactical constraints of the time. The designation of Dutch tactics and drill as a true 'Schoole of War' was accurate in a number of respects, but some innovations originated elsewhere, or were autonomous developments in approximately the same period. It was the 'package' as a whole, including the regular pay and other reforms, that rendered the military organization under Maurice truly unique. Yet as was also demonstrated in the previous chapter, the Dutch 'Schoole of War' quickly lost its lead after peace was signed in 1648.

Increasing standardization and the proportion of firearms

Throughout the sixteenth century Spain's military successes had been based on utilizing disciplined pikemen in massive formations, deployed in infantry squares. In this tactical formation the elite *tercios* were unequalled at the time.[12] By contrast Orange favoured the use of firearms (at that time harquebuses – in Dutch, *roers*) and his companies of 1573 were at least 70 per cent harquebusiers, probably following Huguenot military practice in which even an 80 per cent proportion of firearms had not been uncommon. Smaller, more mobile units had proved effective in the 'petite guerre' of the French Religious Wars and likewise in the early years of the Dutch Revolt. By 1575 Orange had

Table 3.1 Distribution of major arms categories in the Dutch infantry, in percentages, 1572–1621

Years	Firearms		Edged weapons	
	Harquebusiers	Musketeers	Pikemen	Halberdiers and swordsmen
1572–7	76	4	13	7
1578		67		33
1579		58		42
1588		47	47	6
1593	45	18	35	4
1596	40	18	40	2
1598	24	32	38	6
1599	37	25	38	–
1607	–	58	42	–
1609–20	–	54	46	–
1621	–	64	36	–

Source: De Jong, *Staat*, p. 33; Van Nimwegen, *Deser landen crijghsvolck*, pp. 84–7; Swart, *Krijgsvolk*, pp. 145–6

replaced a significant proportion of the harquebusiers by musketeers because the larger bullets of the heavier musket had greater 'stopping power' against the armour of the harnessed cavalry than the harquebus.[13]

Yet the proportion of soldiers with firearms declined with the establishment of the States' army in 1576. The number of men with edged weapons increased; the percentage of soldiers with firearms fell from 67 per cent in 1578 to 58 per cent in 1579 and 47 per cent in 1588 (see Table 3.1).[14] One reason for this decline was the shift from 'small war' to regular war, in which musketeers needed good pike protection against Spanish cavalry attacks. In all probability the soldiers who were equipped with firearms were still poorly trained and the effectiveness of their volley fire will have been limited, to say the least. The limited effectiveness of firearms may not have been so much a problem in guerilla warfare, but in larger formations the efficiency of infantry gunpowder weapons declined. Remarkably, this downward trend ended around 1590. Thereafter the proportion of pikemen was always less than half, and after 1620 their share diminished further, as will be discussed below.

In the cavalry the rapid replacement of lances by firearms was unmistakable, as throughout north-western Europe.[15] Their tactics had become outmoded. In the Low Countries the heavily armoured lancers were impractical, as mounted attacks at full gallop were only feasible on a flat surface in an open field. A 'light' cavalry, called cuirassiers, with small firearms (pistols) appeared more versatile and more suitable for warfare. By the later 1590s lancers had but all disappeared in both the Spanish and States' armies.[16]

The Maurician standardization of weaponry which accompanied these changes was an important step forward, reducing the overwhelming variety in weapons and calibres.[17] The general decree on arms and armour of 1596 issued by Maurice and William Louis specified that cuirassiers were to ride strong horses and carry a cuirass, closed helmets, arm protection, an armoured glove, a short sword and two flintlock pistols. Each company of one hundred should have 25 more fully protected cuirassiers with a heavy cuirass and additional protection for the thighs. As compensation for the weight of their armour these elite horsemen did not need to carry their luggage themselves – that was taken care of by servants or boys on bidets, pack horses. The cuirassiers were supported by harquebusiers, also on horseback, who were protected by an open helmet and a cuirass and carried a sword and a carbine, a gun of about 90 centimetres long that could be fired from horseback.[18]

A comparable set of regulations was introduced for the infantry in 1596, further amplified in 1599. Pikemen were regarded by contemporaries as the elite corps of the infantry; after 1596 their proportion hovered around 40 per cent while other edged weapons (such as halberds and broadswords) disappeared completely. Following the ceasefire of 1607 the harquebusiers were discharged first (no new harquebusiers were hired subsequently) which temporarily increased the proportion of pikemen, but after the Truce of 1609–21 pikemen constituted approximately one-third of the Dutch troops (see also Table 3.1).[19] The best and tallest soldiers were to carry the heavy wooden pikes of 5.5 metres (18 feet), reduced in later decrees to 4.5 metres (15 feet), along with a rapier, a kind of sword. Furthermore, they had to wear a helmet and protection for their neck, breast and back; pikemen in the front rows also wore protection for their arms, thighs and lower belly. Musketeers had preferably to be men with strong legs; the barrel of their gun should measure some 150 centimetres with a calibre of ten to twelve bullets in the pound. In order to reduce the weight of the weaponry they were expected to carry, some pikemen and musketeers shortened their pikes and barrels, but after 1599 they could expect heavy fines during mustering (see also Chapter 2).[20] Gunners gradually evolved into a distinct corps, and from 1599 onwards they were obliged to provide evidence of their proficiency.[21]

Standardization of weaponry for the infantry and cavalry was an outstanding and specific Dutch achievement, unequalled for decades in other European armies. The standardization of heavy artillery came later however, and in this regard a significant degree of interaction was evident: the Dutch first followed the Spanish example and then improved upon their scheme. In 1609 Count de Buquoy, Spain's general of the artillery, reduced the calibres of their cannon to the 48-pounder full cannon, the 24-pounder demi-cannon, the 10 or 12-pounder quarter cannon and the five or six-pounder eighth cannon. The Spanish artillery expert Ufano wrote in 1613:

> There was such diversity and confusion among the old pieces that it cost a great deal of trouble and effort to obtain their ammunition. Nowadays we have but a single range of artillery, all based on the full cannon and its fractions down to the eight. It is truly remarkable to have reduced all our guns to these four calibres.[22]

During the Twelve Years Truce of 1609–21, Maurice followed this example in reducing the casting of cannon to 48, 24, 12 and 6-pound calibres, thus discarding the tens and fives completely. He also conducted experiments on the beach at Scheveningen to establish by how much he could reduce the length of the barrel without diminishing the range. One consequence was a reduction in the weight of the barrel of the demi-cannon by 316 pounds.[23] In addition the Dutch often used mortars to fire shells during sieges.[24]

Regular exercises and new formations

All in all the increased uniformity in the composition of the companies and the weaponry of the soldiers furthered the professionalization of the Dutch army. After 1596 the stadholders controlled armed units that could be used interchangeably to form battalions and regiments. In the Low Countries infantry predominated and tactical improvements therefore centred above all this arm.[25] Time and again the elite *tercios* of the Army of Flanders proved much more experienced – as was obvious, for example, at the battle of Amerongen (1585), when both sides deployed more or less an equal number of troops.[26] The reforms of the infantry introduced by the stadholders were the product of simple necessity: something new was needed to withstand the superior and far more efficient forces of the Spanish.

Spanish preoccupation with France during the early 1590s (see Chapter 1) provided the opportunity for experiments by the Dutch. The *tercios* of the Army of Flanders were formidable and experienced because of their long service. The response of the stadholders was the introduction of regular drill. In particular after July 1592, when the capture of Steenwijk resulted in a relaxation of Spanish pressure in the east, Maurice and William Louis let the troops try out and practise how to turn, advance, retreat, double their lines, and so on, without destroying the order. Thousands of troops, mainly from Friesland, Holland and England, assembled near Giethoorn for this purpose.

Drill in the Dutch forces reached quite different proportions compared to other early modern armies. Elsewhere at this period exercises were usually limited to new recruits and consisted mainly in 'teaching the musketeer the use of his weapon so that it would be a greater hazard to the enemy than to himself'. In fact most soldiers learned their trade through warfare itself and the actual extent of training was dependent upon the inclination of the captain. Drill was usually meant for pikemen and musketeers separately, not in tandem; regular exercises were not government policy, and where it was officially sanctioned it was poorly implemented.[27] Orange had already ordered exercises once a week in the 1580s, though never in large formations. The frequency of drill in the Maurician reforms of the 1590s and the exercises combining pike formations with forces equipped with firearms was undoubtedly a novelty in early modern Europe. Captain Frederik van Vervou noted: 'Whenever the army is at rest the soldiers are trained in the proper use of the arms and how to form the order of battle, which is highly prizeworthy'. A French captain who stayed in

Delft during the winter described in a letter how they exercised every day. Several decades later this had not changed: Turenne, the famous French army commander who served in the Netherlands in order to learn the military vocation, wrote in 1631: 'We are still at the same place and do nothing. All we do is drill the majority of the troops each morning'.[28]

For the larger and more complex formations soldiers needed to know how to obey all commands faultlessly. William Louis found appropriate terms in the writings of the Greek Aelianus Tacticus and the Byzantine Emperor Leo VI and had them translated into Dutch. Although the classics were not only read by the Dutch officers corps, it was the stadholders who transformed the recommendations into a new set of rules for the captains and made them applicable to daily training and the handling of firearms. Maurice also translated the orders into German, French and English, underlining the multi-national composition of his army.[29] The efficiency of these commands was praised in an English pamphlet:

> How be it the practise of Aelians precepts hath long lien wrapped vp in darknes, & buried (as it were) in the ruines of time, vntill it was revived, & restored to light not long since in the vnited Provinces of the low-Countries, which Countries at this day are the Schoole of war, whither the most Martiall spirits of Europe resort to lay downe the Apprentiship of their service in Armes.[30]

Furthermore, Dutch formations were considerably smaller than in most other armies, with the probable exception of the French. The Army of Flanders used the *escuadrón* that could contain as many as 3,000 men, but that tied up a great part of the soldiers in the middle and rendered them redundant during any battle. William Louis and Maurice developed a basic battalion size of 500 to 600 men, which was more flexible and made more efficient use of the available manpower.[31] Following Roman precedent battalions operated independently from one another, deployed in a checkers pattern with alternating front and rear battalions, to permit battalions at the front being relieved by those at the back without creating chaos in the ranks.[32] The benefits of the checkered structure became obvious during the battle of Nieuwpoort: when some units retreated, Spanish soldiers thought the whole army was retreating and broke from their formations, giving pursuit, after which they were easily attacked and quickly routed by the remaining Dutch forces. Despite the importance of these victories, however, the main contribution of the new tactics was the strict obedience which training inculcated.

Training also counted in firing volleys and executing the counter-march. Pikemen stood as a rule in the middle of the Dutch formations, flanked at both sides by the musketeers and harquebusiers. The disadvantage of these firearms was their notorious lack of accuracy. They were most effective when the muskets fired simultaneously, in a volley.[33] As it took some time to reload a musket or harquebus, the firing of a volley by a front row of soldiers was best followed up rapidly by a second row, and then a third row, and so on until the first line could fire again. Such tactics were practiced elsewhere – reported, for example, in the Army of Flanders in 1587.[34] Some kind of interaction might well have been possible between the two belligerents. The countermarch itself, in which the front rank fired, then turned and marched to the rear, followed by the second row and so on, did not originate in the Dutch forces. However, the calculations concerning the necessary lines of retreat and the simultaneity of the movements were innovatory, as was the degree of discipline exhibited by the soldiers. Musketeers retreating with their matches on fire could create enormous havoc among their fellow soldiers, many of whom were carrying powder on their body, but the wide space necessary for safe retreat rendered the whole front of the battalion somewhat vulnerable. A scheme of William Louis signalled a major improvement: the men were not to turn and retreat individually but as a rank of five. Space was thus not essential between every row. Such schemes were improved, and after 1609 the standard battalion consisted of 250 pikemen and 240 musketeers divided over five blocks, with rows of five pike men across and ten deep and six blocks of four musketeers across and ten deep. After firing, half the musketeers went to the left and half to the right, retreating along the lanes between the blocks. In this way the total frontline measured not more than about 57 metres, which significantly reduced its vulnerability.[35]

During the Twelve Years Truce, Dutch involvement in the War of the Jülich Succession was used by Maurice and William Louis to try out alternative formations, with two rows of musketeers preparing to fire within a combination of three battalions into one brigade – which resulted in the simultaneous fire of 72 musketeers (three times 24 per battalion) – and the placing of musketeers alternately before and behind the pikemen. Regular exercises increased the rate of fire, making it a 'unit of continuous production'.[36] With such tactical improvements the fame of the 'Schoole of War' spread further. The innovations were transferred to other armies, among others by John of Nassau who entered Swedish service to train its forces.[37]

In fact, the Dutch rarely utilized such tactical formations on the battlefield and none of the battles of the Eighty Years War were decisive.[38] But the complicated manoeuvres accustomed the troops to operate in coordination with both other infantry units and the cavalry. Above all, Dutch drill and commands minutely regulated the actions of the soldiers and ingrained the habit of obedience, and the reforms were thus responsible for troops that operated in a 'rationally uniform' way.[39] The art of warfare had changed completely since the earlier sixteenth century. With the disappearance of halberdiers and swordsmen and the increasing utilization of firearms, the last remnants of medieval man-to-man fighting were replaced by less personal 'undiscriminating slaughter at a distance'.[40] In much of Europe this transformation took the form of a gradual evolution. In the Dutch army, however, the development had been truly revolutionary.

Later in the seventeenth century the depth of the formation was reduced, first from ten to six lines, and then from six to three. The armour for the foot soldiers was also reduced, which improved their physical coordination. In the cavalry the cuirassiers were gradually replaced by more mobile, even lighter armoured horsemen; in the Dutch army this transformation had taken place by the 1650s. As the musketeers proved increasingly able to repulse cavalry attacks, the number of pikemen decreased further; in addition their guns became lighter, with 14 instead of 12 bullets in the pound. Bayonets were used first by the grenadiers, a new elite vanguard corps established in the Dutch army in 1670, modelled on the French example; in 1674 William III ordered that each company should have 20 grenadiers.[41] None of these later innovations, however, were 'Made in the Netherlands': by then the 'Schoole of War' had migrated to other forces in Europe – first the Swedes and subsequently the French.

After 1650 the Dutch forces lost a great deal of their efficiency due to lack of drill and poor discipline. William III, however, was determined to restore regular training and discipline and he demanded harsh punishment for insubordination or failure to obey orders: the men should fear the Supreme Council of War more than the opposing French army. Indiscipline was still widespread in 1673, when Johan Maurice wrote: 'The negligence of all captains, lieutenants and ensigns and the disdain for their orders is so great that it is hard to believe and insupportable.'[42] Three captains and three lieutenants who had refused to follow orders were forced to pay fines amounting to two to three times their monthly salary; in addition they were humiliated by being reduced to the ranks and forced to serve as pikemen in William's guard. Ten foot soldiers and 14 cavalrymen who had fled to the French during the battle at Lopik had to draw lots to decide who would be hanged; four were executed, while the others had to run the gauntlet three times on three consecutive days. William's disciplinary regulations concerned above all conduct within the army itself. Earlier stadholders had often punished misconduct in military-civil interactions; William cared less about such matters. His primary aim was the absolute obedience of soldiers in order that they would perform better under fire.[43]

Fortresses and fortifications

Disciplined troops constituted an enormous advantage in siege warfare. Sieges always demanded a high degree of patience and restraint on the part of the troops. The difference between the Dutch soldiers' outlook and the more 'heroic' or 'martial' identity of other nations was very evident. For instance, during the siege of 's-Hertogenbosch an attempted assault by French soldiers turned out to be a particular bloody episode. They did not secure and defend the breach as ordered but advanced in a disorderly way, each soldier trying to demonstrate their prowess to Frederick Henry, which led to huge losses.[44]

Both the Spanish and the Dutch improved upon their defences by applying the principles of the *trace italienne*, with thick low ramparts and pointed bastions, artillery platforms that facilitated flanking fire along the ramparts and ditches.[45] The complete fortress with powerful extensive walls reinforced by earthworks that became the hallmark of advanced fortification systems in the

Netherlands was not developed by a single individual but resulted from the interaction of engineering techniques on both sides. Ravelins were an imitation of the Italian original, but the *demi-lune* ('half-moon') form and the hornworks were typically 'Dutch', that is to say, developed in the Low Countries. In the early decades of the Revolt the Brussels government could draw upon expert technical advice from talented Italian engineers such as Bartolomeo Campi, Chiappino Vitelli, Gabrio Serbelloni, Francesco Pacciotto and Properzio Barozzi. But Parma also obtained the support of Master Hanse, a Dutch engineer captured during a siege and who remained in Spanish service. The Dutch were to profit above all from the skills of Adriaen Anthonisz from Alkmaar, a former burgomaster. By 1589 he had been involved in no fewer than 29 different sets of urban fortifications in the Republic.[46]

This practice-based engineering was supported by textbooks on fortification. The first ones had been published in Italian; Spanish and Dutch ones followed in the 1590s. Simon Stevin, the leading advisor of Maurice on military logistics and fortifications, published his *Sterktenbouwing* (fortification construction) in 1594. To improve such knowledge among fellow engineers, a chair of engineering was established at Leiden University. Teaching began there in 1600, carried out in Dutch (not Latin) in order to attract the widest possible range of military talent in the Netherlands. At Franeker University the son of Adriaen Anthonisz, Adriaen Metius, was appointed to teach geometry in 1598; Metius stimulated the study of fortifications and conduct of sieges there. The science of military engineering flourished in the northern Netherlands. Metius wrote *Fortificatie en Stercktebouwinghe*, in which he explained the work of his father and other authors. Other famous scholars in this field were Hendrik Hondius, Samuel Marolois, Adam Freitag and Andreas Cellarius.[47]

Although these scholars were by no means all Dutch by birth, the study of the science of military engineering became increasingly concentrated in the north rather than the south. Dutch-trained engineers became an 'export item' and were in demand all over Europe, in places ranging from English strongholds to Berlin, Hamburg, Bremen, Danzig and even the Russian fortresses of Rostov and Terki. In contrast, the Spanish did not establish a school for engineers before the final quarter of the seventeenth century. As a result the international diffusion of Spanish-Dutch experience, or the 'Old Netherlands System' as it came to be called, was largely achieved by the Dutch. This added significantly to the existing reputation of the United Provinces as a true 'Schoole of War'.[48]

Several decades later, however, the Old Netherlands System proved vulnerable when the French, following the advice of the famous engineer Sébastien Le Prestre de Vauban, aimed their artillery at the bastions instead of the walls, which rapidly destroyed the cannon of the defenders.[49] Again the Dutch were forced to introduce major innovations. In 1676 Naarden was altered to become a modern fortress: the earthen bastions were enlarged with two platforms, one higher and one lower to permit the positioning of more and heavier artillery. The lower part of the bastions, the main rampart and the ravelins were constructed of stone; the upper part continued to be made of earth. Outworks became less important and many were demolished. The new approach came to be called the 'New Netherlands System': it adopted Vauban's innovations and added improvements by the famous Dutch engineer, Menno van Coehoorn. Coehoorn's main innovation was the strengthening of the covered way with half-moon-shaped strongholds, which provided a protected base from which raids against the besiegers were possible but with an open rear to prevent its use by the enemy. In the later 1670s similar fortifications were built at Sas van Gent, Grave, Breda and 's-Hertogenbosch, followed by other towns in subsequent decades.[50]

Yet leadership in the science of fortifications had now passed decisively to France. Following the French example of the *frontière de fer* (along the French northern border with the Spanish Netherlands and the north-eastern border with Germany), a line of fortified towns with Maastricht, Bergen op Zoom and towns in Zeeland-Flanders constituted the main 'rampart' of the Republic after the peace of 1678.

The art of siege warfare

With the advent of the earthen *trace italienne*, the spade often did more to capture a town than firearms. Steenwijk fell to the Dutch in 1592 not because of the latter's impressive rain of shot from the artillery, but because of the way its defences were undermined by trenches. Shortly afterwards, Coevorden's strong walls and ditch of 30 metres wide were only conquered due to the spade. At the 1593 siege of Geertruidenberg Maurice employed as many as 5,000 pioneers (soldiers or peasants hired to do the digging). His siege works were so impressive that visitors flocked to see them during the operations.[51]

The main innovation to warfare in the Low Countries introduced by Alva's engineer Vitelli was to entrench the besieging army within a fortress of its own, thereby making counter-attack much more difficult. An inner line of redoubts and trenches faced the town (contravallation); the outer perimeter (circumvallation) was intended to prevent any attack by a relief army. At the siege of Mons in 1572 Vitelli integrated these as interconnected lines with ditches and redoubts that successfully held off Orange's attempts at relief; as a result Mons was forced to capitulate to the Spanish. This method was further systematized by Spínola, Maurice and Frederick Henry and evolved eventually into surrounding an entire town by these lines of contra- and circumvallation.[52] Over time each side emulated the other, leading to further sophistication of schemes and devices. Count Rennenberg failed with the siege of Deventer in 1578 because he did not seal off the town completely, but Maurice in 1591 did so and succeeded. In 1583, when Dutch rebels tried to take the Wouw castle (near Roosendaal in Brabant), the surprise element of the siege was all but lost as they had to wait so long before the 15 cannons arrived from Antwerp. A decade later Maurice was fully aware of the importance of striking fast and did not begin a siege before the artillery was at hand.[53]

Once the circum- and contravallation lines had been constructed, it was all but impossible to relieve a besieged town. Such lines could be very long: 15 kilometre at the siege of Groenlo in 1627, 30 to 35 kilometre at the siege of 's-Hertogenbosch in 1629.[54] To a significant degree these lines were strengthened by digging ditches and breastworks and by inducing inundations. The abundance of water and the marshy terrain in much of the Low Countries added a specific instrument to the art of siege warfare: strategic flooding. This device had not been unknown in the Middle Ages, but during the Revolt its application was widened and extended over far larger areas than previously.[55] The first inundation of the Revolt was the result of a spontaneous action by Brill's master carpenter Rochus Meeuwisse: he jumped into the water and destroyed a sluice with his axe, thus preventing the recapture of the town by Spanish soldiers in 1572. Sonoy, Orange's governor in North Holland, is credited with the first large-scale inundations – for instance in the successful defence of Alkmaar in 1573.[56]

Thereafter Orange periodically favoured inundations as a tactic, not only to strengthen the defence but also to imperil the encampment of the besiegers and enable the provisioning of the besieged by boat, such as during the siege of Leiden in 1574. With the increasing threat to Antwerp in 1584 Orange advocated opening the sluices and cutting the dykes to the north of the town in order to create an access to enable the supply of provisions and fresh troops should the town be besieged. This scheme was blocked by powerful Antwerp cattle owners who utilized the meadows for grazing. Unfortunately, without such a supply route over water, the town was forced to surrender to the Spanish in 1585.[57]

The Spanish were less reliant upon inundations, but they made ingenious use of waterways. At the siege of Haarlem in 1573 they dug a canal that improved their communications and simultaneously cut the supply line of the rebels. Another canal was dug for the siege of Antwerp of no less than ten kilometres in length to facilitate the transportation of material needed for Parma's spectacular blockade bridge over the river Scheldt. This bridge was truly phenomenal: it spanned a channel about half a kilometre wide and 20 metres deep and was made up of piles and boats, with a musket-proof parapet on top and a fortress at each end.[58]

More than hitherto, mathematical calculation and planning was an essential part of sieges, above all during the digging works. The construction of the approaching zigzag trenches required close coordination with the artillery personnel. At the 1594 siege of Groningen, for example, the Dutch cannon were located too early in their final position, leaving them easy prey for a raid by the defenders. In general, when the approaching trenches had reached the 55-metre line from the town walls and were thus within range of accurate musket fire, the work of specialized sappers began.[59] Soldiers were only willing to perform these risky duties for extra payment: 25 or 26 guilders per *roede* (around 3.5 metres), sometimes even more. In the final days of the 's-Hertogenbosch siege, when trench digging had become truly hazardous, only a few particularly daring sappers were prepared to work, in return for payment between six and ten times the normal wage.[60]

Maurice's scientific insights helped him obtain enormous skill in siege warfare: he captured 45 towns and surrendered 28. But it was his half-brother Frederick Henry (25 towns gained and 12 lost) who acquired the widespread reputation of 'Conqueror of Towns' (*Stedendwinger*) because some of his successes were with towns such as 's-Hertogenbosch that were so heavily fortified and situated in such difficult terrain they were regarded as unconquerable.[61]

The 1629 attack on 's-Hertogenbosch is an example from that time of state-of-the-art siege warfare. The town was considered unconquerable because of the 2,500 soldiers in the garrison and additional 3,000 burgher militia, the strengthened ramparts and bulwarks, the waterlogged, marshy hinterland, the supplementary inundations and the further defence outworks along roads leading to the town. Frederick Henry employed no fewer than 28,000 troops. The prince managed to deceive the enemy as to the true target of the campaign by leading his army east to Schenkenschans (near Cleves) and then to the Mookerheyde (to the south of Nijmegen). In early May (earlier than usual for such campaigns, thanks to provisions stored in advance) his troops rapidly took up positions around the town; boats arrived with artillery and the siege train followed. He was determined to surround the whole town; in the past Maurice had attempted to besiege 's-Hertogenbosch from one side only, which had ended in disappointment. Frederick Henry inspected the area personally to determine the length of the lines of contravallation, and he erected five encampments, all roughly one hour from the town, all headed by able commanders, from where the siege was to be conducted. A sixth encampment, at Engelen, was established in order to take care of the protection of the provision transports from Crèvecoeur. To ease the transport of provisions by ship the dykes were pierced at the village of Empel.[62] Once the five encampments had been established, all major routes to 's-Hertogenbosch were controlled by his army and the town was blockaded.[63]

Next, roads were constructed to ease the transport of provisions and increase the mobility of the besieging troops. The construction of the circumvallation involved numerous pioneers, among whom were more than 2,100 farmers and peasants from Gelderland and Holland. The town was sealed off within two weeks, which was remarkably fast. No fewer than 116 cannons were placed in position and the lines of contra- and circumvallation were further strengthened. The latter were particularly impressive, consisting in part of two ramparts or two ditches, with redoubts, strongholds, and inundations at strategic points. To the west of the town Frederick Henry had a dyke constructed in a particularly wet area. Another dyke shortened the distance between two encampments. In addition, he erected dams across the Dommel and Aa to heighten the water level on the outer side of the circumvallation, providing an extra defence for the besieging forces, while lowering the water level within the contravallation, thus easing the construction of the approach trenches and facilitating the operations of the attackers.[64] Old watermills in the area were repaired and new horse treadmills installed to pump water out, with the assistance of Leeghwater – subsequently one of Holland's famous polder engineers – among others. The besiegers advanced quickly, hardly hindered by sorties from the 's-Hertogenbosch garrison, whose commander, Grobbendonk, could not believe that the town would ever be sealed off completely.[65]

After only four weeks, an incredibly short time in view of the enormous length of the circumvallation, the actual attack on 's-Hertogenbosch started and the artillery opened fire. Frederick Henry decided to establish five lines of approach instead of the usual two, to create confusion in the garrison, but the high water level quickly forced the abandonment of three of these. At one of the other approaches a gallery of several hundred metres was constructed over a particularly wet area. The only approach over dry terrain was divided in two; one branch came under the control of a Walloon company, the other was commanded by an English unit. Competition between the nations was exploited to stimulate the hard and dangerous work.[66]

After three months the attackers had advanced almost continuously by zigzag digging. But then the Army of Flanders sent a relief army. As a precaution Frederick Henry had the Land van Altena inundated. The Spanish troops did not dare to attack the circumvallation, which was too strong. Instead they invaded the Gelderland Veluwe region, to the north-east of 's-Hertogenbosch, trying to divert Frederick Henry (see also Chapter 1). This incursion of the Army of Flanders, which was joined by the emperor's troops under Montecuccoli, caused enormous distress among the Dutch citizenry. But Frederick Henry stayed put and sent some of his men to Wesel, which they took by surprise. This town had guaranteed the provisions for the invading troops; its seizure forced the Spanish to retreat.[67] The very wet August slowed down the pace of the attack, but by early September the besieged garrison asked to negotiate. All along Frederick Henry had shown great skill and generalship, able to direct officers, soldiers, pioneers, engineers and gunners alike in extremely difficult terrain, supporting his attack by means of a series of innovative constructions.

For several decades this way of besieging remained the standard model. But later in the century the celebrated French engineer Vauban developed new methods of approaching a besieged town. A major ditch was dug parallel to the town wall at a distance of 225–50 metres, just outside the range of musket fire, and from there a zigzag of trenches was cut towards another parallel ditch line at a distance of 115–25 metres from the wall, and from there more zigzags led to a line close to the covered road. No redoubts were necessary: in case of raids from the town the soldiers retreated to the last parallel and began the counterattack from there. This implied a wide front instead of one or two salients and brought about a much higher degree of uncertainty on the part of the besieged. One of Vauban's priorities was the destruction of the covered way, to damage the defence there.[68] This change in siege warfare implied a decrease in the use of outworks: indeed, these might well be of more use to the attackers than the defenders, and as a result they were often discarded completely.

It was some time before these new techniques were emulated by the Dutch, who remained wedded to their traditional siege tactics. The fortress of Grave, which had been conquered by the French and subsequently fortified by Vauban, was besieged by the Dutch in 1674. William III approached the walls in the traditional manner, on a narrow, zigzagging front, but Grave's heavy artillery – Vauban's adaptations had resulted in more space for artillery on the bastions – easily spotted the advancing soldiers. As a consequence the Dutch assaults resulted in enormous losses. Grave finally surrendered after three months, but at a cost of between 7,000 and 8,000 Dutch soldiers, against a loss of only 2,000 on the part of the garrison. At the subsequent siege of Maastricht, William III failed once more to appreciate the drawbacks of the old tactics. Progress was too slow, the stadholder devoted too much time and resources to the capture of an outer defence work that was of little use anyway, and once again his narrow frontline proved an easy prey to the garrison's powerful artillery. Almost all his engineers were killed and the French managed to send a relieving force in time.[69] Thus, despite the achievement of individual engineers such as Coehoorn, by the 1670s the Dutch had clearly lost their previous lead in siege craft.

Tactical limits, provisioning and army size

A significant tactical limitation throughout most of the sixteenth and seventeenth centuries pertained to the size of the field army. These troops always constituted less than half of the total on the payroll as many soldiers were required to man the garrisons. Vulnerable points on the frontiers, such as the Dutch Yssel line in the east, needed additional security. But that was not the only reason field armies remained limited in size, not rising above 20,000 to 30,000 men during most of the seventeenth century. All over Europe the provisioning of troops – above all the supply of bread – constituted a significant restraint on army growth. Magazines, wagonloads of supplies, field ovens, bakers from nearby towns, the levying of heavy contributions, requisitions: all these constituted only temporary or partial solutions until the French organized a superior system of magazines in the later seventeenth century.[70]

In its turn, the size of field armies determined the possible strategic objectives. In the 1590s the Dutch army, though quite small, was sufficiently large for the purpose. The Army of Flanders was preoccupied with the political crisis in France and Maurice and William Louis could move their 10,000 to 12,000 soldiers quite quickly from one side of the country to the other, making use of the numerous inland waterways. Maurice also had great pride in rapid troop movements, a reason why he curbed the size of the supply train. His army left Steenwijk on 17 July 1591 and arrived at Arnhem (some 110 kilometres away) only three days later, despite summer heat and a trajectory through the Rouveen marshes that had never been used by an army before. It was an outstanding achievement: the usual distance per day for armies on a march, 15 to 20 kilometres, was easily surpassed.[71]

Unlike its Dutch counterpart, the Army of Flanders did not enjoy the luxury of internal lines of communication and in the 1590s had to travel over much greater distances. Furthermore, after 1568 neither troops nor supplies could be carried by sea because almost every major naval expedition from Spain against the Dutch ended in disaster. Initially Spanish ships were harassed and obstructed by the Sea Beggars, then by Dutch allies (particularly the English in 1588) or the Dutch navy (in 1639 at the Downs), while the Flemish coast was effectively blockaded. Only in 1598 did an expedition succeed in landing – at Calais with 4,000 troops. As a result the Habsburg government had to use the much more expensive 'Spanish Road' that ran over the Mediterranean from Spain to Genoa and then over lands either in the possession of the Habsburgs or allied to them: Milan, Tyrol, Savoy, parts of Burgundy, Franche-Comté, Alsace, Lorraine and Luxemburg.[72]

After 1599 the military centre of gravity of the Eighty Years War moved periodically south into Flanders and Brabant, and then it was the turn of the Dutch to move their troops over the greater distance. With fewer internal communication lines, army strength had to rise. But provisioning, above all in enemy territory, was problematic for larger armies.[73] Not all supply problems were equally difficult. In general Dutch troops had the advantage of an adequate supply of arms and ammunition throughout the Eighty Years War and beyond (see Chapter 8). The supply of money, including small coinage to pay the soldiers, was also notably well organized in the Republic (see Chapter 7). Such items caused recurrent problems in most other armies of the time.[74] But the supply of bread, along with hay and other foodstuffs, was also intermittently a problem for the armies of Maurice and Frederick Henry.

Most foodstuffs were provided by local merchants along the line of march, and from small-scale army victuallers (sutlers, in Dutch *zoetelaars*, or *marketentster*). The field army was forced to rely upon bread produced by local bakers. Few towns in the Low Countries had more than 30,000 inhabitants, so supplying a field army of that size was an enormous challenge. An additional difficulty was that local produce was often insufficient to feed large numbers in the short term, let alone when the army had to stay for a long time in one area. The Low Countries were not renowned for their grain *exports*; the high degree of urbanization instead required considerable grain *imports*. Even when grain was to be had, the population had often disabled the mills by removing the axes and wings to prevent the enemy milling grain or had destroyed them completely. In 1602 Maurice took six mills and 20 ovens along with his army, a capacity adequate to bake bread for the troops, but the initiative failed because insufficient grain could be acquired.[75]

Transporting necessary supplies was an option, but the bulky goods demanded considerable space; as they were perishable, careful planning was also necessary. In 1583 the superintendent-general of provisions, Van Dorp, failed to bring the foodstuffs to the Dutch during the Brabant campaign because the Holland wagons – with a different axis from the Brabant ones – could not be used with the cart tracks.[76] Good timing was crucial too: for the campaign that ended in the battle of Nieuwpoort the States-General had sent bread by sea to the troops, but most of it rotted and had to be thrown overboard. And with the increasing size of field armies ever more wagons were needed, and not only for carrying bread: in 1605, 672 wagons and 200 transport vessels; in 1631, 894 wagons and 232 vessels; in 1634, 1,250 wagons and an unspecified number of vessels. Even these numbers could not carry all the grain, bread or forage required: most soldiers continued to be supplied as they marched. An additional problem was that each year wagoners, draught horses, provision and luggage wagons and transport vessels had to be hired anew: they were not part of the regular army establishment.[77]

The problems of provisioning were reduced when the strategic aims were located close to frontier garrison towns. The siege of 's-Hertogenbosch was planned well in advance by Frederick Henry; stocks of rye had been ordered ahead from merchants; an inventory was made from the available reserves in the countryside; and bread was supplied regularly on wagons from nearby towns like Heusden. In planning the siege of Breda in 1637, Frederick Henry ordered the establishment of a magazine in nearby Terheiden with enough rye to feed the siege army of 24,000 men for one and a half months. This also had a strategic benefit: it prevented the Spanish severing the supply lines of the besieging troops.[78]

Yet such successes were difficult to emulate as the strategic radius expanded. As noted in Chapter 1, the 'natural' limit to field army size (20,000–30,000) was one of the reasons why the Dutch were unable to win major victories in the south. Typically, the Dutch military administration had most of the army well organized, but where foodstuffs were concerned they continued to rely more on the market than France or Spain. The Spanish army, which lacked a regular pay system, recognized the need to provide soldiers with free or cheap bread in order to avert mutinies. In the earlier seventeenth century, the archdukes tried to reduce the discontent of the rank and file by providing cheap bread when regular pay appeared too distant a prospect. In 1622 Maurice reported that bread was available in the Army of Flanders for a reasonable price, never more than three *stuivers* for a of three-pound loaf, while the States' troops suffered from periodic price increases. Later in the century the Spanish improved their magazine system.[79]

In the later sixteenth century the French had already made a start with the installation of magazines containing food supplies for the troops. *Munitionnaires*, merchants under contract, bought the necessary amount of grain, had it ground, baked it in ovens which they either hired or provided, and then transported the bread to the camps where soldiers could buy it at a fixed price. The lack of regular funding meant that the network suffered and eventually disintegrated, but at the end of the 1650s Le Tellier and Louvois reorganized the magazine system.[80] This eventually permitted the emergence of individual armies containing 100,000 men or more during the last decades of the seventeenth century. At the time of the War of Devolution (1667/8) the French magazines were still unable to supply an army of 50,000 men, but the Lorraine campaign of 1670 functioned as 'a dry run' for the attack on the Netherlands. In 1672 the French had sufficient stocks, in seven magazines, to feed the field army for a full six months. The continuing supply of provisions by way of shuttle services enabled the French to maintain considerable military pressure without giving their opponents the respite to reorganize themselves.[81]

The magazine system brought other crucial advantages, such as facilitating the rapid advance of troops through less populated districts and an earlier start to campaigns. Normally field armies did not normally leave before mid-May or even early June, by which time fresh grass was to be had on the way for the horses. French practice was different: the Dutch Council of State noted that

> The French habitually made considerable progress in the Spanish Netherlands in the winter and early spring, before we could subsist in the open field. This advantage is not just a question of superior forces, but proceeds from the practice of making magazines on the borders. On our side, in that season, we lack the fodder.[82]

In February and March 1676 Louvois had installed large stores of hay in Ath, Doornik and Oudenaarde, while in 1677 Louis' army began to attack Valenciennes as early as March. In comparison William III advanced, but he was discouraged, as no forage was to be found: all hay had already been bought or confiscated by the French.[83]

The logistical improvements of the French brought other consequences. The larger field armies which France could now support forced Dutch garrisons to be enlarged. As long as armies contained no more than 20,000 to 25,000 men, as throughout most of the Eighty Years War, garrisons of 2,000 to 2,500 men were adequate to permit the organization of raids on the part of the besieged and to hold out for two months, which – as a rule – would be long enough for a relief army to arrive. Field armies of 50,000 to 60,000 men, however, could overwhelm such garrisons rapidly. Even the 3,500 men defending Doesburg proved no obstacle at all for the French in 1672.[84]

The obvious success of the French magazine system prompted the Dutch to take action, beginning with bread provisioning. A contract was signed in October 1672 with Moses Machado and Jacob Pereira, Sefardic Jews from Amsterdam who controlled sufficient sums to advance the payments that were essential. In the Dutch campaign to relieve Naarden in 1673 they took care of the provisioning for 25,000 men: for each soldier one and a half pound of bread and half a pound of Edam cheese, and for each hundred soldiers a ton of beer. The Naarden campaign proved a success, and in subsequent years Machado and Pereira became so proficient in supplying the army, for example establishing bread magazines in the Southern Netherlands, that other provision merchants had little opportunity to compete for the contracts. William III was delighted with their services and granted them the title *Provediteurs-Generaal van den Staat* (general provisioners of the state). With food provisioning secured, up to a radius of 40 to 60 kilometres from a magazine, the former ceiling of 25,000 to

30,000 men on the size of an individual army disappeared. As a result William secured with his larger forces much greater room for manoeuvre than Maurice, William Louis and Frederick Henry had ever had.[85]

In addition the States-General established rye magazines in 1675. In that year, 150 wagons were involved in bread provisioning alone; next year, with the troops operating further south, 400 wagons were needed. Soldiers still paid for their own bread, but at least they had something to eat: the overhead costs were met by the provinces – above all by the province of Holland – and in due course could then be deducted from the standard provincial tax contribution. As Vauban's scheme for the French northern frontier demonstrated, a line of fortified border towns could also act as excellent magazines for the field army, providing grain, forage, ammunition and heavy artillery. For the Dutch, Bergen op Zoom and later Maastricht constituted strategic magazines of this kind. One area where the Dutch long continued to lag behind was the provision of forage for the horses. Between 1676 and 1678 oats were stored in Mechelen, Diest and Louvain. But oats alone were not sufficient – horses needed hay or straw in addition. Louvois had complete packages of horse food stored, with oats, hay, and straw. In this way the French continued to enjoy significant tactical and even strategic advantages over the Dutch.[86]

Conclusion: the model of a disciplined army

Not all the tactics introduced by Maurice and William Louis in the 1590s were new. But what was different was that they were embedded in an institutional setting characterized by advanced military professionalization, as was made clear in Chapter 2. This permitted other significant benefits, above all much improved drill and discipline. Internalized military discipline fitted well into Dutch society of the period. The American historical sociologist Philip Gorski noted the simultaneous imposition of military discipline and Calvinist discipline. Both had an advantageous effect on state formation in the northern Netherlands; disciplined troops protected the territory, while church discipline kept the citizens morally in line.[87]

The study of fortress design and siege techniques developed in surroundings that encouraged mathematical applications and scientific discovery. This brought an end to the period during which simple experience had been the best way to learn the art of war: henceforth, army commanders required some knowledge of mathematics and how to carry out complex manoeuvring.[88] Some of the innovations were inspired by the French, others by the Spanish. But it was the Dutch 'Schoole of War' that became famous. 'Dutch' tactics were copied by a great number of military leaders throughout Europe; Dutch military instructors were much in demand abroad.[89] The military school at Siegen advertised its course with the slogan: 'Darnach wird man geübt alhier, Im Trillen auff niderländisch Manier' (= then follows the training, to drill in the Dutch manner).[90] Owen Feldham, a popular English author of the time, wrote of the Dutch military: 'There is hardly upon earth such a school of Martial

Discipline. Tis the Christian worlds *Academy* for Arms; whither all the neighbour-Nations resort to be instructed.'[91]

It was not just new ways to perform the countermarch. The Dutch method of manoeuvring fostered the development of automatic obedience on the part of the soldier, which was at least as important as efficient volley fire.[92] Michael Howard summarized this crucial development as follows:

> [T]his period witnessed a development far more important than that of military weapons or techniques: it saw the rise of the professional army … . Self-control and obedience gradually replaced the heroic virtues as the primary military requirement; and such obedience, especially in the firing line, made possible by the beginning of the eighteenth century that coordination of arms on the battlefield.[93]

After the Peace of Münster of 1648, however, the Dutch lost much of their cutting edge. Innovations by the French demanded rapid responses, but apart from bread provisioning the Dutch were slow to adopt new ideas, particularly where siege warfare and the need to organize forage stocks were concerned.

Thanks to increased drill and discipline, mutinies on home soil all but vanished after 1590. However, outside 'Dutch' territory the States' troops were sometimes capable of glaring misconduct. During the capture of Wesel in 1629, the soldiers stole and robbed not only Spanish, Catholic and Jewish goods (which had been sanctioned by the command) but also ordinary shops in the market. Their behaviour quickly got out of hand and the violence and theft brought about great disorder, arousing enormous resentment against Dutch rule among the civilian population. The States' troops behaved equally badly in 1673 during their counter-attack on Cologne. Colonel Van Reede-Ginkel wrote to his father: 'They spare nothing … . Monasteries and churches, all are looted.' The States' troops brutally killed numerous inhabitants and hanged the burgomaster at the town gate.[94]

Nevertheless, these were relatively isolated examples. Within the Netherlands itself soldiers' discipline was relatively good, and within garrisons relations between soldiers and citizens was unusually positive, as the next chapter will make clear.

Notes

1 Roberts, *Military Revolution*, pp. 14–15. The italics are mine.
2 Two examples that recognize Maurice's achievements: Lynn, 'Evolution', pp. 505–45; Parrott, *Military Revolution*, p. 20ff.
3 Black, *Military Revolution*, p. 19, see also Parrott, 'Strategy', pp. 230, 236. Black also notes that usually the larger armies won, not the ones with superior tactics, Black, *Military Revolution*, p. 12. Geoffrey Parker did not deny the importance of the Maurician reforms but regarded the siege warfare earlier in the century as having more crucial impact: Parker, *Military Revolution*, pp. 12, 22.
4 Hahlweg, *Heeresreform*, p. 27; Parrott, *Richelieu's Army*, p. 27; Swart, 'Mythe', pp. 107–8.

5 Lynn, 'Tactical evolution', p. 190; Croxton, 'Territorial imperative', p. 277.

6 Weber, *From Max Weber*, pp. 256–7; see also McNeill, *Keeping Together*, pp. 127, 131; Hahlweg, *Heeresreform*, p. 25; Joas, 'Modernity', pp. 465–6.

7 McNeill, *Pursuit of Power*, pp. 128–31; see also Hale, 'Armies', p. 182.

8 Max Weber: 'The content of discipline is nothing but the consistently rationalized, methodically prepared and exact execution of the received order, in which all personal criticism is unconditionally suspended and the actor is unswervingly and exclusively set for carrying out the command. In addition, this conduct under orders is uniform. The effects of this uniformity derive from its quality as social action within a mass structure. Those who obey are not necessarily a simultaneously obedient or an especially large mass, nor are they necessarily united in a specific locality. What is decisive for discipline is that the obedience of a plurality of men is rationally uniform.' Weber, *From Max Weber*, p. 253. See also Drake, *Problematics*, p. 260; Van Nimwegen, 'Transformation', p. 163; Burschel, *Söldner*, pp. 44, 318.

9 Tallett, *War and Society*, p. 25.

10 James Turner, quoted by Rothenberg, 'Maurice', p. 45 [orig. 1683, on p. 360].

11 Parrott, *Richelieu's Army*, pp. 28–9. The fame of Dutch military reforms was greatest in Calvinist circles.

12 Hale, 'Armies', p. 184; González de León, *Road to Rocroi*, p. 57.

13 Alva introduced the musket to the Low Countries in 1567. The Spanish *tercios* counted proportionally more pikemen than the Dutch troops: 71 per cent in 1571, Parker, *Army*, pp. 235–6. On the Huguenots, see Chapter 2. On French tactics Lynn, 'Tactical evolution', p. 178. On small war, Pepper, 'Aspects', pp. 195ff.

14 Swart, *Krijgsvolk*, pp. 145–6. The English companies had no pikemen at all. Since the army size increased in the meantime, the decline was less in numbers, more in proportion.

15 Jespersen, 'Social change', p. 12; Hale, 'Armies', p. 189.

16 Swart, *Krijgsvolk*, pp. 149–52.

17 Lynn, *Giant*, pp. 181–2; ibid., p. 459: the first standardization of weaponry in the French army dated from 1666; Anderson, *War*, p. 105: in the English army of the 1680s, 14 different varieties of musket were counted.

18 Van Nimwegen, *Deser landen crijghsvolck*, pp. 89–91. Dragoons, foot soldiers on horseback, appeared only in the second half of the seventeenth century (contrary to Wijn, 'Military forces', p. 214).

19 De Jong, *Staat*, pp. 31–4. Roundachiers had a round shield (*rondas*) and a short sword; swordsmen and halberdiers had the task of destroying the pikes of the enemy. After 1596 halberds continued to be carried by sergeants as a sign of their status (and they were handy to control unruly soldiers as well). After the Eighty Years War the proportion of pikes decreased further, disappearing altogether around the turn of the eighteenth century when the implementation of the bayonet combined the capacities of gun and pike in one weapon. In the first half of the seventeenth century the proportion of pikes to musketeers was still higher in the Spanish army, but after 1650 roughly similar to other belligerents: Rooms, *Organisatie*, p. 91.

20 Van Nimwegen, *Deser landen crijghsvolck*, pp. 87–8. The bullets were somewhat smaller than the musket calibre as gunpowder slime used to block the barrel. Lighter muskets existed since 1604 (the French army used considerably smaller muskets, with an enormous range of calibres) but Maurice and William Louis thought their impact was not substantial enough. Furkets were to disappear from the army in the last quarter of the seventeenth century; contrary to Wijn, *Krijgswezen*, p. 145.

21 Davids, *Rise*, pp. 427–8.

22 Quoted by Duffy, *Siege Warfare*, p. 96.

23 The Prince's mathematical insight was praised by contemporaries; the positioning of cannon at sieges was also often very efficient.

24 A serious disadvantage was the mortar's weight, but in 1673 the Dutch engineer Menno van Coehoorn introduced a new invention: small mortars, which were

subsequently named after him (*coehoorns*). On Maurice's reforms: Nickle, *Military Reforms*, p. 5; Parker, *Army*, p. 15. Lynn, *Giant*, p. 502: Sully's attempt at the standardization of cannons did not succeed. The French copied the heavy mortar bomb from the Netherlands, introduced there in 1634 by an Englishman who had been in Dutch service.

25 In the Dutch cavalry the 'caracole' remained the dominant tactic against pikemen, as in other armies of the time: Lynn, 'Tactical evolution', p. 183; Rogers, 'Tactics', p. 229; Tallett, *War and Society*, p. 31. Asch, 'War and state-building', notes that the caracole was by no means as inefficient as is often claimed. The cavalry was also often employed in raids, in misleading and distracting the forces of the enemy, and in securing contributions, provisions or booty from the countryside.

26 De Graaf, *Oorlog*, p. 231.

27 With the possible exception of the Swedes under Gustavus Adolphus, who copied a range of Dutch methods. Hale, *War and Society*, p. 164; Hale, 'Armies', p. 194 (quote); Fletcher, *County Community*, p. 184. González de León, *Road to Rocroi*, pp. 58, 61, 72, 270, on the erosion of drill and discipline in the Army of Flanders. Lynn, 'Tactical evolution', p. 189, mentions that weekly drill was introduced in 1629 under Louis XIII, but Parrott, *Richelieu's Army*, p. 40 sees no documented evidence for that statement; regular drill was subsequently introduced only by Louis XIV. Van Nimwegen, *Deser landen crijghsvolck*, pp. 92–3: the manual of arms published by De Gheyn in 1607 was in all likelihood not used in the regular drill within the army; this book was used for individual recruit training and of great value to military schools elsewhere; contrary to Nickle, *Military Reforms*, p. 145.

28 Quoted by De Graaf, *Oorlog*, p. 424, and Lynn, *Giant*, p. 515. Contrary to Swart, 'Mythe', p. 109, who denies the importance of the Maurician drill, pointing to examples of exercise in other armies. However, elsewhere exercises were not performed on a daily basis.

29 Hahlweg, *Heeresreform*, pp. 49, 70, 279. Van Deursen, *Maurits*, p. 80: William Louis warned that such commands might be 'strange and laughable, and mocked by the enemy', yet he stressed that such was not unusual with innovations.

30 Aelianus, *Tactiks*, preface; see also Tallett, *War and Society*, pp. 26–7.

31 Parker, 'Military Revolution', p. 39; Hale, 'Armies', p. 184. Roberts, *Essays*, p. 60; González de León, *Road to Rocroi*, pp. 292, 322. Rooms, *Organisatie*, p. 93: the tactical formations in the Spanish army were also reduced in the seventeenth century. Parrott, *Richelieu's Army*, p. 52: the number of men in French battalions was roughly similar to that in the Dutch, which again might point to the influence of French army practices.

32 Van Nimwegen, *Deser landen crijghsvolck*, p. 91. Lynn, 'Tactical evolution', p. 179: the French also applied checkerboard formations in the later 1590s, perhaps independently of the Dutch.

33 As had been practiced by other armies earlier in the century; Weir, *Turning Points*, p. 65.

34 Swart, *Krijgsvolk*, pp. 142–8; Gonzáles de León, 'Doctors', p. 73.

35 Van Nimwegen, *Deser landen crijghsvolck*, pp. 94–6.

36 Quote in Feld, 'Middle-class society', p. 176.

37 Frost, *The Northern Wars*, p. 63; Lynn, *Giant*, p. 517.

38 Black, 'Military Revolution', p. 19.

39 Van Nimwegen, 'Het Staatse leger', p. 502. On examples of commands poorly obeyed among the Spanish: Parker, *Army*, p. 188.

40 Roberts, *Military Revolution*, p. 28; see also Corvisier, *Armies*, p. 183. At sea line tactics replaced boarding in the seventeenth century. Even though war became much more impersonal, there was still a place for chivalrous gestures or generous acts, and the numerous skirmishes and raids provided plenty of occasions for individual bravery and enterprise, Hale, 'Armies', p. 207.

41 Lynn, *Giant*, p. 455, named after the grenades that they threw at the enemy (mainly in trenches). Van Nimwegen, *Deser landen crijghsvolck*, pp. 326, 333–7.
42 Quoted by ibid., p. 288.
43 Ibid., pp. 290–1.
44 De Cauwer, *Tranen*, p. 128; Lynn, *Giant*, p. 568, and Parrott, *Richelieu's Army*, p. 73, on the heroic but often reckless tactics of the French who could not get used to the slow, patient siege warfare of the Dutch.
45 Martens, *Militaire architectuur*. See also Chapter 4.
46 Westra, *Nederlandse ingenieurs*, pp. 15–21, 36–44; Duffy, *Siege Warfare*, p. 91.
47 Van den Heuvel, *Papiere Bolwercken*; Westra, *Nederlandse ingenieurs*, pp. 82–9; Postema, *Johan van den Corput*, pp. 88, 148.
48 Davids, *Rise*, pp. 289–92; Braddick, *God's Fury*, p. 392; Fissel, *English Warfare*, p. 170; Vorsters, *Beleg*, pp. 76–8. On the lack of Spanish and Italian military academies: Elliott, *Richelieu and Olivares*, p. 133; Parrott, 'Utility', p. 149; González de León, *Road to Rocroi*, p. 142.
49 Lynn, *Giant*, pp. 556, 562.
50 Van Hoof, 'Nieuwe manieren', pp. 551–2; Van Nimwegen, *Deser landen crijghsvolck*, pp. 328–30.
51 Van Deursen, *Maurits*, pp. 108–9, 125.
52 Duffy, *Siege Warfare*, pp. 70, 80.
53 Holthuis, *Frontierstad*, p. 35; De Graaf, *Oorlog*, p. 229.
54 Van Nimwegen, *Deser landen crijghsvolck*, pp. 121–3.
55 De Kraker, *Landschap*. Leper, *Kunstmatige inundaties*, pp. 103–4, records five strategic inundations in fourteenth- and fifteenth-century Flanders, but the tactic had rarely been applied in Holland.
56 Supported by the famous engineer Adriaen Anthonisz.; Klinkert, 'Water', pp. 455–68. Strategic flooding as a defence line for a larger area was first developed by Sonoy, who employed thousands of peasants to dig a waterline in north Holland. The line successfully halted the march of the Spanish commander Hierges in 1575. Similar tactics were applied to defend whole regions, in particular Holland, in 1629 and again in 1672 (see Chapter 5).
57 Tracy, *Founding*, p. 219.
58 De Graaf, *Oorlog*, pp. 247, 261–2; Duffy, *Siege Warfare*, p. 76. The defenders launched a new device as well: two ships turned into mines that were drifted towards the bridge. Success was limited, though.
59 The Dutch army had employed specialized sappers since 1588, Ten Raa and De Bas, *Staatsche leger*, II, p. 248.
60 Ibid.; De Cauwer, *Tranen*, p. 126; on the payment of the pioneers see also Adriaenssen, *Staatsvormend geweld*, pp. 266–7.
61 De Graaf, *Oorlog*, p. 547.
62 Engelen, Crèvecoeur and Empel are all situated to the north of 's-Hertogenbosch.
63 De Cauwer, *Tranen*, pp. 60, 67–70.
64 The Dommel and the Aa are small rivers to the east of 's-Hertogenbosch.
65 Relief attempts by the Army of Flanders were unsuccessful because of logistic problems and disagreement in the high command (see also Chapter 1). Parker, *Army*, p. 93; De Cauwer, *Tranen*, pp. 8, 47, 61, 70–74, 87, 238.
66 Ibid., pp. 75–82, 224.
67 Ibid., pp. 48, 91, 98, 102, 113. The Land van Altena was a low-lying region between 's-Hertogenbosch and Gorinchem.
68 Lynn, *Giant*, pp. 569–70; Van Nimwegen, *Deser landen crijghsvolck*, pp. 322–3. Vauban also aimed the artillery fire first at the cannon of the besieged. Duffy, *Siege Warfare*, 138: the attack along parallel lines had been practiced in Turkish wars, and parallel trenches had been applied in isolated cases in 1644 and 1645 but had not yet become general practice in Europe.

69 Van Nimwegen, *Deser landen crijghsvolck*, pp. 326–7.
70 Perjés, 'Army provisioning', p. 23; Adams, 'Tactics', pp. 31, 41.
71 Van Deursen, *Maurits*, p. 105. Parma was also keen to curb the size of the army train.
72 Parker, *Army*, p. 49; Goodman, *Spanish Naval Power*, p. 25.
73 Pagès, *The Thirty Years War*, p. 128.
74 Parrott, *Richelieu's Army*, p. 242.
75 Van Nimwegen, *Deser landen crijghsvolck*, p. 305.
76 De Graaf, *Oorlog*, p. 208. See also Chapter 8.
77 Van Nimwegen, *Deser landen crijghsvolck*, pp. 108–14.
78 Ibid., p. 114; De Cauwer, *Tranen*, pp. 175–6.
79 Rooms, *Organisatie*, p. 186; Rooms, 'Bezoldiging', pp. 534–6; Van Nimwegen, *Deser landen crijghsvolck*, p. 111.
80 Wood, *King's Army*, p. 243; Parrott, *Richelieu's Army*, p. 259–60.
81 Lynn, *Giant*, pp. 16, 108–11, 125.
82 Quoted by Lynn, *Giant*, p. 130; see also p. 551.
83 Van Nimwegen, *Deser landen crijghsvolck*, pp. 313–14.
84 Vermeesch, *Oorlog*, p. 227. On the size of garrisons, see also Kingra, 'Trace italienne', p. 436; Lynn, 'Trace italienne', pp. 315–17; Parker, *Military Revolution*, p. 40; Parker, 'In defence', p. 352; Ágoston, 'Empires', p. 128.
85 See also Chapter 8. Van Nimwegen, *Deser landen crijghsvolck*, 306–9. In contrast to their French colleagues, Machado and Pereira did not strive after dynastic power for their individual families; Rowlands, *Dynastic State*, p. 71.
86 Van Nimwegen, *Deser landen crijghsvolck*, pp. 311–15.
87 Gorski, *Disciplinary Revolution*, p. 75.
88 Roberts, 'Military revolution', p. 25.
89 Tallett, *War and Society*, pp. 26–7, 41; Parker, *Thirty Years War*, p. 184; Roberts, *Essays*, p. 63; Manning, *Apprenticeship*, pp. 7, 127, 133, 138.
90 Quoted by Hahlweg, *Heeresreform*, p. 148.
91 Feltham, *Brief Character*, p. 69.
92 Lynn, *Giant*, pp. 515–17; Rogers, 'Tactics', p. 221.
93 Howard, 'Tools', p. 239.
94 De Cauwer, *Tranen*, p. 122; Van Nimwegen, *Deser landen crijghsvolck*, p. 291.

4 Garrisons and urban communities
Strengthening local bonds

[The Eighty Years War] was a war over fortresses whose garrisons, on the
Dutch side at least, paid cash for what they took from the surrounding population
and thus often had a stimulating rather than retarding effect on the local economy.[1]

The fortifications of the *trace italienne* undoubtedly strengthened the ability of
the smaller states of Europe to defend themselves; they raised the prospects of
survival for the Dutch Republic too.[2] But the new-style defences required a large
number of troops to be stationed in garrison towns. In most of Europe the close
intermingling of garrison soldiers and citizens resulted in periodic tension and
violence, emanating from both sides. For example, in the 1630s French soldiers
were reported to have menaced their hosts by smashing their windows,
demanding more services and goods. In response townspeople rose up against
the garrison; in one case, the garrison's commander was even killed as a result.
Similar clashes took place in Habsburg Spain and elsewhere.[3]

All over Europe civilians tried wherever possible to avoid the quartering of
soldiers. In seventeenth-century England the accommodating of troops was even
regarded as an act of monarchical tyranny. During the Thirty Years War no
large German city seems to have accepted such quartering; the burden was
shifted to smaller and less powerful urban communities. In France, entire towns
(such as Grenoble and Boulogne) and even provinces (such as Auvergne and
Burgundy) had managed to exempt themselves from the obligation to provide
quarters for soldiers. The French first minister Mazarin remarked: 'Having
soldiers billeted for three days is more onerous for a man than the *taille*', while
in the 1660s Colbert noted: 'The four generalities of Paris, Amiens, Châlons,
and Soissons, have suffered more from quartering over the last six months than
in the last six years of war.' In Warwickshire during the English civil war, the
burden of free quarter and plunder was reported to equal half the level of
taxation. Such burdens caused towns to beg for a reduction of their garrisons
and if possible, the loss of them altogether. Because Antwerp refused to admit
Parma's troops, they were forced to set up camp on royal and church domains
during the winter of 1582/3. Authorities imposed new taxes in order to recompense the unwilling hosts, yet the schemes repeatedly failed to provide sufficient

funds and the burden of both accommodating and paying the soldiers fell recurrently upon the same (middle and lower) classes. Since the latter were unwilling to pay for a tax while they also had to provide accommodation for the soldiers, the military coercion that accompanied the collection of these taxes was at times more costly than the sums raised.[4]

Since town authorities were so unwilling to admit any garrison soldiers, they armed their own citizens for protection.[5] But by the end of the sixteenth century urban militias were no longer able to stand up to the more professionalized army forces. In addition, the centralized state did not always look with favour upon militia forces because of its fear of urban insurrection. In France the *milices bourgeoises* were regarded with great suspicion; towns were not even entrusted with major fortifications and numerous French fortifications were destroyed in the seventeenth century.[6] Obviously, such policies and antagonisms undermined not only protection capabilities but also the political power of French urban communities.

In the United Provinces some forty garrisons were maintained, primarily along the frontiers but also in the interior, with a further thirty or so in 'conquered areas' such as Brabant and in friendly adjoining territories such as East Frisia. The number of troops stationed in the garrisons was substantial: usually amounting to between 10 and 25 per cent of the total urban population, to which the town militias should be added.[7] Yet it was a remarkable fact that these soldiers largely remained on peaceful terms with the inhabitants of the Dutch Republic, in contrast to the tensions and periodic outbreaks of violence elsewhere. The French commander Condé complained to Mazarin in 1648 about the strength of the alliance between garrisons and citizens in the Low Countries: 'The enemy fortresses are defended by the townspeople as well as the garrisons, whereas in our fortresses the citizens are our mortal enemies.'[8] Strict discipline and drill (see Chapter 3) contributed significantly, as did Orange's reforms regarding the method of weekly pay, advanced through a system of town loans (see Chapter 2). Article Six of the Union of Utrecht had imposed the Holland pay arrangements on the whole Republic: 'That the Frontier Towns shall be bound to receive or dismiss all Garrisons by the command of the States, as likewise to pay them their pay out of the publick Money'.[9] As a result, by the later 1570s hostilities between citizens and soldiers had faded away in Holland and, with some time lag, also in the other provinces of the Republic (after the introduction of regular provincial contributions in the 1590s, see Chapter 7). These relatively harmonious relations, however, ultimately depended on the fact that – unlike the billeting which prevailed in many other countries – these arrangements were not compulsory and townspeople were reimbursed for the costs involved.

The peaceful co-existence between military and civilians permitted towns to benefit from the potential positive consequences of boarding soldiers. Urban authorities even repeatedly asked for an increase in the number of soldiers. The garrisons created positive economic demand, and a further positive side effect came from providing quarters to soldiers, as will be demonstrated below. In addition, the building of fortifications entailed significant expenditure on part of the central state institutions, which served local contractors and labourers extremely well. The chapter also re-evaluates the common notion that earthworks were cheap.

The participation of the burghers in the civic militias was increased by the war. Although the on-going professionalization of the military rendered regular forces more effective than urban militias, their role was by no means insignificant. All in all, the presence of the garrisons strengthened town communities and shored up the existing political culture of Dutch urban society. After the Peace of Westphalia, however, some of the positive benefits enjoyed by urban communities as a result of war expenditure disappeared, as will be shown below.

To explain the unusual situation of the Dutch garrisons, this chapter employs recent detailed research, predominantly concerning Gorinchem (with around 6,000 inhabitants, located in Holland), Deventer (comparable to Gorinchem in size, located in Overijssel) and Doesburg (with around 2,000 inhabitants, in Gelderland).[10] Data from garrisons in the far north-east (Groningen) is added in order to present an overall view of the situation prevailing in the United Provinces. The particular advantages of the Dutch garrisons did not appear overnight, however. The chapter first sketches some of the problems which arose from the presence of soldiers in the early decades of the Revolt.

The difficult early decades of the Revolt

To a significant extent the Dutch Revolt was fuelled by popular hatred of the misconduct of Spanish soldiers.[11] But in the early decades of the war Dutch soldiers were not that much different. All underpaid soldiers were likely to provoke disruption in the towns or undertake raids into the neighbouring countryside, often driven by the sheer need to survive.

Holland experienced its share of such problems. In February 1574 Captain Hendrik van Broekhuysen was wounded by aggrieved citizens in Hoorn. In November of that same year the unruly behaviour of the garrison triggered an uprising by the Medemblik burghers.[12] In view of problems of this kind, the Provincial States of Holland decided to sanction the presence of garrisons in the province's towns only on the condition that in each town a sergeant major (*wachtmeester*) was appointed to supervise the troops' conduct (see also Chapter 2). Two years later, in 1576, the governments of Holland and Zeeland further stipulated that soldiers were never to interfere with the political or juridical affairs of the town.[13] The Union of Utrecht of 1579 specified in addition:

[T]hat both Captains, and Souldiers, shall besides the general Oath, make particular oath also to the Town, or Citie, and Province, where the Garrisons is to bee layd; and that this same shall bee inserted in their Articles; and that likewise there shall bee such order taken, and such discipline kept among the Souldiers, that the Burghers and inhabitants of both Town and

Countrie, whether Church or Lay-men shall not bee burthened beyond reason, nor suffer any molestation.[14]

This oath of allegiance thus not only related to the paymaster of the troops, as in most of Europe, but extended to the local authorities. In the late 1570s the relationship between garrisons and citizens improved in Holland and Zeeland, as a consequence of the reforms of Orange. Occasional funding shortages, however, did not disappear; in the 1580s lack of cash still resulted in hostility towards the garrisons. In 1588 the soldiers in the Woudrichem garrison complained that irregular payment and hunger had made beggars of them. The nearby garrison at Heusden stood on the brink of mutiny for the same reasons.[15] Yet before long the difficulties in Holland were contained.

In the landward provinces, the problem of unruly garrisons took longer to remedy, as not all provincial authorities were able to introduce the system of regular pay as quickly as Holland. In Zutphen (Gelderland) the soldiers of the States' company of Captain Van Brienen behaved so oppressively to the urban inhabitants that the town government had the burghers secretly armed. On 11 February 1583 the majority were evicted; only 70 soldiers remained behind. When the Spanish commander Taxis learned about Zutphen's weakened defences, he attacked the town in September 1583 and plundered it.[16] Such violent and destabilizing incidents were recurrent in the eastern Netherlands up to the 1590s.

Religious strife was a particular difficulty of some new garrisons. In Doesburg (Gelderland) the arrival of (mainly Calvinist) States' soldiers caused a major transformation in the religious structure of a predominant Catholic urban settlement. Despite protests by the local population, the Calvinists were assigned two churches in 1578/9. In the autumn of 1580 the population was nearly doubled by the stationing of 1,100 English soldiers, together with a sizable army 'train' consisting of wives, children, servants, prostitutes and all kinds of traders. Army trains caused problems everywhere, but particularly in smaller communities. The Doesburg citizens had little chance to protest since the position of *richter* (bailiff) was held by an army officer, Captain Balthasar van Rossum, whose own soldiers extorted the money from the population.[17]

The burden of paying for Doesburg's garrison thus fell upon the shoulders of local citizens and farmers; they also had to billet the soldiers without any compensation. In the first half of the 1580s underpaid and mutinous troops were once again stationed in the town. In 1585, provoked by the ill-disciplined garrison and dissatisfied with what they viewed as anti-Catholic measures over the two previous years, a number of town magistrates, burghers and farmers conspired with the Spanish. The States' soldiers were driven out and immediately replaced by a garrison from the Army of Flanders. When Leicester recaptured Doesburg with his States' army, however, he retaliated by forcing the new urban government to strictly implement the regulations that forbade all public Catholic services. The problems remained: the new garrison was paid so poorly and irregularly that it remained permanently on the brink of mutiny, and complaints about soldiers' appalling behaviour continued until 1590. In contrast to Holland, only a handful of towns received a *wachtmeester* to control discipline. The few district *wachtmeesters* who were appointed in the eastern Netherlands in the later 1580s could do little to restrain the undisciplined troops.[18]

Civic militia and urban community

Where efficient provincial tax structures made possible the collection of funds for soldiers' pay, a garrison did not need to cause such hardships for the populace. Already in the 1570s, when local funds fell short in Holland, non-frontier towns sent part of their tax yields to garrison towns. Dordrecht, Rotterdam and Delft in this way supported the Gorinchem garrison.[19] Urban governments also took care to cultivate cordial relations with the army contingents. Town accounts reveal considerable expenditure on meetings at which officers of the garrison could socialize with representatives of the urban authorities and the local militia. In Gorinchem Captain Robinson was particularly loved by the urban community; when he died in 1573 the authorities commemorated the excellent relationship they had enjoyed with this officer and recommended Robinson's lieutenant – who was also popular among the local population – for the post. To a certain degree urban governments could also negotiate the number and composition of soldiers making up the garrison. For example, in 1586 the Gorinchem town council asked the Provincial States of Holland to replace the two companies of English troops in their garrison with units comprising 'good [= more reliable] Dutch soldiers'.[20]

The Dutch Wars of Independence also revived the urban militias. Former militia institutions were overhauled and, where necessary, replaced.[21] The Gorinchem authorities divided the town into eight areas, each responsible for the levy of a militia company of 200 men. These men received arms and training and swore an oath of allegiance to the town. Their main task was to stand guard during the night in order to relieve the garrison of its duties. Each night about two hundred burghers carried out sentry duty. This was a substantial obligation: every militiaman was on duty once a week, not only on the Gorinchem walls but also in the nearby strongholds and villages. When danger threatened the guards were doubled.[22]

However, armed citizens could not always be relied upon. During the siege of Venlo in 1637, for example, after the Spanish artillery had set the town on fire, the citizens – armed to support the defence – conspired together. As soon as the regular States' soldiers were stationed in the outworks of the fortifications, they captured the governor, occupied the marketplace, the magazine and the gate, and shut the army out. Venlo capitulated the next day.[23] Neither were all citizens willing to serve in the militia. In Doesburg, where the sudden changes in religious and political conditions had caused great difficulties in the 1580s, the authorities were obliged to impose fines for failure to appear for sentry duty. Peasants from the surrounding area were forced to fill the gaps in standing guard.[24] But in the main the increased duties imposed upon burghers during the Dutch Wars of Independence strengthened the notion of local citizenship.

Citizenship could be forfeited if an individual had fled the town when an opposing army threatened. Citizens were expected to help shoulder the burden of burgher obligations, especially during periods of emergency. Splinter Cornelisz van Voorn, clerk of the Gorinchem town council, had fled and taken refuge in 's-Hertogenbosch because of the troubles. When he returned he found his house had been seized by the urban government and used to accommodate soldiers. His request to have his former property restored was declined, the argument being that for several years he had failed to perform his duties as a burgher. Similar policies were noted in Deventer. Following the capitulation to the States' army in 1591, the urban authorities ordered those burghers who had fled to return within one month, under pain of being deprived of their citizenship.[25]

Militias defended primarily their own town and district, but occasionally they also served farther afield. Service in other garrison towns was quite common. For example in 1602, 100 Gorinchem militiamen were sent to nearby Woudrichem; Woudrichem's garrison soldiers could then move on to Breda, in turn releasing Breda's garrison soldiers for service in the field army. During the invasion of the Veluwe in 1629, 5,000 Holland militiamen left their home towns to bolster the defences in the frontier garrisons: 1,000 from Amsterdam, 500 from both Leiden and Haarlem, 400 from Rotterdam, 300 from Delft, and so on, down to 75 from the small town of Schoonhoven. For duties performed outside their own town the militias were paid 12 *stuivers* a day.[26]

Occasionally, militiamen even served in field armies. In 1578 two hundred Doesburg militiamen were sent to Deventer to assist the defence on the redoubts. The next year nearby Doetinchem was captured by the Spanish commander Maarten Schenk, but an army consisting of militias from Deventer, Doesburg and Zutphen successfully stormed the town, even before professional reinforcements had arrived. The toll was heavy though: a great number of the citizen-soldiers died. Because of their inadequate training, militiamen were quite vulnerable, and the effectiveness of militias diminished with the increased professionalism evident among the regular units.[27] Even in 1637, during the siege of Breda, Frederick Henry made some use of militias, but this seems to have been the last occasion on which Dutch militiamen were involved in a major military operation outside town walls.[28]

The economic benefits of garrisons

That garrisons could offer significant opportunities for local business was well known. In the 1550s, for example, an Antwerp company had made the staggering sum of 250,000 guilders supplying 11 garrisons.[29] In addition, during the Dutch Wars of Independence a significant portion of the tax revenues were spent paying for garrison soldiers and providing for their housing, and for the

Table 4.1 Reconstructed annual budget of the expenditure of the Dutch Republic broken down in detailed categories (*c*.1641), in percentages

Army, of which:		51.5
cavalry, pay	8.5	
infantry, pay	32.8	
salary higher officers	4.2	
housing	3.1	
transportation	0.8	
magazines/ammunition	2.2	
Navy		26.0
Pensions		3.3
Fortifications		8.7
Administration		5.6
Debt service		4.4
Miscellaneous		0.5
Total (23.7 million guilders)		100.0

Sources: 't Hart, *In Quest*, pp. 43, 51; 't Hart, *Making*, p. 62.

fortifications. Table 4.1 summarizes the annual expenditure of the Dutch Republic in the early 1640s.

The other elements in this expenditure will be considered subsequently; what is of interest in this chapter are the enormous sums that ended up in the pockets of garrison soldiers, their suppliers, their hosts, and the contractors and labourers at the fortifications; in Table 4.1 this is represented by the amounts for the pay of cavalry and infantry, their housing, and the fortifications.

The Dutch army was in fact the largest single employer of the period. Over 41 per cent of the Republic's budget was devoted to paying for the infantry and cavalry ranks, all of whom stayed in garrison towns over the winter, while in summer a majority of the troops remained in the towns (the field army usually constituted a smaller proportion of the armed forces). The ordinary infantry soldier received some 11.5 to 12 guilders per month (42 days).[30] This pay was not high in comparison with that for other occupations demanding a certain minimum of skill and training, yet it was paid regularly and also continued during wintertime, when casual labourers were usually laid off. Pay in other armies was often higher but it was seldom paid fully or on time; by contrast, Dutch soldiers usually received what was promised. Dutch soldiers could also earn significant additional sums by digging, fortification repairs, convoy duties and assisting with tax collection.[31]

Not all Dutch soldiers received the same pay; the older and more experienced men usually received higher amounts. The elite pikemen obtained up to six guilders extra per month, the best musketeers up to one guilder extra. The average pay for a cavalryman was around twice that of an infantry soldier, since he had to provide for a horse too. On average, captains withheld 1.5 to 2 guilders per soldier per month to provide for clothes and weapons.[32]

As noted before, soldiers received these sums in weekly instalments, which usually amounted to a quarter guilder per day, rather than monthly as in other armies of the time. The advantage of weekly pay arrangements can hardly be overestimated. Monthly payments had often been gambled away; in contrast the smaller weekly instalments encouraged peaceful co-existence with civilians, since soldiers usually had a small amount to spend. Thus, an English soldier in the Flushing garrison reported in 1606 that his unit lived 'in love' with the local population.[33]

The regularity of soldiers' spending ensured that local artisans enjoyed an important and regular boost to demand for their products because of the presence of a garrison. This increase was considerable due to the regulation that the States' soldiers should not themselves engage in a civilian trade. This contrasted with much of the rest of Europe where soldiers were often permitted to pursue their own trade alongside their military profession.[34] This prohibition in the Netherlands was a further sign of the high degree of professionalization in the military, and it had the effect that even a small garrison created continuous greater demand for local produce; it also reduced friction with local craftsmen and tradesmen. Following the construction of the Bourtange fortification in the far north-east, for example, the village of nearby Vlagtwedde experienced a major increase in the number of artisans and shopkeepers.[35] In the much larger garrison town of Deventer, the trades of baking, blacksmithing and weapon-making flourished; the number of tailors among the new immigrants increased and the textile industry revived thanks to the soldiers' need for clothing.[36] In Gorinchem the beer industry also experienced a period of prosperity due to the expansion of the garrison. The town's trade in general expanded to such an extent that the market became too small for the number of stalls which proliferated; the fish bridge even collapsed under the weight of the goods brought to market.[37] In some cases the garrison exerted a significant stimulus for new goods; for example Maastricht's resident soldiers turned tobacco into a mass product.[38]

Dutch garrison regulations were also distinctive in that the soldiers were not exempted from taxation, unlike garrisons elsewhere. The Union of Utrecht of 1579 had stipulated that 'the said Garrisons shall bee no more privileged or exemted from paying of Excise or impost, then the Burghers and inhabitants are of the place, where they com to lie.'[39] The troops thus paid taxes on commodities, just like citizens, unlike in many other countries where the military were exempted from such duties. For example, in the Spanish Netherlands the soldiers were free from local excises on wine, beer and brandy. Some soldiers even sold those items to the burghers at a profit, to the detriment of the income of government.[40] The effect of soldiers' presence in the northern Netherlands was quite different, as was noted by the London pamphlet of 1664, *The Dutch Drawn to Life*:

> By their Excise, ... the more mony they [the Dutch] pay, the more they receive again, in that insensible but profitable way: what is Exhaled up in

Clouds, falls back again in Showers: what the souldier receives in pay, he payes in Drink ... for every day he payeth his sutler, and he the common purse.[41]

The considerable proceeds of the beer excises in garrison towns once again supported the local and provincial authorities through the boost provided to their revenues. Small wonder, then, that urban governments frequently requested an enlargement of the garrison. A larger garrison implied a higher budget; a higher budget brought enhanced prestige to the town authorities as well as a boost to the local economy. Thus, in addition to the economic motive behind those requests for enlargements, the fact that the political and administrative room for maneouvre of local authorities was enhanced must also be taken into account.[42] To these reasons another benefit can be added: the profitability of housing soldiers.

Housing the soldiers

Another 3 per cent of the budget of the United Provinces was devoted to housing the troops the garrisons required (see Table 4.1). This might not seem a particularly large amount, but the sums constituted a net transfer from the central authorities to those who actually provided lodgings for the soldiers, which contrasted sharply with the practice elsewhere in Europe.

Under the Habsburgs, as in most of early modern Europe, inhabitants of garrison towns had been required to provide soldiers with free quarters: one room with a bed for two soldiers or a soldier and his wife, plus heating, lighting and a place to cook, together with salt, vinegar and oil.[43] Together this was called the *servitium*, in Dutch *servies*. For these services soldiers were required to compensate their hosts from their own pay, but since this was frequently in arrears these arrangements regularly led to disputes. Different interpretations as to what constituted the actual *servitium* caused widespread problems: some soldiers also expected candles and tableware, for example. Difficulties of this kind were a significant reason why urban authorities shied away from billeting troops.

In the first years of the Revolt the quartering of troops in Holland and Zeeland followed traditional Habsburg practice. Quartermasters (*foeriers* among the landsknecht companies) billeted the soldiers on households; no-one could refuse. The hosts sometimes received compensation, sometimes not, depending on what was left of soldiers' pay.[44] Orange's reform of the pay structure brought about significant improvement, as did his efforts to reduce the army train by permitting only lawful wives and reducing the numbers of servants or boys to three per company.[45] A major advance was the direct link established between the army's local expenses and the sums raised in the immediate locality by the improved provincial taxes. From June 1577 onwards the *serviesgeld*, the financial compensation for the *servies*, was paid out of local tax funds (and then deducted in turn from the sums the town had to advance to the province).

Table 4.2 Payment for military lodgings, in guilders per 32-day month

	Infantry	Cavalry
Captain	6.0	6.8
Lieutenant	4.0	4.8
Ensign/Cornet	5.0	5.8
Sergeant	1.7	
Corporal	1.5	2.0
Soldier/Horseman	1.2	1.8

Source: Vermeesch, *Oorlog*, p. 109

A crucial innovation was that the households received the funds directly from the urban authorities, not indirectly via the soldiers, which ensured more reliable and regular payment. This significantly reduced disputes between soldiers and civilians.[46] After January 1578 the payments were as presented in Table 4.2.

Towns appointed *serviesmeesters* to deal with the payment to households of the substantial sums involved. The Union of Utrecht of 1579 extended these measures to the entire Dutch army:

> Order also to bee given, that the Generalitie shall pay the Burghers and inhabitants for the lodgings, in the same manner, as hath hitherto been practised in Holland.[47]

Orange's advice led to the introduction of additional regulations in 1580. In return for *serviesgeld* hosts had to provide only a bed with bedding. Heating, lighting, oil, vinegar, salt, lard, oats, hay, straw, pots or pans were no longer included in the *servies*. Henceforth many soldiers had their meals at inns and did not burden their hosts in the kitchen or with further demands. Ordinary soldiers slept up to a maximum of six in a room with three beds; officers were entitled to their own room, again with a bed; captains were to have a room with two beds, together with a kitchen. When the army departed on a campaign, soldiers' wives and children remaining behind were to receive half the standard instalments.[48]

During the 1580s the detrimental aspects traditionally associated with the billeting of soldiers vanished in Holland and Zeeland. The system of providing regular payments for soldiers' lodgings via the military or local authorities proved an enormous improvement on the previous Habsburg practice. This system was not extended to the garrison towns of the other provinces until 1595, when payment for accommodation became a standard item in the States-General's budget.

The Spanish Netherlands lagged significantly behind their Dutch adversaries in finding solutions to the billeting of troops. Some improvement was noted after the arrival of Archduke Albert. His advisors had warned him 'that if he wished to master and overcome his enemies he should set his affections more upon the people than upon the soldiers'. The obligation to house soldiers was then changed in part into a money payment made directly to the government and passed on to the soldiers, who could then pay their hosts. Citizens unable to pay this levy had no choice: they were obliged to provide accommodation for soldiers free of charge. They were promised compensation, but the real costs were always higher than the reimbursements, and payment came in late, if at all. The regulation was further hampered by the considerable scale of tax exemption, and nobles, church officials and urban councillors contributed nothing at all. Thus, the presence of soldiers in the frontier garrisons of the southern Netherlands remained a fertile source of problems and complaints throughout the war.[49]

The failure to solve the problem of billeting in the Spanish Netherlands led to the solutions that were gradually taken up in other countries as well, though not in the northern Netherlands: the building of barracks. These were built in 's-Hertogenbosch (1610), Dunkirk (1611), Lier (1613), Maastricht (1616) and Breda (1630), among other towns. This attempt to relieve the local population of the burden of housing soldiers, however, was unpopular among the soldiers themselves. They preferred to stay at private houses, which were more comfortable and where they were less vulnerable to the spread of disease.[50]

Also contrary to the usual European practice, Dutch soldiers were not forcibly billeted upon households. Maurice stipulated in 1595 that burghers could never be compelled to provide accommodation. This fact encouraged military discipline and endowed the would-be hosts with significant freedom in negotiating with troops. They had the right to decide upon how many soldiers they wished to house, they could refuse to have any at all, and they could select those for whom they were prepared to provide quarters and reject those they did not like. The French Captain Puységur described the quartering of soldiers in Gorinchem (1636):

> One does not give any billets for housing soldiers, the men and women choose them on the market-place: some pick two, others four, but not all from the same company ... . Usually, only the worst looking and worst clothed remain without lodging, but after being smartened up they find always someone to stay with, yet never are they forced, nor by billets or by any other means.[51]

The willingness to provide quarters for soldiers increased substantially with the introduction of the *serviesgelden*; they created above all a regular source of potential income for numerous townspeople, above all middling and lower-income households. An English soldier in the Flushing garrison reported that many poorer inhabitants made a living primarily through the housing of soldiers.[52] Soldiers often ended up year after year with the same family, like Luym Smit who always stayed with Jan Otten in Doesburg. Other hosts, like Bernt Dumenbrinck, Vrouw ten Bergh and Wessel Schaep, regularly accommodated four soldiers or even more. Even the local urban elite provided quarters, usually for the higher ranks. One commanding officer always resided at the house of the prominent regent Herman Baerken.[53]

These peaceful conditions and the harmonious relations with townspeople which they fostered permitted soldiers to engage in leisure activities. Edmund Verney, a cavalryman, improved his Latin and French while staying in the Utrecht garrison; Captain Jan van der Meulen pursued his hobby of experimenting with plant seeds in the Meurs garrison; while in Doesburg Lieutenant Johan Bentinck, who had earlier served in Brazil, introduced brazilwood furniture and South American tablecloths to fellow citizens.[54] Such relaxed reports stood in sharp contrast to the practices of billeting and garrison towns elsewhere in Europe.

Fortifications: costs and payments

Garrison towns received yet another kind of funding from the States-General: payments for fortifications. At the start of the Revolt relatively few towns in the north were fortified according to the recent advances of the *trace italienne*. Improvements had mostly been piecemeal – the building of a bastion here and a ravelin there.[55] Within a couple of decades all that had changed. Former towers were lowered and flattened and the high brick walls that were so vulnerable to cannon fire were replaced by thick ramparts made of earth, first in Zeeland, then in Holland, and subsequently in the other parts of the Republic. Where the ramparts were surrounded by deep water the earthen construction was faced with stone. Bastions, not usually further apart than the maximum range of musket fire (225 to 235 metres), were broadened to permit the positioning of cannon. Bastions were also built with five angles to enable flanking fire along the ramparts. A wet ditch (not a dry one, as was more usual in Italy) prevented storming by enemy troops. Island forts, called ravelins, and hornworks (two demi-bastions) constituted additional protection at vulnerable points. A 'covered way', protected by breastworks, encircled the fortress to connect the outworks and permit the organization of outward raids. The fortifications as a whole, including outworks, were to be further defended against attack by a glacis, a gentle slope descending downwards from the town walls and free of habitation or other permanent buildings. As a result the outlook of many Dutch towns changed radically. In addition to these urban fortifications, sconces (*schansen*) were built in the countryside, mainly to control dykes and river crossings. In this way Maurice constructed a chain of fortified towns and redoubts, first along the Maas and Waal in the 1590s, then along the Yssel and the north-eastern border.[56]

Such fortifications were costly. Traditionally, towns were responsible for their own defences. In the early days of the Revolt urban communities paid themselves for the constructions, often assisted by a tax on the surrounding countryside, such as the *walgeld* in Gorinchem. Yet these solutions were inadequate for really large-scale reconstructions. Gradually the provincial authorities and States-General stepped in and arranged more regular funding.[57] In 1596 the States-General decided that all provinces should shoulder the burden of paying,

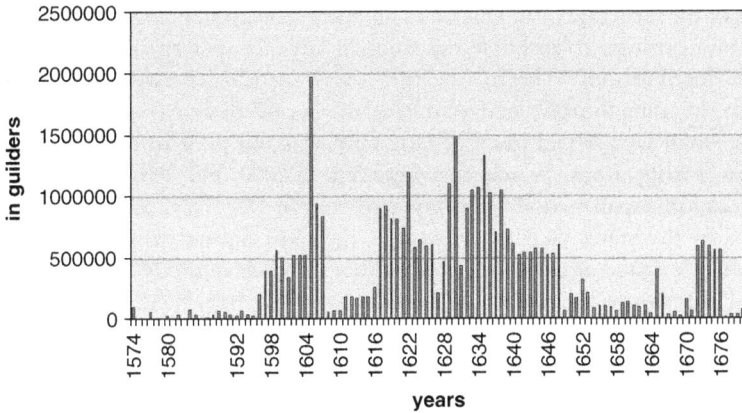

Figure 4.1 Expenditure on fortifications, 1574–1680
Source: Van der Ent and Enthoven, *Gewestelijke financiën*; Fritschy, *Gewestelijke financiën*; Liesker and Fritschy, *Gewestelijke financiën*; Veenstra, *Gewestelijke financiën*; Trompetter, *Gewestelijke financiën*

initially a sum of 100,000 guilders a year, but as more money was urgently needed the provinces soon decided to increase Generality support. From 1605, 500,000 guilders was voted annually. This was a substantial amount, particularly when compared to, for example, France, a country that spent far less on its fortifications.[58] Individual provinces added considerable sums on their own account, which resulted in expenditure peaks of around two million guilders annually (see Figure 4.1). In addition to these expenses, towns also devoted significant portions of their own budgets to the new ramparts. The provinces and the Generality only paid for fortifications along the frontiers; non-frontier towns (such as Amsterdam) had to provide all the funds themselves.

The significant sums involved are apparent from the example of Gorinchem. Large-scale construction started in 1584; its total costs can be estimated at some 250,000 guilders. The Provincial States of Holland provided two-thirds of the funding, paid out of local revenue raised by the new provincial land tax (*verponding*). The town funded the remainder, which consumed almost 25 per cent of the urban budget during the period of construction. Within 16 years the town's ramparts were renewed. The defence works contained no fewer than 11 new bastions together with a new rampart; the number of gates was reduced to four; at the same time the area contained within the town walls expanded significantly, from 27 to 56 hectares.[59]

The new construction at Deventer, the inland commercial centre on the Yssel, cost the same as Gorinchem's, between approximately 225,000 and 290,000 guilders. Building started in 1597; by 1621 the new fortifications were ready. Subsidies provided by the States-General ranged between 47 to 61 per cent of the expenses; the town itself thus provided between 39 and 53 per cent.

Much of the Generality funding was significantly delayed, but the town authorities were in a position to disburse the sums in advance, permitting steady progress on the fortifications. The fortification costs absorbed between 10 and 20 per cent of the annual urban budget during the period of construction.[60]

The small Gelderland town of Doesburg was too poor to contribute itself to its new fortifications, which cost between 150,000 and 200,000 guilders. The construction began in 1597, the same year as in Deventer, and was completely funded by the States-General. However, the sums did not come in soon enough and the restricted urban budget (as little as 5,000 guilders per year) did not permit the gap to be temporarily bridged as had happened in Deventer; contractors abandoned the works in 1598.[61] But Spínola's offensive in the early 1600s spurred on the fortification programme along the eastern frontiers and came to the town's aid. Maurice himself closely supervised these plans. In 1607 Doesburg's brick wall was demolished to make room for an earthen rampart. Within a couple of years the town had new ramparts, nine bastions, three ravelins and two major outworks.[62]

With the expiry of the Truce it became clear that the fortification funds of the States-General had been well spent. In the winter of 1623/4 enemy soldiers passed through the Yssel area but did not dare to attack Doesburg or the other newly fortified towns. Throughout the remaining decades of the war fortifications remained high on the agenda of the provincial governments and States-General.

Earthen defence works might be cheaper to construct than brick ones, but the difference was not as substantial as is assumed in the standard historiography, which sometimes suggests the costs were one-twentieth of those for traditional brick walls.[63] The brick bastioned constructions of Antwerp had cost over one million guilders in the mid-sixteenth century; 100 years later the new earthen bastioned walls of Amsterdam carried a price tag of no less than 21 million guilders.[64] But by then Amsterdam had grown into a large metropolis, significantly larger than Antwerp. A better comparison might be found in the Deventer accounts. A comparable brick construction was estimated to have cost around three times more than the actual earthen one.[65] Although less expensive, the cost of new earthen defences was still considerably more than is generally assumed.

In addition, earthen constructions had the disadvantage that they were much more costly to maintain than brick ones due to problems of sagging and crumbling. The ramparts' angle of 45 degrees necessitated the planting of thorny hedges that needed regular trimming. Furthermore, a palisade of sharp-pointed poles, some two to three metres long, had to be inserted horizontally just under the parapet, which was quite labour intensive; these poles needed replacement at regular intervals to prevent them rotting. For Maastricht's defence, for example, no fewer than 30,000 poles were needed.[66] A striking example can be given of the continuing costs involved. In the far north-east, along the eastern border of Groningen, three new fortresses were constructed, Bourtange (1594), Bellingwolderschans (1603, later called Oude Schans) and Langakkerschans (1629, later called Nieuwe Schans). Ammunition-masters, convoy-masters (to collect custom duties), overseers, and building and dyke contractors were

Table 4.3 Generality expenditure 1603–53 on fortresses on Groningen's eastern frontier, for construction and provisions, in guilders

Period	Bourtange	Bellingwolderschans	Langakkerschans
1603–10	6,136	7,013	–
1611–20	43,925	25,489	–
1621–30	16,209	53,762	21,127
1631–40	13,292	34,253	50,862
1641–53	22,844	39,437	45,064
Total	102,406	159,954	117,053

Source: *Ordonnanties op gemene middelen Wedde en Westerwolde*

appointed. Excluding their salaries and soldiers' pay, these three fortifications received some 375,000 guilders between 1603 and 1653, mainly spent on ramparts, dykes, buildings, canals, bridges, ironworks, spades and buckets (see Table 4.3).

Until the very end of the Eighty Years War, there was regular funding for the maintenance of existing fortifications and the construction of new ones. In the later 1640s the States-General continued to reserve 300,000 guilders annually for such expenditure, while the provinces furnished at least a further 200,000 guilders (see Figure 4.1). Expenditure on this scale always had a considerable positive economic effect, in particular for the local contractors and their labourers. In Deventer, for example, 33 to 41 labourers worked on the ramparts each year; shippers, wagoners and victuallers of food and drink were also involved.[67]

The fortifications were inspected regularly by provincial controllers, and on an annual or bi-annual basis by a committee of the Council of State. The town authorities welcomed such inspections since they usually involved additional spending and a transfer of sums by the Union and the provincial authorities. In Holland itself the fortification master and provincial representatives inspected the ramparts and bastions together with the local authorities. Captains of the garrison, local polder officials and inhabitants all had the opportunity to put forward specific requests. Gorinchem secured almost 90,000 guilders for the maintenance of its fortifications between 1625 and 1648 through these inspections. The contract for any remedial work was usually sold to the lowest bidder, but earlier experiences with the contractor were also taken into account.[68]

In 1648, however, these rather advantageous arrangements came to an abrupt halt. Expenditure on fortifications plummeted because the Provincial States of Holland decided that subsidies were no longer necessary. The small peak in 1652 in Figure 4.1 was caused by expenditure on the part of Zeeland and Groningen.[69] Although some individual contractors managed to obtain substantial maintenance contracts since annual or bi-annual inspections along the frontiers continued,[70] the great age of expenditure on fortifications has passed.

The impact of declining subsidies was felt above all in the inland provinces, for example in Doesburg. Jacob Muys, who had earned an annual 3,400 guilders for maintaining the town's fortification during the Eighty Years War, secured a similar contract in 1649, but now for only a third of that sum, 1,130 guilders per year. The covered way was soon overgrown; parts of the rampart and bastions were excavated by the inhabitants, who established gardens in their stead. The maintenance contracts were unattractive; in 1658 not a single contractor in Doesburg was willing to undertake the repairs needed. Soon the fortification weakened; ramparts, bastions and thorny hedges had been partly washed away by the river; the ditch itself was full of sand; inhabitants cultivated not only parts of the rampart but also areas on the hornwork and breastworks. Since private contractors could not be found to undertake the maintenance, individual officials of the urban government or local army officers fulfilled the repair contracts – men like Artillery Master Jan Ooms, Captain Maerten Haesten and the clerk Johan Mentingh.[71]

The Peace of Westphalia also changed the position of the urban militias, which immediately lost their military function. In Gorinchem the urban authorities reduced the formation from eight to four companies. All male inhabitants were still formally required to participate, but many preferred to purchase exemption at a rate of five guilders a year. This changed early in 1672, when the threat of war prompted the sudden revival of the militia companies. The Provincial States of Holland ordered their regular exercise in April. But numerous burghers were unwilling to take up arms. Gorinchem experienced enormous difficulty in filling the eight companies now required. Apparently the community solidarity evident during the Eighty Years War had faded away. By January 1673 the Provincial States of Holland decided to take firm action; over twenty thousand citizens were mobilized; they were compensated when they were sent for service in another town. In moving militias between towns the danger of local militias turning against their own urban authorities was reduced. Gorinchem's militia departed for elsewhere and the town received 750 militiamen from Haarlem and 250 from Alkmaar.[72] These attempts to introduce some kind of compulsory military service proved short-lived, however, and disappeared when the direct war threat of the 1670s had subsided. In contrast, France started at exactly this period to create a military reserve, partly based upon the former urban militias.[73]

Popular willingness to support the cause of the Republic was obviously much reduced after 1648. The decreasing size of garrisons in the wake of the Peace negatively affected urban prosperity in all frontier areas. In 1648–50 the number of soldiers in most garrisons was reduced to a third. In addition, payments for housing soldiers were halved.[74] As a result towns suffered from an economic downturn; the revenues of the beer excise dropped and local artisans and traders suffered from reduced demand.[75]

These developments weakened morale in the frontier towns and further undermined their defences. When the French army arrived in Doesburg in 1672 the town appeared sufficiently fortified, the fortifications having been repaired in time, with batteries in place and a reinforced garrison of 3,500, plus the urban militia. But the town surrendered remarkably quickly. At a certain point during the siege a number of burghers, farmers and town soldiers planted a white flag on the ramparts. The governor ordered it to be taken down, but the urban authorities supported the inhabitants, and then the military command decided to surrender. The consequences were disastrous; the French destroyed 33 houses and another 55 were set on fire; troops were forcibly billeted on the population: even the burgomaster had to house four cavalrymen. But most far-reaching was the destruction of the fortifications, which left the town an easy prey in the future.[76] The great period of profitable subsidies from the Union and provincial institutions – such a feature of the Eighty Years War – had passed.

Conclusion: the strength of the urban community

From the 1590s onwards fortifications and garrisons strengthened the Dutch urban communities. This is in itself noteworthy, since the presence of even friendly troops usually increased the risks for local populations in sixteenth- and seventeenth-century Europe and imposed an economic burden. After a difficult start in the 1570s the Holland arrangements for garrisons turned out to be quite favourable. In the 1590s their reforms were extended to the whole Dutch Republic. Together with the drill and discipline discussed in earlier chapters, the measures regarding the housing of troops, the prohibition of soldiers engaging in another trade and the obligation for troops to pay excises and other taxes all encouraged peaceful co-existence between army units and the local population.

Thanks to this non-violent co-existence the town inhabitants were in a position to benefit from the numerous transfers of resources from central and provincial authorities to their local garrisons. To lodge soldiers or not was optional; the opportunity to earn some money by providing lodging for soldiers served as a welcome additional income for the middle and lower classes. The considerable expenditure on the earthen fortifications – which was more substantial than usually thought, not least because of the additional maintenance costs – provided ample opportunities for local contractors and labourers. Throughout the Eighty Years War there was a high level of cooperation between garrison and burgher militia. This is not surprising since soldiers stimulated local demand, which profited artisans and traders, and at the same time the presence of troops meant increased revenues from excises as well as essential defence. To a significant degree the military expenses of the Dutch Republic involved sizeable positive effects for the garrison towns.

The Peace of Westphalia brought about a sudden change in this regard. With the reduction in the numbers in the garrisons the frontier towns experienced substantial economic decline. Once the direct threat of fighting faded away, the population was less willing to serve in the militia. All kind of advantageous payments (fortification construction and maintenance, serving in the militia, the housing of soldiers) were cut significantly. Even though much of the former garrison arrangements continued – such as the regular fortification inspections by central and provincial authorities, which were usually accompanied by new spending – the economic benefits were much reduced. By the time of the French invasion of 1672 the local bonds between garrisons and their urban populations had undoubtedly weakened; the Franco-Dutch War was too short to boost the loyalty of the Dutch citizenry to a level comparable to that in the Eighty Years War.

Even so, the state of the Dutch Republic demonstrated a resilience that continued to rely upon such sentiments. The Wars of Dutch Independence had resulted in a distinctive form of state, one in which the role and even power of individual urban communities remained considerable – even after 1648. The way in which war expenditure could benefit local communities had earlier been observed in highly commercialized Italian city-states like Florence and Venice.[77] The wartime financial transfers in the Netherlands also strengthened local governments; the garrisons contributed to larger urban budgets and the fortifications attracted men and money, while the new ramparts were awesome and prestigious. The question remains, though, whether the Revolt was as profitable for the inhabitants of the countryside as it was for the burghers in the towns. This issue will be considered in Chapter 5.

Notes

1 Anderson, *War*, p. 73.
2 See also Arnold, 'Fortifications', p. 222.
3 Parrott, *Richelieu's Army*, pp. 432, 524–5; White, 'Experience', pp. 36–7.
4 Tallett, *War and Society*, p. 149 (Mazarin quote; *taille* = heavy tax on land); Swart, *Krijgsvolk*, pp. 177–8; Lynn, *Giant*, pp. 162–8, 193 (Colbert quote); Braddick, *God's Fury*, pp. 396–7; Parrott, *Richelieu's Army*, pp. 271–3, 511; Rooms, 'Bezoldiging', p. 544; Kroener, 'Soldat', p. 111; Schennach, 'Soldat', p. 61; Göse, '*Landstände*', p. 208; Fletcher, *County Community*, p. 198; Gaunt, 'One of the goodliest', pp. 193, 197; Vermeesch, *Oorlog*, p. 107; Childs, *Armies and Warfare*, pp. 175ff.
5 Gunn, Grummit, and Cools, *War, State, and Society*, p. 75; Corvisier, *Armies*, pp. 29–31.
6 Lynn, *Giant*, pp. 372–3. Only later in the seventeenth century did the French state again revive urban militias, in a new and centralized setting.
7 Zwitzer, 'Soldaat', p. 181. In the southern Netherlands the Spanish maintained a comparable number of garrisons, see the lists in Rooms, *Organisatie*, pp. 374–417.
8 Quoted by Duffy, *Siege Warfare*, p. 130.
9 Aglionby, *Present State*, p. 64. See also Tracy, 'Holland's new fiscal regime', p. 54.
10 Gorinchem is also called Gorkum.
11 Rooze-Stouthamer, *Opmaat*, pp. 97–9.
12 Swart, *Krijgsvolk*, p. 176. Medemblik is located to the north of Enkhuizen, on the Zuiderzee.
13 Ibid., p. 177.
14 Aitzema, *Notable Revolutions*, p. 13.
15 Vermeesch, *Oorlog*, pp. 47–8.
16 Ibid., p. 69. The town remained in Spanish hands until 1591.
17 Ibid., pp. 65–6.
18 Ibid., pp. 67–76.

19 Ibid., p. 56.
20 Ibid., pp. 47, 52, 54.
21 Knevel, *Burgers*, p. 92–8; Van Nierop, *Verraad*, p. 73; on the militia in the southern Netherlands: Despretz, 'Stadsversterkingen', p. 14ff.
22 Vermeesch, *Oorlog*, p. 97; see also Rooze-Stouthamer, *Opmaat*, pp. 94, 157, 185, for Zeeland militias. In addition, the militia could be strengthened by soldiers hired by the urban government or provincial authorities. Town soldiers hired by the province were called *waardgelders*. Their pay was somewhat higher than the ordinary soldier's, seven *stuivers* a day instead of five, because their service was discontinued during the winter when the field army returned to the garrison. Wagenaar, 'De waardgelders', pp. 211–30; Van Nimwegen, *Deser landen crijghsvolck*, pp. 46–7. One guilder = 20 *stuivers*.
23 Ibid., p. 123.
24 Vermeesch, *Oorlog*, pp. 50, 75, 98.
25 Ibid., p. 48; Holthuis, *Frontierstad*, p. 39.
26 Vermeesch, *Oorlog*, pp. 67, 74, 97–8.
27 Ibid., p. 67.
28 Knevel, *Burgers*, p. 255. In other armies the role of militias diminished too, see Parrott, *Business of War*, pp. 98–100.
29 Soly, 'Antwerpse Compagnie', p. 358; see also Gunn, Grummit and Cools, *War, State, and Society*, p. 81; Kroll, *Stadtgesellschaft*, p. 476; Corvisier, *Armies*, p. 81.
30 On the standard number of days in the pay month, see Chapter 2.
31 On digging, see also Chapter 2. Adriaenssen, *Staatsvormend geweld*, pp. 164–8.
32 Van Nimwegen, *Deser landen crijghsvolck*, pp. 59, 62.
33 De Graaf, *Oorlog*, p. 396.
34 Thompson, 'Money', p. 289; Kroener, 'Modern state', pp. 215–16.
35 Post and Van Oorschot, *Middelen*, pp. 108, 114, 127. See on the Bourtange fortress also Chapter 5.
36 Holthuis, *Frontierstad*, pp. 164–6, 172–6.
37 Vermeesch, *Oorlog*, p. 164.
38 Steegen, *Kleinhandel*, pp. 264, 290.
39 Aitzema, *Notable Revolutions*, p. 13.
40 Rooms, 'Bezoldiging', pp. 542–3; Rooms, *Organisatie*, pp. 253–4.
41 Anon., *Dutch Drawn to Life*, pp. 50–1.
42 De Graaf, *Oorlog*, p. 561; Holthuis, *Frontierstad*, p. 45; Vermeesch, *Oorlog*, p. 114.
43 Rooms, 'Bezoldiging', pp. 537ff.; Groenveld, *Van vyanden*, p. 15.
44 Rooze-Stouthamer, *Opmaat*, pp. 86, 193.
45 Swart, *Krijgsvolk*, pp. 182–4. Holthuis, *Frontierstad*, p. 102, estimates the army train at some 40 per cent of troop strength. On average one in four soldiers was married, De Graaf, *Oorlog*, p. 201.
46 Tracy, *Founding*, pp. 131, 172; Vermeesch, *Oorlog*, pp. 53–6.
47 Aitzema, *Notable Revolutions*, p. 13.
48 Swart, *Krijgsvolk*, pp. 178–9; Vermeesch, *Oorlog*, p. 108; Van Nimwegen, *Deser landen crijghsvolck*, p. 63.
49 Rooms, 'Bezoldiging', pp. 540–1; Rooms, *Organisatie*, pp. 238–46. The burden of housing soldiers fell on the less well-off in Germany too: Kroener, 'Soldat', p. 111. Fletcher, *County Community*, pp. 195, 199, notes that in early seventeenth-century England the costs of billeting should be reimbursed, but this was rarely effectuated.
50 Rooms, 'Bezoldiging', pp. 541–2; Rooms, *Organisatie*, p. 250. See also Black, *European Warfare*, p. 225, on barrack building; for French barracks see Lynn, *Giant*, p. 159, and Parrott, *Richelieu's Army*, p. 505. Lier is located to the south-east of Antwerp.
51 Quoted by Vermeesch, 'Organisation', p. 286.
52 In 1589, De Graaf, *Oorlog*, p. 396.

53 Vermeesch, *Oorlog*, pp. 53, 109–11; for the lodging of soldiers in the small town of Doesburg in 1661–8 almost 36,000 guilders were paid by the Council of State; ibid., p. 122. A minority of the troops preferred to stay at inns; as such, they boosted the business of the innkeepers.

54 De Graaf, *Oorlog*, pp. 556, 565; Frijhoff and Spies, *Hard-Won Unity*, p. 156. The garrison of Meurs was located on the Rhine, near Wesel.

55 Westra, *Nederlandse ingenieurs*, pp. 13–14; Soly, *Urbanisme*, p. 202; Gunn, Grummit, and Cools, *War, State, and Society*, p. 70.

56 Van Hoof, 'Met een vijand', pp. 629–39.

57 Vermeesch, *Oorlog*, pp. 119, 121–4; Veenstra, *Gewestelijke financiën*, p. 258.

58 On the limited expenditure on fortifications in France, Lynn, *Giant*, p. 592; see also Kingra, 'Trace italienne', p. 441.

59 Vermeesch, *Oorlog*, p. 125; the Gorinchem budget was around 20,000 guilders annually.

60 Holthuis, *Frontierstad*, pp. 85–6; the annual urban budget amounted to 22,500 guilders on average.

61 Vermeesch, *Oorlog*, pp. 127–9.

62 Ibid., pp. 130–4.

63 Duffy, *Siege Warfare*, p. 91.

64 Soly, *Urbanisme*, p. 223; Koenen, *Voorlezingen*, p. 27.

65 Holthuis, *Frontierstad*, pp. 83, 91.

66 Van Nimwegen, *Deser landen crijghsvolck*, pp. 119–20; Vermeesch, *Oorlog*, p. 135.

67 Holthuis, *Frontierstad*, p. 90; on the significant numbers of workers employed in fortifications elsewhere, see also Soly, *Urbanisme*, p. 268; Tallett, *War and Society*, p. 227, even mentions 6,000 workers on Milan's fortifications in 1657.

68 Vermeesch, *Oorlog*, pp. 135–6.

69 Ten Raa and De Bas, *Staatsche Leger*, V, pp. 373, 380, 389.

70 Vermeesch, *Oorlog*, p. 200.

71 Ibid., pp. 222–5.

72 Ibid., pp. 196, 203–4; Knevel, *Burgers*, p. 257. The compensation amounted to ten stuivers a day, which was remarkably less than in the Eighty Years War, when such payments had been 12 stuivers a day. The militia also had to support the fortification repairs, but this was done only reluctantly.

73 Which signalled the start of the *Grande Armée* based on conscription, see Lynn, *Giant*, p. 381.

74 Ten Raa and De Bas, *Staatsche Leger*, V, pp. 393–4; a temporary increase was evident in 1667–8.

75 Vermeesch, *Oorlog*, pp. 113, 195, 218. The numbers increased temporarily in Doesburg in 1665. See also Steegen, *Kleinhandel*, p. 265, for comparable negative economic effects after the decrease of the numbers in the Maastricht garrison.

76 Vermeesch, *Oorlog*, pp. 227–30.

77 Caferro, 'Warfare and economy', pp. 204–5.

5 Warfare in the countryside and the threat to farming communities

> In order to accurately comprehend the Eighty Years War we must actually differentiate between three parties: the two war parties and the countryside. The first two had at least the advantage that the blows came only from one side; the strength of the third was tried by blows coming from both sides at once.[1]

Previous chapters have demonstrated how the Dutch Revolt advanced the professionalization of the military. This process was accompanied by thorough disciplining and by state formation; the increased capacity of the army to protect benefitted the urban communities of the Dutch Republic – above all in Holland, which had introduced favourable arrangements for the payment and housing of soldiers at an early stage. The relationship between army and countryside was altogether more ambiguous. The operations and even the presence of the States' army increased farmers' risks and uncertainties, while simultaneously levying duties ('safeguards' and 'contributions') with the promise not to set fire to the village. In such instances soldiers were not much different from robber bands; they might even be labelled racketeers, as argued by the American historical sociologist Charles Tilly in his famous essay on 'War making and state making as organized crime': 'Someone who produces both the danger and, at a price, the shield against it is a racketeer.' Tilly concluded his historical analysis: 'Governments' provision of protection, by this standard, often qualifies as racketeering.'[2]

In Europe the main victims of the violence of underpaid soldiers lived in villages and hamlets, not in the fortified towns. The sieges of Haarlem, Leiden or Ostend, the sacks of Magdeburg, Mechelen or Antwerp were horrendous events, yet they were unusual: most towns were spared such a fate. For the countryside, each army on the march constituted a plague, an army remaining in the neighbourhood a disaster. When pay failed to arrive in time, pikes and muskets were employed to guarantee subsistence for the military. During the English Civil War rural inhabitants had to provide free quarters and provisions; a petition from Sussex claimed that 'by free quarter and plunder of soldiers our purses have bin exhausted, corne eaten up, cattell plundered.'[3] *En étappe* French troops acted as highwaymen, even in their own country, and extorted money, goods, and sex from the inhabitants.[4] The seventeenth-century French *Mercure* noted: 'One finds enough soldiers when one gives them the freedom to live off the land, and allowing them to pillage supports them without pay.'[5] Hungry soldiers either became deserters or thieves, while treating 'friendly' civilians in the same violent manner as they treated 'enemy' populations.[6] The disruptive and demoralizing effects of such 'legalized robbery' were huge. Moreover, as armies grew larger, they also became potentially less manageable and more dangerous. David Parrott has emphasized the 'true human tragedy' which occured across France when the increase of Richelieu's army in 1635 was coupled to the overall ineffectiveness of French administration.[7]

Rural experience of war was exacerbated by conflicts that lasted more than just one or two years and campaigns that coincided with poor harvests, on-going economic decline, adverse weather conditions, famine and/or epidemics. The fact that the climatic deterioration associated with the Little Ice Age struck particularly hard in the late sixteenth and early seventeenth centuries created extremely unfavourable conditions for farming communities all across Europe. But the effects were not the same for everyone. Military violence often pushed the poorer peasants over the edge of subsistence while allowing the richer ones to survive. In addition, the resilience of a farming community depended strongly on the existing institutional network and village solidarity. In the Thirty Years War, for example, the worst effects of soldiers' quartering might be reduced if village representatives were able to enter into discussions with army officers before the troops arrived.[8]

In the longer term such hardships for the peasants often implied a transfer of the countryside's wealth to burghers in the towns. When armies arrived, numerous peasants fled to nearby walled towns, selling their cattle and stock at low prices to the burghers; the burghers could sell these assets at high prices to the military; when the army left and the farmers wished to re-establish their farmsteads, the burghers once again provided the necessary capital, but at a high rate of interest.[9]

With regard to the Dutch Revolt, such effects have seldom been studied. Historiography is concentrated on urban history; much of the rural experience of war has been ignored. Furthermore, the sorry tales of peasants as victims of extortion are usually ascribed to the enemy invaders, not to Dutch soldiers. Northern Netherlanders continue to be characterized as unwarlike; this notion was advanced particularly after 1648 when Dutch political leaders promoted the idea of the Republic 'as a peace-loving nation, oriented toward freedom and trade, averse to war and belligerence.'[10] Yet as will be shown below, that characterization is totally unjustified.

This chapter discusses recent evidence concerning the Dutch countryside's experience of war, and begins with an examination of the general vulnerability of the peasantry during hostilities. The inundations in Holland and Zeeland receive particular attention, followed by the ravages of war in northern Brabant. No other area of the northern Netherlands experienced such a war-related demographic collapse as the Meierij, the district of 's-Hertogenbosch. Payments in the form of safeguards and contributions were a way to avert the most terrible war threats. Such solutions only worked, though, when strong village institutions were at hand, as will be exemplified by a case study of Tilburg (northern Brabant) and a range of villages in the north-east of the Netherlands. Finally, the chapter's conclusion discusses the question of whether the Dutch Wars of Independence were accompanied by a shift of wealth from countryside to towns.

The vulnerability of the peasantry

The countryside was open to all kinds of threat from armies and soldiers passing through. After the invasion of Louis of Nassau in the northern Netherlands and his victory at the battle of Heiligerlee in 1568, Spanish troops retaliated by setting fire to entire villages. Rebel forces brutally extorted money from innocent and harmless villagers. Garrison soldiers, from both sides, just took what they needed, above all when they did not receive their pay. This remained a problem until the late 1580s, even in Holland. In 1584, hundreds of starving soldiers from the States' army travelled through the Gooi district to the south-east of Amsterdam seizing food and extorting money, until driven away.[11]

Throughout the Dutch Wars of Independence the countryside lay unprotected. Sconces were built to protect communications between the towns; they were not intended to provide a defence for the peasantry. In fact sconces constituted additional burdens for the farming population because of the obligation to contribute in kind (labour, such as making hurdles and gabions, and wagon services for the transport of provisions or building materials); *ad hoc* land taxes were levied to pay for them. Orange himself did not shy away from subjecting the countryside to burdensome demands when necessary. In 1574 all inhabitants of the Rijnland, Delfland, Schieland and Alblasserwaard regions, which made up the larger part of south Holland's countryside, were ordered to vacate their residences within three days and take all cattle and goods with them, for fear that they might provision the Spanish. What remained would be confiscated as booty for the States' soldiers. Parma's typical siege tactics did not spare the peasants either; he usually drove the inhabitants of the surrounding countryside into the town with cavalry raids, to reduce the town's supply of provisions.[12]

Cavalry raids were the greatest threat to villagers. Heeze, on the road from 's-Hertogenbosch to Maastricht, was pillaged in this way on no fewer than three occasions in 1577; in early 1580 the village was even attacked four times by French mercenary soldiers from the States' garrison at Herentals. During the last raid eight villagers were killed, women and girls were raped, 108 houses burned down and 27 men taken as a hostage. Following prolonged argument the latter were released after a ransom of 4,090 guilders was paid. Extortion methods were brutal; a shoemaker was hung in his burning hearth and hauled up and down to enforce a demand for a large ransom in Dongen (near Tilburg) in 1579.[13] To meet the costs of such ransoms villagers were forced to sell goods or even part of their farms. In December 1586, probably because the village had failed to supply peat for the Doesburg garrison, around 40 English mercenary horsemen in States' service attacked the Veluwe village of Veenendaal as a reprisal. They took seven hostages, one of whom was shot on the spot when he declared himself unable to pay the sum demanded (950 guilders per head).[14] Cattle could also be seized and held hostage. Pietro Boboca, the Italian commander of the Spanish garrison in Tilburg, took oxen grazing in the Langstraat (southern Holland); the beasts were returned to the owners at a rate of 15 guilders per head, which produced the considerable sum of 3,000 guilders. Such funds were necessary to provide pay and provisions for a garrison, but many soldiers also operated entirely on their own account. Ygrom Aerts for example, originally from the village of Heesch (Brabant), had taken up service in the States' garrison of Tiel (on the Waal river, Gelderland). He took Goort Jacops de Lender of Heesch as a hostage to extort a significant ransom from him, presumably in revenge for his fathering an illegitimate child with Ygrom's stepdaughter.[15]

It has been argued that soldiers were as much victims as victimizers, risking destruction just like the peasants, both standing on the step of an 'existential crisis'.[16] However, their weaponry and training rendered them unquestionably more powerful than the average peasant. But not all peasants were passive victims. At times they took up arms, as in 1579 when, in revenge for troops' plundering, farmers near Alost and Dendermonde (Flanders) disarmed two French companies and defeated three Scottish companies in the States' service. In Drenthe, Overijssel and Gelderland there were widespread peasant uprisings against States' troops in 1580. The revolt was probably instigated by Stadholder Rennenberg, who was plotting to side with the Spanish king. At first the armed peasants only wished to chase out the marauding and plundering troops, but their success inspired new ambitions and in Overijssel the peasants (around 5,000-strong and commanded by professional soldiers) even managed to defeat the States' forces.[17]

Such successes against professional soldiers were transient, however, and in the cases mentioned above the troops soon managed to take bloody vengeance of their own. In Overijssel the States' soldiers – if contemporary reports are to be believed – killed over 1,000 armed peasants. Peasant militias had at best mixed success. Against vagrant soldiers peasant militias were quite effective; in the area bordering Westphalia numerous Spanish deserters were killed by armed farmers. Occasionally they received instructions to side with regular soldiers, such as in 1576 when the peasant militia from the Doesburg district participated in a military expedition to subdue the mutineers of the nearby Army of Flanders. But for longer campaigns peasant militias were of little use. Apart from their poor level of professionalization, peasants were not always strongly motivated to serve. In the district of Zutphen, for example, the authorities compelled all villages to arm their farmers and have them stand guard, imposing fines when they failed to turn up. Numerous complaints about sleeping guards and ignored emergency calls testified that the scheme did not work out as expected. Another defence measure was the erection of barriers in the road, to halt troops temporarily so that negotiations could start before the soldiers actually entered the village. The Brabant village of Oirschot alone was reported to have over a thousand such barriers.[18]

Yet neither barriers nor militias could stop the spread of diseases carried by soldiers as they marched. One soldier affected by the plague signalled the start of a major epidemic in Brabant in 1603; in the small town of Grave (Brabant) as many as a third of the population died. The worst disaster occurred in 1622–5 as a result of the 'Mansfeld disease', named after the Bohemian soldiers of the military entrepreneur Ernst von Mansfeld (see also Chapter 1). In Vught (Brabant) bodies remained on the streets for days; there was no one to bury the dead because so many households were affected. In 1635/6, the Veluwe was devastated by an epidemic after friendly French mercenary soldiers passed through; so many died in the little village of Veenendaal that the peat works declined and never recovered. Such epidemics did not stop at town walls either, and because of the numerous trade links even towns far removed from zones of conflict were affected.[19]

The lasting burden of inundations

Such horrors were atrocious, yet if temporary might still be bearable for a village community as a whole. Military pressure of longer duration constituted a totally different matter; prolonged armed conflicts caused farms to stand empty and lands to lay fallow for years on end. From this perspective the large-scale inundations in the Low Countries were particularly important; it took years, long after the hostilities had ended, before the lands could be tilled again. The repair of breached dykes and destroyed water mills was always expensive, and local funds were hard to come by since hardly any cultivation had been possible and many of the cattle had been sold, stolen or killed.

Inundations were fairly common in the low-lying regions. Many fields of pasture flooded over the winter and were only usable in the summer, particularly in the northern parts of Holland. But the strategic inundations were a different matter altogether because they involved all kinds of land – not only pasture but also fields for cereal cultivation, horticulture and peat extraction. Even during the summer the lands could not be tilled. In the vicinity of strategic areas, adjoining polders often flooded since numerous smaller inner dykes became saturated with water and broke down. The resulting damage was always great since many dykes were at the same time roads that constituted essential rural communications; inundations thus disrupted the peasants' local trade networks.[20]

In addition, the flooded area was much more extensive than usually thought. The terrible flood of All-Saints' Day in 1570 had drowned vast coastal regions, but several years later approximately two-thirds of Holland's countryside was flooded. The infamous Leiden siege (1574, see also Chapter 1) caused the flooding of no fewer than three major polder boards' districts: Delfland, Rijnland and Schieland, together constituting the majority of south Holland's countryside.

Even streets in Rotterdam, Delft and Gouda were under water. The same year further flooding near Gorinchem drove the Spanish out of the region. In the next decade inundations struck particularly hard in Gelderland and Brabant. In 1588 the Betuwe and Tielrewaard, the Gelderland districts between the Meuse and Rhine, were inundated. The adjoining polders of North Brabant suffered from recurrent inundations along the river Meuse throughout the final two decades of the sixteenth century.[21]

Farmers in the estuaries of Zeeland and northern Flanders that consisted of a set of polders and islands protected only by sea dykes were even more vulnerable. Inundations in this region carried the additional burden of flooding by *salty* water. Recovery not only depended upon the repair of dykes; in addition the soil needed years for the high content of salt to be reduced. An aggravating factor was the sale of numerous monasteries in this district during the Calvinist dominance of Ghent (1577–84), which removed a major source of institutional support for the local water authorities. Rebels also demolished monasteries and churches in order to obtain building materials for strongholds.[22]

In 1572 rebels from Flushing and Veere opened the sluices and pierced the dykes in an attempt to threaten the livelihood of powerful Middelburg, which remained loyal to the Spanish king until 1576. Three polders near Veere were flooded.[23] Further, States' troops cut the sea dykes of Saeftinghe and the nearby districts of Hulst and Axel in 1583 and 1584, acts that immediately threatened the adjoining polders too. Soon larger areas were flooded; some villages and towns even became islands. The continuing military operations in the neighbourhood of Antwerp prevented repair of the dykes. Within two years the cumulative infrastructural damage amounted to 20 times the annual income of the local water authorities. In some cases repairs had become impossible; the fertile farmlands of Saeftinghe including four villages were thus permanently lost to the sea.[24]

The resulting costs for the villagers were enormous, above all in the early decades of the war when dykes were often cut indiscriminatingly and without thought for the consequences. In Brabant near Rosmalen no fewer than 34 or 35 breaches of the dyke were discovered and the costs of repairs estimated at 20,000 guilders, too high for the local water authorities.[25] Following Leiden's siege (1574), the damage to the Holland dykes was calculated to be worth as much as six million guilders. The Provincial States of Holland decided to pay for the repair of the dykes, but since money was desperately needed for the soldiers, no funds actually materialized. The only compensation for the landowners consisted of tax reductions and tax remittances.[26]

After the Leiden siege it took at least six years for Holland's polder infrastructure to be restored; all that time the access of farmers to their lands was limited, their trade destroyed and rent collectors received no income at all from those lands. Near Gorinchem, the dykes still contained major breaches nine years after the inundations and local farmers were unable to harvest anything. Heavy autumn storms added to the misery in this district, since these destroyed the recent repairs.[27] Holland rural rent levels declined drastically during the 1570s as a result.

In the meantime towns seemed to have thrived because of the inundations. In 1574 an infantry captain in the north of Holland wrote during the countryside's misery from inundations and marauding soldiers: 'Here are many towns wishing that the war may last longer, because they are enriched by it. A house that was rented at 20 guilders now yields a hundred'.[28] Such prices must have been prohibitive for the poorer refugees from the countryside. A town like Gouda only permitted refugees with sufficient funds to enter, probably to prevent overcrowding.[29] In this process numerous cottiers and landless peasants lost their livelihood, particularly in the clay area along the rivers; this brought about a landscape change from numerous small-scale holdings to predominantly medium and large-scale ones after 1580. Peat exploitation, however, permitted the return of the smallholder to the vast boggy regions of Holland, also advanced by church institutions disappearing as major landowners in this province.[30] Monasteries and the gentry lost their grip on the land; large-scale farmers and burghers investing in lands were the beneficiaries. Much of the capital for restoring farms came from the towns, which again enabled wealthy burghers to profit.[31]

Due to the considerable damage experienced by farmers and the limited system of compensation, it is little wonder that country dwellers frequently opposed the military-strategic policy of inundations. In the far north the construction of the new fortress of Bourtange (1594) on Groningen's eastern border involved a sudden new threat to the livelihood of local farmers. The *marke* (the organization of the commons) of the hamlet of Wollinghuizen lost about a third of its common fields, which became the territory of the new Bourtange-*marke*. But even more contentious was the maintenance of the area around the new fortress as wetland. It was a matter which the Council of State regarded as of the highest importance and its deputies ordered the construction of new dykes to raise the water level of the moors as a strategic device. Yet local farmers regarded the moors as fields for growing buckwheat and sabotaged the policy by digging canals in order to drain the land again.[32]

Inundations continued to take their toll after the end of the Truce. The fields of 17 villages near Sluis and Cadzand (on the coast of States-Flanders) were flooded as a defence measure in 1621. In connection with the siege of Breda in 1624 lands were inundated near Heusden, Bergen op Zoom and Steenbergen (to the north of Bergen op Zoom). During the siege of 's-Hertogenbosch (1629) Frederick Henry had the Land of Altena, to the north of Brabant, flooded. During the war threat from the Veluwe in 1629 (see also Chapters 1 and 3) the famous Holland waterline was created for the first time: all the land along Holland's eastern border, including major parts of Utrecht, was to be flooded with the help of thousands of pioneers to prevent the enemy advancing. Luckily for the Dutch, the invading army was forced to retreat from the Veluwe district after three months, a fortunate occurrence as both pioneers and local farmers were extremely unwilling to contribute to the destruction of the lands. In 1672 a similar tactic was applied to the region, on this occasion proving extremely helpful for the defence (see also Chapter 1). However, once again the local population sabotaged the works; landowners constructed new dams and secretly drained their flooded fields. Only the threatened imposition of the death penalty for such actions by William III enforced cooperation. After each occasion – 1629 and 1672 – farmers complained for years about their damaged lands, but no compensation was paid and only occasional tax remittances were granted, ensuring minimal relief for the damage incurred.[33]

Virtually all these inundations were undertaken by the Dutch. The regime in the southern Netherlands was much more hesitant in this regard, perhaps because they had less experience with water management, perhaps because their power base depended more on a rural elite than it did in the more urbanized north. In 1574 Philip II's advisors considered the option of flooding all of Holland and Zeeland. But the king rejected the plan as it would almost certainly earn Spain a reputation of extreme cruelty. The Dutch themselves were apparently less afraid of undertaking actions of this kind: the interests of the (wealthy) burghers clearly dominated political debate; above all, the defence of the towns counted, not the defence of the countryside. Instead of inundations, however, Philip II ordered the burning of Waterland, the rich agricultural region north of Amsterdam. The district narrowly escaped this ordeal because of a serious mutiny in his army that year.[34] Yet scorched earth campaigns soon returned to other areas of the Low Countries, principally carried out by the States' soldiers themselves.

Scorched earth campaigns

Several parts of the northern Netherlands suffered from the presence of both States' and enemy troops. Throughout the 1580s great stretches of northern Flanders, Brabant, Friesland, Groningen, Overijssel and Gelderland were depopulated as military operations took over the region; no taxes were collected and the civilian administration all but collapsed. The threat did not only come from marauding soldiers: the new Dutch state added to the dangers. When the States-General suspected the population of a particular territory was paying or supplying the enemy, extremely harsh measures followed. In 1584 the Republican government announced that scorched earth tactics would be adopted in the Zutphen district to punish the farmers for their alleged support of the enemy, but prominent Overijssel noble delegates managed to amend this decision and in the event only a small part of the countryside was burned.[35]

Areas that were not represented in the States-General had less opportunity to defend themselves. The Brabant Meierij, a district near the frontier around the powerful city of 's-Hertogenbosch, suffered from prolonged military operations. The territory experienced several rounds of scorched earth action during the 1580s, authorized by Orange and the States-General, and carried out by famous commanders such as Hohenlohe and Maurice.

The militarization of the Meierij had begun in 1567 with the building of forts, redoubts and strongholds; villages were fortified; soldiers were lodged in village garrisons that had to be supported by the local farmers. The idea behind garrisoning the countryside was not protection of the farming communities but keeping open the important trade routes between 's-Hertogenbosch, Antwerp, Maastricht, Liège and the territory of Jülich. As soldiers' pay was slow to arrive at this early stage in the war, the garrisons often simply seized what they needed from the surrounding countryside. Orange's 1572 campaign to plunder the Brabant countryside marked the true beginning of large-scale violence in the region. This attack was countered by the arrival of the Duke of Holstein's troops the same year, but his forces were unable to advance beyond the Meierij. Holstein's soldiers subsequently carried out a true reign of terror in the countryside. The wealthy woollen textile-producing village of Oisterwijk was pillaged; Holstein's horsemen robbed farmers in a wide arc up to the Holland borders, the barony of Breda and the territory of Cuijk (to the south of Nijmegen, on the Meuse). In 1576 the Spanish army mutinied; once again, mutineers found no obstacle to the exactions they visited on the Meierij peasantry. Two years later the rebel troops of Johan Casimir, Count of the Palatinate (a Dutch ally), once more terrorized the country.[36]

This burden, severe though it was, might have been bearable for the rural communities if only the atrocities had halted there. But circumstances in the Meierij worsened considerably after 1579 as military operations were intensified by the signing of the Union of Utrecht. That year 's-Hertogenbosch decided to switch sides and join the Spanish king, and the Dutch army then openly attacked the town and its surrounding district. The interests of the countryside became totally subordinated to the Republic's war aims. Oisterwijk was plundered again in 1581, this time by no fewer than seven thousand States' soldiers; at the same time the mutinous States' troops of Ernst Casimir roamed through the Kempen district, plundering as they went. 's-Hertogenbosch strengthened its defences and enlisted two hundred town soldiers on foot and one hundred horsemen; their pay was to come from new taxes on the Meierij region. In the countryside, mounting insecurities led to increasing difficulty in collecting the necessary sums, and the town soldiers – whose pay depended upon money extracted from the peasantry – then suffered, which led to further uncontrolled raids on the countryside.[37]

Parma now sent additional Spanish troops under the command of Haultepenne into this precarious situation. Since 's-Hertogenbosch refused to lodge them, a number of outer garrisons emerged, located in the fortresses and villages of the Meierij, intended to strengthen the military position of 's-Hertogenbosch and assist in the collection of contributions in the countryside. Thousands of inadequately paid soldiers were soon roaming through the countryside on their own account; complaints about misbehaving soldiers quickly multiplied. The arrival of new Spanish units, including those of Karel van Mansfeld, brought about another increase in the burden of war. The farmers were forced to house the soldiers and pay for the cost of these troops through new taxes, while at the same time suffering from the uncontrolled exactions of the numerous underpaid and undisciplined garrison troops. Parma deplored the fact of his soldiers pillaging but acknowledged their need to loot in order to survive, because Madrid once more failed to prioritize the war in the Low Countries and simply did not send sufficient funds. Things came to a head when Mansfeld's Spanish troops laid siege to the rebel town of Eindhoven in 1583. Since money was lacking his soldiers simply lived off the land, looting widely: for example, seizing virtually all the horses, cattle and sheep from the village of Bladel, as well as all its provisions, and burning nearby Eersel, leaving as few as three out of three hundred houses standing. In addition, Haultepenne's troops mutinied and rampaged uncontrollably through the countryside while the States' garrison in Eindhoven organized raids to secure provisions, thus confronting the local population with a further attack, once more from the opposite side.[38]

's-Hertogenbosch should really have come to the defence of the inhabitants of 'its' Meierij, but completely failed to do so.[39] On the contrary, the town imposed additional demands on the surrounding countryside, requiring labour and requisitioning grain deliveries. The economy of the Meierij was actually too weak to endure such compulsions. The farmers were part of a traditional subsistence economy and its grain had never been exported. There was an almost complete absence of meadow to provide fodder for horses. Most cattle were reared in stables for the manure; when soldiers stole the cattle, the lack of manure resulted in a sharp decrease in the grain harvest. Meanwhile the town paid no taxes to support the soldiers, leaving the bulk of war costs the responsibility of the countryside – even the expenses of its own garrison and fortifications. As a result the tax burden per head of the population was two to four times heavier in the countryside than in the town.[40]

On top of that, in the early 1580s the States-General launched scorched earth campaigns, aiming to ruin the economic base of Spanish military operations. Hay and rye were destroyed in the fields, farms were burned, cattle stolen and peat stocks set on fire. The States' campaign of 1583 was even more barbarous and also logistically better planned than the previous ones. The population was warned beforehand to gather their belongings and leave the area. That year Dutch soldiers, numbering between 500 to 600, even burned whole villages to the ground.[41]

Scorched earth operations were carried out again in the Meierij in 1584 and 1586, but a particularly draconian campaign was launched in 1587 with some four to five thousand troops – professional soldiers together with militiamen from Amsterdam, Leiden, Delft, Gouda, Woerden, Oudewater, Tholen, Willemstad, Zevenbergen and Tiel. They initially aimed to assault 's-Hertogenbosch, but, recognizing that to be impracticable, the States-General decided to ravage the countryside of the Meierij instead. Maurice received instructions to destroy all agriculture and confiscate all horses and cattle, wagons and carts, ploughs, scythes and any other items of farming equipment. Some 500 farmers of Veghel rose up in revolt but they were simply massacred. Thirty or forty villages, including the large settlements of Helmond and Eindhoven, were burned to the ground. The following year Maurice was ordered to repeat the campaign, but this time the operation was uncompleted because Spanish troops managed to prevent the arrival of the States' soldiers. Even so, large parts of the

Meierij were devastated, plague broke out and lands lay fallow. The formerly wealthy village of Oisterwijk never recovered from the devastation of these years. Ironically, these campaigns were of little value: 's-Hertogenbosch was not deprived of food because it continued to receive provisions by river, despite the blockade on the Meuse.[42]

The Meierij district was thus dealt blow after blow. Soldiers committed atrocities elsewhere and almost everywhere the peasants suffered from the presence of nearby garrisons, but rarely to the same extent or over such an extended period, and certainly not accompanied by repeated scorched earth campaigns carried out with professional precision by disciplined troops. Although few country dwellers died from direct confrontation with soldiers, the uncertainties and disruption caused by repeated raids, continual demands for pay by the garrisons, the theft of cattle and grain, inundations, village fires and prohibitions put on selling goods to the enemy combined to significantly reduce economic opportunities. Fertility declined, marriages were postponed and famine and a general physical enfeeblement resulted in increased vulnerability to disease. In the period 1572–1609 the demographic loss for the Meierij is calculated at a staggering 68.5 per cent, comparable to the most severely affected areas in Germany during the Thirty Years War.[43]

The fall in the population was much higher in North Brabant than in South Brabant or Flanders, or for that matter any other area in the Low Countries. The years 1586 and 1587 were the absolute nadir, as war, famine and disease reinforced each other. The harvest had been extremely poor in 1585 and again in 1586 due to adverse weather conditions, and the scorched earth policies removed viable agricultural support. This demographic loss was not entirely due to death or declining fertility, however; out-migration was also substantial as local inhabitants fled the presence of armies. Farmers and village elites usually returned after an interval, but the departure of many of the peasant-artisans proved permanent. Wool workers from Tilburg and Oisterwijk fled to Rotterdam; linen workers left for 's-Hertogenbosch, Breda, Antwerp, Harlingen and Goch, but above all Haarlem. The population loss through migration to Haarlem was sizeable; between 1579 and 1609 no fewer than 904 heads of household left the Meierij, mostly from Eindhoven and Helmond.[44]

Such military jurisdiction as did exist was unable to provide protection against all the abuse, hostage-taking, rape and manslaughter going on in areas experiencing 'total war' such as the Meierij. The Articles of War were insufficient to curb the widespread excesses of the soldiers; the Brabant civilian authorities had no influence whatsoever on soldiers outside their town walls. As many bailiffs had themselves fled, there was little opportunity to even begin legal proceedings. The lawsuits that did come before the military courts and the Council of State were costly and often disappointing, usually only resulting in a reprimand for the troops involved. In dealing with illegal plundering the Council of State was anxious not to create precedents and usually rejected the claims of the peasants. When sufficient evidence existed, theft and extortion by soldiers was certainly condemned, but a judgment that the goods should be restituted was often a dead letter as the commodities had already been sold or consumed.[45]

After 1588 the pressure of States' troops on the Meierij relented. To limit the burdens imposed in provisioning the field army, Maurice decreed that troops were only permitted to march through the countryside with a clerk who had to *buy* the necessary provisions, not seize them. Another regulation specified that no company was to stay longer than one night in any single village.[46] But the recurrent presence of soldiers caused temporary hardships again, above all during sieges. In 1622, during the siege of Bergen op Zoom, States' soldiers had extracted money from the nearby peasants under the pretext that they had given food to the Spanish, contrary to Dutch orders. Maurice sighed: 'The poor are much hard-pressed and extorted, first by the one and then by the other; as soon as they give something to one side, the other is again at the door.' In 1624 in the neighbourhood of Breda the Spanish besiegers demanded food from the farmers, but again this was likely to provoke retaliation by the Dutch, since the States-General had forbidden any such supply. During this episode the Frisian stadholder Ernst Casimir remarked:

> The poor peasant has nothing left. They lost everything they had in the world, and are daily tormented both by the enemy and by us; it is virtually impossible to serve two armies at the same time.[47]

While these facts about the Meierij war experience have only recently been uncovered by the study of Adriaenssen, the example of the Veluwe district (Gelderland) is much better known. This area was invaded by the Imperial troops of Montecuccoli in operations linked to the siege of 's-Hertogenbosch (1629, see also Chapter 3). The subsequent atrocities committed by these units are an established Black Legend in Dutch historiography. Most historians follow the standard account of the contemporary historian Pieter Bor, who described in detail the butchery that took place in numerous villages, depicting for instance the Catholic 'Croats' as a cavalry of 'a people black of hunger and little horses'.[48]

Recent studies of this historical episode, however, reveal no evidence of such barbarities, apart from damage of an economic nature. On the contrary, a certain degree of normalcy seemed to have prevailed. Contemporaries observed farmers working their fields, despite the orders of the Court of Gelderland and the States-General to evacuate the countryside, take all cattle into towns, burn all grains in the field, remove the shafts from the mills and destroy all brewing kettles in order to prevent supplies reaching the enemy. Plundering did occur, mainly because the enemy troops were poorly provisioned, but outright violence against civilians seems to have been extremely rare. In Amersfoort a man died of his wounds when the town was captured; an 80-year-old died in a prison; and, out of frustration because the small town of Hattem could not be taken, a couple of innocent civilians were killed. That was probably the sum total of 'direct' fatal casualties. No large-scale killing of civilians has been revealed.[49]

What must have happened is that images of suffering from other wars were transplanted to the Veluwe case. In the Thirty Years War, for example, historians have shown that several traditional accounts of armies wandering around *sengend und brennend* ('scorching and burning') could not be substantiated. The Black Legend of the Croats was also found in Germany. These horsemen were particularly skilled in rapid raids, but their cruelty consisted more of hostage-taking and occasionally setting fire to a farm than massacring the population, as mainstream historiography suggests. The locals were not guiltless either. A closer look at the Veluwe episode revealed that Timen Henricksz from Amersfoort had tried to profit from the war by buying up the hostages taken by the Croats. He attempted to extract larger sums from the villagers for their release, allegedly acting out of mercy but in reality making handsome gains from the transactions.[50]

Increasing financial burdens

Relief from such depredations could be purchased by paying bribes, ransoms, fire taxes, safeguards or other contributions to the military. These moneys were usually exacted under threat and therefore not counted as taxes but as a kind of tribute from an enemy population. The Brabant village of Tilburg paid in this way regular bribes in money and wine to Christoffel van IJsselstein, the States' governor of the nearby Heusden garrison, who obviously had a drinking problem. Another way of preventing troops from choosing your village as a place to stay was to present the soldiers upon arrival with a sum of money on condition that they ride on to the next village. The Tilburg village accounts of 1597–8 show no fewer than 28 examples of such *doorkoop*, which was sometimes accompanied by the provision of a guide to point the way to another unhappy community.[51]

A more official solution consisted of safeguards (*salva guardia*) issued by the army's high command. These contracts were purchased by individuals, villages or institutions, in return for which they were free (at least in theory) from *brandschatting* or 'fire tax', the exacting of money from a community under threat of burning it down.[52] Several Holland districts bought safeguards from Orange – for example, the Alblasserwaard in 1574 and villages in the neighbourhood of Haarlem in 1576 – to prevent pillaging and extortion by States' troops. Rural communities outside Holland, such as in Gelderland, Utrecht and North Brabant, also bought safeguards from Dutch troops. A sack by underpaid and undisciplined soldiers occasionally followed, however. Orange ordered the apprehending of those violating the safeguards and tried to restore the damage. For example, Captain Michiel Caulier, whose cavalrymen had stolen cattle from farmers around Utrecht, was compelled to return the animals or pay for them.[53]

But not all military commanders were as considerate as Orange. From the town of Hulst the Dutch army organized regular *brandschat* campaigns; these involved thousands of soldiers roaming freely across Flanders between 1591 and

1596, with the sole purpose of selling safeguards for monetary gain. The Hulst captain, Charles Everwijn, was hated for his violent behaviour during these campaigns, not only by the 'enemy' population but also in the frontier town itself. Following an incident in 1593 he was almost beaten to death by his fellow townsmen.[54] Safeguards were also sold by the Spanish; for example, prior to the invasion of the Veluwe in 1629, the Spanish military commander Hendrik van den Bergh asked the Infanta for a safeguard for Castle Annendael near Roermond, where his sisters lived.[55]

Some safeguards were written down, others took the form of paintings to be placed at the boundary of the property, while sometimes soldiers were positioned as safeguards, such as the two halberdiers left by the Count of Bossu, the stadholder for the Spanish, in Tilburg in 1587. The agreement had to be renewed twice a year, accompanied on each occasion by the payment of an extra month's contribution. From 1596 onwards such safeguards became a permanent source of income for the Council of State. A supposedly 'unwarlike' statesman, the pacific Johan Van Oldenbarnevelt, ordered a couple of houses to be set on fire in 1602 as an example, to encourage the purchase of safeguards in order to increase state revenues.[56]

The payment of contributions was another financial solution. Contributions were usually levied across larger districts or even whole provinces. The power to collect taxes was in fact delegated to the soldiers themselves and generally carried out to cover the costs of a local military unit. A major difference between safeguards and contributions was the degree of choice. A safeguard was a more or less free option to prevent a possible *brandschatting* in the future, but refusing to pay a contribution meant immediate and inevitable violent action on the part of the soldiers. Once regularized, however, such contributions had the advantage that they were often levied in cooperation with the local estates or the political representatives of the district, which ensured a reasonable levy, while safeguards had been rather individualized, *ad hoc* arrangements. Contributions could also be levied in instalments, per week or month, instead of annually or every six months as was the practice with safeguards. However, although contributions appeared like taxes paid to a lawful sovereign, they remained a kind of a tribute, paid to a foreign power. The threat of a violent (cavalry) attack was always imminent, though the menace decreased once contributions were systemized and levied in a regular manner. Non-payment of contributions was usually dealt with by taking hostages until the sums were paid; only in the worst cases would pillaging and burning follow.[57]

During the last two decades of the sixteenth century contributions were levied in almost all frontier areas of the northern and southern Netherlands. By the 1590s they had turned into a routine financial burden of the war. As a result they changed in character and were looked upon by the rural population as ordinary taxes, while the individual cavalry attacks became significantly fewer. The amount was decided on after negotiations with the local authorities, who became more involved and increasingly took care of the collection themselves.

Once established such payments proved beneficial to all concerned: the farming population was relieved of the distress caused by individual raids and local garrisons received more regular funds to pay the troops.[58]

The exact date of the imposition of such regular contributions is unclear, however. Numerous historians point to Wallenstein, during the Thirty Years War, as the inventor of the system.[59] This is certainly wrong. A more persuasive chronology is put forward by Geoffrey Parker, who argues that the levying of contributions introduced by Spanish commander Requesens in 1574 in Flanders and Brabant was a 'regular, permanent and rational contributions system, perhaps the first of its kind in Europe'.[60] This provides a reason to return to the case of the Meierij – to consider such a suggestion, and also because the contribution levy of this district has been well studied.

The administration of the superintendent of contributions in the Meierij, Juan Andrea Cigogna, might have given a favourable impression on paper, but closer inspection shows little of regularity, permanence or rationality. First, Cigogna failed to administer the payments correctly; several villages were forced to pay twice, whereas others did not contribute at all. Second, the lawful authority – the Provincial States of Brabant – had not been consulted regarding either the imposition of the contributions or the amount to be collected. Third, the territory from which Cigogna was to collect the contributions was poorly defined; he subsequently demarcated the area in an extremely wide and general way that made no sense. Fourth, no centralized control existed: several villages paid contributions to Cigogna while also continuing to provide funds to nearby Spanish garrisons.[61]

A 'rational' contribution system should optimize the likelihood of communities actually being able to pay the sums demanded in the prevailing circumstances, but Cigogna's unjust and irrational conduct made him one of the most hated men in Brabant. Being a captain of a company his methods of collection were harsh and unreasonable; his soldiers drank wine for free when visiting a village, stole chickens and generally took whatever they could; they extorted tolls from wagons or simply seized them along with their contents. Following the death of Requesens in 1576, mutinies broke out and the Spanish soldiers began to fend for themselves again; the levying of contributions ceased altogether for some years and in 1577 Cigogna was declared 'persona non grata' by the Brussels government because of his violent and irregular behaviour.[62]

The counter-offensive of Parma that began in 1579 badly needed financial levies, however, and Cigogna was once again appointed superintendent of contributions. One improvement on the early 1570s was consultation with representatives of the Meierij, who in 1580 assembled specifically for this purpose. As a result local authorities – the bailiffs of the districts – participated in the collection. But this improvement was short-lived as the meetings ceased the following year. The levies still were unauthorized by the Provincial States of Brabant and, just as before, there was no centralized direction. Without any intervention by Cigogna, the Spanish military commanders Alberto Caponotti, Camillo Capizucchi and Karel van Mansfeld and the governors of 's-Hertogenbosch and of other garrisons demanded and collected contributions on their own account. Among the Spanish military commanders there were even disputes over the contribution of a particular 'wealthy' village they each claimed for their own garrison. The Cigogna contributions were increased after 1582, reaching a staggering 700,000 guilders per year in 1587. Side by side with these 'ordinary contributions', 'extraordinary contributions' were also levied to pay, for example, for the sieges of Eindhoven, Antwerp and Geertruidenberg. Despite all those increases the sums raised were still insufficient to pay all the soldiers in the area, and the discipline of the troops thus hardly improved.[63]

The result was a tangle of uncontrolled and confusing levies, with individual local military commanders free to enforce their own demands. Since the military were their own collectors, their response when confronted with resistance or inability to pay was invariably violent and cruel. Improvements only came about in the later 1580s after Parma ordered an investigation into the manifold abuses of Cigogna's administration. It turned out that there had been no fixed system or practice in the raising of contributions; instead, 'he fixes their amount on his own, according to his pleasure, in every village or town.'[64] Cigogna was eventually dismissed in 1590, and, in recognition of his harsh and unusual demands, the Meierij was granted relief from one-third of the contributions. In 1592, this time in consultation with the Provincial States of Brabant, a new division was established and the methods of collection considerably improved. Some deficiencies remained: for example, one commander, Count Nicolo Cesis, continued to levy 'his' funds in 'his' villages; in addition, mutineers continued to oppress the countryside with their own demands. But such acts became increasingly rare; it is thus possible to argue that the Spanish levying of contributions in the Meierij was 'regular and rational' after 1592.[65]

Alongside the Spanish levies, the Dutch were raising their own. Initially these too were neither rational nor centralized. Between 1577 and the early 1580s the States' army commander Hohenlohe imposed duties on his own account. The French commander Bonnivet, in Dutch service, enforced the levy of 'his' contributions after he captured Eindhoven in 1583. But the final mention of Meierij contributions imposed directly by individual States' forces dates from 1587. The Dutch levies came to be administered by Van Eyck, a civilian administrator and not a military commander like Cigogna. Van Eyck was also an agent of the Provincial States of Brabant, which suggests cooperation with the lawful authorities. Van Eyck's administration did not survive, but the town accounts of Tilburg show the considerable sums extracted by the Dutch (see Table 5.1).[66]

Although the Dutch military administration was more orderly than its Spanish counterpart, this did not preclude the violence that underpinned all contributions. Thus, the Brabant village of Wommelgen, which had not paid its dues to the Dutch, was sacked in 1589 by the States' company of Captain Marcelis Bacx of Bergen op Zoom. The church tower where many had taken refuge was set on fire; 33 inhabitants died. In October 1596 the States' cavalry of Sergeant Major Sedlintcky attacked the Brabant village of Werchter to provide unwilling tax

Table 5.1 Contributions to the Spanish and Dutch troops and (mostly Spanish) mutineers paid by Tilburg, in guilders, 1583–1608

Year	Spanish troops	Dutch troops	Mutineers
1583–4	9,871	10,379	
1586–7	11,987	10,226	
1587–8	11,043	13,386	
1591–2	6,124	7,798	
1599–1600	3,616	12,400	6,492
1600–1	3,883	13,094	7,521
1601–2	9,307	15,173	4,323
1602–3	2,652	7,881	15,910
1603–4	6,903	12,263	10,784
1604–5	3,553	9,743	873
1606–7	2,766	9,482	
1607–8	2,305	8,179	

Source: Adriaenssen, *Staatsvormend geweld*, p. 251; not all accounts survived, which explains the absence of certain years

payers with an example; in fact, this was carried out in error since the unhappy village had paid its contributions on time. Maurice also permitted the Spanish mutineers from Hoogstraten to collect contributions on their own account (see Table 5.1).[67] In 1622 Frederick Henry pillaged the countryside of Brussels, Mechelen and Leuven to encourage the payment of contributions, earning himself the nickname *Boerenplager*, punisher of country folk, because of his war against defenceless peasants.[68]

On the whole, however, by the early 1590s the imposition of contributions in the Meierij had become quite regulated, on both sides, and farming communities started to show signs of recovery. Although the annual financial burden remained high (see Table 5.1), reductions in the sums demanded in the case of extreme circumstances (such as during inundations, sieges or harvest failures) became increasingly negotiable. With the normalization of the levy of war duties the collectors and receivers acquired an unexpected role as intermediaries between local communities and the rulers in The Hague. The receiver of contributions in the Meierij even became a sort of spokesman for the countryside.[69]

The sums raised by Dutch levies were usually higher than those of the Spanish (see also Table 5.1) because they included the clergy, whereas monasteries were exempted by the Spanish. But the Dutch also practiced what they called *retorsie* politics (retaliation). When Dutch authorities learnt that the peasantry paid contributions to the Spanish, they responded with countermeasures, usually in the form of duties at least as high as those levied by the enemy.[70]

Contributions were also imposed in other frontier parts of the Netherlands. In the district of Zutphen Johan van Lamzweerde (a civilian, not a military officer) was the receiver for the Spanish contributions after 1589. His administration exhibited a high degree of regularity and rationality, much more than

Cigogna's organization at that time. The level of the demands was decided upon in consultation with the local authorities; the communities that paid were to be left strictly in peace, as his uncompromising letters to the military commanders Verdugo and Van den Bergh attest. Between 1621 and 1630 the Zutphen district paid around 30,000 guilders to the Spanish and a comparable though somewhat higher sum to the Dutch. Over the years the levies had become systemized to such a degree that several receivers for the Spanish lived in the Republic – for instance, Bernard Boncamp in Oldenzaal and Bartolomeus van Egmond in Deventer. After Frederick Henry's capture of Rheinberg in 1633 the threat of Spanish cavalry raids diminished considerably in the eastern Netherlands, but several farmers and even whole villages continued to pay the Spanish receiver in secret because they feared the situation would change again.[71]

Village institutions and the urban connection

It might seem surprising that despite all the ravages of war, such as in the Meierij, it still seemed possible to extract taxes and contributions from the farming communities. In reality numerous villages were not in a position to pay; they were simply overburdened, with debts of more than 40,000 guilders at the time of the Truce, sometimes with rates of interests as high as 21 per cent. This indebtedness increased rural dependency on wealthy town-dwellers who provided loans. In Eindhoven the linen merchant Mathijs van Taterbeeck became the administrator of several villages; he assumed responsibility for the debts and set about clearing them.[72] Some villages sold part of their common land in order to free themselves of the sums involved. In Twente (Overijssel), a massive sale of forestry on common land was needed in order to pay off the loans. As a result the nearby town of Almelo became a major timber trading centre.[73]

How individual villages fared during the war depended to a large extent on the resilience of their institutions. Tilburg in the Meierij is an example of a community that managed to cope with the heavy demands of war thanks to a well-organized treasury. In 1575, the year when war exactions began to increase in the Meierij, their administration became permanent. The new treasury awarded compensation for war damage, distributed the war burden fairly and could make funds for war available quickly when necessary. One advantage was that the per capita burden of ordinary taxation was comparatively low because Tilburg's sixteenth-century population growth had not been recorded in the outdated Brabant tax distribution. By contrast the level of contributions soared, up to seventeen times the level of taxation before the Revolt. Tilburg debts were high too, but interest rates were relatively low because of the efficient village administration.[74] Tilburg also held another trump card: a strong proto-industrial sector, which suffered less than the agricultural sector from the war (see Chapter 8) and also profited from the village's careful financial management. The two factors were in all probability self-reinforcing.

Thus, in the case of Tilburg a well-organized treasury supported the resilience of the peasantry. These findings are compatible with Myron Gutmann's study of a late seventeenth century war-stricken Meuse district to the south of Maastricht. He observed a greater degree of continuity among communities with institutions that permitted flexible survival strategies. A strong degree of local ownership and robust inheritance structures encouraged farmers to return to their villages.[75] A case study of Westerwolde to the far north-east of the Republic confirms these conclusions. Like the Meierij, this was not a particularly fertile region. In 1568 war hit the area hard with the battle of Heiligerlee, when soldiers on both sides plundered lands and farmsteads. The territory continued to be contested throughout the following decades and the local population had to bear the brunt of the devastating *Groninger Schansenkrijg*, the Groningen 'War of the Sconces', but by 1594 Westerwolde was regarded as Republican territory.[76] Military campaigning affected the district again in 1623–4, 1665–7 and 1672–3.

As in much of the Netherlands' sandier areas, the land was divided in *marken*, commonage organizations in which the rights were shared by the *eigenerfden* of the village.[77] The Westerwolde peasant-owners with a commonage-bound *erve* ('full' farm) also held a certain portion of rights in the common land. This in turn conferred official political status; these farmers could be elected as local judges, had a voice in the election of the local priest, and when grievances arose, they sent deputies to the political representatives of their province or even the authorities in The Hague. The farms typically carried the family names of the peasant-owners; when the farm changed hands, the new farmer adopted the traditional name of the farm.

In the Westerwolde parishes an institutional safety net existed which reinforced solidarity among the peasant-owners. When high war-related death rates threatened the system of inheritance because heirs were still minors, local judges appointed custodians. These were usually peasant-owners of the same commonage with a family connection of some sort; they took care that a tenant farmer was appointed to manage the farm for the time being and/or had the inheriting daughter married. Women enjoyed almost equal inheritance rights to men; although sons generally succeeded their fathers, girls could also inherit the farm.[78]

This communal solidarity was less strong in Wedde, the only Westerwolde village with a distinct social structure. The Wedde farmers owned their houses but not their fields; for these they paid rent to a landlord who did not live in the district itself.[79] The Dutch Wars of Independence eroded the capacity of the landlords to support their farmers; as a result, Wedde farms were regularly put up for sale and at the same time the commonage rights were subdivided or sold to outsiders. Virtually all other Westerwolde *marken* entered the nineteenth century with a majority of the original *erven* still extant as owners of the pasture rights, but not Wedde.[80]

Information on other wartime village administrations is scant, but local institutions elsewhere also played a significant role. With regard to inundations a disparity was evident between the districts in Flanders conquered by the Spanish and those conquered by the Dutch. States-Flanders, which was Dutch territory, managed to recover more quickly from flooding than comparable Spanish-dominated regions. One important difference lay in the organization of local water authorities. Traditionally, monasteries had played a major role when urgent dyke repair was necessary, but – as was shown above – the Revolt had destroyed much of this formerly important resource, through either military damage or the impact of the Reformation.[81] When no aid was forthcoming from the ecclesiastical side, farmers in the south turned to the Brussels government, but this could not make funds available because of pressing war demands. The institutional structure under the Provincial States of Zeeland was different; fair taxes and duties encouraged the repair of dykes, which was mainly carried out by the farmers and authorities of the area themselves. The farming communities may not have received sufficient financial aid from the Dutch Republican state in the case of inundations, but the polder administrations helped develop a sense of local responsibility and local solidarity, which was useful when the higher authorities were unable to provide adequate support.[82]

Another important source of support was, somewhat paradoxically, located in nearby towns. The Dutch Revolt was accompanied by a general increase in the urban population, caused by higher net migration from both the surrounding countryside (undoubtedly spurred on by inundations and scorched earth campaigns) and regions further away. In addition, legislation in Holland favoured the urban economy over its rural counterpart. The Provincial States stipulated that all foodstuffs not for local consumption had to be stored in the towns, not in the countryside. Henceforth, all butter and cheese needed to be traded on urban markets. It was prohibited to run breweries in the countryside and brewing became concentrated in large-scale urban plants. The powerful town of Delft even organized armed raids to destroy village beer production.[83]

The presence of strong towns in a locality ensured that support for farming communities could increasingly be secured from nearby. This was very much more a matter of individual burghers taking an interest in the farms than a formal, institutional response. Particularly in the clay soil regions of Holland, the profitability of the average farm had risen substantially. As was noted above, the military destruction of the first two decades had driven out numerous smallholders from those areas. One positive side effect of inundations had been to raise the general fertility of land, provided the flooding had not been by salty seawater. The expanding towns created a ready (export) market for farm produce and encouraged the commercialization of rural production. Burghers were thus willing to invest in land; polder administrations were increasingly financed by urban funds; there were even vigorous draining programmes. In the 1620s and 1630s millions of guilders were pumped into the creation of new polders, mostly in the northern part of Holland, the funds mainly provided by wealthy townsmen.[84]

These circumstances were not, however, found throughout the Republic. To take one example, Northern Brabant experienced no significant urban growth in the seventeenth century. In contrast to the rich clay areas of Holland, there was no general increase in the size of landholding there either. Most peasants continued to produce within a subsistence economy, with some proto-industry on the side. The recovery of the countryside was thus much slower in Brabant than in Holland.[85]

Conclusion: the subordination of peasants' interests

The historiographical neglect of wartime experiences in the countryside provides a mere handful of case studies for this chapter. Yet some general trends emerge. In several distinct ways the Dutch Wars of Independence turned out to be much more burdensome for the countryside than for the towns, above all during the first two decades of the struggle. This had to do with the generally greater vulnerability of the rural population during any fighting, but also with the tactics of inundation and scorched earth campaigns, as well as the high level of financial demands – in the form of safeguards and contributions – made upon rural inhabitants.

Yet after the first two decades, when warfare lost its civil war character and became a more regularized conflict, a development which coincided with the consolidation of 'Republican territory' (see Chapter 1), conditions improved for farming communities. After 1588 the Dutch Council of State moved away from tactics of complete destruction (scorched earth campaigns) and took up methods that ensured a regular revenue through contributions. A similar change was apparent on the Spanish side. After the 1590s even the poorest war-stricken regions were in a position to negotiate with the military. This process was evident elsewhere in Europe too, albeit several decades later. Much of Germany suffered from the indiscriminate levying of contributions during the early stages of the Thirty Years War, but these became increasingly regularized. In France the reforms of the 1660s and 1670s, including the famous magazine system, constituted fundamental innovations and brought about a notable decline in the disorderly and violent behaviour of French soldiers suffered by rural inhabitants. Myron Gutmann concluded that in the course of the seventeenth century the direct burden of armies on the countryside grew less because of improved provisioning methods and the greater discipline evident in more professional armies.[86]

Troops still often caused destruction, even when merely passing through a region. But farmers could now return to their homesteads within one or two years, while population and agrarian production levels recovered quite rapidly. There were also, as this chapter has made clear, positive structural outcomes of warfare that helped promote rural economic growth in the long term, such as higher average farm size, at least in areas of clay soil, and increased soil fertility following fresh-water inundations or longer periods of fallow caused by campaigning. These trends were also evident in other European countries. Wars in general seemed to have weakened feudal control and encouraged the sale and cultivation of common lands and forests, while market integration was advanced by heavy wartime taxation.[87]

However, in the Dutch Republic the countryside benefited less than towns from state largesse (Chapter 4). The latter received payments for the housing of soldiers and funds for the building and maintenance of fortifications. Throughout the war urban political and economic interests prevailed, particularly during inundations and scorched earth campaigns; such tactics could save a town but always severely damaged the farming community. Most Dutch historians have overlooked the greater vulnerability of rural dwellers to soldiers' activities, not least because of the still-prevailing myth of the 'unwarlike Dutch'. This is exemplified by the following verdict in a recent biography of Maurice: 'When Maurice led the field army, the damage for the country folks was limited to apples and pears and the grain in the fields.'[88]

On the contrary: Dutch troops behaved particularly ruthlessly during the recurrent scorched earth campaigning in northern Brabant. The destruction of the Meierij countryside was not collateral damage but carefully planned and professionally executed. These campaigns followed a longer period during which farmers suffered the presence of numerous underpaid garrisons and consequent monetary exactions. The further addition of plague and poor harvests made the years 1586–7 the absolute nadir, resulting in a major outflow of migrants to Holland and a dramatic fall in population.

The strength of village institutions turned out to be of crucial importance in explaining the resilience of some rural communities. Tilburg was an example of a village that was able to render the war burden sufferable. A similar finding was noticeable in certain German parishes during the Thirty Years War, where strong village institutions alleviated the most troublesome demands of the armies, while villages with less competent institutions were overwhelmed by the soldiery or war debts.[89]

A transfer of wealth from countryside to towns was noticeable in several ways. Towns seemed to have flourished during inundations – they were less burdened by contribution payments, while urban moneylenders profited from village war debts. But at the same time the countryside often managed to recover more rapidly when there was a strong and growing urban network nearby, as in Holland after the 1590s. The farmers there were probably in a more favourable situation than their counterparts in the eastern and southern parts of the Republic. Overall, the state formation that accompanied the Revolt benefited particularly the rich burghers of the Holland towns. This bourgeoisie was also simultaneously profiting from new trade opportunities and new admiralties, which are the subject of Chapter 6.

Notes

1 J.W. Wijn quoted and translated in Fishman, *Boerenverdriet*, p. 3.
2 Tilly, 'War making', pp. 170–1; see also Asch, 'War and state-building', p. 324.
3 Fletcher, *County Community*, p. 274.
4 Lynn, *Giant*, pp. 185–6.
5 *Le Mercure François*, quoted by Tilly, *Contentious French*, p. 123.

6 Manning, *Apprenticeship*, p. 215, on English soldiers in England; White, 'Experience', pp. 28, 36, on the Spanish soldiers in Spain itself; see also Gutmann, *War and
   Rural Life*, pp. 77ff.
7 Parrott, *Richelieu's Army*, p. 516.
8 Theibault, *German Villages*, pp. 181–3; Schögl, p. 362; Kroener, 'Soldat', p. 116;
   Gutmann, *War*, pp. 109, 197–200, 130; Kleinehagenbrock, 'Einquartierung als Last',
   pp. 176, 184.
9 Kroener, 'Soldat', pp. 110, 112; Tallett, *War and Society*, pp. 154–5; Caferro, 'Warfare
   and economy', p. 191; Hale, *War and Society*, pp. 196–7.
10 Frijhoff and Spies, *Hard-Won Unity*, p. 136; see also Price, 'State', p. 183, and
   Zwitzer, *Militie*, p. 137.
11 Parker, *Army*, p. 187; Van Nierop, *Verraad*, pp. 69, 97, 100, 157–61; Noordegraaf,
   Hollands welvaren, p. 135; Rooze-Stouthamer, *Opmaat*, pp. 86, 144; De Graaf,
   Oorlog, p. 194.
12 Tracy, *Founding*, p. 122; Swart, *Krijgsvolk*, p. 195; Vermeesch, *Oorlog*, p. 44; Hale,
   'Armies', p. 207. After the massacre of Zichem's garrison, Parma explained in a letter
   to his (worried) mother than this was to teach other towns to surrender quickly.
   Gabions are wicker baskets filled with mud or sand.
13 Adriaenssen, *Staatsvormend geweld*, pp. 142–3, 162. On the enormity of rape in early
   modern wars, Parker, *Spain*, p. 178.
14 De Graaf, *Oorlog*, pp. 292–3.
15 Adriaenssen, *Staatsvormend geweld*, pp. 147–8, 154.
16 Kroener, 'Soldat', pp. 108, 113, 122; Croxton, 'Territorial imperative', p. 277; Redlich,
   German Military Enterpriser, I, p. 511.
17 Trompetter, *Leven*, pp. 28–30; Swart, *Krijgsvolk*, pp. 196–7. In October 1645 south
   Netherlands peasants killed hundreds of French soldiers in revenge for their taking
   all their cattle and horses, see Van Nimwegen, *Deser landen crijghsvolck*, pp. 128–9.
18 Van Nierop, *Verraad*, pp. 98, 100, 103; Vermeesch, *Oorlog*, p. 99; Adriaenssen,
   Staatsvormend geweld, pp. 401–5. The peasant militiamen often received some form
   of compensation.
19 Ibid., pp. 274–5; De Graaf, *Oorlog*, p. 582. Most war casualties were caused by disease,
   above all epidemics. See also Ergang, *The Myth*, p. 24; Braddick, *God's Fury*, p. 395.
20 Groenveld, *Van vyanden*, p. 11.
21 Ibid., p. 18; 't Hart, 'Rijnlands bestuur', p. 21; Klinkert, 'Water', p. 463; Feitsma,
   Delft, p. 40; Swart, *Krijgsvolk*, p. 195; Vermeesch, *Oorlog*, p. 45; Lesger, *Handel*,
   p. 117; Van Nierop, *Verraad*, p. 157; Adriaenssen, *Staatsvormend geweld*, pp. 372–4.
22 De Kraker, *Landschap*, pp. 320–1, 328, 333, 352.
23 Rooze-Stouthamer, *Opmaat*, pp. 154, 222–3.
24 De Kraker, *Landschap*, pp. 129–35, 144.
25 Adriaenssen, *Staatsvormend geweld*, pp. 291, 374–5.
26 Arentz, 'Schadevergoeding', p. 69; Tracy, *Founding*, pp. 96–7, 112; Koopmans,
   Staten, pp. 166–7; De Kraker, *Landschap*, pp. 341–2.
27 Klinkert, 'Water', p. 463; Vermeesch, *Oorlog*, pp. 45–7; Groenveld, *Van vyanden*, p. 24.
28 Quoted by Snapper, *Oorlogsinvloeden*, p. 32.
29 Groenveld, *Van vyanden*, p. 22.
30 Van Bavel, 'Rural development', pp. 180–2; Van Tielhof, 'Turfwinning', pp. 113–16;
   Van Dam, 'Fuzzy boundaries', p. 111.
31 Enthoven, *Zeeland*, p. 346. The large-scale reclamation projects that started in particular in the 1620s furthered the dominance of urban investors once again. Van
   Zwet, *Lofwaerdighe dijckagies*, pp. 414–58; Stol, 'Schaalvergroting'.
32 Joosting, *Marken*, pp. 128–9.
33 De Cauwer, *Tranen*, p. 91; Klinkert, 'Water', pp. 467–70; De Graaf, *Oorlog*, p. 527.
34 Parker, *Army*, p. 114; Van Nierop, *Verraad*, p. 101; on scorched earth campaigns in
   the sixteenth century, see Hale, *War and Society*, pp. 184–5.

35 Trompetter, *Leven*, pp. 33–4; Vermeesch, *Oorlog*, pp. 71–4, 95; Swart, *Krijgsvolk*, pp. 194–6; De Graaf, *Oorlog*, pp. 196, 288, 291.
36 Adriaenssen, *Staatsvormend geweld*, pp. 88, 91–4, 131.
37 Ibid., p. 98.
38 Ibid., pp. 96–101, 105–8, 149.
39 In the Thirty Years War, too, numerous towns failed to perform their duty of *Schutz und Schirm* in the countryside; Theibault, *German Villages*, p. 225.
40 Subsistence economy: producing only enough food for local consumption, not for the market. Adriaenssen, *Staatsvormend geweld*, pp. 112, 398. The different tax burden is an important observation and confirms the general shift of wealth from the countryside to the urban economies, as already noted in the section on inundations.
41 Ibid., pp. 133–5.
42 Ibid., pp. 136–40, 408; see also De Graaf, *Oorlog*, p. 288. The small towns of Woerden and Oudewater are located in Holland, Willemstad and Zevenbergen are located in Brabant but belonged to the territory of Holland, Tiel is a town in Gelderland and Tholen is situated in Zeeland.
43 Pagès, *Thirty Years War*, p. 198; Kamen, 'Economic and social consequences', p. 49; Gutmann, *War and Rural Life*, pp. 163ff.; Adriaenssen, *Staatsvormend geweld*, pp. 271–3.
44 Ibid., pp. 269, 411–12; De Graaf, *Oorlog*, p. 296. Haarlem increased in population from 18,000 in 1572 to almost 40,000 in 1622. Tallett, *War and Society*, p. 161, also notes the significant role of out-migration in population losses during war.
45 Adriaenssen, *Staatsvormend geweld*, pp. 176–7, 206–8.
46 De Graaf, *Oorlog*, p. 363.
47 Both quotations in Van Nimwegen, *Deser landen crijghsvolck*, p. 128.
48 Van Deursen, *Kopergeld*, p. 81.
49 De Graaf, *Oorlog*, p. 580; De Cauwer, *Tranen*, pp. 110, 197–200.
50 Ibid., p. 204; Schlögl, *Bauern, Krieg*, p. 67; Pepper, 'Aspects', p. 196; Kroener, 'Soldat', p. 114.
51 Adriaenssen, *Staatsvormend geweld*, pp. 357–8.
52 Parker, *Army*, p. 121.
53 Swart, *Krijgsvolk*, pp. 190, 194; Captain Nicholas Ruychaver was likewise reprimanded by Orange for taking cattle in the Gooi area (1574).
54 De Kraker, *Landschap*, p. 347. The sums raised were disappointing owing to the high cost of paying the soldiers who enforced the *brandschatting*.
55 De Cauwer, *Tranen*, p. 207.
56 Van Nimwegen, *Deser landen crijghsvolck*, p. 130; Adriaenssen, *Staatsvormend geweld*, pp. 172–3, 202, 238–9.
57 Redlich, 'Contributions', pp. 249–50; Tops, 'Heffing'; Theibault, *German Villages*, p. 138; Van der Ent, 'Oosterse contributiën', pp. 36–7; Parrott, 'From military enterprise', pp. 83, 93.
58 Swart, *Krijgsvolk*, pp. 191–2; Vermeesch, *Oorlog*, pp. 76–7, 141; Van Nimwegen, *Deser landen crijghsvolck*, p. 129.
59 Kroener, 'Soldat', p. 105. Lynn, *Giant*, pp. 197 and 205, notes that France started to collect regular contributions in the 1660s; most was coming from the Spanish Low Countries, which were used to these sort of taxes.
60 Parker, *Thirty Years War*, p. 183; Parker, *Army*, pp. 120–1; see also Parrott, *Richelieu's Army*, p. 282.
61 Adriaenssen, *Staatsvormend geweld*, pp. 226–8; see also Swart, *Krijgsvolk*, p. 19.
62 Adriaenssen, *Staatsvormend geweld*, pp. 229–30.
63 Ibid., pp. 230–4, 396–7.
64 Quoted by Parker, *Army*, p. 121.
65 Adriaenssen, *Staatsvormend geweld*, pp. 231–2, 235, 238.
66 Ibid., pp. 239, 241–3.

67 Ibid., pp. 112, 208–11, 224; Van der Ent, 'Oosterse contributiën', p. 42; Parker, *Army*, pp. 160, 175.

68 Fishman, *Boerenverdriet*, p. 15.

69 Adriaenssen, *Staatsvormend geweld*, pp. 217, 245.

70 Ibid., pp. 212–16.

71 De Cauwer, *Tranen*, p. 208; Vermeesch, *Oorlog*, pp. 65, 142–6. The regularity in contribution levy by the Spanish in the Zutphen district (1589) thus preceded the one in the Meierij (1592). On Verdugo's administration, see also Parrott, *Business of War*, p. 92.

72 Adriaenssen, *Staatsvormend geweld*, p. 335.

73 Trompetter, *Leven*, p. 392. The timber was increasingly sold to Holland.

74 Adriaenssen, *Staatsvormend geweld*, pp. 246–8, 351.

75 Gutmann, *War and Rural Life*, p. 80, 204.

76 Lepage, *Vestingen*, p. 59; Van Winter, *Westerwolde*.

77 Bieleman, *Boeren*, p. 37; Hoppenbrouwers, 'Use and management of commons', pp. 104–6.

78 Based on my analysis of 145 full farms listed in Wegman and Wegman, *Westerwolders*, I-VI; see also Joosting, *Marken*, pp. 103–42.

79 Huizing, 'Inkomsten', pp. 7–14.

80 Wegman and Wegman, *Westerwolders*, VI, p. 519.

81 Groenveld, *Van vyanden*, p. 26.

82 De Kraker, *Landschap*, pp. 348–9, 353.

83 Aten, *Als het gewelt*, pp. 287, 293, 295, 318; Yntema, 'Entrepreneurship', pp. 185–201; Van Zanden, *Rise*, pp. 25, 35–6; Van Bavel, *Manors*, p. 364.

84 Ibid., p. 260; Van Bavel, 'Rural development', pp. 183, 188; Van Zwet, *Lofwaerdighe dijckagies*, pp. 415, 423, 425, see also Van Tielhof, 'Financing water management', p. 217.

85 See also Chapter 8. In contrast to Flanders, where the average size of farms had increased because of the war and where the urban-based economy also revived to a greater extent than in Brabant. In addition, many of the Flanders lands had remained fallow for a couple of years, which had increased their fertility and so added to the rather rapid recovery after the war; see Thoen, 'Oorlogen', pp. 367–70. In Oberbayern, the regeneration after the Thirty Years War (within thirteen years) was called 'erstaunlich'. Labour was more productive, as peasants could concentrate on the better lands; with fewer mouths to feed, the pressure of population had diminished; see Schlögl, *Bauern, Krieg*, pp. 67–8, 356–66.

86 Rowlands, *Dynastic State*, p. 210; Gutmann, *War and Rural Life*, p. 54.

87 Theibault, *German Villages*, p. 181; Schögl, *Bauern, Krieg*, p. 362; Thoen, 'Oorlogen', pp. 363–78; Gutmann, *War*, pp. 109, 130; Kamen, 'Economic and social consequences', pp. 53–7.

88 Van Deursen, *Maurits*, p. 90.

89 Theibault, *German Villages*, p. 226.

6　Admiralties, privateers and the colonial connection

War fed trade and trade fed war.[1]

The northern Netherlands was a region which lived by seaborne commerce and this proved to be of huge benefit in the struggle with Spain. During the Dutch Wars of Independence the economy turned even more than previously to the seas. Trade connections over water were vital to survival; direct links to the sea enabled trade and thus the securing of provisions.[2] But it was by no means uncomplicated. In the late 1560s and early 1570s the activities of the Dutch Sea Beggars increased the danger in coastal waters to all vessels, including those of Dutch merchants. Since pirates and privateers roamed the seas some sort of protection was clearly necessary. While the state of the northern Netherlands was in its infancy (1570s) no regular navy existed and merchants had to arm their own vessels.

The process of state formation in the Republic and the assumption of firm control by the States-General in the later 1570s made it more and more possible to fit out navy vessels, which was in the interest of the merchant communities. The expansion of trade networks was impossible without coordinated armed support by the state. The merchants and armed forces were thus thrown together.[3] At first the major challenge was providing defence against Spanish warships in European waters, but soon the international rivalries extended into more distant regions. The mercantilist conviction that the world's wealth was ultimately finite underpinned new struggles for foreign markets and resources. Growth and expansion, it was assumed, must always entail someone's loss. Economic warfare was thus an important dimension of the struggle of the Dutch Wars of Independence. Tactics that aimed at damaging enemy commerce became increasingly sophisticated, with the imposition of trade prohibitions, differential custom duties and impressive blockades.[4] Any thought of free trade in this context was unlikely; almost all colonial trade was controlled by companies that exercised some form of monopoly.

Maritime historians of the Eighty Years War have long emphasized the problems of the Dutch navy with its decentralized establishment of five separate admiralties. They have depicted the navy boards as riven by corruption and fraud, prone to decision-making delays and unable to provide adequate protection against Spanish privateers. And while the Dutch East India Company (VOC) has been heralded as a success, in the historiography the Dutch West India Company (WIC) has usually been looked upon as a failure.[5] Recent scholarship, however, has shown that the Dutch navy was actually quite efficient in comparison to its opponents. This chapter examines how the Dutch merchants continued to expand their overseas networks during the Wars of Independence. The Dutch navy modernized, initially under pressure from the Spanish and then because of the English threat. Meanwhile the local admiralty boards and colonial companies made significant economic demands on their home communities. Privateers damaged Dutch trade, but Dutch privateers did well too – not least thanks to the infamous West India Company. The new colonial links were testimony to an essential widening of the Dutch trade networks. Military professionalization at home stimulated this extension, keeping other Europeans away from Dutch trading posts and colonies. The chapter closes with an overview of the numerous ways in which the admiralties and colonial companies benefitted both economic warfare and the domestic economy.

The precocious efficiency of the Dutch navy

In 1573, while Orange was dismantling the unruly Sea Beggars' fleet, a new council for the admiralty was set up. In the following years Rotterdam was assigned the central navy organization, but the decentralization of political power led to the establishment of no fewer than four additional admiralty boards. These five boards continued in existence up to the end of the eighteenth century. Mighty Amsterdam demanded a board of its own, refusing to be subordinated to a Rotterdam admiral. Zeeland housed one board, at Middelburg, and in the north of Holland another board was established with a seat that moved every six months between the towns of Hoorn and Enkhuizen. Friesland then secured a navy administration, located in Dokkum; before long the board moved to the more easily accessible harbour of Harlingen.[6] Each navy board controlled the collection of custom duties in its district; these revenues were then employed for the fitting out of ships.

The five boards were nominally under the authority of the States-General but they all evolved into rather independent institutions, with strong links to local mercantile elites. The Amsterdam admiralty soon became the most prominent. Its customs officers gathered most revenues, which were obviously connected to the size and wealth of its district and reflected the trading strength of Amsterdam (see Table 6.1). By the end of the century Amsterdam collected as much as two-thirds of all custom revenues, while the Middelburg admiralty sank to the level of a second-class establishment. This also mirrored the declining trading opportunities in Zeeland, which will be discussed further in Chapter 8.

The revenues collected do not reveal the complete extent of trade conducted because the navy boards suffered significantly from fraud and tax evasion.

Table 6.1 Distribution of yield of custom duties in the Dutch Republic by the five admiralties, in percentages, 1586–1700

Admiralty/seat	1586/99	1601/25	1626/50	1651/75	1676/1700
Amsterdam	31.4	42.7	47.1	53.1	64.6
Meuse (Rotterdam)	26.5	24.3	21.1	19.6	19.5
Northern quarter of Holland (Hoorn and Enkhuizen)	5.8	6.9	6.4	7.6	6.0
Zeeland (Middelburg)	30.1	21.8	22.7	17.3	7.6
Friesland (Dokkum, later Harlingen)	6.2	4.3	2.7	2.4	2.3
Total	100.0	100.0	100.0	100.0	100.0

Source: 't Hart, *In Quest*, Appendix

Decentralized regulation had its drawbacks; control of revenue collection was difficult. Custom duties on their own did not yield enough to maintain all the warships that were needed, particularly after the 1620s, and additional financial support from the provinces was required, paid out of provincial taxes (see Chapter 7). But difficulties persisted: in the crisis year of 1672, for example, the warships of the three smaller admiralties were commissioned only after significant delays.

Such problems, however, were also familiar to other early modern navies. Corruption in custom collection was conspicuous everywhere. Decentralization also hampered the Spanish; their fleet consisted of regional squadrons that expressed and perpetuated provincial loyalties.[7] In England too the navy was hindered by factional struggles. The most pressing problem there was to find sufficient financial credit to fit out the ships; victualling and manning were other major difficulties for England in the seventeenth century. In comparison to the centralized naval organizations of countries such as England and France, this kind of 'resource extraction' (loans, victualling, manning) proved much easier in the Netherlands.[8] During the Eighty Years War the Dutch navy required on average the service of 8,000 sailors annually (with another 4,000 in the VOC and WIC companies); during the Anglo-Dutch wars the total number in naval service rose to between 20,000 and 24,000.[9] These crews were predominantly made up of volunteers, in contrast to, for example, the men on board English ships.

The Swedish maritime historian Jan Glete, who died recently, argued that the highly complex nature of navies, requiring short-term support from a number of different entrepreneurs, shippers, merchants and financiers, was better served by local networks than by centralized state bureaucracies. All early modern navies were dependent to a large extent on private providers for their ship-building, recruitment and supplies; local links in these fields turned out more effective than national organizations. The Dutch case confirms the importance of such decentralization, with the Republic enjoying close connections between navy boards and essential suppliers. The decentralized admiralties thus furthered what Glete termed the 'interest aggregation' between the central state and local elites.[10] In a similar way the Venetian Arsenal had supported the maritime republic's traders; its navy had hired out warships to private shipping companies, which relieved Venetian merchants from the need to maintain their own expensive armed vessels.[11]

The principal task of the navy was the protection of overseas trade. Individual navy boards organized regular convoys along the trade routes most frequently taken by their local merchant communities. Professionalization in the navy advanced; by 1626, 60 captains were commissioned in regular service, earlier than in any other European navy. In 1629 new regulations brought about a reorganization of pay, the supply of victuals and officer hierarchy.[12] In addition, occasional *Directiën* emerged, convoy services for specific trade routes; they operated in close cooperation with the navy boards.

In consequence, shippers and merchants often reaped direct benefits from their cooperation with nearby naval establishments. This may seem inefficient, but because of the shared interests with local mercantile networks vessels could be hired or confiscated on a short-term basis. The privately owned merchant fleet, numbering around 2,000 to 3,000 ships, was easily the largest in Europe. The maritime Netherlands enjoyed a particularly strong market in shipping and naval stores, thanks to its age-old involvement in fisheries and overseas trade. This was a rich source from which to draw in order to fit out vessels that could be turned into armed men-of-war.[13]

The navy boards further shored up Dutch shipping by hiring out cannon, arms, ammunition, sails, anchors, maps and so on from their arsenals. Fishermen received assistance, as well as traders to the Mediterranean, West Africa, and the East and West Indies. The local admiralty even hired out sailors and vessels. In 1601, for example, the merchant Jacques Lampsins was completely supported by the Zeeland admiralty when fitting out his ships for the Newfoundland cod fisheries. The whale fisheries provide another example. This trade was seriously threatened by English privateers, but the Amsterdam admiralty provided protection in the shape of three armed convoy vessels and also helped out with low-priced cannon. Such ready and inexpensive provisioning of cannon by the navy boards also permitted Dutch merchants to obtain a secure foothold in the Mediterranean. This kind of activity reached a peak during the Truce when such items were less in demand by the admiralties themselves. During these years navy boards sold cannon and vessels at reduced prices; this facilitated the rapid expansion of Dutch overseas trade in the 1610s.[14]

In addition, the Dutch admiralties provided regular financial support to the major trading companies and fisheries; they assisted with loans and managed the subsidies from the Provincial States of Holland and the States-General. In this way the herring fisheries secured sums amounting to over 20,000 guilders per year before and after the Truce; the sums were only lower in 1609–21

Table 6.2 Subsidies from the States of Holland, States-General and admiralties for the herring fisheries and the East India Company (VOC), in guilders, 1609–17

Year	Herring fisheries	VOC
1609	12,000	20,000
1610	12,000	100,000
1611	12,000	145,000
1612	12,000	125,000
1613	10,000	225,000
1614	10,000	225,000
1615	17,000	300,000
1616	0	300,000
1617	18,000	300,000

Sources: De Jong, *Staat van Oorlog*, pp. 115–16; Van Vliet, *Vissers*, pp. 251–2

because the direct threat in the North Sea was less. The Dutch East India Company (VOC) also received substantial support from the admiralties, in both money and kind. Protection costs are always high when breaking into new markets. During the first years of its existence, the VOC had to invest heavily in the application of force and no dividends could be paid. Between 1615 and 1617 the subsidies were so high that the company was able to fit out one ship without any charge to itself (Table 6.2).[15]

From 1611 the Dutch admiralties maintained a garrison at Fort Nassau on the West African coast, the frequently used route of colonial companies. This fort reduced the costs of protection and provisioning for Dutch merchants in the area, as well as the Dutch East India Company. Thanks to the precocious efficiency of the Dutch navy the VOC rose rather rapidly to prominence in the early seventeenth century, in contrast to its English counterpart, which started to prosper only later in the century.[16] The Spanish navy had little opportunity to inflict damage on the well-protected Dutch in their overseas trade. Only twice did the Spanish king send a fleet north, in 1588 and 1639; both attempts ended in failure.

Naval shipbuilding and its economic impact

At home, in their local communities, the facilities and storehouses of the navy establishments meant there was significant demand for suppliers of victuals and essential items such as cannon, gunpowder, ammunition, timber, rope, sails, tar and pitch, anchors, nails and bolts, glass, lanterns, copper, plumbing, flags, compasses and masts. Shipbuilding was a well-established and strong capital-intensive industry in the northern Netherlands, with ample provision for ship construction and repair. It probably gave employment to as much as 5 per cent of Holland's industrial labour force. One advantage enjoyed by the Dutch navy was that ship construction was cheaper than in neighbouring countries, thanks to the significant Dutch-Norwegian timber trade and technological advances, including the innovation of the sawmill later in the century. By 1669 the construction of the same vessel would cost 8,000 guilders in Holland but 13,000 guilders in England: more than 60 per cent more expensive. Several rivals of the Republic even bought their warships in Holland.[17]

The naval dockyards, able to repair ships at short notice or construct new ones, provided additional employment for hundreds of shipwrights and other labourers; their numbers increased to more than a thousand during periods of intensive shipbuilding.[18] Particularly after 1650, the Amsterdam navy dwarfed all others; its board was one of the largest employers in the Republic.[19] This positive economic impact was also evident around other naval establishments. A naval base was consistently one of a country's main productive enterprises, as exemplified by Deptford and Chatham (England), Rochefort (France), Kronstadt (Russia) and Ferrol (Spain).[20] Since the Dutch navy was spread over five establishments, its positive economic impact was dispersed across several local communities. One example is the way in which a large part of the Holland naval subsidies went to the admiralty board at Rotterdam; this contributed significantly to this small town becoming one of the largest cities in the Republic. By 1600 Rotterdam had already surpassed powerful Dordrecht in wealth. The town of Harlingen, in Friesland, benefitted economically from the demand by the Frisian admiralty for victuals, especially meat from butchers, and the repair of vessels, and so forth.[21]

The need for warships gave a substantial boost to an already thriving industry. Calculated in tons the fighting navy comprised about one-tenth of the combined volume of the naval, merchant and fishing fleets.[22] Table 6.3 lists the numbers of the larger warships.

Because of the shallow coastal waters of the Low Countries, the warships constructed by the Dutch admiralties were initially rather small, in sharp

Table 6.3 Size of the Dutch navy in larger warships, selected years, 1587–1680

1587	44
1596	91
1616 (Truce)	34
1621	86
1628	110
1631	125
1642	120
1650	62
1655	101
1660	97
1665	115
1670	129
1675	110
1680	93

Sources: De Jong, *Staat*, p. 59; Glete, *Navies*, pp. 156, 639.

contrast to the average English or Spanish fighting vessel.[23] The construction of larger warships became imperative, however, when the tactics employed in warfare at sea started to involve the deployment of more and heavier artillery. The challenge was to design a ship able to access Dutch harbours but large enough for expeditions lasting five months or more and with sufficient stability to carry a variety of heavy guns. The design of such vessels was actively encouraged by Maurice of Nassau. The prince consulted closely with Pieter Jansz Liorne, the designer of the successful flute ship, as well as master carpenters and representatives of the admiralty boards. The result was a vessel with a strong hull, like the flute ships, which permitted heavy artillery to be mounted on the stern and prow and along the board sides as well. Their large amount of storage allowed them to remain at sea for five to six months. This standardization of warship design occurred at the same time as the standardization of army weaponry, around the turn of the seventeenth century (Chapter 2).[24]

During the Truce a major shipbuilding programme was launched; by 1621 the Dutch fighting navy consisted of a core of large, heavily armed, specialized warships, to which hired merchant vessels were added during wartime. Despite its small population, the United Provinces thus became one of the strongest naval powers in the world (see Table 6.4).

At the battle of Downs (1639) the Dutch admiral Tromp was the first fleet commander known to deliberately use line-of-battle tactics when he bombarded the Spanish enemy from the broadside of ships sailing in a line behind each other. This innovative tactic resulted in a fundamental transformation of sea warfare, labelled by some authors as a 'military revolution at sea'. From then on Europe's sea battles were generally fought not in the mêlées which had hitherto been fashionable but from a greater distance, and preferably using the guns from the broadside. The traditional method of transforming merchantmen into warships by mounting cannons gave way to permanent navies with purpose-built ships.[25] But these new tactics did not change Dutch shipbuilding practices for more than another decade, because the leaders of the Republic were convinced they could depend upon hired merchantmen when the necessity arose.

Table 6.4 Navies (displacement in 1,000 tons) and population of the Netherlands, England, France and Spain, 1600–1700

	Population (millions)	1600	1630	1650	1675	1700
Dutch Republic	1–2	20	40	29	88	113
England	6–8	27	31	49	95	196
France	18–20	–	27	21	138	195
Spain (incl. Portugal)	10–11	50	50	30	18	20

Sources: Glete, *War and the State*, p. 164; for population, Cipolla, *Before the Industrial Revolution*

After peace was signed in 1648 the States-General decided to sell a number of warships; they retained the vessels needed for convoy duties and the West India Company. Despite this significant reduction the Dutch navy remained prominent on most European trade routes and provided adequate protection for the seaborne trade of the Netherlands.[26] Paradoxically, the Spanish also profited from the strength and effectiveness of the Dutch convoys. Particularly after the early 1640s the presence of the Dutch in the Mediterranean was said to have brought about a significant reduction in the threat from pirates and privateers.[27]

By then the English had replaced the Spanish as the main rivals at sea. In the late 1640s the English had launched an impressive shipbuilding programme that took full advantage of the new line-ahead tactics at sea; the vessels now built contained at least two and sometimes three gun decks. The outcome of the First Anglo-Dutch War (1652–4) was disastrous for the Dutch. The superior English vessels swept away the hastily armed merchantmen of the United Provinces, which often had only one gun deck. Such vessels had served the country well during the battle at Downs in 1639, but by the 1650s they had been overtaken by shipbuilding developments and become hopelessly outmoded.

Responding swiftly, the Council of State decided in 1652 to construct new men-of-war. Two million guilders were provided for the purpose; another two million guilders were voted in the following year. This impressive shipbuilding programme came too late to influence the outcome of the First Anglo-Dutch War, but by its conclusion in 1654 the Republic's navy had been transformed. Converted merchantmen became a thing of the past; by 1655 the navy of the United Provinces consisted of 115 specialized warships, almost as powerful as the English fleet (130). In addition, 60 new men-of-war were constructed in the 1660s, followed by a further round of shipbuilding in the 1670s. The vessels were still generally smaller than their English counterparts, but the greater versatility this gave them allowed the Dutch to use the numerous shoals of the North Sea and shallow coastal waters of the Netherlands as a tactical refuge. In addition, by the time of the Third Anglo-Dutch War the Dutch were able to maintain a higher rate of fire than the English.[28]

It is impossible to study the full economic impact of the new shipbuilding programme because most naval records were destroyed by fire in 1844. Luckily, many of the Zeeland admiralty accounts survived. Not all vessels were built on admiralty wharves; in order to improve competitiveness, the construction of some warships was subcontracted to yards in nearby towns. In the period 1650–74, 24 warships were built in Zeeland. This provided employment for on average 1 per cent of the labour force. During years of major construction this percentage increased in smaller towns like Flushing (8,000 inhabitants) to 6 per cent of the labour force, or even 14 or 15 per cent in the case of Veere (3,000 inhabitants). Compared to the average wage level shipwright's wages were quite high; 1.8 guilders a day in summer, 1.5 guilders in winter (because of the shorter workday), while an ordinary master craftsman earned on average 1.35 a day in summer.[29]

Table 6.5 Make-up of expenditure for a warship, 1653–5, in percentages

Shipwrights (including block makers)	27.6
Timber merchants	23.5
Smiths (including coppersmiths, plumbers)	16.1
Roperies	12.4
Sail makers	3.8
Woodcarvers and painters	0.8
Cannon and arms dealers	13.8
Administration	2.1
Total (*c*.75,000 guilders)	100.0

Source: Otte, 'Zeeuwse zeezaken', pp. 152–5

Analysing the expenditure involved in warship construction, it is obvious that a large proportion of the subsidies ended up in the pockets of shipwrights, timber and arms merchants and artisans such as smiths and rope-makers (see Table 6.5). The presence of an admiralty board thus brought significant economic benefits to artisans and traders in the vicinity.

Commercial prohibitions and trade with the enemy

The destruction of an opponent's economic base was an important dimension of any war. Trade blockades contributed substantially to the rebels 'persuading' Amsterdam and Middelburg to join the Revolt in the 1570s; during the next decade, similar tactics brought Ypres, Ghent and Bruges once again under the king.[30] Madrid and Brussels issued numerous trade bans intended to damage Dutch trade. The Dutch for their part preferred the direct tactic of blockades; after the fall of Antwerp in 1585, the Dutch restricted trade on the river Scheldt and blockaded the Flemish coast with their warships. Throughout the Dutch Wars of Independence the Spanish were unable to send the Army of Flanders provisions by sea.[31]

Despite these trade bans and blockades, not all commerce stopped. Already in 1573 the Provincial States of Holland and Zeeland had introduced the possibility of trading with the south at the cost of buying a license, the *licent*, which amounted to a heavy customs duty. Items of strategic importance (bullion, arms, ammunition, gunpowder, ships and ship parts such as masts, and crucial foodstuffs for the army, like grain) were proscribed, but a substantial amount of trade was condoned. The southern Netherlands responded with a similar license system, but Spanish kings tended to be critical of such 'lax measures' and repeatedly suspended licensed trade to the north, much to the chagrin of the southern Netherlands merchants.[32]

There was considerable disagreement among the rebels over these trade licenses. Despite official 'total' trade bans by the States-General in the 1580s, the Provincial States of Holland often continued to permit commerce with the south. The Hollanders argued that if they did not, 'others' would profit from this rewarding trade; and indeed, Cologne, Wesel and Hamburg all profited from sending supplies to the Spanish when Holland failed to do so. But the rebels in the south attributed the fall of Antwerp and other towns to the greediness of the Holland merchants. The *licenten* trade continued throughout much of the war, since the revenues were extremely profitable; among other benefits the income facilitated the establishment of the new admiralties in the north. Alongside the licensed trade, covert transactions and smuggling continued; between April 1586 and August 1588 Dutch merchants even shipped silver to Antwerp, which eased the payment of *asientos* that were used for the financing of the Army of Flanders.[33]

Economic warfare was revived in particular after 1625, because Philip IV preferred this tactic to large-scale military operations to bring the Dutch Republic to its knees (see Chapter 1). In addition to putting a stop to all Iberian-Dutch trade and increasing the scale of Dunkirk privateering, a series of river blockades were established on the Rhine and Meuse. These struck hard at Dutch towns that profited from river commerce, such as Dordrecht and Deventer. However, the bans always harmed the Spanish troops more than the Dutch because of the Republic's ability to secure provisions for its soldiers from a wide variety of sources.

In the northern Netherlands such trade bans enabled some to profit while others lost out. The Spanish river blockade of 1627 lasted longer than necessary because several Holland and Zeeland towns refused to lift the Dutch trade ban issued in reprisal; they obviously profited from the inland towns' decline in trade (see also Chapter 8).[34] But blockades also prevented the export of herring to the hinterland, which was why herring merchants were anxious for the prohibitions to be lifted as soon as possible. At the same time poorer people in Holland benefited from the declining price of fish, which became a welcome addition to their diet during the difficult years of the 1625–7 trade bans.[35]

Despite the intensification of prohibitions on trade after 1625, numerous rich Holland merchants managed to gain substantially from commerce with the enemy. They soon regained admission to Iberian ports, and by the early 1640s about three-quarters of all goods in Spanish harbours were transported on Dutch ships. Portuguese exiles in Amsterdam financed a major part of the Spanish *asientos*. After 1644 the transport of bullion from Spain to Dunkirk and Antwerp was insured by Amsterdam merchants; in 1646 the famous burgomaster-merchant Bicker even shipped the silver required to pay the Army of Flanders.[36]

Privateering: costs and benefits

The principal aim of the war at sea was that of *petite guerre*, locating enemy supply ships and capturing or destroying them.[37] Even the 1588 Armada was intended to send soldiers and provisions to the Army of Flanders, while the battle of the Downs was actually an attack on another Spanish supply fleet. The main Spanish threat at sea, however, consisted of privateers from Dunkirk.

Parma began to fit out these small, versatile, armed vessels as soon as he captured this harbour on the Flemish coast.[38] The Dutch sent out privateers too, initially merchantmen ordered to protect themselves, with the taking of enemy vessels or their goods as a profitable side effect. After 1598, the year that Philip III issued a major trade ban against Dutch commerce, the States-General started to commission vessels to engage in privateering as a dimension of offensive warfare. Privateering became big business, above all in Zeeland.

Despite Dutch efforts to blockade the Flemish coast, the small Dunkirk vessels managed to sneak out from time to time. Their attacks multiplied after 1625, and because of the sheer size of the Dutch commercial fleet (2,000 to 3,000 vessels) their search for booty was often rewarded. The Dunkirk campaigns were at their peak in the early 1630s and again from 1642 to 1646 when over five hundred Dutch vessels were captured, which yielded their admiralty 4.5 million guilders. The economic historians De Vries and Van der Woude calculated the value of Dutch shipping lost to these privateers at 22 million guilders or more.[39] As a reprisal, cruiser squadrons of the Dutch navy destroyed Dunkirk ships – for example, 23 in 1633, 16 in 1645 and 8 in 1646. But the Dunkirkers were not the only problem: between 1641 and 1653 the Dutch lost vessels worth together between ten and eleven million guilders to French privateers in the Mediterranean, where Algerian pirates were also a significant threat.[40]

The difficulty of establishing a clear picture of the value of privateering to the war effort is that net losses on one side never constituted a net gain on the other. Despite the substantial Dutch losses, the Dunkirk prizes never represented an important source of revenue for the Spanish crown. Goods seized were not always needed on the local market; merchants from the northern Netherlands frequently bought goods at the public sales, profiting from prices which were extremely low. Several Zeeland and Holland merchants even invested in the fitting out of privateers from Dunkirk and thus reaped the fruits of damage inflicted on their own countrymen. To make matters even more complicated, the predominance of privateering also had adverse effects on Flanders' trade. Numerous Antwerp merchants employed Dutch vessels for their commerce with Italy, Portugal and France; in 1638 the Antwerp-based Jeremias Cock went bankrupt because of the activity of Dunkirk privateers.[41]

Certain trades were obviously more vulnerable than others, and Dunkirkers above all inflicted damage on the Dutch herring fleet. The herring busses had grown in number since the early sixteenth century; by 1630 they amounted to some six or seven hundred. By the end of the war their number had declined to around 550.[42] Many vessels were taken by the Dunkirk privateers, of course. But the story is more complex than that. Recent research has shown that not all fishing communities suffered to the same extent. The fishermen sailing from the Meuse estuary, in south Holland, suffered particularly severely; those departing from Enkhuizen in north Holland were much more fortunate – though they in turn would suffer disproportionately from the subsequent Anglo-Dutch wars. Within the Meuse estuary the economic effect was again highly unequal.

Fishermen from Delft, for instance, suffered significant losses, while those from Rotterdam fared much better. The Rotterdam authorities endeavoured to create new opportunities for the fishermen affected; many were helped to launch other fishing or shipping ventures. The loss of fisheries could thus be compensated for by increased activity in other areas, given the active support of the local authority. In nearby Schiedam numerous former fishermen also found ready employment in the developing brandy distilleries.[43]

In addition, biologists have suggested that the decline of the Dutch herring fisheries in this period might also have been caused by overfishing or by the migration of herring to the Baltic or other seas. Although there is no proof for such claims, it is true that even after the 1670s, when fishermen experienced far fewer threats from privateers, the herring fisheries continued to decline.[44] The most plausible conclusion is that warfare reinforced an existing trend (generally declining opportunities within the herring industry) rather than causing a new one.

The losses on the part of the herring fisheries must be balanced against the privateering profits from Zeeland, which amounted to around two million guilders per year between 1621 and 1646, in total around 48 million guilders. The Dutch East India Company also proved rather successful; in the first 20 years of its existence its prizes yielded at least ten and perhaps as much as 20 million guilders. Thereafter the VOC reduced its role as privateer and became more orientated towards trade (see below). In addition, the WIC won rich Spanish-Portuguese prizes every year from West Indian trade: between 1623 and 1637 no fewer than 609 ships; the loss to the enemy was estimated at 118 million guilders. During 1647 and 1648 the WIC was again very successful, taking as many as 220 enemy vessels.[45]

Whatever the net results of Dunkirk privateering and the Dutch response, the fact is that shipping from the northern Netherlands continued to grow during the Wars of Independence. The merchant fleet of the United Provinces reached a tonnage larger than the fleets of England, France and Spain combined. The effects of privateering on Dutch overseas trade were undeniable, but it seems to have been more of an inconvenience than a serious problem.[46]

The limited nature of the damage inflicted upon the Dutch was due to both the wide array of shipping and alternative trading opportunities enjoyed by the maritime provinces and the existence of institutions that spread the risks and reduced the losses of individual investors. The *partenrederij*, the division of vessel ownership into as many as 32 or even 64 parts, making for a large number of shareholders, resulted in a spreading of the risks. This system dated back to the fifteenth century and may have been copied from certain Italian cities. From the final decade of the sixteenth century, moreover, new institutions were created that dealt with insurance. Amsterdam set up a special Chamber of Insurance to regulate the business; in the mid-1630s this institution registered premiums that amounted to over 400,000 guilders. The intensification of Dutch privateering in the early 1630s, above all from Zeeland, to combat the increased pressure of the Dunkirkers, resulted in a lowering of the premiums paid for trade to Bordeaux, La Rochelle and Nantes to a mere 3 per cent from their previous level of between eight and ten. Even enemy vessels were insured, remarkably enough, although that was not officially sanctioned.[47] At a local level, additional insurances came to be provided. Sailors and fishermen, for example, set up mutual funds for their widows or in case they were taken hostage by the Dunkirkers.[48]

Privateering was to remain an important tactic for decades to come, not least in the three Anglo-Dutch wars of the seventeenth century. During the first (1652–4), English privateers captured over a thousand Dutch vessels, but many of these were small and of relatively little value. Dutch privateers captured far fewer prizes, but the vessels were on average larger and yielded better returns. Although the war ended in a victory for the English, they were more affected by their losses than were the Dutch because of the size of their merchant fleet, which remained modest. In 1665–7 the English captured around 450 ships, the Dutch some 400, but once again the English vessels were rich ones returning from the colonies, while the Dutch prizes were much lower in value, carrying wine, brandy, fish or salt. For example, the capture of nine English merchantmen alone yielded some two million guilders; as a result of Dutch successes the price of fuel and food went up in London. Dutch privateers continued to outperform the English in terms of captures in the Third Anglo-Dutch War.[49]

However, although the successes of Dutch privateers in the Anglo-Dutch wars were substantial and, particularly during the 1670s, more profitable than those of the English, the Dutch were ultimately the losers in these three conflicts. This had little to do with the war at sea or privateering. Since the English pursued an economic policy based on protectionism, and were followed in this by the French, the Dutch lost their competitive edge in international shipping and trade.[50] The wealth of the northern Netherlands had been based on free access to foreign ports and markets, but all over the world territories were increasingly burdened by state regulations. The Anglo-Dutch wars were not the source of this trend, but they did precipitate the rise of national states with ever more effective navies. International shippers thus became less dependent on the Dutch merchant networks and services, although it would still take another century before London replaced Amsterdam as Europe's foremost financial centre.

The role of colonial warfare

Repeated strategic trade bans imposed by the Spanish kings, together with a general weakening of Portuguese colonial networks, caused pepper prices to rise in the 1590s. This stimulated Dutch merchants to find their own shipping route to the Far East. The first expedition took place in 1597; soon there were a number of companies engaged in the profitable spice trade. But fierce competition among these companies threatened the Dutch position relative to other colonial powers, and also weakened their position vis-à-vis the indigenous rulers in the region. Urged on by a number of merchants, the influential statesman Van Oldenbarnevelt intervened and ensured that in 1602 the States-General granted one company the monopoly of the United Province's trade in the Far East: the Dutch East India Company, the VOC. Its capital (6.4 million guilders) was quickly subscribed by, amongst others, wealthy refugees from the southern Netherlands.

Though the monopoly granted to the VOC was an obvious centralizing force, the effect in the Netherlands itself was inevitably more decentralized. The company created six chambers, divided between the six major spice-trading towns; Amsterdam's was the largest. The directorship was made up of a collective of 17 deputies sent by the six chambers.[51] As with the admiralties, this was an example of the Dutch Republic managing to combine the interests of local elites with one of its war enterprises.

The VOC's charter conferred far-reaching powers. Full autonomy was granted in the management of the overseas trading posts and territories; the directors had the right to conclude peace with or declare war on Asian rulers; and the company could recruit soldiers on its own account. This construction of 'a state within a state' speeded up the decision-making process in the VOC, which was truly run as a mercantile enterprise. Economic interests came first; political considerations second. This constituted one of the secrets of the VOC's staying power. One novelty was the length of its charter: 20 years, regularly renewed thereafter. Before the creation of the VOC, shipping contracts were usually for one voyage only, after which the capital had to be returned. This permitted the directors to decide whether to re-invest the profits or pay dividends to the shareholders. Investors who disagreed with a postponement of dividends could sell their stock at the Bourse.[52] Since the initial capital was never returned, the VOC became the first joint-stock company of the world.

Compared to the earlier Dutch strategy (1580s–1590s) of blockading the enemy with squadrons stationed between the Azores, the Canary Islands, and the Iberian peninsula, the advanced new strategy of utilizing semi-independent colonial companies proved to be much more efficient, cheaper and also more successful.[53] But initial results were mixed. The VOC strategy hovered between two extremes: privateering and forced trading on the one hand and peaceful, legal commerce on the other. Numerous Portuguese vessels were taken as prizes and the harbour of Malacca (dominated by the Portuguese) was blockaded. During the Truce the belligerent policy continued, including a blockade of Spanish-dominated Manila. In addition, Chinese ships were attacked; one expedition yielded 800,000 guilders-worth of silk alone. This strategy brought rich prizes but was also very costly, since the Dutch found themselves at war with almost everybody. During the Truce the costs of equipping vessels (3.8 million guilders annually) were always higher than the revenues (3.4 million). By around 1622 the military expenses alone had risen to five million guilders per annum. In these years, supplementary support by the States-General and its admiralties was indispensable.[54]

The VOC's transition from privateering to trade occurred in the early 1620s. In 1621 the revenue from prizes yielded around two million guilders; trade brought in almost twice that figure, 3.8 million guilders. By 1627 the relative proportions had changed: booty amounted to 3.2 million guilders, trade 12.3 million, almost four times as much.[55] Increasingly the company moved from a strategy of securing crucial positions in the spice trade to one of developing strong footholds in the main hubs of Asian trade. A quarter of the VOC ships (the smaller ones) remained permanently in the Far East, used more and more for intra-Asian trade.

It was the VOC's economic position within East Asian trade that gave the Dutch such enormous leverage. None of the VOC's competitors was able to assess the relative price of silver in China, Japan, Persia, Surat and Amsterdam in the way that the company's headquarters in Batavia (Djakarta) could. The decisions were frequently beyond the scope of most directors and investors at home. In fact, the VOC behaved rather like a multinational corporation. Each year bullion and goods for exchange arrived from the Netherlands, with a list of desirable goods to be acquired for the six chambers, but managers in Batavia decided on the final distribution of the available assets; when silks from Persia yielded more in exchange within Asia itself, then the VOC in the Netherlands simply had to wait for silks in the following cargo.[56]

The Dutch trade network within Asia depended on four major hubs, in addition to Batavia itself. The first centred on the Moluccas. Significant victories were gained over the Portuguese in Amboina, Tidore and Ternate in 1605; Banda was won by brutal force in 1621. This gave the VOC a monopoly over spices such as cloves, nutmeg and mace, which were in demand not only in Europe but also within Asia itself. The second hub was Pulicat (conquered in 1612) on the east coast of India, which guaranteed a steady flow of Indian cottons that were greatly in demand all over Asia. From there, trade links to the coast of Bengal were established, and in 1639 the Portuguese were ousted from Ceylon (present-day Sri Lanka), which gave the VOC another spice monopoly: cinnamon. The third hub had been in Dutch hands since 1616: the town of Surat, a permanent settlement on the west coast of India. This port provided access to the markets of Malabar India, Persia and Arabia, and gave the Dutch enormous leverage in the west Asian seas. In particular the Dutch secured a near-monopoly in indigo, sharing control of the European market for the precious commodity with the English. By the 1660s the VOC dominated most of the maritime trade of south-west India. The fourth hub gave them direct access to trade with Japan. With the establishment of a trading post in Formosa (Taiwan) in 1622, the Dutch gained a crucial position, connecting Chinese and Japanese trade, isolating the Spanish at Manila and securing access to the silver exported by the Japanese, which was in great demand in the region. From Japan the VOC obtained military *matériel* and soldiers too, necessary not only for wars against other Europeans but also to subjugate the spice islands of the Moluccas, which rose in revolt against the imposition of the Dutch trade monopoly. In 1639 the VOC secured the monopoly on European trade with Japan through the island of Decima. The Dutch network thus extended from the Red Sea to Japan. No trading complex as extensive as this, controlled from one commercial centre, had ever existed before.[57]

By the 1630s the VOC's position was well established. The company's surplus of revenue over equipment costs in the Dutch Republic came to exceed two million guilders per year. The investors received steady dividends, while the directors regularly re-invested significant portions of the proceeds in the further build-up of the fleet; VOC shares achieved excellent prices on the stock market. By 1650 total dividend payments amounted to over eight times the initial investment. In Batavia the VOC made increasing profits from its intra-Asian trade; its capital stock in Asia had risen to over 20 million guilders by the 1660s. Japan was a ready market for hides, cotton textiles and porcelain, shipped by the VOC from the Coromandel Coast, Bengal and China. Ceylonese elephants, a VOC monopoly since 1658, were highly priced in India. To pay for the products of the Coromandel Coast of India the Dutch used gold from China, which they obtained in Formosa. The Indian market for spices was twice as large as the market in Europe. Indian textiles were bartered for pepper, gold and camphor from Sumatra; in Siam, spices, pepper and coral were exchanged against tin (which was exported to Europe too) and hides, necessary for the trade with Japan, and gold. Although the trading post at Timor was run at a loss, its sandalwood fetched high prices in China and Bengal. Bengal offered silk, rice and saltpetre, the latter being increasingly important for the Dutch arms market. The revenues needed for the expansion in Asia came increasingly from the profits of trade in Asia itself and thus relieved the Dutch state and navy from direct involvement in colonial exploitation.[58]

The expansion of the VOC continued after 1650, but at a slower pace. In the 1670s the English East India Company (EIC) increasingly became a competitor, which caused pepper prices to fall sharply in Europe.[59] New rival companies were set up in both France and Denmark. In Asia the Chinese empire re-established itself under the Qing after 1644, and this reduced the need for the Dutch to act as a trading link with Japan. As a result, VOC debts rose. Even so, while the English EIC went bankrupt in 1683, its Dutch counterpart remained one of the world's most important commercial enterprises until the late eighteenth century.[60]

Once established, it proved extremely difficult for other Europeans to drive the Dutch from their Asian trading posts. Only in the final decades of the eighteenth century did the British surpass its rival. The considerable tenacity demonstrated by the Dutch in the Far East was undoubtedly assisted by the advanced military techniques developed during the Dutch Wars of Independence. Around 30 per cent of the company's budget was spent on wars and coercion. VOC fleets destroyed the outdated Portuguese ships in numerous trading posts and simultaneously blockaded the Spanish at Manila. After the peace of 1648, over 10,000 troops discharged from the Republic's army were hired for Asian forts. With England becoming a more significant competitor in the colonial sphere, the number of soldiers serving the VOC grew from 8,000 in 1625 (30 per cent of all employees) to 22,000 in 1688 (47 per cent). These troops were well trained and highly disciplined, like the soldiers in the Netherlands.[61]

The Dutch built some of their strongest forts and maintained their mightiest garrisons on the spice islands of the Moluccas. The military engineers who served the VOC and WIC (between 1602 and 1700 they totalled 100 for the VOC, 16 for the WIC) were drawn from the same tradition of Stevin and the *mathématique* schools as the fortification-builders in the Republic. In the colonies the Dutch preferred small fortified citadels, 'Dutch cities', with less fortified – or even unfortified – outer parts for the indigenous population. This approach was relatively inexpensive and worked extremely well. Between 1613 and 1692 the cost of fortifications amounted to around 4 per cent of VOC expenditure in Asia.[62] The British recognized the value of these Dutch fortifications, not simply for defence but as one element of a system of armed trading, and began to construct fortifications of their own later in the seventeenth century.[63] They also began to promote regional trade networks in the colonies, instead of simply using the EIC as an instrument of extraction for the home community, thus emulating one of the keys to Dutch success.

The situation regarding trade in the Americas and Caribbean was completely different. Established in 1621 with a charter similar to the VOC but with five chambers instead of six, the West India Company had a problem raising the necessary capital (17 million guilders). The early 1620s were rather bleak years for the Republic due to renewed (and considerable) military pressure from the Army of Flanders; investors were hesitant over all new ventures. Another impediment was the absence of key hubs of local trade in the Americas that might be occupied. It was impossible to create the kind of near-monopoly of the spice trade which sustained the VOC in Asia. Nor could a monopoly of trade to and from the Netherlands be enforced either, since too many Dutch traders were already involved in profitable Atlantic commerce dominated by salt and sugar.[64]

Even so, the strategic role of the WIC should not be underestimated; nor should one undervalue the revenues that became possible for the Dutch merchant community thanks to the expansion of trade links within the Atlantic world. Initially the WIC was most successful in West Africa.[65] The company extracted more gold from Guinea than the private companies that had previously dominated this trade. Twelve million guilders in gold was extracted before 1637; as much as nine million in just the three years between 1645 and 1647. Gold remained the most profitable trade for the WIC throughout the seventeenth century. From 1623 to 1636 the Dutch also exported goods worth 14 million guilders to West Africa. An impressive series of forts were constructed along the Gold Coast. The slave trade took off in the 1640s; in the later 1650s the WIC shipped on average 1,300 slaves per year, which increased to 4,900 by 1674; this was enhanced by control over the strategically located island of Curaçao, which evolved into the largest slave market in the Caribbean.[66]

The WIC posed a serious threat to the Spanish trading monopoly within its Atlantic empire throughout the 1630s. At the centre of this challenge was privateering; as noted above, between 1623 and 1637 over 600 Iberian vessels were taken, the rich silver fleet captured by Piet Heyn in 1628 (yielding 11.5 million guilders) making one of the largest prizes. Together these seizures amounted to a loss of 118 million guilders for the Spanish crown and produced a total revenue of 81 million guilders for the Dutch. After deducting the costs of the expedition – sailors' wages and so forth – there was still a clear profit of 36 million guilders.[67]

Around the Atlantic settlements, with their rich plantations, the Dutch encountered fierce competition from the English, Portuguese and Spanish. It was the establishment of plantations that counted in the Americas and Caribbean; trading posts were altogether less important. But unlike Spain, the small Dutch Republic had little surplus manpower to populate the colonies. And while numerous dissenters left England, providing a solid base for British expansion in North America, the Dutch Republic's pragmatic religious policy did not drive out any major religious groupings from their European homeland.

The capture of Brazil, completed in 1635, granted the WIC control over the sugar trade and was a temporary Dutch success. During the next decade, sugar imports boosted the refineries of Amsterdam, Rotterdam and Middelburg. The colony was lost, however, and an attempt to gain control over the profitable salt trade from the Caribbean also failed.[68] Around 1650 46,000 furs were traded annually in the WIC colony of the New Netherlands, primarily through New Amsterdam, but the Dutch were driven out by the superior colonial organization of the English. Despite such setbacks the WIC's profits were still greater than its losses during the 1670s and 1680s.[69]

In addition, numerous individual Dutch merchants continued to prosper through their participation in the fur trade conducted from what was now renamed New York. Goods from the Americas increasingly arrived at markets in the Netherlands, in volume terms second only to imports from the Far East. The WIC might not have been particularly successful, but in its wake the Dutch merchant community extended their trade networks across the Atlantic. The Dutch increasingly occupied lucrative intermediary positions in that part of the world.

One estimate is that in the 1770s the VOC conducted 13 per cent of the United Provinces' total foreign trade. Several scholars have used this relatively low figure as proof that colonial trade was not that important to the Republic, while others argue that merchants in the southern Netherlands had not been excluded from Spanish-dominated colonial trade.[70] The enrichment of individual merchants is different from the establishment of a trade centre advantage, however. The fact that the Dutch controlled direct access to luxury colonial goods gave the entire merchant community of the VOC and WIC chamber towns an undeniable advantage over other commercial centres. Most of the colonial goods did not remain in the Netherlands but were re-exported. And while the scale of industrial exports to the colonies was modest, it should not be neglected: high-quality woollen textiles from Leiden continued to make up a significant part of the cargoes shipped to China and Japan.[71]

In addition, and broadly like the five admiralties, the VOC and WIC maintained warehouses and wharves in their chamber towns. The VOC was actually the second largest employer in the Republic after the Dutch army. Its warehouses and wharves employed thousands of workers and created a strong demand for ropeworks, slaughterhouses, timber yards, smithies, coopermen, tailors, shoemakers, bakers, breweries and the like. An annual 580,000 guilders was spent on the fitting out of ships in the small north Holland town of Hoorn; the huge Amsterdam chamber spent as much as 5.4 million guilders on fitting out in 1700 alone. Between 1602 and 1699 approximately 710 ships were built on VOC wharves, of which 367 were constructed in Amsterdam. A significant proportion of the wages of the tens of thousands of employees on the ships and in Asia was paid within the Republic, mostly to sailors' wives and families.[72]

Conclusion: the fruits of maritime warfare

The navy was extremely important for the 'protection-selling capacity' of the Dutch Republic, to employ Frederick Lane's term. Dutch convoys in European waters were crucial; their presence lessened the risk of enemy attack and thereby lowered the protection costs faced by Dutch merchants, thus increasing profit margins. Numerous local elites, above all in the maritime provinces, consequently regarded the Dutch state as an institution worthy of support. In this respect, the Spanish navy performed much less well.[73]

Economic warfare was an important dimension of the Eighty Years War. But trade blockades did only limited damage to the Dutch.[74] Dunkirk privateers were more destructive, but Dutch privateers were quite successful as well. However, these activities increased risks at sea and resulted in a considerable loss of capital. Capital accumulation, permitting steady economic growth, was generally better served by ordinary trade than by privateering. In this regard the establishment of the two colonial companies added significantly to the wealth of the Dutch Republic, not only via the traded goods but more in terms of the boost to Dutch prestige within Europe and the stimulus to related trades.

Numerous scholars have pointed out that the European military revolution was only of limited importance in the conquest and acquisition of colonies overseas. This may be true, but the Dutch advances in military professionalization was of tremendous importance in the competition with other European powers to establish and maintain overseas trading posts. In this respect the WIC was not a 'total failure', as is often suggested in historiography; the company contributed significantly to the income from booty and facilitated access for individual Dutch traders in the Americas and the Caribbean. In addition, the Dutch colonial companies were supported by the Republic's navy in various ways; this again contributed to their notable resilience.

The degree to which the navy and the colonial companies were closely meshed together undoubtedly spurred on the Dutch Golden Age. The wealth which resulted also supported the military system of the United Provinces, allowing the army to be regularly paid, as will be shown in Chapter 7.

Notes

1 Fruin, *Tien jaren*, pp. 199–200.
2 Rooze-Stouthamer, *Opmaat*, p. 152.

3 Mann, *Sources of Social Power*, p. 473; Enthoven, 'Mars en Mercurius bijeen'; Adams, 'Trading states, trading places'.

4 Roberts, 'Military revolution', p. 26.

5 Van Vliet, *Vissers en kapers*, pp. 248–55; Bartstra, *Vlootherstel*, pp. 10–16; Braunius, 'Oorlogsvloot', pp. 322–3.

6 Oosterhoff, *Leicester*, p. 142; Van Vliet, 'Staatse vloot', pp. 45ff.; Raven, 'Naval organization', pp. 155–7.

7 In particular after 1617, see Thompson, *War and Government*, p. 275. Goodman, 'Armadas', pp. 70–3 on the continuing problems in arming and victualling Spanish warships.

8 Glete, *War and the State*, pp. 167, 172; Jones, *Anglo-Dutch Wars*, pp. 45, 56, 59–60.

9 Bruijn, *Dutch Navy*, p. 131; Raven, 'That expensive asset', p. 167. Many came from abroad. Jones, *Anglo-Dutch Wars*, p. 47, notes that Dutch sailors were paid more regularly than sailors in the English navy. Soldiers on board came from the army establishment; only after 1665 did a special navy regiment come into being that remained permanently in service; see also Diekerhoff, *Oorlogsvloot*, pp. 55, 59.

10 Glete, *War and the State*, pp. 52ff., 154, 167.

11 Lane, *Profits*, p. 81.

12 Rodger, 'Military revolution', p. 61; Bruijn, *Dutch Navy*, p. 44; Anderson, *War*, p. 57; Van Vliet, 'Staatse vloot', pp. 52, 54. In England the professionalization of the navy advanced much earlier than that of the army: Manning, *Apprenticeship*, p. 434; Bruijn, 'States', p. 83. On the efficiency of the convoys, see Van Tielhof, *Mother*, pp. 221, 226; Clark, *English Provincial Society*, pp. 119, 127.

13 Harding, *Seapower*, p. 61.

14 Van Vliet, *Vissers*, p. 251; De Jong, *Staat*, pp. 109, 113, 117–21.

15 De Jong, *Staat*, pp. 140, 149. On the importance of protection costs in trade being taken care of by governments, see Lane, *Profits*. Towns provided ordnance support to the companies too, sometimes guaranteed by the States-General.

16 Snapper, *Oorlogsinvloeden*, p. 61; De Jong, *Staat*, p. 115. The fortress was handed over to the WIC in 1623.

17 Davids, *Rise*, pp. 184–5; Van Beylen, *Schepen*, p. 30; Kleij, 'Scheepsbouw', pp. 10–14; De Vries and Van der Woude, *First Modern Economy*, p. 297. Building ships for the enemy was not allowed, but the impediments could be avoided, for example by using the Hamburg-route; Enthoven, *Zeeland*, p. 224; Jones, *Anglo-Dutch Wars*, p. 52.

18 Based on the estimation that around thirty men were needed to build a warship; see Strubbe, *Oorlogsscheepsbouw*, pp. 74–5. In that respect the wharves were quite large establishments, since on average most other workshops employed no more than 5 employees.

19 Brandon, *Masters of war*, p. 170; Bruijn, *Admiraliteit*.

20 Anderson, *War*, p. 142; Bruijn, 'States', p. 86; Jones, *Anglo-Dutch Wars*, pp. 60–2; Nef, *War and Human Progress*, p. 209.

21 Snapper, *Oorlogsinvloeden*, p. 50; Roodhuyzen, *Admiraliteit*, pp. 10–12.

22 Glete, *Navies*, p. 157; De Vries and Van der Woude, *First Modern Economy*, p. 297.

23 De Jong, *Staat*, p. 65. At the time of the Armada of 1588, the English galleons measured some one hundred to three hundred tons, those of the Spanish eight hundred to thousand tons. Their cannons, though, were not that effective as yet: the shot of the English was too light to do much damage, the one from the Spanish too inaccurate. Hale, 'Armies', pp. 203–4.

24 De Jong, *Staat*, pp. 66–8; Davids, *Rise*, p. 412; Elias, *Vlootbouw*, pp. 17–18; Sicking, 'Naval warfare', pp. 250–3, 258; Van Vliet, 'Foundation', p. 165.

25 Parker, *Military Revolution*, p. 99; Bruijn, 'Mercurius'. Goodman, *Spanish Naval Power*, p. 257, on the slow adaptation by the Spanish with regard to new tactics in sea warfare.

26 Elias, *Vlootbouw*, pp. 72–3; Glete, *War and the State*, p. 170. The campaign for Brazil failed, though: Den Heijer, *Geschiedenis van de WIC*, pp. 51–2.
27 Glete, *War and the State*, pp. 88, 107, 115–18.
28 Sicking, 'Naval warfare', pp. 257–9; Bruijn, *Dutch Navy*, pp. 73–4; Hart, 'Scheepsbouw', p. 76. On the advantage of these Dutch tactics: Jones, *Anglo-Dutch Wars*, pp. 18–21, 42, 52; Glete, *Navies*, p. 199. Figures given in table 6.3 differ from the ones in the text since the table excludes smaller warships.
29 Otte, 'Zeeuwsche zeezaken', p. 123; Strubbe, *Oorlogsscheepsbouw*, p. 72; De Vries and Van der Woude, *First Modern Economy*, pp. 144, 614.
30 Kernkamp, *Handel*, pp. 20, 40, 45.
31 Van Vliet, 'Staatse vloot', p. 49; Stols, *Spaanse Brabanders*, I, p. 18.
32 Kernkamp, *Handel*, pp. 32, 105, 127, 137, 140, 204.
33 Decavele, 'Willem van Oranje', p. 85; Tracy, *Founding*, p. 271.
34 Holthuis, *Frontierstad*, pp. 58–9.
35 Van Vliet, *Vissers*, p. 256.
36 Klein, *Trippen*, pp. 201–2; Stols, *Spaanse Brabanders*, I, pp. 43–6; De Graaf, *Oorlog*, pp. 197, 241, 481.
37 Pepper, 'Aspects', p. 198, on the 'small war' at sea.
38 Stradling, *Armada*, p. 12. See also Goodman, *Spanish Naval Power*, p. 122.
39 De Vries and Van der Woude, *First Modern Economy*, 404; totalling the losses to Dunkirk privateering from the late 1620s to the mid-1640s. See also Stradling, 'Spanish Dunkirkers', p. 555.
40 Snapper, *Oorlogsinvloeden*, pp. 105, 110; Van Vliet, 'Foundation', pp. 161, 169; Van Vliet, *Vissers*, pp. 27, 130–1, 202–5, 246; Clark, *English Provincial Society*, p. 108; Stradling, *Armada*, p. 218.
41 Ibid., pp. 217ff., 224–6; Van Peteghem, 'Vlaanderen', p. 339; Baetens, 'Organisatie', p. 119; Stols, *Spaanse Brabanders*, II, p. 187; Parrott, *Business of War*, pp. 245–6.
42 Parker, 'Spain', p. 199; on the figures (a significant improvement on former estimates, which had always been far too high); Van Vliet, *Vissers*, pp. 34, 157; Willemsen, *Enkhuizen*, p. 55.
43 Van Bochove, 'Hollandse haringvisserij', p. 22; Van Vliet, *Vissers*, pp. 60–2.
44 Richards, *Unending Frontier*, p. 51; Bochove, 'Hollandse haringvisserij', pp. 13, 16; Van Vliet, *Vissers*, pp. 82–91, 150, 189–203.
45 Wijffels and Van Loo, 'Zealand privateering', p. 636; Van Loo, 'For freedom', pp. 180, 183, 192; Frijhoff and Spies, *Hard-Won Unity*, p. 29. The WIC also lost few vessels to enemy privateers in those years: Wätjen, *Holländische Kolonialreich*, p. 336 finds no more than five or six vessels lost to privateers during the 1630s and 1640s.
46 De Vries and Van der Woude, *First Modern Economy*, pp. 403–4, 490; Snapper, *Oorlogsinvloeden*, pp. 75, 111.
47 Van Tielhof, *Mother*, pp. 213ff., 221; Lane, 'Family partnerships'; Israel, *Dutch Primacy*, p. 136; Snapper, *Oorlogsinvloeden*, p. 96. On insurances in the southern Netherlands, see Stols, *Spaanse Brabanders*, II, pp. 315–19.
48 On ransoms for sailor hostages, see Van Deursen, *Kopergeld*, p. 94.
49 Rommelse, 'English privateering', pp. 28–9; Bruijn, 'Dutch privateering', p. 93; Rommelse, *Second Anglo-Dutch War*, pp. 125–6, 196; Jones, *Anglo-Dutch Wars*, pp. 29–30; Bruijn, *Dutch Navy*, p. 90; Snapper, *Oorlogsinvloeden*, pp. 127, 180, 289; Stradling, *Armada*, p. 220; Van Gelder, *Sailing Letters*, pp. 14–15.
50 Rommelse, 'Role of mercantilism', p. 609.
51 Gaastra, *Geschiedenis*, pp. 19–23.
52 Glamann, *Dutch-Asiatic Trade*, p. 7.
53 Glete, *War and the State*, p. 169.
54 Israel, *Dutch Primacy*, p. 103; Enthoven, *Zeeland*, pp. 201–7, 253.
55 Ibid., p. 211.

56 Gaastra and Bruijn, 'Dutch East India Company', pp. 179–80; Gaastra, *Geschiedenis*, p. 109; De Vries and Van der Woude, *First Modern Economy*, p. 392.

57 Ibid., p. 387; Gaastra, *Geschiedenis*, p. 124; Israel, *Dutch Primacy*, pp. 178–9, 187, 248, 251.

58 De Korte, *Jaarlijkse financiële verantwoording*, pp. 50–1; Chaudhuri, *Trade and Civilisation*, p. 90; Steensgaard, *Asian Trade Revolution*, pp. 95ff.; on saltpetre see also Glamann, *Dutch-Asiatic Trade*, p. 19.

59 Ibid., p. 14; Israel, *Dutch Primacy*, p. 249.

60 Ibid., pp. 254, 333–5. De Vries and Van der Woude, *First Modern Economy*, p. 457. Between 1640 and 1680, the value of VOC goods traded averaged eight to nine million guilders per year; in the period 1750–80 this figure stood at 18 to 21 million guilders. For over a century and a half the VOC constituted the most important European power in the Far East. Towards the end of the eighteenth century, however, the costs of protection simply outran the capacity of the company and the British navy-*cum*-EIC proved a superior device. Gaastra and Bruijn, 'Dutch East India Company', pp. 180–1, 205; Mann, *Sources of Social Power*, p. 481.

61 Gaastra, 'Sware continuerende lasten'; Israel, *Dutch Primacy*, pp. 175, 185–7, 245, 250; De Vries and Van der Woude, *First Modern Economy*, pp. 431–2.

62 Zandvliet, *Mapping for Money*, pp. 78–9, 84, 197; Jayasena, 'Katuwana', p. 142; Floore, 'Bouw', pp. 161–2; Bonke, 'Eiland Onrust', p. 49; Van Beek, 'Zout', p. 77; De Korte, *Jaarlijkse financiële verantwoording*, p. 50.

63 Watson, 'Fortifications', pp. 70ff.

64 Wätjen, *Holländische Kolonialreich*, p. 288; Den Heijer, *Geschiedenis van de WIC*, p. 33.

65 For a more negative view, see De Vries and Van der Woude, *First Modern Economy*, p. 466.

66 Den Heijer, *Goud, ivoor*, p. 70; Den Heijer, *Geschiedenis van de WIC*, pp. 73, 79–80, 96, 151.

67 Ibid., pp. 63, 65. It should be noted that during the war with France (1672–8), WIC losses to French privateers were considerable; ibid., p. 135.

68 Ibid., pp. 41–8, 53–4; Van Beek, 'Zout', p. 80; Israel, *Dutch Primacy*, p. 163.

69 Den Heijer, *Geschiedenis van de WIC*, pp. 88, 185.

70 Stols, *Spaanse Brabanders*, pp. 141–2.

71 De Vries and Van der Woude, *First Modern Economy*, pp. 458–9.

72 Kist, 'VOC op Oostenburg', pp. 29–30; Gaastra, 'Arbeid', p. 67; Gaastra, *Geschiedenis*, pp. 161, 163; De Korte, *Jaarlijkse financiële verantwoording*, pp. 16, 19; Glamann, *Dutch-Asiatic Trade*, p. 41; De Vries and Van der Woude, *First Modern Economy*, pp. 461–2, 643. Alongside these advantageous distributional effects, however, the VOC also intensified the divide between rich and poor. The dividends increasingly ended up in the hands of a small group of affluent families; see ibid., p. 464.

73 Glete, *War and the State*, p. 115. O'Brien, 'Nature and historical evolution', p. 438, shows how, similarly to the Dutch Republic, the British navy of the eighteenth century managed to preserve external security while protecting trade and safeguarding property rights for private investments, thus supporting economic development.

74 Contrary to the arguments of Israel, *Dutch Primacy*, p. 125.

7 Warfare and the strength of Dutch public finance

> I know very well, that the country is in urgent need of funds, and that warfare is
> very costly, but I know also, that costs as such are not opposed to making
> profits ... and even if the country has no money, it still has its credit, and the
> enemy has neither funds nor credit... .[1]

Previous chapters have shown how regularity of soldiers' pay reinforced the discipline and professionalization of Dutch military forces. Its importance can hardly be overestimated. Fiscal systems that enabled an efficient extraction of the necessary funds to pay troops regularly did not exist in early modern Europe. Income taxes as such still lay in the future, and the property registers which did exist were almost always seriously incomplete and hopelessly outdated.[2] The secrecy and inefficiency that characterized all financial administration eroded the willingness of wealthy individuals to pay their share, since in times of crisis they might be burdened with unforeseen war taxes or forced loans.

The absence of a regular tax system, however, did not preclude the bringing of an enormous army into the field. *Ad hoc* financial contributions, loans and donations together permitted the assembling of military forces. But maintaining an army in the field for a long period of time was a totally different matter. Military effectiveness was repeatedly weakened by defaulting governments.[3] The noted French statesman Cardinal Richelieu was clear on this point: 'History knows more armies ruined by want and disorder than by the efforts of their enemies'.[4] Mighty Spain raised enormous armies, but periodic defaults by the crown prevented its armed forces from maintaining pressure on the Dutch and French. Mutinies were part of the standard repertoire of the Army of Flanders during much of the sixteenth and early seventeenth centuries.[5]

The cumulative impact of prolonged warfare increased the danger of arbitrary and unsystematic exactions by the state. In exchange for emergency loans, creditors demanded high rates of interests; in return for a rapid transfer of the tax funds, tax farmers demanded increasing autonomy. Such demands inevitably increased the burden upon state finances, and not least in the future. When no funds were to be had from taxes or loans, rulers resorted to mint manipulation and debasement. Such policies hindered the accumulation of capital by financiers large and small and weakened confidence in economic transfers in general.[6]

Regular ordinary taxation, on the other hand, might be burdensome too, yet scholars have pointed out the advantages of standarized and predictable burdens. Early modern taxation contributed to the monetization of the economy and rationalization of state administration. Regular taxes permitted the rise of a secured public debt since they provided the funds needed for interest payments, while the increased tax burden is said to have brought underutilized land resources into cultivation.[7]

Chapter 2 demonstrated how towns in Holland had time and again survived the severe financial pressures of the early decades of the Revolt. Throughout the Eighty Years War the urban-based maritime economy proved a cushion that could absorb much of the high cost of war. Of course, fiscal strength and resilience had behind an advanced and commercialized economy. But in view of the fact that rich societies elsewhere operated with much less financial efficiency in times of war – and sometimes none at all – the strength of Holland's financial system should by no means be taken for granted. The province contained around 40 per cent of the Republic's population but paid approximately 60 per cent of the cost of war.

How it was that a decentralized polity like the Dutch Republic managed to coordinate the financing of a war against the most powerful monarchy of the age is explained in this chapter. In Holland, public loans were supported by regular taxation, over and above excise duties. The innovations in financial administration of this particular province had its roots in the early sixteenth century, as will be explained. The war caused a rapid increase in taxation. How and why the Dutch accepted a new and heavy tax burden, while they had been prepared to fight Alva for much lower duties (the imposition of the 'tenth' penny, see Chapter 1) will be discussed. A number of Holland's financial institutions were copied by the other northern provinces, but after 1648 the powerful 'moral economy' that had accepted such a large financial burden (the Dutch were the most heavily taxed people in Europe) started to show some serious cracks. Yet the mechanisms of war finance continued to function. This can be explained at least in part by the fact that wartime expenditures brought about a certain redistribution of the wealth, which stimulated economic demand across a broad societal base and so fuelled a constant expansion of the economy.

Sources of Holland's financial power

Friends and foes alike admired the strength of Dutch public credit. William Temple, a former English ambassador to the northern Netherlands, wrote in the early 1670s:

> Besides the debt of the Generality, the province of Holland owes about sixty-five million, for which they pay interest at four in the hundred; but

with so great ease and exactness, both in principal and interest, than no man ever demands it twice; they might take up whatever money they desired.[8]

To explain the 'ease and exactness' of the financial administration of Holland, though not of any other province of the Low Countries, it is necessary to go back to the early decades of the sixteenth century. Under the rule of Charles V the province had been forced to develop a strong provincial government. In the regular meetings of the Provincial States, convened at the request of the ruler with the aim of funding his incessant costly wars, the Holland towns had learned to cooperate closely in the collection and administration of provincial taxes and loans.

Such meetings of the Provincial States only became well developed in the larger provinces of the maritime core of the western Low Countries that had been part of the Burgundian territories in the earlier fifteenth century – that is to say, Flanders, Brabant and Holland. In contrast to Holland, the southern provinces failed to develop a coherent financial administration at the provincial level. Good governance was difficult because of the numerous layers involved in decision making. Guilds and other corporate institutions held voting rights within urban governments. The clergy continued to be taxed separately and the major towns jealously guarded their particular (tax) privileges over their rural districts. Cooperation between towns was hampered since the major cities were engaged in long-standing inter-city rivalries, with Ghent pitted against Bruges, Bruges against Antwerp, Louvain against Brussels, and so on. Louvain chose to support the nobility in trying to curb Brussels' influence, for example, exactly because of such rivalries. The traditional privileges and exemptions of the nobility, clergy, larger cities and urban officials caused the tax burden per head of the population to be substantially lower than in Holland. At the same time these exemptions pushed up the size of the burden on those who did pay.[9]

While Ghent in the south showed an ambition to rule over Flanders and even replace Brussels as the centre of government, in Holland the political relationships were quite different. Urban institutions had a shorter history and corporate privileges were less articulated and important. In most towns guilds were unrepresented in urban government; towns were usually controlled by a single oligarchic body of burgomasters and aldermen supported by the *vroedschap*, a council of former burgomasters and aldermen. Election to this body was by co-option. Urbanization was more recent, and instead of being dominated by a few large cities – as was the case in the south – Holland contained a larger number of medium-sized towns that more or less balanced each other. Urban rivalry was by no means absent, but politics were dominated by shifting urban coalitions, with towns choosing and changing sides for *ad hoc* reasons, not because of membership of a rigid bloc. Amsterdam, though much smaller than Antwerp, Ghent or Brussels, soon became the largest town in the province, yet its trading interests also served other urban communities in the region. The nobility was much weaker than in the southern Netherlands; no extended landholding was possible; no powerful court was nearby. Because the clergy held no political power in the Provincial States, the nobles had no 'natural' ally in the struggle with urban interests. The Holland nobility, therefore, tended to vote along with the towns, which rendered the provincial government rather transparent and effective, promoting the collective interests of the whole urban community.[10]

In the early 1540s, in both the north and the south, Charles V had granted substantial autonomy to the provinces in order to regulate their finances. In the south this autonomy did not result in the centralization of provincial financial administration. Flemish and Brabantine taxes and loans continued to be managed by a traditional mixture of corporate, urban and district institutions, in which privileges and tax exemptions held sway. Cities continued to rule over their own rural hinterland. Since the incidence of the fiscal burden was highly uneven, resource extraction was not as flexible as in Holland.

The patchy financial system of the southern provinces had revealed its limitations in the later 1540s, when the numerous provincial loans had not been adequately supported by regular taxation. The damage to provincial credit hampered the raising of loans in subsequent decades. In contrast, Holland managed to fund borrowing without any major difficulty, at least up to 1572. The loans were supported by ordinary revenues. For the payment of interest, the six larger voting towns (Dordrecht, Haarlem, Delft, Leiden, Amsterdam and Gouda) acted collectively as security guarantors of their highly productive urban excises.[11] In the 1540s, new provincial excises strengthened the fiscal base. A great number of large and small domestic investors readily purchased these provincial bonds, trusting in the management of provincial officials and the support of the larger towns.

By the 1550s the final remnants of forced loans were abolished in Holland. Henceforth, voluntary provincial loans supported by provincial excises and administered by the major towns gave provincial government a powerful and flexible base. Scholars have called this development in public finance a 'financial revolution'; during wartime it enabled an extremely efficient extraction of funds. Perhaps paradoxically – in view of the strong opposition to the 'tenth penny' and the subsequent outcome of the war (in which the north became independent) – Alva experienced less difficulty extracting funds from Holland than from the southern provinces due to Holland's earlier familiarity with organized central taxation.[12]

The years 1572–5, however, were a period of severe financial crisis. Amsterdam remained loyal to Spain; Haarlem was conquered and Leiden besieged by its armies; numerous important financiers fled the country; trade was disrupted, not least because of strategic flooding; uncertainty and insecurity caused by mutinous soldiers and political crises hampered the raising of provincial loans. The payment of interest on funded provincial annuities was halted (essentially a bankruptcy) and the provincial authorities decided to reinstate the system of forced loans. Even the currency was debased; coins were only valid with a stamp of the province, which increased their value by 10 to 15 per cent.[13]

Despite these difficulties Holland's earlier financial revolution seems to have left a strong legacy. Data regarding provincial finances for this period are scarce and not always reliable, but during 1572–5 Holland probably raised 929,000 guilders from taxes, as well as at least 1,030,000 guilders from the *repartitiën*, a system dating from the early sixteenth century in which necessary public loans were divided between towns in proportion to the revenue of their property taxes.[14] In July 1572, moreover, in addition to these funds, 13 Holland towns agreed to grant Orange a massive loan of half a million guilders, which was badly needed to finance his campaign against Mons. The towns declared they would stand security collectively, exactly as in earlier decades. On this occasion smaller towns were involved too, not just the larger cities.[15] Orange's military commanders and their creditors only accepted this simple piece of paper because of Holland's historical reputation for reliability where loans were concerned.

Although the years 1572–5 were extremely difficult, inter-city solidarity held firm. Chapter 4 has described how provincial excise revenues collected in the Holland towns of Rotterdam and Dordrecht supported the pay of Holland's Gorinchem garrison. The taxes that had been imposed during Charles V's reign were increased and their range significantly expanded. These 'general means' (mainly excises on consumer goods) yielded 71,000 guilders in 1572; in 1575 they raised 540,000; by 1585 the total was one million guilders; by 1625, six million guilders.[16] Part of these tax increases were spent in the towns in which they were collected, to finance the troops. Although this might look like fiscal decentralization, it was not: the management of the funds was coordinated and ultimately decided upon by the central authorities of the province.[17] The cooperation by a large number of urban communities in the Provincial States signified the extent of efficient centralization, alongside the decentralized dispersal of some revenue.

Holland's finances thus improved due to the remarkable increase in taxes imposed, but also because the earlier financial revolution had created trust in the system of public loans and in public administration in general.[18] After 1584 Amsterdam once again sold voluntary loans for the province on a large scale. By 1594 voluntary provincial loans were issued in other Holland towns too. Within two decades the financial problems of the early 1570s had been solved.[19] Until 1585, moreover, part of the rebels' financial support was coming from the south, often from *ad hoc* borrowing in Antwerp, although the backing of such loans was weak. Debt servicing was cumbersome and made investors hesitate, remembering the failure of the Flemish and Brabantine provincial loans of the 1540s. There was no provincial tax structure in Brabant that could be transformed to raise the sums needed to meet the swelling burden of wartime interest payments. In Flanders and Brabant the raising of provincial taxes lagged significantly behind what could be achieved in Holland. New taxes were levied in revolutionary Ghent in the later 1570s, but these were not provincial levies: they were destined only for Ghent.[20]

The role of small and medium-sized towns in Holland and their willingness to cooperate in the common provincial effort was thus key to explaining the performance of the province and the rapid restoration of public credit.[21] In the south the smaller towns had lost their political rights in the fifteenth and (early) sixteenth centuries because of the way large cities were able to dominate the countryside. Towns in Holland did not dominate their rural districts; the distance between medium-sized towns was simply too small to allow a rural district to be demarcated as belonging to a particular town.[22] In the sixteenth century small Holland towns still had the right to participate in the Provincial States, alongside the traditional six.[23] In 1572, some of the initial revolutionary fervour came from small towns such as Brill and Enkhuizen (see Chapter 1). The network of small and medium-sized towns meant that Holland's urban communities could be readily mobilized in opposition to Spain. At the time of Amsterdam's decision to support the Revolt (1578), no fewer than 18 Holland towns had the right to vote in the Provincial States, leaving only one vote for the nobility, many of whom were also loyal to the common cause.

Decision-making in Holland could be cumbersome at times, involving numerous urban centres and shifting coalitions, but provincial decisions ultimately reflected a broad political base. The new Provincial States of July 1572 had also assumed sovereign powers, taking on competencies that actually belonged to their overlord, the Spanish King; these included the election of a new stadholder (William of Orange), the subordination of supra-provincial institutions (the Court of Holland as court of appeal and the Chamber of Accounts as financial control mechanism), the confiscation of émigré and church property, and the signing of treaties with England and France.[24] In fact, the progressive administrative and financial structures that had been developed under Charles V and Philip II proved surprisingly adequate for revolutionary ends as well.[25]

Other provinces in the northern Netherlands, acquired more recently by Burgundian or Habsburg rulers, had not been pushed to develop a comparable administration. Neighbouring Zeeland, though, had been part of Burgundian core territory since the early fifteenth century. However, decision-making in this small province was strongly dominated by the *Eerste Edele*, the 'Fist Noble', in the Provincial States, who represented the gentry but also the king. The impact of urbanization was also far more uneven; Middelburg was much larger than other Zeeland towns. As long as it sided with the king (as it did up to 1576) it was virtually impossible to hold an independent Provincial States. But Zeeland soon copied several of Holland's successful fiscal institutions and increased its taxes in a similar manner.[26]

Tax increases in the other provinces, by comparison, lagged greatly behind. But even there the tax burden became substantially higher than before the war. In a town like Doesburg (Gelderland), no regular provincial taxation at all had been collected before 1572. In 1583, after being overwhelmed by the huge cost of garrisons, the Doesburg authorities saw the advantages of the new 'general means' and decided to vote for excises on condition that 50 per cent of the yield could be used to pay the local garrison. The imposition of the new duties strengthened the provincial tier of government; in addition, the administration became more active, while the imposition of taxes became more efficient. Gelderland also began to participate regularly in the meetings of the States-General. In the 1620s and 1630s the last remnants of tax privileges for the nobles were abolished. Henceforth the tax system resembled Holland's, although the rates remained lower. Towns were allowed one-fifth of the revenue raised by the excises, to be used to compensate households providing accommodation for soldiers and pay the expenses of the local militia.[27] This gradual acceptance of new taxes furthered the transition towards more efficient financial administrations throughout the Republic.

War budgets and the mobilization of funds

While Holland's provincial finances could draw on experiences from before the war, the newly unified provinces of the Union of Utrecht of 1579 could not. The statesman Van Oldenbarnevelt should be credited with the successful organization of central infrastructures at Generality and Union level. The expenditure for the fighting rose from 1.5 million guilders in the early decades to over twenty million guilders in the final phase of the Eighty Years War. The bulk of the funds were used to pay the military (see Table 7.1; see also Chapter 4).

These expenditures were met by revenues from various sources, as can be seen in Table 7.2. The funds for the navy came mainly from customs revenue, while part of the costs for administration and the servicing of debts was covered by central revenues and taxation levied upon Generality lands.[28]

The federal structure of the Republic ensured that central revenues were limited. They consisted of a salt tax, fees for passports and safeguards, along with the Generality stamp duty. Generality lands (the conquered areas in Flanders, Brabant, and Westerwolde) yielded some 5 per cent of the revenues, mostly from taxes and contributions. The provincial admiralties collected the customs, which yielded around 12 per cent of the total. But the bulk of the revenues (almost 82 per cent) had to come from the provinces. They had to provide the funds for the most expensive part of the war budget, the army and fortifications, plus sums for the navy, administration and servicing of debts. As can be calculated from the totals in Tables 7.1. and 7.2, the ordinary

Table 7.1 Reconstructed annual budget of expenses of the United Provinces (*c.*1641), in percentages

Army	51.5
Navy	26.0
Fortifications	8.7
Administration	5.6
Debt service	4.4
Miscellaneous (including pensions)	3.8
Total (23.7 million guilders)	100.0

Sources: 't Hart, *In Quest*, pp. 43, 51; 't Hart, *Making*, p. 62

Table 7.2 Reconstructed annual budget of revenues of the United Provinces (*c.*1641), in percentages

Central revenues	0.8
Taxes: Generality lands	5.2
Customs	12.2
Provincial taxes	81.8
Total (22.6 million guilders)	100.0

Source: 't Hart, *Making*, p. 86

revenues fell short by some 1.1 million guilders; public loans had to make up this deficit.

The provinces remained fiscally autonomous. Each year the Council of State calculated essential war expenditure, the *Staat van Oorlog*, to be approved by the provincial deputies in the States-General. After approval each province was allotted a certain portion, which in the later 1580s became a fixed distribution. Holland was responsible for by far the largest part (58 per cent), Friesland came next with 12 per cent, Zeeland paid 9 per cent, and so forth, down to the smallest contribution by Drenthe of 1 per cent.[29] The Chamber of Accounts in The Hague registered the payments of the provinces. Not all funds came in as quickly as desired; in case of emergency the Receiver General of the Union raised loans that were ultimately guaranteed by Holland's powerful credit. In addition, the States-Provincial of Holland and the Council of State kept some secret funds that could be employed when needed.[30]

Voting in the States-General was made easier by the division between ordinary and extraordinary war expenditure. The ordinary budgets remained more or less the same, year in, year out; they provided the bulk of the funds and were approved with little discussion. Extraordinary war budgets were proposed for specific campaigns, fortifications, ordnance, or additional support for the navy. When the expenses recurred over extended periods they could be transferred to the ordinary war budget. Thanks to the influence of Van Oldenbarnevelt, the established ordinary budget became customary in the 1590s and considerably facilitated the mobilization of funds for the war.[31]

The straightforward way in which funds for the army were raised contrasted sharply with war funding in the southern Netherlands. This can be illustrated by looking at the raising of funds during the 's-Hertogenbosch siege of 1629 (see also Chapters 1 and 3). Although the rate of economic growth in the southern Netherlands had slackened, the country remained one of the wealthiest parts of Europe. But the Brussels government could not extract more than 10 per cent of its wartime expenses from this area, the remainder had to be supplied by Spain and its overseas territories; these were an important source of wealth, especially their precious metals. In 1629 the Spanish king prioritized the Mantua crisis over the war in the Low Countries, creating immense problems for Brussels' finances. The problem was exacerbated by the Dutch capture of the Spanish-American silver fleet in 1628, which hurt the financing of the Spanish loans needed to bridge the gap between expenditure and collection of funds (see also below).[32]

A kind of division of taxation existed in the south too, but no standard ordinary budget facilitated provincial consent. All sums required complicated deliberations. Wealthy Flanders usually provided a third of the amount demanded in taxation, Brabant somewhat less, while the other provinces raised significantly smaller amounts. But the periodically inadequate or delayed pay of soldiers caused disturbances, notably in 's-Hertogenbosch, and rumours of mutinies impeded the willingness of urban authorities to comply with the demands from Brussels. New tax proposals intensified the considerable discontent regarding the huge exemptions enjoyed by the nobility and clergy, who owned perhaps half the land. Representatives of the guilds in Antwerp justified their refusal to consent by pointing to the disastrous consequences of the trade ban that had shut off commerce with the enemy (see Chapter 6); no less than two-thirds of the sailors had abandoned the Antwerp merchant fleet. Instead of agreeing to additional taxes, they suggested opening up trade with the enemy again, as that would undoubtedly mean rich rewards from extraordinary custom duties (*licenten*). The trade ban was also detrimental for the provisioning of the army, since no supplies were to be had from the north.[33]

But the trade ban was not lifted. Only after long and difficult deliberations, during which it was agreed that some provinces could spend a substantial portion of the funds raised for local military purposes, together with voting manipulations that circumvented the negative response of the guilds, did the provinces concede. Even then the sums raised were insufficient and a myriad of additional measures were necessary. An impressive range of initiatives were attempted to support the war effort financially, underlining the extent of support for the struggle with Spain. A fundraising campaign was launched, resulting in loans from the Brabant church and nobility (100,000 guilders), the Council of Mechelen (50,000 guilders) and the chancellery of Brabant (400,000 guilders). The chancellor of Brabant himself went to great pains to sell some of his furniture and personally borrowed funds that he transferred to the government; the county of Mons financed an infantry company; and various monasteries and wealthy individual burghers provided additional loans. Furthermore, the government imposed forced loans on the high nobility and the officers of central government and church institutions.[34] The difference in economic conditions between the southern and the northern provinces was important here. An English nobleman Sir John Suckling, acting initially as a volunteer in the defence of 's-Hertogenbosch and then travelling through the Low Countries, wrote that the south was considerably poorer than the north, for in the south 'the private purses are drawne dry, there [in the north] onely the publique'.[35]

Brussel's fundraising campaign of 1629 was impressive, but the fact that those funds were raised not through regular taxation but by various extraordinary means revealed that the wealthier classes in the south were actually undertaxed. War finance in the south thus retained a much more *ad hoc* character, which was difficult to sustain year after year. The contrast was clear. In the north, Holland alone mobilized 8.8 million guilders from regular taxation that year, together with 3.2 million in loans.[36] Both sides had to support enormous financial burdens to sustain the war, but in the north there was much greater willingness to pay taxes and invest in loans, with the result that necessary funds were more easily raised.

Taxation: burden and compliance

Since the provinces remained fiscally autonomous, the tax burden varied through the Dutch Republic. Excises yielded the bulk of the funds in highly urbanized provinces such as Holland, Zeeland and Utrecht; land taxes contributed significantly more in inland provinces such as Overijssel and Gelderland. Table 7.3 shows that the Holland excises were particularly important throughout the Eighty Years War, although they declined in relative terms after the conclusion of peace in 1648.

Until the late 1640s new duties were added to the already existing taxes on beer, wine, spirits, peat, flour, meat, fish, woollen goods, salt, oils, vinegar, coal, candles, wood, soap, bricks and other items; new taxes were introduced, for instance on wagons, the keeping of servants and tobacco. The wide range of options – to levy a duty here or raise a tax there – contributed to the flexibility of the provincial administration. After the resumption of war in 1621, extraordinary taxes on property were also rapidly increased to 0.1 per cent, 0.2 per cent or 0.5 per cent of the value of the property of 'half capitalists' (owning 1,000–2,000 guilders) and 'whole capitalists' (owning 2,000 guilders or more). A stamp duty on legal documents was introduced in 1624. Ordinary land and house taxes rose as well; after 1632, houses were assessed at 12.5 per cent of their rental value, up from 8.3 per cent: an increase of 50 per cent. In particularly difficult years, land and house taxes were levied more than annually: sometimes twice and even four times. The extraordinary duties on property rose considerably in 1665–7, during the Second Anglo-Dutch War, but they increased

Table 7.3 Tax revenues of Holland in categories, 1578–1680, in percentages of the total

	1578–85	1621–30	1671–80
'General means' (mainly excises)*	65.4	69.5	51.6
Land and house taxes	24.9	21.0	18.3
Extraordinary property levies, transfer taxes** and other duties	9.7	9.5	30.1
Total	100.0	100.0	100.0
Per annum, in million guilders	1.4	8.7	17.1

Source: Liesker and Fritschy, *Gewestelijke financiën*, pp. 160, 162
Notes: * proportion of excises in 'general means': 92 per cent in 1650, mainly beer, peat and flour; 11 per cent taxes on the keeping of servants, horses, cattle, ships
** A transfer tax is a tax on the passing of the title of property from one person to another

above all during the Third Anglo-Dutch War and the war with France in the 1670s. These duties were then imposed so regularly that they became part of the ordinary tax burden. Table 7.3 shows that these property taxes had become quite substantial.

The consequence was that the population of Holland became the most heavily taxed people in Europe. The burden per head in the province increased from 5 to 15 per cent of annual income between 1575 and 1630.[37] At the turn of the eighteenth century the Englishman Ellis Veryard wrote about the Dutch: 'Though the people boast of their Free State, I am confident no subjects in the world are more burdened with more taxes than they [are].'[38]

Why did the Dutch accept such a large tax burden? The first thing to say is that not all inhabitants did. Between 1600 and 1680 Holland witnessed at least thirty tax revolts.[39] Yet such disturbances were relatively common throughout early modern Europe. And in contrast to the large-scale revolts in neighbouring France, most of the Dutch uprisings were minor protests, limited in time and space. Thus, relatively speaking, tax compliance was indeed quite high.

The impressive growth of Holland's economy after about 1585 must have sweetened the pill, but it cannot explain the full extent of this compliance. Neither can it explain support for the levying of taxes in the early decades of the Revolt. The fact that urban elites supported the imposition of the duties and contributed their share is a significant part of the answer. Elsewhere in Europe tax revolts were spurred on by local elites taking sides with the insurgents, even providing leadership.[40] In Holland no fewer than 18 urban governments were represented in the Provincial States; they had thus been consulted beforehand and were able to influence the decision about the actual spending of the sums collected. This consultation in the Provincial States was vital for the high degree of tax compliance by urban elites and guaranteed the rapid suppression of any disturbance caused by the lower classes. The Englishman Fynes Moryson, who travelled through the Low Countries in the 1590s, observed:

> The Tributes, Taxes, and Customes, of all kinds imposed by mutuall consent, – so great is the love of liberty or freedome – are very burthensome, and they willingly beare them, though for much lesse exactions imposed by the King of Spaine – as they hold – contrary to right, and without consent of his Subjects, they had the boldnesse to make warre against a Prince of such great power.[41]

The 'mutuall consent' to impose higher duties also enhanced the power of the local authorities. Large sums were now transferred through their hands and their role as mediators increased; at times urban administrators were able to obtain priority for certain payments, for instance for householders providing accommodation for soldiers (above, Chapter 4) or local shippers transporting troops. Cooperation between local elites and the provincial government was extremely close. In Gorinchem, for example, captains of the militia, town councillors and burgomasters all participated in the collection of the land and house taxes. The involvement of leading citizens enhanced the efficient collection of the levies, not least among the upper classes.[42]

While land and house taxes were collected by the local administration, excises were as a rule farmed out. This might appear inefficient, but recourse to tax farming gave the authorities some certainty over revenues that could fluctuate sharply and relieved them of the cost and responsibility of collection. Excise farming thus augmented the public services provided by provincial and urban governments and even helped the poorest members of society, since a standard minor levy on farm contracts (a duty called 'rantsoengeld') helped fund local poor relief agencies.[43] Also, the rise of the new provincial debt relieved local communities of the traditional management of loans for the sovereign that continued to burden towns in the southern Netherlands. Holland towns had the option to contract further debts for specific local purposes, which gave them greater freedom in their financial management than was possible in the south.[44]

The fact that the majority of public funds came from excises is another reason why the tax burden caused relatively few disturbances. Additions to an existing excise were not apparent to the public; they usually resulted in higher prices, but the exact amount of taxation within the price was unknown. Furthermore, urban governments took care to distribute bread to the poorer classes in periods of high prices.[45] The risk of fiscal disturbances was also reduced because the tax-collecting agency was diversified and decentralized. In contrast to France, where in many provinces powerful *financiers* took on the management of numerous excises for a long period of time and over an extended area, Dutch tax farmers were men (and even, occasionally, women) of modest means. In Holland the excises were auctioned to the highest bidder two or three times a year; usually only one or a very few excises were sold off at any one time, and covering only one (part of the) town or district. Thus, each year as many as six to eight hundred tax farmers were responsible for collecting the Holland excises, all under individual contracts. The auctions were supervised by representatives of other towns in order to avoid local arrangements. This institutional arrangement prevented the formation of a wealthy group that might rouse the resentment of a large number of unhappy tax payers. Dutch tax revolts were usually aimed at just one of these minor tax farmers and therefore were restricted in time and space.[46]

Safety-valves: domestic investors and military solicitors

The high degree of compliance with taxation was reinforced by the fact that much of the money paid as taxes returned in some form of positive transfer to the taxpayers. Chapters 4 and 6 have already described how sums provided for items such as soldiers' pay, housing, provisions, the navy and fortifications often ended up in the communities that housed garrisons or had admiralty boards. This mechanism of economic transfer, by which military expenses were to a considerable extent immediately pumped back into the economy again,

Table 7.4 Expenditure of Holland in 1623, broken down into categories, expressed in percentages

Army		65.0
Pay for troops and salaries for officers	53.2	
Housing	5.7	
Transport and provisions	2.3	
Magazines, ordnance and ammunition	3.8	
Navy and WIC		3.0
Fortifications		4.0
Administration		7.9
Debt charges		16.2
Other (including pensions)		3.9
Total (10.4 million guilders)		100.0

Sources: Liesker and Fritschy, *Gewestelijke financiën*, p. 523; 't Hart, *Making*, p. 48

worked most notably in Holland, particularly with regard to expenses related to the management of the public debt.[47]

Table 7.4, which sets out the wartime expenditure of Holland in 1623, demonstrates this point.[48] The province spent most of its funds on the upkeep of the troops, but by that date the proportion of debt service charged was significantly larger for Holland than for any of the other provinces. This share was to increase steadily, rising as high as 50 per cent of the provincial budget later in the century.[49]

That scale of debt burden could be supported because of low interest rates. In the early decades of the Revolt these rates had been quite high, even on forced loans (12 per cent), because of the provincial government's financial problems. Many of those emergency loans were never repaid; the bondholders received interest year after year, while the bonds were eventually converted into regular provincial annuities giving lower returns. Merchants and troop captains accepted obligations on the part of the provincial government as payment; credit was obtained on the basis of such bonds.[50] By the 1590s, as has been noted, Holland bonds were once more being sold on a large scale; the rate of interest fell to 8 per cent in the 1580s and then to 6.25 per cent in the first decade of the seventeenth century. Thereafter the Dutch Republic enjoyed the advantage of cheap loans (see below), overwhelmingly voluntary in nature, in contrast to the earlier forced borrowing. Contrary to most other European countries, where the public purse relied on the credit of a limited number of merchant bankers, often powerful foreigners, loans in Holland depended on a wide range of domestic creditors. Government bonds were also traded on the market and usually made a good price there.[51]

Small-scale arrangements predominated; the high proportion of bonds of less than a hundred guilders enabled even people of modest means to invest. At a time when no savings banks existed, investment in a government-backed annuity was a useful way to save something for a rainy day or provide an income for a relative or friend. Loans of thousands of guilders also existed; these attracted the richer merchants and senior members of urban and provincial government. Bonds were issued by the different tax district receivers, making for a wide distribution of these highly desirable investments. Receivers prioritized interest payments over all other expenditure. The public auctions of the tax farms made potential investors aware of the money available to pay interest, which increased trust in government bonds. Urban institutions also profited from the opportunity to invest funds in secure loans. In Gorinchem about 9 per cent of the loans issued by the local receiver were held by institutions like the orphanage, the hospital and the old men's home. In this way the operations of war finance bolstered the services provided by the urban government.[52]

Investors thus came from all classes and groups of Holland society. The great variety of financial options for the provincial government – from taxes of all kinds to different sorts of bonds – founded on a substantial public able and willing to invest ensured a flexible system of war finance. Among its benefits, flexibility of this kind permitted the gradual conversion of bonds to bring down interest charges. The rate of interest declined further, first to 5 per cent in 1640 and then to 4 per cent in the 1650s. The lower rates allowed for an extension of the amounts contracted. By the time of the Truce, Holland's long-term debt stood at 17.5 million guilders; the resumption of war in 1621 brought about an enormous rise that peaked at 130 million guilders in 1652.[53] After 1648 the debt was reduced and contained, but the French attack in 1672 plunged Holland into another financial crisis and for a time brought about a return to forced loans. However, the crisis was brief and after the Peace of Nijmegen (1678) Holland engaged in a further round of reforms, which restored the efficiency of the financial system.[54]

Holland's credit system also inspired Sir George Downing, England's finance minister. In the 1660s he reformed English borrowing by assigning a specific tax to each new loan as support. These bonds were quite successful and enjoyed a high degree of confidence among investors. However, Downing's system defaulted in 1672 because of war preparations; Charles II arbitrarily suspended the payment of interest, damaging the property rights of creditors and bankers.[55] The English were obliged to wait till the 1690s, with a Dutch king on the throne, for a true financial revolution.[56] Meanwhile, although the Dutch were occasionally obliged to introduce forced loans, after the early 1570s they never had to violate creditor property rights.

Long-term provincial debt, with its roots deep in domestic society, thus constituted a major safety valve, able to provide for soldiers' pay in times of emergency. Loans oiled the wheels of warfare, not least because they were needed to plug the gap between expenditure required and taxes collected. Its importance cannot be gauged from the 4.4 per cent figure in Table 7.1 alone. This figure was to grow rapidly, becoming a burden that was disproportionally taken care of by Holland. By 1665, debt service amounted to half the expenditure in Holland's provincial budget.[57]

The actual transfer of funds to the army was supported by another shock absorber: regulated short-term credit by intermediaries. In the early decades of the Revolt the towns had advanced the weekly loans needed to pay the troops. Such arrangements were usually only applicable in garrisons, though, and in the field, as with all other European early modern armies, captains were expected to advance their own funds in order to prevent disorder due to irregular payment. After the early seventeenth century, States' companies employed military solicitors for this purpose. These semi-private financiers mobilized and advanced the necessary sums, took care of the actual transfer of the cash to the companies, and then collected the funds from the provincial tax receivers.[58] The position of the military solicitors was improved in 1622, when the Provincial States of Holland decided to reduce their risks by granting them preferential treatment among all other creditors of the company.[59] A contemporary noted the enormous advantage of this 'Agitatour':

> It is very observable in these *Provinces,* that though there be no Money in the Treasury, yet the Souldiers receive their pay every week or moneth; for every Regiment chooses an Agitatour, who resides near the *States* to sollicite the payment of those he represents; and when there is no Money in the publick Treasury, he may confidently, and does borrow and take up Money for the present necessity; and it is repaid him again with interest by the *States* order.[60]

The solicitors' interest rates fluctuated; they were usually higher than the current market rate, and rose when arrears accumulated, such as in the 1630s following the expensive campaigns of Frederick Henry.[61] Difficulties arose when captains chose solicitors with insufficient means to bridge financial gaps. This was a widespread problem during the crisis of 1672–3. To repair the safety valve of the military solicitors the Provincial States of Holland therefore took action. A reform programme was introduced that established limits to the interest rates charged (6 per cent) and required a solicitor guarantee of 5,000 guilders. The number of solicitors was also reduced.[62]

Other provinces copied these Holland arrangements to ensure regular payment, and in this way the Dutch found a solution to the problem of transferring monies to soldiers in a timely fashion, a problem that confronted all early modern armies. Elsewhere in Europe the intermediaries who carried out such tasks enjoyed much less backing; the risks they personally assumed were therefore much greater. Individuals carrying out the task of transferring sums to the troops – such as Barthélemy Hervart for companies in French pay during the Thirty Years War, or Hans de Witte for Wallenstein's army – were able to earn massive sums.[63] The Spanish army used *asientos*, after 1609 *anticipaciónes*, which were not very different from the loans provided by the Dutch military solicitors. Several private bankers were involved, at first Spanish and Italian, but increasingly merchants from the southern and even northern Netherlands too.[64] The principal difference to the service offered by Dutch military solicitors was the high rate of interest on the *anticipaciónes*, as much as 18 to 36 per cent, which constituted a significant additional burden for the Council of Finance in

Brussels. No regular taxation and no secure long-term public debt supported these short-term loans. As a result the troops often failed to receive their pay on time. The men of the Army of Flanders had every reason to complain; Etienne Rooms has calculated that they received as little as 32 per cent of their promised pay between 1660 and 1700.[65] Such failures obviously damaged the discipline and efficiency of the troops (see also Chapter 3).

Fault lines in tax compliance

The enormous financial burden of war obviously had an impact on Holland's economy. Military expenditure must have amounted to between 5 and 8 per cent of the province's gross annual income.[66] As was noted previously, much of this expenditure took place within the province itself. But after 1648 the war budget was reduced, and the positive redistribution effects apparent in Table 7.4 diminished accordingly. For example, the standard payment for housing soldiers was halved, while expenditure on wagons and barges decreased from 30,000 to 10,000 guilders.[67] The number of soldiers in the garrisons dropped; demand for local provisions fell correspondingly. Meanwhile, the pressing debt charges ensured that the tax burden itself hardly reduced. The 1650s and the 1670s both witnessed a significant series of revolts in which tax protests mingled with faction struggles and politically motivated riots.

The provincial government of Holland also wished to reduce the public debt, so opportunities to subscribe to new public loans diminished; it was predominantly only the strategically located elite (richer merchants and the ruling oligarchy) who invested in new bonds. Between 1652 and 1665 more than ten million guilders' worth of debt was repaid. The redistributive effect of debt servicing diminished and instead there was an accumulation of capital among the leading circles of the towns. Several studies demonstrate that about half of the urban oligarchs' assets usually consisted of government bonds. The significant accumulation of cash as a result of continuous interest payments in the hands of fewer and fewer people may have fuelled the explosive speculation on the financial market and real estate boom of the 1660s.[68] While the tax system above all burdened the lower classes (excises are by nature economically regressive), the financial system now increasingly entailed a hidden transfer from the poor to the rich.

Tax compliance had begun to show some minor cracks even during the Eighty Years War. With the conclusion of peace and the disappearance of the direct military threat, citizens gradually took longer to pay the taxation due on their lands, houses and other property. The direct involvement of the local authorities in the collection of the duties had decreased, although burgomasters still visited households to keep records up to date and surprise visits by the magistrates could follow in case of grave tax arrears.[69] The problems multiplied particularly after 1648. The situation in Gorinchem, the small Holland frontier town, can again serve as an example. During the 1650s, tax farmers experienced especial difficulties in this town. People called them names and threw stones, clods of earth, vegetable tubers and the like; the tax farmer of flour was even shot in the eye. The receiver of the land and house tax was accused of fraud; his house was pillaged. Difficulties in tax collection were exacerbated by increased political squabbling, which damaged the credibility and efficiency of the urban government. Even the local garrison became involved in the faction struggles. Only the arrival of troops sent by the provincial government could restore order. Harsh new measures were needed against the recalcitrant tax payers. From 1657 onwards the receiver could take the front door away in case of tax arrears; if payment did not follow within 24 hours, the furniture of the unwilling taxpayer would be sold in public.[70]

In the year 1672 the tax burden again rose suddenly. All kind of extraordinary taxes and forced loans were imposed during the emergency of the French invasion – in Gorinchem as in the rest of the province. The urban government was itself purged following the political changes that reinstated William III as stadholder (see Chapter 1). The new inexperienced local magistrates were unable to inspire taxpayers, however, and revenue came in exceptionally slowly. The receiver of taxes Van Ulft was suspected of fraud; this further lowered willingness to pay. In 1674 inhabitants smashed the windows of the farmer of the shoe tax, one of the novel new duties.[71] The military threat on its own had obviously not prompted greater compliance with taxation demands; the relationship between urban government and townspeople had deteriorated to such an extent that the whole financial system of Holland showed considerable cracks.

The situation was hardly better in other provinces; in places it was even worse. The Gelderland town of Doesburg was occupied by the French. Soldiers were billeted on the inhabitants, to be accommodated and fed for free; fires destroyed a large part of the town; the fortifications were demolished. Every three months the French required a monetary contribution of 4,500 guilders – 50 per cent more than the town's usual tax contribution in the 1660s – and made additional demands for beer and cattle. To raise the money the town issued loans in 1673, confiscated the houses of those who had fled, and the next year imposed a forced loan. But the funds did not come in as quickly as the French desired, and took hostages to enforce payment of the arrears. After the French left the area (early 1674) the situation hardly improved; debts were high; numerous well-to-do inhabitants had fled the town; tax farms were sold for significantly lower sums than hitherto (almost half); and throughout the 1670s further extraordinary taxes were imposed that could not be met, resulting in a new round of enforcement by the district authorities.[72]

Yet such difficulties in raising taxes were minor in comparison with most other European states. By and large the discipline of the Dutch army remained high because soldiers' pay continued to be guaranteed by the military solicitors, and the presence of troops did not in general entail a negative economic burden on society. In Spain expenditure on the war constituted a much more damaging drain since the discipline of soldiers in the garrisons was so poor. Castile provided the bulk of the funds, but around 20 per cent of the expenditure was sent to the Netherlands, never to return. Of the remaining 80 per cent, about half went to pay off (long-term) loans; but many of these *juros* were held by foreigners, not by Castilians. Only 4 to 5 per cent of the war expenditure was spent in Castile, the rest went to outlying regions (Aragon, Catalonia, Cantabria, and above all Galicia). Despite the fact that such expenditure stimulated the economy in the Spanish monarchy's more peripheral areas, these regions contributed little to the overall war effort.[73]

Conclusion: public finance and its positive distributional effects

The Dutch Wars of Independence were prolonged and costly, for both sides. But the Netherlands held one trump card: the financial power of Holland. In comparison with other regions in the Low Countries this province had the advantage of a precociously rational and efficient organization. Earlier in the sixteenth century its urban oligarchs had learned to cooperate; the provincial government advanced the collective interests of the towns. In connection with the already high degree of monetization and commercialization, such an environment rendered the extraction of resources much easier than anywhere else in early modern Europe, with the possible exception of a couple of city-states.[74] At the outbreak of the Revolt, Holland already had a financial system that levied regular duties on a great variety of items and enjoyed an established tradition of high public credit.

Of course, the northern Netherlands also suffered from financial crises and difficulties in paying the troops on time. But in comparison with Spain, England and France, such crises were relatively unimportant, thanks to the large number of financial options available and safety valves in the form of a wide range of domestic investors, to which the short-term credit of the military solicitors could be added.

The British state was the first to adopt Holland's innovative system of public debt, in the last decade of the seventeenth century.[75] The British even improved on Dutch methods, rendering the extraction of taxes and loans nationwide, while the Holland financial system remained within its provincial borders because of the fiscal autonomy enjoyed by other provinces. Spain's finances, meanwhile, moved in exactly the opposite direction; in the course of the seventeenth century increasing decentralization and privatization reduced the monarch's ability to tap the country's resources to the full.[76] Continuous warfare thus did not advance Spanish state formation but rather contributed to the weakening of government. The wearing down of Spain's fiscal strength also had a lot to do with the poor distributional impact of war expenditure: Castile contributed the bulk of military costs but received little economic benefit in return. This stood in sharp contrast to Holland.

Due to the efficient financial system, Dutch citizens were very willing to pay the taxes that reduced the threat of mutinies and plunder. The advantage of loans was obvious; they spread the military costs over a long period and at the same time ensured that the numerous investors in the bonds received income from the state, while the bonds could be traded on the market or used as collateral in transactions. This flexible financial structure secured the discipline of the troops, which in turn made possible bolder and more responsive deployment of the soldiers in the States' army. The impact of the Eighty Years War was thus by no means only negative. Most important of all, positive distributional effects served to strengthen the economy of Holland. The Dutch Wars of Independence also promoted the direct trading interests of the province, as will be described in the following chapter.

Notes

1 Dutch pamphlet *Treves-krack* (1630) quoted by 't Hart, *In Quest*, p. 112.
2 Howard, *War*, p. 38.
3 Landers, *Field*, pp. 305, 377.
4 Quoted by Jones, 'The Military Revolution', p. 155; see also Parrott, *Richelieu's Army*, p. 266, and Wood, *King's Army*, pp. 295, 304.
5 Parker, *Army*, pp. 116, 126–7. The bankruptcies of the Spanish Habsburgs started in 1557 and were repeated in 1560, 1575, 1596, 1607, 1627, 1647 and 1653. Drelichman and Voth, 'Serial defaults' and Drelichman and Voth, 'Sustainable debts', explain that not all defaults by the Spanish Habsburg government were necessarily disasters for investors, but their analysis focuses on a restricted time period only and on Spanish bankers and does not consider southern Netherlands investors such as the famous Fuggers, whose position was substantially weakened by the repeated financial crises. Neither do they explain the continual poor payment of the Army of Flanders.
6 Tallett, *War and Society*, p. 176; on the difficulties faced by territorial states trying to contract loans, see Stasavage, *States of Credit*, p. 34.
7 McNeill, *Pursuit of Power*, p. 74; Theibault, *German Villages*, p. 195; Thompson, *War and Society*, II, p. 5; III, p. 269.
8 Temple, *Observations*, p. 188.
9 The sums extracted from Flanders and Brabant were still substantial, though, due to the area's high degree of urbanization and commercialization. Blockmans, *Metropolen*, p. 542; Gunn, Grummit, and Cools, *War, State, and Society*, p. 173; 't Hart, 'Democratische paradox', pp. 377–81; Bos-Rops, *Graven*, pp. 248–54.
10 Lesger, *Handel*, p. 65; Tracy, *Holland*, p. 103. Only in Dordrecht did guilds exercise their privileges in urban government.
11 The system of collective support dated from the later fifteenth century, see Zuijderduijn, *Medieval Capital Markets*, p. 181. On the tax differences between north and south, see also Swart, 'Field of finance', p. 1054.
12 Tracy, *Financial Revolution*, pp. 1–2; 't Hart, 'Democratische paradox', p. 382. The term 'financial revolution' is borrowed from Peter Dickson's work on the financial institutions of early eighteenth century England. It indicates, first, the establishment of a centralized responsibility regarding the guaranteeing of public loans; second, funded debt, for which regular tax funds are necessary to pay interest charges; and third, a system of largely voluntary loans within a broader financial market, instead of the forced loans that prevailed in much of Europe at that time.
13 Van Gelder, *Nederlandse munten*, p. 78; Vermeesch, *Oorlog*, p. 55. Forced loans were imposed upon certain groups of investors – for example, government officials, urban authorities, particular guilds and ecclesiastical institutions.
14 Liesker and Fritschy, *Gewestelijke financiën*, p. 160; Tracy, *Founding*, pp. 105, 263; Hibben, *Gouda*, p. 161. The *repartitiën* might be levied as voluntary or forced loans, depending on the discretion of the individual towns.
15 Tracy, *Founding*, p. 85.
16 Fritschy, 'Financial revolution', p. 83.

17 Contrary to Tracy, *Founding*, pp. 261ff., who stresses financial devolution (instead of financial revolution) because of the increased power with respect to finances of the urban authorities and the decline of provincial authority during the period 1572–90. While towns used much of the provincial tax funds for local expenses, coordination remained strongly in the hands of the province.

18 Fritschy, 'Financial revolution', introduces the term 'tax revolution', which rightly points to the notable stepping up of taxes. But her suggestion that one should discard the notion of 'financial revolution' in these decades is beside the point. War expenditure is rarely paid out of current taxation; numerous loans are needed to bridge the gap between the imposition of taxes and their actual collection and transfer to the troops. Her analysis is based on the tables of Liesker and Fritschy, *Gewestelijke financiën*, p. 160; see also Figure 2, Fritschy, 'Financial revolution', p. 66. But those tables only include bonds not directly backed up by taxes (see Liesker and Fritschy, *Gewestelijke belastingen*, pp. 180–1, for an explanation of this omission), which thus underestimate the role of loans in the 1570s and 1580s; the figures for loans in the first decades are calculated by extracting tax revenues from expenses. The reason for this misrepresentation is a lack of sources, but there is evidence that more loans were levied than is suggested by Fritschy's tables; see also Vermeesch, *Oorlog*, p. 59; Tracy, *Founding*, p. 251; and Van der Heijden, *Geldschieters*, p. 278.

19 Van der Burg and 't Hart, 'Renteniers', p. 214.

20 't Hart, 'Democratische paradox', p. 386; Swart, 'Field of finance', p. 1062.

21 See also Prak and Van Zanden, 'Towards an economic interpretation', p. 140.

22 Dordrecht's dominance over the surrounding countryside reflected to some extent the situation in the south. Dordrecht was able to carve out some particular political and financial privileges for its hinterland, but these were limited and exceptional.

23 The 'traditional six' (Dordrecht, Leiden, Haarlem, Delft, Amsterdam, Gouda) were always present at the meetings, but smaller towns maintained the right to appear and be heard.

24 Tracy, *Founding*, p. 109; Koopmans, *Staten*, pp. 122, 144.

25 't Hart, 'Democratische paradox', p. 363. Both Zagorin, *Rebels*, and Tracy, *Founding*, rightly stress the provincial character of the Dutch Revolt.

26 Lemmink, *Ontstaan van de Staten*, pp. 131, 139, 146–7.

27 See Chapter 4; Vermeesch, *Oorlog*, pp. 82, 85–6, 153–6.

28 Administration costs remained quite low throughout the time of the Republic, see Van Deursen, 'Raad van State', p. 61.

29 See 't Hart, *Making*, p. 80, on the exact amounts and temporary changes.

30 For example, the one million guilders secret fund in 1629, De Cauwer, *Tranen*, p. 151.

31 Israel, *Dutch Republic*, pp. 234, 291–2.

32 Enthoven, 'Oorlog', p. 66; De Cauwer, *Tranen*, p. 44. The capture of the silver fleet facilitated the raising of funds in the north by enabling the States-Provincial of Holland to borrow funds from the West India Company. Vermeir notes the sharp fall in revenues from Spain in the 1640s; the contributions of Flanders and Brabant increased and, after 1645, remained higher than the contribution from the Crown. See Vermeir, *In staat*, pp. 256, 282, 332.

33 De Cauwer, *Tranen*, pp. 45–6.

34 Ibid., pp. 153–65.

35 Quoted by ibid., p. 166.

36 Liesker and Fritschy, *Gewestelijke financiën*, p. 162.

37 Fritschy, 'Financial revolution', pp. 72–3; De Vries and Van der Woude, *First Modern Economy*, p. 109. Scholars have used the high tax burden of Holland as an explanation for slow industrialization in the eighteenth century, see Wilson, *Economic History*, pp. 114–27, and Mokyr, *Industrialization*. This view has been refuted, however, by Van Zanden and Van Riel, *Strictures*, p. 9.

38 Quoted by Van Strien, *British Travellers in Holland*, p. 137.
39 Dekker, *Holland*, pp. 28, 177; Van Deursen, *Kopergeld*, p. 61. The number of riots is different from Van Zanden and Prak, 'Towards an economic interpretation', p. 131: they count only 24 tax riots between 1600 and 1795, but obviously failed to consult the list in Dekker's Appendix.
40 Zagorin, *Rebels*, I, pp. 126, 247–9, 215–20; Te Brake, *Shaping History*, p. 15; Merriman, *Six Contemporaneous Revolutions*, pp. 15–16.
41 Jacobsen Jensen, 'Moryson's reis', pp. 214–305, 267.
42 This elite participation was strongest in the early decades of the war. Vermeesch, *Oorlog*, pp. 59–61, 90, 151, 164; Van der Heijden, *Geldschieters*, p. 55. Van Zanden and Prak, 'Towards an economic interpretation', stress the greater degree of tax compliance in communities with citizenship because of the lowering of transaction costs between state and citizens; see also Prak and Van Zanden, 'Tax morale'.
43 Van der Heijden a.o., *Serving the Urban Community*.
44 Van der Heijden, *Geldschieters*, pp. 96, 113; 't Hart and Limberger, 'Staatsmacht en stedelijke autonomie'.
45 De Vries, 'Political economy of bread', pp. 103–4.
46 De Vries and Van der Woude, *First Modern Economy*, p. 103; Van Deursen, *Kopergeld*, p. 27. The cost of collecting Dutch taxes was rather low, whether they were farmed out or collected directly; see Fritschy, 'Efficiency', p. 63; De Vries and Van der Woude, *First Modern Economy*, p. 123. The tax revolts of 1748 were a different matter since they were linked to widespread political opposition.
47 Caferro, 'Warfare and economy', p. 206, concluded that Siena, Padua, Luca and Pisa relied on credit from foreigners, so their war loans represented a drain on their economy. This stood in contrast to Milan, Venice and Florence, which enjoyed positive benefits from debt services because their creditors were predominantly domestic.
48 The proportion of funds needed for the navy was still quite low at this time (compare Table 7.1); customs still took care of most admiralty disbursements. A decade later the navy required a larger share in Holland's public expenditure. Bruijn, *Admiraliteit*, p. 78.
49 Liesker and Fritschy, *Gewestelijke financiën*, p. 37.
50 Tracy, *Founding*, pp. 108, 181–2, 249, 255–6; Tracy, 'Holland's new fiscal regime', p. 48. Gelderblom and Jonker, 'Completing', argue that the financial revolution was only partial before 1610 because the trade in VOC shares was much more important than trade in government bonds in the early seventeenth century. In my view, Gelderblom and Jonker underestimate the extent of all kind of public bonds on the Holland market (numbering tens of thousands) and overestimate the trade in VOC shares before the 1630s (only a minority of them were traded on the market). Between 1584 and 1604 Amsterdam issued at least two million guilders in bonds. See also Fritschy, 'Holland's public debt', pp. 53–4.
51 Gelderblom and Jonker, 'Public finance', pp. 12–13.
52 Vermeesch, *Oorlog*, pp. 173–7; Gelderblom and Jonker, 'Public finance', p. 12. In a larger town like Amsterdam the bonds were at least three times larger, which served the richer merchant classes and the wealthier urban officers well. 't Hart, 'Public loans and lenders'; 't Hart, 'Mutual advantages', pp. 130ff.; Van der Burg, 'Rotterdamse stadsfinanciën'; Van der Heijden, *Geldschieters*, p. 181. The spread of investors was much more limited in other countries, but the French crown used the intermediation of Paris and had Parisian annuities issued for national purposes, see Beguin, 'Circulation'; in the 1660s a new intermediary arose, the Burgundian Estates, which managed annuities for the king in a comparable annuity system, see Potter and Rosenthal, 'Politics'; Potter and Rosenthal, 'Development'.
53 Dormans, *Tekort*, pp. 26, 45, 65–6. In comparison James I could only issue short-term debts at much higher interest rates; Ashton, 'Deficit finance', p. 26; Wheeler, *Making*

of a World Power, p. 97. By 1650 the Austrian Habsburgs still had no long-term consolidated debt at all, see Bérenger, *Finances*, p. 561.

54 Fritschy, 'Efficiency', pp. 64–74.

55 Jones, *Anglo-Dutch Wars*, pp. 95, 222; Browning (ed.), *English Historical Documents*, pp. 352–3; see also Wheeler, *Making of a World Power*, pp. 57, 98, 109.

56 Dickson, *Financial Revolution*; Brewer, *Sinews of Power*.

57 Liesker and Fritschy, *Gewestelijke financiën*, p. 37.

58 The admiralties also employed solicitors, comparable to the military solicitors, who earned around 5 per cent over the pay of the sailors. Roodhuyzen, *Admiraliteit*, pp. 20–1. For the dependency on the credit of captains during the early years of the revolt, see Nolan, *Sir John Norreys*, p. 64: captains had maintained soldiers at their own expense for periods sometimes running into months.

59 Zwitzer, *Militie*, pp. 91–9. In particular, the weapons of the soldiers were regarded as security for the solicitor's advances; De Jong, *Staat*, p. 43.

60 Aglionby, *Present State*, p. 121.

61 See Chapter 1; Van Nimwegen, *Deser landen crijghsvolck*, pp. 68–70; see also Van Deursen, *Kopergeld*, p. 45.

62 Zwitzer, *Militie*, pp. 93–4; Brandon, *Masters of War*, p. 223.

63 Badalo-Dulong, *Banquier*, p. 32; Ernstberger, *Hans de Witte*, p. 62; Ebben, *Zilver*, pp. 149 ff. For examples in England: Judges, 'Philip Burlamachi'; Baker, *Life*, pp. 46–9; Johnson, *Princely Chandos*, pp. 39–40; Tawney, *Business*, pp. 69–71.

64 Thompson, *War and Government*, pp. 99; Thompson, *War and Society*, IV, p. 22.

65 Rooms, *Organisatie*, pp. 165, 178–9, 217. The Spanish pay was further complicated by the fact that two financial systems existed – a Spanish one and a southern Netherlands one – which increased administration costs.

66 Calculated with the help of figures from Liesker and Fritschy, *Gewestelijke financiën*, p. 154; De Vries and Van der Woude, *First Modern Economy*, pp. 702, 710; and Van Zanden, 'Economie van Holland', p. 607.

67 Ten Raa and De Bas, *Staatsche Leger*, V, pp. 372–4, 393.

68 Dormans, *Tekort*, p. 66; Vermeesch, *Oorlog*, pp. 190–1, 197; 't Hart, 'Mutual advantages'; De Jong, *Met goed fatsoen*, p. 260; Kooijmans, *Onder regenten*, p. 223; Prak, *Gezeten burgers*, p. 276; De Vries and Van der Woude, *First Modern Economy*, pp. 105, 117–19. Gelderblom and Jonker, 'Public finance', pp. 16–17, describe the harmful effects of lowering interest rates and redemption plans in the 1660s. Lane, *Profits*, pp. 74, 79, shows that the effect of public debt was comparable in Venice: the well-to-do paid less in direct taxes than they were paid in interest; see also Caferro, 'Warfare and economy', pp. 181, 184–6.

69 Vermeesch, *Oorlog*, pp. 148–50, 165.

70 Ibid., pp. 191–5.

71 Ibid., pp. 205–9.

72 Ibid., pp. 228–33.

73 Thompson, *War and Society*, II, pp. 7–13, 17–20; Goodman, *Spanish Naval Power*, p. 258.

74 Caferro, 'Warfare and economy', p. 182.

75 Brewer, *Sinews of Power*; O'Brien, *Fiscal and Financial Preconditions*, pp. 35, 37.

76 Thompson, *War and Government*, pp. 275, 283; Elliott, *Richelieu and Olivares*, pp. 117, 160.

8 Warfare's new economic opportunities

> You would be surprised about the shipping and trade which is here with all parts of the world. Here no talk about war; one travels all through the country, from Emden to Middelburg in Zeeland, without carrying a gun.[1]

The Dutch Wars of Independence destroyed lives and capital assets but also created new economic opportunities. The quotation above is from Hans Thijs, a young merchant who migrated from Antwerp to Amsterdam in 1584. The letter to his family dates from 1594 and demonstrates that the economic prospects for the northern Netherlands must have seemed quite promising despite the intensive warfare of that decade, even before the 'garden' of the Dutch Republic was closed (see Chapter 1). It was also the decade during which Maurice and Van Oldenbarnevelt introduced the reforms that improved military discipline and the Republic's efficiency in war finance (see Chapters 3 and 7).

The political scientist Henry Barbera enumerated six ways in which wars might encourage new economic opportunities. Intensive military conflicts could 1) encourage the development of managerial skills; 2) tap new credit resources; 3) concentrate capital in increasing taxation; 4) create new industries; 5) standardize output; and 6) exploit underused natural resources. But Barbera warned that these developments were not preordained in all countries. Much depended on the situation before fighting began. In particular, a significant degree of control over the environment (energy resources), a certain level of pre-war economic performance, and the existence of a wide variety of institutions and resources (social and political structures) were essential for wartime growth. Pre-war economic performance and pre-war social and political institutions were thus of great importance. Following Barbera, Seonjou Kang and James Meernik in their article 'Civil War Destruction and the Prospects of Economic Growth' emphasized the importance of political organization; in the twentieth century post-war recovery was most rapid in democratic nations because of the greater respect for law together with a more suitable environment for investment, entrepreneurship and capital formation. They also pointed to the advantages of pre-war economic growth and the availability of pre-war capital stock.[2]

Barbera's view corresponds remarkably well to the experiences of the Thirty Years War, the economic impact of which was extremely differentiated. Military violence seemed to have aggravated pre-war negative trends, while post-war economic booms occurred in areas that had experienced economic growth before the fighting began. Towns like Hamburg and Bremen, which had been on the rise before 1618, profited from the war and from the shift of economic activity away from war zones towards the more peaceful north-west. On the other hand, towns like Augsburg and Nuremberg barely recovered. These formerly important centres of trade suffered from the fact that wealth and goods from the Italian peninsula and the Middle East were increasingly carried by sea rather than overland. The Thirty Years War seemed to have accelerated and intensified this trend. Italy's wars of the sixteenth century produced similarly mixed results, with only a couple of commercially advanced city-states gaining from the fighting and numerous other communities losing out. Likewise, in the case of the Dutch War, pre-war commercialization facilitated rapid recovery in the war-stricken Meuse region. Most warfare appears to have reinforced economic trends; only rarely were new developments initiated.[3]

But wars could spur on the development of certain economic branches – above all the arms industry and mining; this is exemplified by the copper mines and the vast export of guns that bolstered the small economy of Sweden throughout the seventeenth century.[4] But the provisioning and equipping of an army also created strong economic demand. Michael Braddick makes clear that shoemakers, carters and carriers gained from the English Civil War: 'The war machine was also a customer, not simply a burden'.[5] The Duchy of Friedland is an excellent example of this link between war and economy. In the later 1620s the home base of Wallenstein's 100,000 troops could deliver 10,000 pairs of boots and 4,000 uniforms to the Prague magazines within ten weeks. The Friedland peasants and artisans also operated with astonishing efficiency in the provision of bread, forage and beer.[6] As a result the duchy's economy blossomed.[7]

In view of the importance of pre-war economic trends, this chapter looks at the economic development of the northern Netherlands in the earlier sixteenth century. The first two decades of the fighting had a devastating impact, not least because the Eighty Years War was very much a civil conflict in these years. By the early 1580s some recovery was possible, but the pace of revitalization was highly uneven. The chapter explores the background to the different rates of recovery in Holland, Overijssel (Deventer) and Brabant (Tilburg). But the war also represented a direct stimulus for arms producers and army provisioners. Not every factor on Barbera's list can be addressed in this chapter. However, several have already been examined, such as the exploitation of new credit resources and the concentration of capital in increasing taxation (Chapter 7) and the exploitation of underused natural resources and opportunities (in particular with regard to the extension of trade routes and the establishment of colonial companies), to which the substantial demand created by naval establishments should be added (Chapter 6). This chapter pays particular attention to the impact of army demand, examining the extent to which Barbera's points regarding new managerial skills, new industries and the standardization of output are supported. Overall, two main developments can be identified: first, the concentration of (new and old) economic opportunities in Holland; and second the commercialization of warfare, or more precisely the ability to make money from waging war.

Rapid and sustained recovery in the maritime west

The economy of the northern Netherlands had been expanding since at least the fifteenth century. Above all in the coastal provinces, urbanization advanced, while commerce and industry expanded. Holland's labour market was characterized by a high degree of flexibility as only a quarter of the population was engaged in agriculture: a tiny proportion by the standards of the day. In the countryside the main proto-industrial employment was in peat, fishing, shipping and shipbuilding, brick production and bleaching.[8] Wind and peat provided abundant energy for all kinds of enterprise. In the towns, the labour force worked in a large and diverse number of industries. Trade flourished because of the multifarious connections over land and sea, to which the trading links of the vast Spanish empire were added from the early sixteenth century. Overall, the economy of the maritime Netherlands was growing and exhibiting a high degree of commercialization.

In the mid-sixteenth century, however, the pace of economic development slowed down. A major depression began in 1557 following a default by the Spanish government. The financial crisis experienced by Antwerp affected the whole of the Low Countries because of the Scheldt town's central trading role; virtually all other towns in the region (including those in Holland) depended to a considerable extent on Antwerp's prosperity and economic links. In the 1560s a war in the Baltic added to the difficulties by disrupting the grain trade; prices rose sharply. The flood on All Saint's Day in 1570 inundated vast parts of coastal regions, and the following year the failure of the harvest throughout north-western Europe created near-famine conditions. Alva's embargo on trade with England further increased prices and unemployment and brought about a substantial drop in the standard of living of the lower classes.[9]

The fighting in the early 1570s initially intensified this downward trend. Wealthy royalist burghers abandoned the towns of the northern Netherlands for the south; wealthy dissenter merchants fled to Germany or England; trade was disrupted by the Sea Beggars; the fisheries were almost brought to a halt as no salt could be imported; and sieges, inundations and undisciplined soldiers menaced property rights everywhere. But after 1576, by which time Spanish troops had effectively disappeared from Holland's soil, economic recovery was remarkably rapid. This was to be expected, following Barbera, because of the province's advanced and diversified economy, the favourable policies adopted by the provincial and urban authorities which furthered growth, and civilian control over an army that also demonstrated an increasing degree of professionalization and discipline (see Chapters 2 and 3). Unemployment was rampant in the early 1570s, but the army and navy offered alternative vocations, as they did for those who had to flee the countryside because of flooding.[10] Soldier's pay was not high, but it was at least regular, thanks increasingly to the buffer of loans from local elites and the broad tax base (see Chapter 7).

In Holland, standards of living improved rapidly after the 1570s as unemployment declined and wages were paid on a more regular basis. This trend continued throughout the war, although both the early 1620s and early 1630s witnessed temporary blips due to high prices linked to poor harvests and economic warfare (trade blockades, Chapter 6). Existing industries recovered, expanding even beyond former levels, and new ones emerged. Labour productivity increased thanks to the high level of technological development and more intensive use of energy, further stimulated by an almost continuous flow of people, knowledge and capital into Holland. That province was notable for experiencing substantial per capita growth between 1580 and 1650, when almost all other European countries were plunged into crisis, their economies damaged by civil and international warfare.[11]

In the meantime, the victories of Maurice, William Louis and Frederick Henry created and maintained a safe buffer zone behind which Holland's economy could develop. After the 1590s the other provinces became the contested frontier territory. This security was shored up by institutions that protected property rights and lowered transaction costs, as was summarized neatly by Jonathan Israel:

> The merchant élite of Holland and Zeeland had at their disposal financial institutions and resources, and a degree of specialization in financial, brokerage, and insurance techniques, such as none of their rivals possessed and which together afforded an immense and continuous advantage in the international arena.[12]

Holland's entrepreneurs thus needed to spend less on protection, an advantage that has been labelled by Frederic Lane as 'protection rent'.[13] The expansion of the buffer zone also created new opportunities for Holland's traders. For example, the 1597 capture of Lingen, located to the east of the Republic, permitted the rise of a flourishing direct Holland-Denmark trade in cattle stimulated by on-going urbanization in the west and the increasing demand for meat – not merely in the growing towns but also by colonial companies. Before the war Danish cattle had arrived in Holland only through merchants in the southern Netherlands and in relatively small numbers.[14]

The disappearance of the traditional merchant connections through Antwerp, in particular after 1585, necessitated the development of a new long-distance trade network. Amsterdam was able to take up the challenge because of its extensive links with the Baltic and its available spare capacity to expand across the Atlantic. Its pre-eminent position within Holland's trade meant it controlled the supply of goods for export – goods manufactured in nearby towns like Haarlem, Leiden or Delft. Amsterdam's own industries also expanded and diversified. The Republic's political independence together with the high degree of urban autonomy gave its merchant community significant advantages. No trade route was hampered by monarchical or imperial institutions; even trade with the enemy was possible, albeit requiring the payment of a high license fee (*licent*) or conducted covertly when a trade ban was in force.[15] The practical toleration offered to all faiths was striking and attracted numerous foreign merchants. New institutions like the Bourse, printed price sheets and the Bank of Amsterdam were all crucial for the prosperity of the merchant community. Refugees who had fled the south and initially preferred ports like London, Hamburg and Middelburg now increasingly opted for Amsterdam.[16]

The blockade of Antwerp's trade undoubtedly encouraged Amsterdam's development. But the enormous influx of merchants from the south did not mean a mere continuation of Antwerp's trade from a new location away to the north. Antwerp's trade was not completely halted after 1585. The blockade rendered in particular its seaborne trade risky and inconvenient and the town now looked more towards its hinterland for long-distance connections. That was nothing new: the Scheldt town's long-distance network had always favoured the routes east overland to German and Italian cities. Antwerp's merchants had few ships of their own; the harbour was dominated by the vessels of merchants from Italy and the Hanse.[17] Amsterdam, though, had focused on seaborne trade from the start and had a strong merchant shipping network of its own even before the war. The town's economy was stimulated by not only the relative decline of Antwerp but also the decline of the Hanse network, along with the general shift in European trade routes from land to sea. Its merchants increasingly sailed to the Mediterranean themselves and at the same time developed new routes. In this way Amsterdam's trade network came to be a blend of old and new – based on both established links and commercial innovation.[18]

The arrival of migrants from the south did not represent a simple influx of Antwerp's wealthy merchant elite, contrary to the argument of the standard historiography. Recent research has indicated that those who left for the north were usually younger merchants, entrepreneurs at the start of their careers. Most made their fortunes only *after* they became established in Amsterdam. Their links to capital and technologies from the south facilitated the founding of new businesses, but Antwerp's former leading merchant and entrepreneurial circuits in fact stayed put.[19]

The economic contribution of migrants from the south differed according to the conditions in the various towns. Contrary to what is often believed, the new migrants did not introduce the 'new draperies' of fine wool (as opposed to the 'old draperies' of coarser wool). This industry did boom in Leiden thanks to the influx of southerners, at the expense of the traditional draperies that had used coarse wool, but it built on important existing foundations: new draperies had existed before that date. In Amsterdam, migrants from the German lands dominated manufacturing and finishing of luxury textiles, not incomers from the south. Remarkably, in that town a totally new industry arose, sugar refining, which was manned by southern migrants, though not a single sugar refiner from the south had settled there. Obviously the immigrants brought skills and knowledge from an Antwerp branch of industry in which they had not worked themselves. In all, the new political circumstances, the different opportunities in the various towns, together with the openness of Holland society, offered numerous possibilities in which innovations from indigenous background mixed with innovations of newcomers. The result was a thorough modernization of industry within the north, particularly in Holland and above all in Leiden and Amsterdam.[20]

In the midst of industrial expansion, new overseas trade routes opened up, again not caused by the simple migration of an Antwerp network but by the blending of experience from Holland and Brabant into a new innovative whole. The temporary peace with the Spanish of 1609–21 permitted a rapid expansion of commerce – with the East and West Indies as well as within Europe itself. After the 1610s, Holland merchants occupied central positions in virtually all Europe's long-distance trade networks. The remark by a Spanish courtier, that the Truce had made the Dutch richer but the Spanish poorer, was all too true.[21]

It is of interest at this point to consider again Antwerp's trajectory during the war. Antwerp lost its primary position in international trade not only because of the Dutch Wars of Independence or the blockade from 1585. As already noted, a downward economic trend had started in the 1550s. The crisis of 1557 (the first Spanish-Habsburg government bankruptcy) had dealt a fatal blow to the city's financial market. Genoa initially took over Antwerp's key position in international finance; Amsterdam had to wait until the early decades of the seventeenth century to become supreme. Antwerp's cloth industry had also begun to contract in the 1550s, not with the start of the Revolt. Antwerp was unable to profit from the general shift in European trade towards overseas routes in the same way as London, Hamburg or Amsterdam did. Indeed, the economic blockade prevented further imports of overseas resources and the whole of the 1580s was a period of severe economic crisis. Yet the Brabant town did not only experience misery. Recovery was surprisingly rapid in the 1590s, and before long the economy of Flanders and Brabant showed renewed vitality. After all, the country enjoyed the advantage of a previously commercialized and diversified economy. By the 1660s the level of industrial production achieved during the 1560s had been regained. Growth rates were lower than in Holland, however, while the standard of living declined in Antwerp after 1615, in contrast to the north where it continued to grow during the war.[22]

Holland's expansion prompted the rise of new ports in the north and the expansion of existing ones.[23] After the Truce, commercial expansion slowed down because of a Europe-wide depression. Within Holland itself economic growth continued, however, albeit at a lower rate until about 1670. The growth rates of the domestic economy slowed after 1650, with a particular crisis in 1663, but true stagnation only began in the 1670s. By that time England and France had begun to levy high import duties on Dutch goods. Its rivals' improved protectionism ensured that several branches of industry in the United

Provinces lost their position in foreign markets, even though some branches (potteries, luxury textiles) maintained or even increased their levels of production. At the same time, the Dutch also experienced growing competition from the English and French in the East and West Indies.[24]

The Dutch Golden Age thus came to an end only in the last decades of the seventeenth century, although the United Provinces maintained the highest per capita income in Europe until the end of the eighteenth century. In the meantime, other maritime regions in the north experienced a somewhat less golden age. Zeeland had recovered rapidly after the 1570s, profiting from the increased volume of trans-shipments required for the Antwerp trade, but after 1585 fewer and fewer goods arrived from there and Zeeland's economy declined. The damage caused by the temporary 1598 trade ban turned into a permanent disaster for the region and the province did not even recover during the Truce. Only the colonial companies generated a significant surplus; numerous Zeeland shippers turned to privateering, which developed into a major economic activity and source of employment.[25]

Wartime recovery had been rapid in north Holland and in Friesland too, but the Golden Age there was of shorter duration than that in Holland's core area (below the line Haarlem-Amsterdam). A sharp decline set in after 1650, which damaged towns like Enkhuizen, Hoorn and Alkmaar in north Holland, as well as Groningen and Frisian towns like Harlingen and Dokkum. This downturn coincided with a general decline in agricultural prices, described by Braudel as European-wide during the second half of the seventeenth century.[26] This particularly damaged these regions since they were so agriculture-dependent, and also caused Zeeland to fall further down the wealth-scale.

The highly urbanized core of Holland suffered far less from lower agrarian prices after 1650. Towns remained vital because of (peasant) immigration, and also because they were the places where soldiers secured their clothes and boots and obtained arms and ammunition. The grip of towns on the political system was strengthened, while inundations and scorched earth campaigns had eroded the economic position of the landed nobility and monasteries.[27] Holland's urban and maritime core continued to attract more migrants, knowledge and trade until the 1670s. The Golden Age was thus very much a (south) Holland Golden Age.

The decline of inland commerce

Overall, the maritime core of the Republic benefited most from the positive economic trend. Before the Revolt Holland's economy already enjoyed advantages over the other provinces, but during the course of the Dutch Wars of Independence the gap increased and became more apparent. Holland's rapid development was also accompanied by a decline in economic opportunities in the rest of the Republic. Periodic trade blockades and high new custom duties levied on the river trade damaged commercial hubs inland. Deventer's economy provides an illuminating case study of exactly this evolution.

This Yssel town thrived before the Revolt because of its central place in inland trade. The fighting brought about the closure of several of its most important trade networks and weakened numerous others. The effects of the trade blockades imposed after the 1590s proved long-lasting. Merchants shunned the Deventer market because of the temporary higher costs and found permanently cheaper alternatives. In 1599 the transport of a barrel of Frisian butter between Lingen and Amsterdam via Deventer cost 183 *stuivers*; if carried by sea via Emden (East Frisia), only 141 *stuivers*: almost a quarter less. Salt cost even three times as much when shipped through Deventer instead of Emden. It was not only a matter of higher duties: convoys also involved extra expense. Armed horsemen had to accompany goods from Holland destined for Münster, Cologne, Frankfurt-am-Main, Augsburg, Nuremberg and so on. The difficulties for Deventer were exacerbated by structural trends. Alongside the already mentioned factor of cheaper sea transport, the famous traditional fairs – the network on which much of the Yssel town's wealth depended – also became a less important part of long-distance trade. In this way warfare both revealed and accelerated already established trends.[28]

Deventer, like other Dutch river trade centres, also languished because several traditional trade centres in the German hinterland suffered during the war. Cologne entered a period of commercial and industrial decline because of repeated closures of the river trade. The number of tolls increased on the Rhine; no fewer than 30 customs stations were to be found between Strasburg and the frontier of Holland. Wine and wheat shipped from Mannheim to the Dutch border trebled in price; timber was almost the only thing that could be moved down the river to Holland with any profit. For their foreign trade, Cologne, Mainz, Krefeld, Mannheim, Düsseldorf and Coblenz became dependent on overseas transport, which was increasingly dominated by Holland merchants. The Thirty Years War thus destroyed traditional long-range economic linkages, producing an enduring regionalization of the interior German economy.[29]

After the Truce and accelerated by the river blockades of 1623, 1625, 1627, 1628, 1629 and 1635–6, the trade that formerly passed through Deventer, Zwolle and Nijmegen came to be diverted through Hamburg and Bremen and often ended up in these towns only after being shipped through Holland. This dislocation also damaged Dordrecht, in the south-east of Holland, by tradition the province's foremost centre of river trade. The frustration of river-trade merchants due to repeated trade bans became evident in 1636, when townsmen from Nijmegen and Dordrecht destroyed the Schenkenschans, the fortress strategically located at the confluence of the Rhine and Waal and used to enforce the trade bans and custom duties. This fortress had only recently been reconstructed by the States-General. This violent act caused widespread uproar in the Republic.[30]

In addition to the relocation of trade routes, the Deventer woollen industry also suffered increasingly from competition in its export market, above all by Leiden cloth. The urban authorities encouraged the manufacture of a new cloth, bombazine (a mixture of silk and wool), to counter this development. They attracted new migrants, mainly from German territories, by promising them freedom from certain impositions. But the success of Deventer bombazine was short-lived because town regulations limited the number of looms to four per master. Leiden competition was soon irrelevant; bombazine from Amersfoort (Utrecht), where bombazine masters experienced fewer limits on the number of looms, drove the Deventer textiles out of the market.[31]

Deventer's decline was not merely economic. Until 1578 the town had cherished its position as a free imperial city with a long-established direct link to the Holy Roman Empire. Due to the war, however, in political and economic terms it became distinctly subordinate to the Republic, and above all to Holland. But although the town became less important as a transit centre for international trade, it remained significant for local trade. The population even increased again after the difficulties of the late sixteenth century. The reconstruction of the town after the military destruction resulted in a growing number of migrants; redevelopment involved not only the fortifications but also the repair of quays, cranes and churches, along with the construction of a new bridge, meat hall and other public buildings. Not all this work was absolutely necessary; the embellishments showed renewed urban pride and a strong faith in the future. The fighting also had an indirect positive impact since the demands of the local garrison supported the workshops of local blacksmiths and cloth producers.[32]

In general it can be concluded that although the economic opportunities available to inland towns did not completely disappear, Holland's development limited the options. Blokzijl, originally a small fortification on the eastern border of the Zuiderzee, turned into a flourishing harbour for peat and the cattle trade only because it could so directly meet Holland's strong demand for these goods.[33] For the products of long-distance trade, local merchants became increasingly dependent on Amsterdam and other Holland towns because high customs duties on river trade remained in place even after the war.

Agrarian production and proto-industry during the war

Again, rural communities inland fared quite differently. Chapters 2, 3 and 5 described how better troop discipline and military governance gradually improved the situation of the peasantry. The financial burden imposed by the war was high, but thriving urban economies could contribute to the recovery of the countryside through financial support and strong market demand.[34] But, with the declining opportunities in trade, inland towns expanded far less than towns in Holland.

An analysis of the accounts for the collection of rent in rye of the *Geefhuis*, a charitable institution in 's-Hertogenbosch with numerous farms in the region, illustrates some of the agrarian difficulties of the Meierij district (see Figure 8.1). Interestingly, decline had already set in before the war, with very poor harvests in the later 1550s. The plundering by soldiers in the 1570s and 1580s thus took place during a period when the farming community had few reserves. The rent books show how revenues dropped dramatically in the 1580s

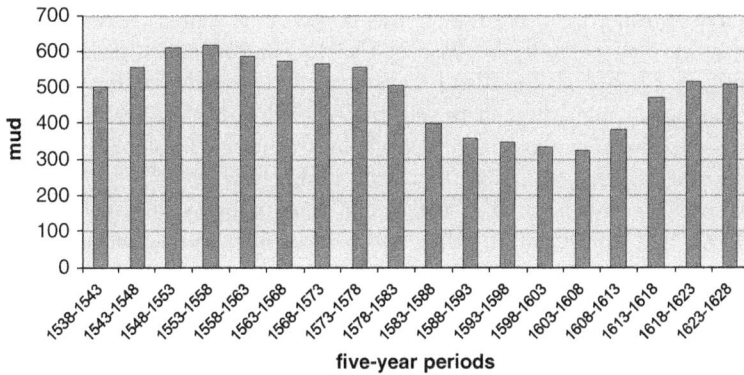

Figure 8.1 Average annual income from Geefhuis in rye from its farms, 1538–1628
Source: Adriaenssen, *Staatsvormend geweld*, p. 291

following the scorched-earth campaigns. Interestingly, 1590s rye rent levels were even lower than those of the 1580s. Real recovery was only possible during the Truce, but even then the pre-war level was not achieved. Not all accounts have survived, so a continuous analysis is not possible, but evidence from the 1660s indicates that the levels of the 1560s were not equalled even then. By that time, the general agrarian crisis mentioned earlier, which lowered agricultural prices after 1650, precluded any improvement.[35] Because of poor agrarian prices in the second half of the century, farmers in the Almelo district of Overijssel also experienced great difficulty in recovering from the damaging impact of the 1672 invasion.[36]

In the Meierij, the proto-industry also suffered during the war because Brabant cloth was burdened by extremely high custom duties. Meierij peasants increasingly sent their cloth for finishing to Holland rather than Brabant. As was noted in Chapter 5, several Brabant linen merchants, including some from 's-Hertogen-bosch and Eindhoven, migrated north and took up bleaching in Haarlem, accompanied by numerous migrant weavers from the countryside, taking with them the latest techniques and thus contributing significantly to that industry's 'Golden Age'.[37] In the midst of all the misery in the Meierij, the rise of proto-industry in Tilburg was a rare positive development. The village even experi-enced population growth during the Wars of Independence; by 1638 it had 6,000 inhabitants, comparable to towns like Deventer and Gorinchem. Tilburg's rise is explained by a number of separate but collectively crucial factors. To begin with, its trump card was fine woollens and not the linen cloth that was pro-duced by most of the Meierij farms. The village of Oisterwijk produced wool too, like Tilburg, but its peasants used coarse materials and thus belonged to the 'old draperies', while Tilburg's more modern looms made it part of the 'new draperies', the latest fashion trend, and utilized fine wool. From the beginning, Tilburg's export markets were located in the north, in the expanding market of Holland, while Oisterwijk cloth producers were traditionally orientated south, where the market was contracting. Thus, Oisterwijk's proto-industry declined not only because of the devastation which accompanied the fighting (see Chapter 5) but also because war accelerated a decline (old drapery cloth was increasingly difficult to sell) that was already in progress. In addition, Tilburg's production was not held back by the restrictions imposed by guilds and cloth halls that dominated the textile trade elsewhere.[38]

A second factor is related to the extent of its vulnerability in times of war. Oisterwijk was an urbanized village with a distinct centre. During attacks by marauding foot soldiers or cavalrymen its wealth was easily located; a single fire might set the whole village ablaze. In contrast,Tilburg consisted of several widely dispersed hamlets and production was distributed between a host of small-scale workshops engaged in the teaseling, spinning and weaving of wool. This spread the risks when attacked by mutinous or marauding soldiers. The village had no merchants with large stocks and no entrepreneurs with expensive filling-mills or dye houses that could be pillaged and destroyed. The leading merchants who dealt in Tilburg cloth lived in nearby Breda, from where they supplied the peasants with high-quality wool – initially from German territories and later from Spain.

The third factor in Tilburg's emergence was linked to advantageous pre-war economic developments. Prior to the war the village had seen an expansion of the cattle trade, the cattle being fattened on the nearby meadows of the Holland Langstraat district. The fattening of cattle was stimulated by Holland's urban-ization and generated substantial wealth for individual Tilburg farmers. This encouraged trade and investment in other products, including wool. But most importantly the available capital stock also reduced vulnerability in war. Tilburg managed time and again to purchase safeguards from the armies in action during the critical period of 1584–8, and thereby avoid the worst of hit-and-run and scorched earth campaigns. The village budget was carefully managed, which permitted compensation payments to local people in case of losses or costs resulting from the payment of ransoms, lodging of soldiers, supply of carts or sentry duty. War was a burden, but it was bearable. The wages earned by pioneers and wagoners was determined by the market; some made it their trade – for instance Adriaen Symons van Oeckel, who secured almost 900 guilders from the Tilburg treasury for serving with wagons and horses at the sieges of Grave, Loon op Zand, Neuss and elsewhere. In Tilburg labour was scarce because of the demands of the wool trade and the village preferred to hire labour to perform the duties demanded by the garrisons of Spanish or Dutch troops. Such expenditure increased the village war debt, which amounted to almost 24,000 guilders by the beginning of the Truce. But thanks to the capital available it was possible to secure loans from local creditors such as Jan Cornelis Gerrit Hermans van Heijst, a cloth merchant whose investments in village bonds totalled a substantial 3,580 guilders. Thus, the expenses incurred in interest payments once again largely served the local community rather than far-away *renteniers* in 's-Hertogenbosch or Antwerp, who were the source of loans for most other Meierij villages with spiralling war debts.[39]

In the early seventeenth century Tilburg continued to enjoy advantages that allowed the villagers to recover from temporary setbacks occasioned by sieges conducted nearby. The finishing of the wool was carried out in Holland, and Amsterdam's interest in this trade resulted in Tilburg's woollens being granted freedom from heavy *licent* duties in 1622. Leiden opposed this policy, fearing competition from cheap rural production, but the voice of Amsterdam's dyers and cloth merchants simply carried more weight.[40]

During the 1630s the trade in fine woollens was transformed into a mass production enterprise; increasingly powerful merchant-entrepreneurs (*reders*) and their sub-contractors controlled the whole process, from the provision of raw materials to the supply of goods to foreign markets. Numerous smaller traders lost their independence, even in Tilburg, and a proletarianization occurred as independent peasant-weavers became wage labourers for a number of big Tilburg and Holland merchants. This mass trade in woollen cloth was a new phenomenon, dominated by Amsterdam. Tilburg cloth ended up in Russia and South America, often under the name of Leiden or Holland cloth. But for Tilburg weavers this connection meant strong and steady demand for their product, and after 1648 Tilburg was the second largest textile centre in the United Provinces after Leiden.[41] But it should be remembered that this development resulted from an unusual, even unique, series of advantages not easily emulated by other villages in the Dutch Republic.

Prosperous dealers in death[42]

The economic stimulus which accompanied warfare also gave rise to opportunities for local industries. A strong commercialization of warfare was noticeable, above all in the field of arms provisioning. New munitions industries were created; during the Eighty Years War the United Provinces even became the centre of the international arms market. In 1688, the English consul at Amsterdam, William Carr, noted the strong competitive position of the Dutch armaments industry:

> It hath inconceivable store of all manner of provisions for war, insomuch, that England and divers other Nations send to Amsterdam to buy arms, buff-coats, belts, match, &tc. Yea, here are several shopkeepers who can deliver arms for four or five thousand men, and at a cheaper rate than can be got any where else.[43]

Holland's strong commercial networks provided essential materials such as saltpetre, sulphur and iron plating. During the seventeenth century the weapons industry made up at least 5 per cent of Dutch GNP.[44]

At the start of the Dutch Wars of Independence the local arms industry was virtually non-existent. Mechelen, to the south of the Republic, was a famed centre of arms production, followed soon by Liège, both mainly supplying the Army of Flanders. But within two decades the number of workshops in the northern Netherlands engaged in manufacturing armaments increased, fuelled by the continuous substantial demand from the army and navy. Stimulus was also provided by the numerous town soldiers, the urban militias, the fortifications and the fishermen and merchantmen who were ordered to arm themselves. The establishment of magazines channelled the supply of munitions. Orange erected a central magazine in Delft in 1573; the provincial governments followed his lead by installing their own. These magazines purchased gunpowder, balls, weaponry and so on, but also wagon parts, spades and axes for use during sieges. In 1574 Delft's magazine alone spent 115,000 guilders; this sum had risen to 600,000 guilders by the early seventeenth century.[45] In addition, captains continued to buy directly from workshops – edged weapons (pikes and swords) above all.

The Mauritian *Ordres op de Waapeninghe* of 1596 and 1599 (see Chapter 3) were important steps towards standardization in the arms industry. The Delft magazine commissioners distributed at least 64 moulds for standard muskets to workshops throughout the Republic; in addition, the repair of standard muskets informed local artisans about the desired calibre. Within just five years Dutch arms producers had become accustomed to the new model musket standard of 12 bullets in the pound. Central control through the magazines prompted further homogeneity and standard designs were produced for the equipment needed to conduct a siege: spades, pickaxes, shovels and sandbags, as well as gabions (wicker baskets to be filled with mud or sand). The magazines also prepared ready-made kits for field fortifications consisting of palisades, beams and nails. To further standardization, Maurice occupied himself with the development of a grenade and design of a wooden shaft to fit all pickaxes and axes and another for spades and shovels.[46]

As a result, an open and transparent market for arms grew up. The fact that soldiers received regular pay at least from the early 1590s was an important boost to demand, as artisans were guaranteed to receive their money. In the navy iron guns replaced bronze cannon since they were cheaper to produce. Maurice set up a gun foundry in The Hague in 1589; similar foundries were established slightly later near the location of the provincial admiralties – that is to say, in Amsterdam, Rotterdam, Middelburg, Leeuwarden and Enkhuizen. Following the standardization of cannon in 1611 (see Chapter 3) the States-General laid down that the Boards of Admiralty should only order 24, 18, 12 and 6-pound iron guns. The number of heavy cannon on board Dutch warships increased rapidly after 1594, facilitated by the construction of larger warships; by the time of the Truce the level of armaments had surpassed those on English men-of-war.[47]

At the same time there was a significant demand for exports, above all from France, which did not have many armaments producers of its own. These orders were made possible by the Dutch subsidies to that country, its ally in the struggle with Spain (Chapter 1). In April 1599 Van 's-Gravensande, the Delft storage clerk, was able to provide straight away a complete set of arms and armour for 15 French companies, including banners and drums. The export trade in munitions soon gathered speed, taking in above all the northern

German ports, the Baltic, Italy (particularly Venice) and England. The Thirty Years War provided a major new boost and numerous weapons were exported to the Protestant allies. During 1625–9 Denmark was completely dependent on the Amsterdam market for its arms. But Dutch arms were also exported to Russia, Morocco, the coastal kingdoms in Guinea and further afield to South Africa, Asia, native tribes in North America and European colonies in the West. Exports to the enemy were not permitted, but Dutch weapons reached the Spanish troops via French ports, and during the Anglo-Dutch wars Amsterdam merchants exported gunpowder to Hamburg, knowing full well that it would be re-exported to the English. Preparing for their 1672 invasion, the French too bought gunpowder and ammunition on the Amsterdam market.[48] Thus, this branch of Dutch industry also profited from the arms their adversaries used to defeat them.

In addition, artisans working in the arms industry received active support from the Dutch authorities. Gun founders in The Hague, Rotterdam and Enkhuizen were given buildings to use as workshops and provided with housing, equipment and an annual salary of 200 guilders. This aided the establishment of new industries and mitigated the effects of foreign competition. The Provincial States of Holland and the VOC provided saltpetre to gunpowder mills in Amsterdam, Delft, Rotterdam, Brill, Flushing and Hoorn in return for the future provision of a given quantity of gunpowder. More and more gunpowder was manufactured in the Netherlands itself, increasingly in larger horse- or wind-powered workshops that replaced the one-man firms. A similar system prevailed in the gun foundry, with entrepreneurs being given copper and tin in return for the future delivery of an agreed number of cannon to the navy, the army or colonial companies. Urban governments further supported the arms business by appointing inspectors to regulate the saltpetre trade. All major transactions were registered with notaries; trade disputes were resolved in town courts, with the possibility of an appeal to the urban government, or by *ad hoc* committees composed of members accepted by both parties. Such institutions significantly lowered the risks involved in the production of and trade in armaments.[49]

Partly due to the support of the authorities, the number of workshops multiplied; since capital and skilled labour was to be found above all in Holland, it was there that the arms industry was concentrated. Specialization advanced, increasing the efficiency of production. After 1602, for example, the forks for the muskets were made only by the gunmakers Jan van Kempen and Daniel van Marle in Dordrecht. Numerous artisans in Gouda concentrated on the production of matches; bronze guns usually came from The Hague; and Utrecht workshops specialized above all in armour and grenades. Increasingly, artisans assembled parts such as barrels, locks, rifle butts and brass rings into guns; sword blades and pike heads became edged weapons; craftsmen assembled armour parts into complete sets of armour. The parts came from workshops all over the United Provinces or were imported from other countries. The magazines also stockpiled damaged and worn-out arms for use in repairs, and in this way saved money. All these developments enhanced efficiency and speeded up production and supply. As a result the Dutch army and navy – unlike those of their enemies – rarely suffered from shortages of arms or ammunition.[50]

These favourable developments encouraged several entrepreneurs to adopt innovative management techniques. Middlemen (themselves arms producers or arms dealers) took on the task of setting up contracts with small workshops; thus, Aert Meynaes, speaking on behalf of the Dordrecht arms makers, agreed to deliver 500 muskets at nine guilders each to the magazine in Delft. Some merchants even acted as intermediaries with foreign powers, selling and hiring admiralty vessels to Venice, for example. Others purchased ships taken as prizes from privateers, recovering their costs directly by means of gunpowder deliveries to the admiralty boards. But the most far-reaching innovations were in the area of package deals. Merchants specializing in such deals acted as intermediaries between the arms producers, the sources of raw materials and the export markets. In this way Count Christian of Brunswick received all the equipment – from arms and armour to shovels and axes – for his 7,000-strong army in a single delivery.[51]

The close links between merchants, magazines, admiralties and the colonial companies facilitated such package deals. Amsterdam above all constituted the hub, acting as the major entrepôt for equipment destined for the army, navy and colonial companies, while the town contained an increasing number of arms manufacturers.[52] Its market was always a useful source of information about prices, products and suppliers, which resulted in significantly lower transaction costs. Due to their diverse and wide-ranging connections, several Dutch armaments exporters developed into general army purveyors for foreign states, providing arms and ammunition but also taking care of the transfer of subsidies and loans. This business was extremely profitable; in 1622, for example, the consortium of Philippo Calandrini and Andries van der Meulen earned 18,750 guilders in a single transaction between Venice and Amsterdam.[53]

The most powerful armaments dealers were even allowed to borrow equipment from the admiralty for their own purposes; Elias Trip, for example, secured weapons for his expedition to Guinea in 1615 in return for a promise to come back with saltpetre for the admiralty. In 1624 Louis de Geer, who had excellent connections with Swedish copper and iron mines, set up an arms trading company with the Trip brothers; the capital was 72,000 guilders in 1624 but had grown to 400,000 only two years later. Increasingly, such traders were allowed to employ the stockpiles in the government magazines of the Dutch state as export reserves; these provided the dealers with arms and ammunition that was not immediately required for the army or navy. This relieved the arms exporters of the need to maintain significant stores of their own and provides an excellent example of the interplay between private capital and public institutions in the Dutch Republic.[54]

Innovative management was less obvious in fields outside arms provisioning. There was strong consumer demand from the garrisons, as shown in Chapter 4, but clothing for uniforms and large-scale supplies of package goods still belonged to the future. Local artisans such as tailors, bakers and shoemakers took care of most of the provisioning, after army victuallers (sutlers) who followed in the train of the army.[55] Attempts to regulate such provisioning on a larger scale encountered major difficulties. In the 1580s the office of the *super-intendent-generaal van de vivres* was discontinued because of the complex nature of his duties; he had had simultaneously to regulate the transportation of the troops on campaign, buy rye, barley, oats, flour, fish and cheese for the soldiers, and deal with all kind of financial transactions.[56]

Army victuallers (sometimes soldiers' wives, or even soldiers themselves) came under the authority of the quartermasters. In 1593 Maurice ordered that each company was to have no more than one (soldier-)victualler. These individuals enjoyed certain privileges, such as freedom from taxation; compensation could be paid in case the sutler's ship or wagon suffered war-related damage. Army officers were not permitted to combine their post with that of a victualler. Clerks of the Council of State were assigned specific tasks, such as keeping sufficient stores in particular magazines or buying grain or hay in advance.[57]

Chapter 3 described how the Dutch were overtaken by the French after Le Tellier established his impressive magazine system. Following the invasion of 1672, William III of Orange installed a *provediteur-generaal*, who was to supply bread to all the soldiers in the field army, in an attempt to keep the French at bay. Other large-scale contracts were signed with suppliers of wagons or horse fodder.[58] Contrary to the *superintendent-generaal* of the late sixteenth century these *provediteurs* were contracted for one specific item. It was an initiative which more and more drew rich entrepreneurs into the army organization.

One firm became pre-eminent in this respect: the firm of Machado-Pereira. Antonio Alvares Machado, a merchant of Portuguese-Jewish descent, began his career as a bread supplier in 1673, when Stadholder William III contracted him to deliver bread and cheese to the 's-Hertogenbosch garrison. The next year Machado provided a hundred wagons for the transportation of bread, grain and flour. In 1676 he was assigned the task of supplying the rye magazines for the army, a contract that was renewed regularly for decades to come. Machado and his associate Jacob Pereira (also of Portuguese-Jewish descent) bought grain on the Holland markets in massive quantities and took care that it was ground, made into bread and transported to the troops.[59]

Holland's strong judicial tradition ensured that such contracts were quite elaborately framed. They not only stated the duties and tasks of the suppliers but also limited their risks. The *provediteurs* were exempted from all kinds of tax, whether custom dues or excises associated with the milling. If the suppliers encountered problems in finding storage, the local authorities were obliged to requisition sites for them. These authorities also had to assist with the transportation and handling of grain, flour and bread intended for the troops. Military escorts were to be hired at reasonable rates. Should goods be stolen, or destroyed by the enemy, the Council of State was to recompense the merchants for their losses. In order that they should be able to buy grain in time, the Council of State also provided the *provediteurs* with loans at low interest.[60]

Significantly, the bread-provisioning contracts were never promised to the Machado-Pereira combination. Every year they had to compete with other potential suppliers, with the result that their prices had to remain competitive and their profits not unreasonable. But prices were not the only consideration: the reliability of the suppliers mattered too. The Machado-Pereira firm managed to build up a strong network of magazines and bakers, which increased the likelihood that they would secure the contract time and again. Such circumstances facilitated the rise of large-scale capitalist enterprises that developed new managerial skills and standardized output. The revenues could be considerable; a foraging contract in 1703 worth 1.6 million guilders yielded Machado a net profit of almost 200,000 guilders: around 12 per cent.[61] Yet these mega-suppliers of wagons, bread and forage only appeared in the last decades of the seventeenth century, when armaments merchants had already been growing in scale and offering package deals for decades.[62]

All these large-scale suppliers profited from the clout and continuity provided by clear and reliable contracts. Dutch practice here was in sharp contrast to most of seventeenth-century Europe. In Spain all the larger military contractors were eventually disgraced or bankrupted. The French monarchy was known for always paying its bills late, or not at all; this significantly weakened the position of indigenous army suppliers.[63] After 1650, with the advent of shorter wars and the rise of competing industries in other countries, the Dutch armament exports ceased to expand. But even so the United Provinces remained a major supplier of arms and thus continued to generally profit from warfare.[64]

Conclusion: wartime protection of capital accumulation

The impact of war on the economy in the northern Netherlands was extremely mixed. It depended not only on the nature of the destruction caused by the fighting but perhaps even more on the economic structure and trends in place before and after the war and the resilience of the region's social and political institutions. It was important that the area was already commercialized when fighting began. Holland contained some 40 per cent of the population of the region, but a much higher proportion of its wealth. The city of Amsterdam prospered most notably. Its seaborne commerce recovered quickly in the 1580s, fuelled by a powerful mix of immigrant skills and incoming wealth and existing advantages, links and traditions.

Holland's exceptional and sustained rates of growth were achieved partly at the cost of economic contraction in the interior provinces. Indeed, the example of Tilburg demonstrated that, for the communities inland, only a strong orientation towards Holland's networks guaranteed economic growth during adverse wartime conditions. But even then war often only accelerated existing trends; in the end Tilburg would probably have expanded and Deventer lost its dominant position anyway, simply more slowly.

The economic growth in Holland's urbanized core was remarkable, based on a political structure that favoured the interests of the merchant and entrepreneurial classes. This ensured a secure environment for continuous capital accumulation. Typical of Dutch economic development was its decentralized structure, permitting flexibility, pragmatism and the contribution of local expertise. Provincial and local authorities supported a great variety of economic sectors, not least the arms industry. Standardization of military equipment furthered the rise of the armaments trade and encouraged innovations in management. But compared with France or Spain, large-scale provisioning of bread and rye came about quite late. Firms in this area only emerged during the 1670s, spurred on above all by the war with France.

Wartime stimulation of certain sectors of the economy was not unknown in Europe, as witnessed by the examples of Sweden and Friedland mentioned earlier. Significantly, both flourished thanks in part to merchant-financiers with strong connections to the Dutch Republic such as Louis de Geer and Hans Witte. The major difference with the Duchy of Friedland was the degree of continuity; after the boom of the 1620s came the catastrophe of the 1630s, which was directly related to the rise and fall of Wallenstein. Indeed, continuity of war demand and social-political setting was everywhere vital for sustained profitability. Almost everywhere in Europe wartime suppliers made enormous profits, but making this sustainable was altogether more difficult.[65]

The capital accumulated during the first phase of growth, 1585–1621, contributed to the steep decline of interest rates thereafter.[66] Wartime shifts in economic opportunities towards Holland strengthened this tendency. 'Because Holland prospered, its citizens and inhabitants had more to give in taxes and loans', remarked James Tracy.[67] The sound system of Holland-centred public finance (Chapter 7) made the Dutch state (and its army and navy) a reliable customer; this was bolstered then by economic expansion which continued until the 1670s. The protection of capital accumulation, even during wartime, was of primary importance for the unbroken profitability of army and navy suppliers. At the same time society was not burdened with unruly soldiers who threatened property rights. The 'turn to the sea' – and away from Antwerp's long-distance connections over land – proved particularly advantageous for the Dutch; it significantly expanded the area from which resources could be drawn and permitted them to profit from the growth in overseas trade. Such considerations are crucial to explaining why and how the Dutch Republic could wage such long and costly wars while maintaining strong civilian control over the military and achieving a high degree of professionalism among its soldiers.

Notes

1 Quoted by Gelderblom, *Zuid-Nederlandse kooplieden*, p. 131.
2 Barbera, *Rich Nations*, pp. 6, 34, 43–4; Kang and Meernik, 'Civil war', pp. 104–5.
3 Tallett, *War and Society*, p. 231; Ergang, *Myth*, pp. 28–30; Kamen, 'Economic and social consequences', p. 61; Wilson, *Thirty Years War*, pp. 798ff.; Rabb, 'Effects', pp. 49–51; Lane, *Profits*, p. 81; Caferro, 'Warfare and economy', pp. 204–5; Gutmann, *War and Rural Life*, p. 7.

4 Hale, *War and Society*, pp. 220, 224; Sombart, *Moderne Kapitalismus*, II, pp. 1, 534; Roberts, *Swedish Imperial Experience*, pp. 49–52.
5 Braddick, *God's Fury*, pp. 397, 399; see also Tallett, *War and Society*, pp. 220–1; Soly, *Urbanisme*, p. 334; De Vries, *Economy of Europe*, pp. 204–5; Sombart, *Krieg und Kapitalismus*, pp. 71, 131.
6 Polišenský, *War*, pp. 137–9, 150–1; Pagès, *The Thirty Years War*, pp. 102, 145.
7 But only until Wallenstein's death, after which it fell apart. The example of Friedland is unusual, perhaps even unique, yet it shows the possible impact of war demand on the economy. On Hans Witte, Wallenstein's financier, see Ernstberger, *Hans de Witte*, in particular pp. 62, 105; Parrott, *Business of War*, pp. 216–19, 231–6.
8 In addition, Holland markets had less institutional barriers than other provinces; see Van Bavel, *Manors*, pp. 239–40, 248, 375, 392–3; Van Bavel and Van Zanden, 'Jump-start'.
9 Van der Wee, *Low Countries*, pp. 275–7; Noordegraaf, *Hollands welvaren*, pp. 136–7, 170; Kaptein, *Hollandse textielnijverheid*, pp. 183–4; Lesger, *Handel*, pp. 45, 113, 134; De Vries and Van der Woude, *First Modern Economy*, p. 364.
10 Swart, 'From landsknecht', p. 77. The influx of silver in the southern Netherlands caused a rising of prices, but in the north it stimulated industry and trade. For example, in west Friesland the shortage of coins came to an end and riches were augmented; Fruin, *Tien jaren*, p. 241.
11 Davids, *Rise*, pp. 73, 533; Noordegraaf, *Hollands welvaren*, pp. 157, 170–5; Van Zanden, 'Economic growth', p. 17; Noordegraaf, 'Dutch industry', p. 142; De Vries and Van der Woude, *First Modern Economy*, p. 341. The period of economic growth was accompanied by a growing polarization between rich and poor; however, the poorer sections of society still managed to maintain a reasonable standard of living.
12 Israel, *Dutch Primacy*, p. 79.
13 Lane, 'Role'; Lane, *Profits*, p. 57; for a discussion of this term see Glete, *War and the State*, pp. 54ff. See also Chapter 6.
14 Gijsbers, *Kapitale ossen*, p. 60.
15 Van Dillen, *Rijkdom*, pp. 103–7; Israel, *Dutch Primacy*, p. 12. See also Chapter 6.
16 Lesger, *Handel*, pp. 130, 168, 176.
17 Israel, *Dutch Primacy*, p. 41; De Vries and Van der Woude, *First Modern Economy*, p. 369.
18 Fruin, *Tien jaren*, p. 201; Ergang, *Myth*, p. 31.
19 Gelderblom, *Zuid-Nederlandse kooplieden*, pp. 64–70, 117–19, 149, 153; Gelderblom, 'From Antwerp'.
20 Kaptein, *Hollandse textielnijverheid*, pp. 188, 190–1, 255; Poelwijk, *In dienste*, p. 132; De Vries and Van der Woude, *First Modern Economy*, p. 367.
21 Ibid., p. 672; Haan, 'Prosperität', p. 114; Anderson, *War*, p. 73.
22 Van der Wee, 'Stedelijke economie', pp. 116–19; Van Houtte, 'Onze zeventiende eeuw', pp. 4–8, 16–17; Verlinden, 'En Flandre', p. 28; Thijs, *Van werkwinkel*, p. 170; Dambruyne, *Mensen*, p. 351; Noordegraaf, *Hollands welvaren*, p. 157.
23 Gelderblom, 'Organization', pp. 233, 248; Israel, *Dutch Primacy*, pp. 93, 137; Davids, *Rise*, p. 101; De Vries and Van der Woude, *First Modern Economy*, pp. 368, 376, 405.
24 Ibid., pp. 336, 344, 403, 411–12, 673; Snapper, *Oorlogsinvloeden*, pp. 76, 111.
25 Enthoven, *Zeeland*, pp. 162, 178–213, 228–31; Lesger, *Handel*, p. 136.
26 Van der Woude, *Noorderkwartier*, p. 610; Faber, *Drie eeuwen Friesland*, p. 392.
27 Also in the Thirty Years War the agricultural economy was hurt more severely than urban commercial enterprises. Redlich, *German Military Enterpriser*, I, pp. 499, 508; Kamen, 'Economic and social consequences', pp. 50–1. See also Chapter 5.
28 Hemann, 'Beziehungen', pp. 149–50; Holthuis, *Frontierstad*, pp. 136, 143, 147, 196. The cost of convoys in the Meierij added on average 20 per cent to transport costs, see Adriaenssen, *Staatsvormend geweld*, pp. 165–6.

29 Ergang, *Myth*, pp. 30–3; Friedrichs, *Urban Society*, p. 82; Landers, *Field*, p. 353.
30 De Graaf, *Oorlog*, p. 535.
31 Holthuis, *Frontierstad*, p. 171.
32 Ibid., pp. 120–1, 145, 164–9, 179–84, 197. See also Chapter 4.
33 Gijsbers, *Kapitale ossen*, pp. 125–7.
34 See also Hale, *War and Society*, p. 212.
35 Adriaenssen, *Staatsvormend geweld*, pp. 299–300.
36 Trompetter, *Leven*, pp. 42, 393. On the agrarian depression that set in around 1650, see Van Dillen, *Rijkdom*, p. 497; Bieleman, *Boeren*, p. 28, and footnote 26, above.
37 Adriaenssen, *Staatsvormend geweld*, pp. 313–16.
38 The peasant-weavers encountered fewer guild-like restrictions than weavers in towns. Another proto-industrial village that experienced major growth was Geldrop, in Brabant; ibid., pp. 254, 317–24, 335; Adriaenssen, 'Hoe Tilburg', pp. 16, 21–4, 28–30.
39 Adriaenssen, *Staatsvormend geweld*, p. 334. See also Chapter 5 for the Meierij village debts.
40 Ibid., pp. 326–30; Adriaenssen, 'Hoe Tilburg', p. 27. Another town that was allowed customs privileges was Maastricht; Steegen, *Kleinhandel*, p. 84.
41 Davids, *Rise*, p. 127; Adriaenssen, *Staatsvormend geweld*, pp. 333, 336; Adriaenssen, 'Hoe Tilburg', pp. 17, 31.
42 Wilson, *Thirty Years War*, p. 137, called the Dutch true 'dealers in death' because of their ability to deliver arms-based package deals.
43 Quoted by De Jong, *Staat*, p. 14; see also Wilson, *Thirty Years War*, p. 137.
44 Vogel, 'Arms', p. 210; Klein, *Trippen*, p. 195; Davids, *Rise*, pp. 146–9; on the calculation of the share of GNP, see also Westera, 'Geschutsgieterij', p. 575. Poland exported saltpetre, but this stagnated in the later seventeenth century and Indian saltpetre (via the VOC) became more important; Anderson, *War*, p. 74. On the centrality of Amsterdam in this trade, see also Parrott, *Business of War*, p. 216.
45 De Jong, *Staat*, pp. 35–8.
46 Ibid., pp. 29–30, 40–1, 49–50; Swart, *Krijgsvolk*, p. 68. On the advantages of standardization of arms, see McNeill, *Pursuit of Power*, pp. 75, 140. Standardization in weaponry in the other early modern European armies was poor. Attempts in England in the 1620s and 1630s to arrive at standardization of weaponry came to nothing; see Fletcher, *County Community*, pp. 175, 186–7, 200; some sort of standardization only occurred in the 1660s.
47 Westera, 'Geschutsgieterij', pp. 578, 588; Adriaenssen, 'Amsterdamse geschutsgieterij', p. 52; Sicking, 'Naval warfare', p. 252; Cipolla, *Guns*, p. 49; De Jong, *Staat*, pp. 75–8, 83, 142. After the 1640s the English men-of-war were again usually better armed than the Dutch.
48 Ibid., pp. 38, 49, 158–60, 174; Vogel, 'Arms', pp. 202–9; Jones, *Anglo-Dutch Wars*, p. 68; Edwards, 'Low Countries', p. 160, on the boost in demand for Dutch arms arising from the Civil War in England.
49 Westera, 'Geschutsgieterij', p. 591; Davids, *Rise*, p. 147; De Jong, *Staat*, pp. 48–9, 143, 286–7, 293. In comparison, in both the Spanish Netherlands and in Spain gunpowder manufacture was a monopoly, which precluded economic gains by private entrepreneurs, see Clark, *English Provincial Society*, p. 61; Thompson, 'Money', p. 289. On the importance of the lowering of transaction costs for economic growth: North, 'Transaction costs'.
50 Vogel, 'Arms', p. 198; Enthoven, *Zeeland*, p. 224; Cipolla, *Guns*, pp. 56–62; Davids, *Rise*, pp. 147, 237; De Jong, *Staat*, pp. 46–9, 122. France, in contrast, suffered from an inadequate supply in this respect, see Parrott, *Richelieu's Army*, p. 67. The army and the militias in Spain also suffered repeatedly from limited supplies of arms, gunpowder and shot, see White, 'Experience', pp. 10–13.
51 In 1622. Klein, *Trippen*, p. 208; De Jong, *Staat*, pp. 170–1; Vogel, 'Arms', pp. 200–1, 205. On Count Christian, see also Chapter 1.

52 Adriaenssen, 'Amsterdamse geschutgieterij'.
53 Glete, *War and the State*, p. 172; De Jong, *Staat*, pp. 240–7, 279–81, 332–4.
54 Ibid., pp. 45–8, 87–90, 148–9, 172; Klein, *Trippen*, p. 247. Leasing warships was also an available option, but only for the richest merchants; see also Chapter 6.
55 See also Parrott, *Business of War*, p. 203. The Dutch term is *zoetelaar* or *market-entster*.
56 Swart, *Krijgsvolk*, p. 51. On the role of women among the victuallers in the Thirty Years War, see also Wilson, 'German Women'.
57 De Graaf, *Oorlog*, pp. 200, 209, 354–5; Aitzema *Notable Revolutions*, p. 470.
58 Schulten and Schulten, *Leger*, p. 86; Van Nimwegen, *Subsistentie*, p. 24; Ten Raa and de Bas, *Het Staatsche Leger*, IV, pp. 13, 28, 42.
59 Ibid., IV, pp. 28, 42, 51, 54; Van Nimwegen, *Subsistentie*, pp. 26–8. William III held excellent relations with Sephardic Jews, a wealthy group of investors that permitted him to circumvent the influence of Amsterdam's oligarchy. See also Chapter 3.
60 Ibid., pp. 29, 52–5, 63.
61 Ibid., pp. 128, 354.
62 Despite the growing home manufacture the Dutch remained a major importer of arms; many of the weapons were re-exported. For their supply the Dutch became less dependent on Suhl, Solingen and Liège, regions with vulnerable lines of supply along the Meuse and Rhine; instead, Sweden and India (Coromandel Coast) became important. The workshops in Suhl and Solingen were hampered by guild regulations that specified, among other stipulations, that they should sell their products only to local merchants; the number of arms produced per workshop was limited, too; see Clark, *English Provincial Society*, p. 62; De Jong, *Staat*, pp. 218, 252.
63 Thompson, *War and Society*, III, p. 270; Lynn, *Giant*, pp. 182–3; Parrott, *Richelieu's Army*, pp. 389–90. Parrott, *Business of War*, pp. 223–5, notes that for military entrepreneurs career considerations were often more important than simple economic benefits: 'financial services might also be a lever for bargain for high military office'. Milan and Venice, however, were examples of places that achieved great profit from the arms industry, comparable to that of the Netherlands, see Caferro, 'Warfare and economy', p. 198.
64 Davids, *Rise*, p. 148; Anderson, *War*, p. 150.
65 British wartime suppliers fared much better in the eighteenth century, thanks also to the improved political-institutional environment; see Bannerman, *Merchants*, pp. 126–37.
66 See also Chapter 7. Cf. De Jong, *Staat*, p. 23; Klein, 'De Nederlandse handelspolitiek', pp. 189–212.
67 Tracy, *Founding*, p. 295.

Conclusion

The advantages of military discipline and commercialized warfare

> And it is just eight years ago that [… I resolved …] to retire to a country such as this [i.e., Holland] where the long-continued war has caused such order to be established that the armies which are maintained seem only to be of use in allowing the inhabitants to enjoy the fruits of peace with so much the more security.
>
> René Descartes, 1637[1]

It was and is a paradox that the Dutch Wars of Independence coincided with a true Golden Age for the Dutch Republic. Early modern warfare was usually destructive, exhausting the financial capacities of rulers and their states, depleting countries' available resources, and increasing risk for everyone involved. War-related violence increased the death toll all over Europe; harvests seized by soldiers induced famines; widespread epidemics reduced manpower. Poorly paid soldiers had to fend for themselves and their poor discipline menaced local farmers and trade. Even societies not overrun by troops suffered. The cumulative cost of maintaining increasing numbers of mercenary soldiers caused taxes to rise and brought about arbitrary exactions by the state. Property rights were threatened – by, for example, debased currencies. Dangers along trading routes mounted, particularly affecting goods traded over a long distance.

The Dutch Republic thrived midst this war-related misery, which dominated much of Europe in the later sixteenth and early seventeenth centuries. Before the reasons for this paradox are outlined, it's worth remembering that numerous inhabitants of the northern Netherlands paid a high price during the Dutch Wars of Independence. Herring fishermen lost their vessels to Dunkirk privateers, Meierij farmers suffered for decades from marauding troops, and the owners and tenants of low-lying fields experienced substantial losses from strategic inundations. High custom duties disrupted established continental, inland-orientated long-distance trade networks. The risks at sea escalated, and war expenditure led to an unprecedented level of taxation. And, of course, war-related violence resulted in the loss of lives, above all during the early decades of the Revolt – for instance in the sacks of Zutphen and Naarden but also in numerous skirmishes and sieges.

By comparison with the other belligerents, however, the Dutch Republic suffered relatively little. Its rise in prosperity went far beyond the usual (but generally only temporary) wealth accrued by war profiteers. Its impressive economic growth lasted from 1585 to the mid-seventeenth century.[2] Warfare apparently created new economic opportunities, yielding profits in the longer term that on the whole eclipsed the losses from war. The Dutch turned out to be masters of exploring and utilizing these opportunities: they constituted the first *territorial* state to successfully engage in commercialized warfare.

In order to be able to sustainedly profit from warfare, public authorities needed first of all to act as reliable employers. This meant they had to pay their troops on time. Because of regular pay, soldiers submitted to discipline, enabling civilians to enjoy the fruits of peace in the middle of war, to employ the phrase of the famous French philosopher, René Descartes, who lived in the northern Netherlands between 1628 and 1649.[3] The remarkable level of discipline was without doubt the most important aspect of the military revolution in the northern Netherlands, which began in the early 1570s when William of Orange set in motion the professionalization of troops, bringing the landsknecht tradition to an end. A well-trained force was the result, under firm civilian command, a not inexplicable outcome in view of the powerful influence of urban authorities in Dutch politics.

By the late 1580s the basic structures of the decentralized state were well established, permitting Maurice to pursue the work of his father within a much stronger institutional setting. Among other innovations, he introduced the standardization of command structures and weaponry and imposed more regular drill. Alongside a stupendous rise in taxation in Holland, made possible by a flexible system of excises and the broad tax base, the leading province's financial transformation secured the flow of soldiers' regular pay. Difficulties with rioting troops or resources that did not arrive quickly enough certainly existed, but the previous chapters have shown that they were of a relatively modest nature. Maurice's reforms may not have been all that new or original, but the aggregate outcome of the reorganization rendered the Dutch military structure outstandingly effective, at least by the standards of the time. In all probability, it was exactly this reorganization and associated efficiencies that enabled the Dutch to continue the struggle against mighty Habsburg Spain.

The state was not only the country's largest employer, it was also its largest customer. The public authorities also turned out to be quite important in this regard, and the army, navy and building of fortifications stimulated producers and traders. The 1595 and 1599 standardization of armaments did much to improve the regulation and transparency of the arms market. Artisans and merchants in the arms trade received support in the form of raw materials, access to government stocks and outright subsidies. The provincial admiralty boards were also active in their support of shippers and companies, and their presence stimulated wharves and ship suppliers in the neighbourhood. And last but certainly not least, soldiers created demand for food, merchandise and services. Dutch soldiers may not have been the highest paid in Europe, but they were known to receive their pay much more regularly than others. As a result, military suppliers received payment with less delay than their counterparts in other countries, who might even never obtain their due. In addition, Dutch families were confident that they would receive a secure income if they provided rooms and bedding for soldiers.

Other belligerent states were rarely such reliable employers or customers, and the contrast with the Dutch Republic was striking.[4] Numerous rulers hired large numbers of soldiers, but only a handful managed to pay their troops on time. Everywhere, armies and navies created huge demand for supplies, arms, ships, fortifications and so on, but only a few fulfilled their side of the bargain. Soldiers were usually quartered on households without sufficient payment. While some rulers and commanders engaged in the reform of military logistics, not unlike Maurice and William Louis in the Netherlands, that process was invariably more piecemeal and evolutionary in character, relating to just one aspect or one section of the military. Since armies tended to grow larger all the time, the potential for the military to constitute a burden for society increased accordingly. In the Dutch Republic, however, the military reforms gathered a true revolutionary momentum, enabling army growth without disturbing good relations between inhabitants and soldiers. A substantial number of improvements (in the fields of finance, discipline, tactics, housing, fortification-building, sea warfare, armaments and so on) were concentrated within one or two decades, approximately from the end of the 1580s. For the Dutch Republic, therefore, the term 'military revolution' remains applicable; the developments in professionalization were rapid and they coincided with far-reaching societal and institutional reforms.[5]

One could argue that if there had been no Dutch Wars of Independence, the Golden Age might well have been even more glorious. Indeed, periods of peace generally tend to promote trade. Manpower locked up in the army and navy could have been put to more productive use in agriculture, industry and the service sector. Funds that were spent on warfare might well have been invested in more rewarding, non-violent purposes. True, the war did not create the general positive economic trend in Holland; economic growth had been under way since the late fifteenth century. But war was ubiquitous in early modern European society. If there had been no Dutch Wars of Independence, the northern Netherlands would have been dragged into the numerous wars of the Spanish Habsburg monarchy, which would have meant high taxes, disrupted trade routes and increased risks at sea exactly as during the Eighty Years War. Actual war expenditure might have been lower, but it would probably have been accompanied by economic disruption due to repeated state bankruptcies, the pressing burden of supporting unruly soldiers, and the disorderly behaviour of troops. Moreover, such warfare would hardly have furthered the interests of the numerous local industries and trades in the northern Netherlands. For example, no Dutch colonial company would have existed since the monopoly of that trade was held by the Spanish government, and no admiralty boards would have prioritized the convoys for local merchants' trade routes. In other words, no commercialization of warfare would have been possible.

Independence, therefore, was a *conditio sine qua non* for the institutional-social-economic-military system that came to fruition in the 1590s in the Dutch Republic. Strict civilian control over the army would have been much more difficult within a political setting in which dynastic glory dominated strategy and tactics. Dutch state finance was only reasonably efficient because priorities in war-related expenditure were decided upon by local elites who actually controlled the major flows of cash and credit. The wartime stimulation of various trades would have been difficult in a more centralized setting where local urban authorities had less power and autonomy. Only an independent state favourably positioned in terms of seaborne routes could engage fully in colonial trade and establish new global trade connections. In short, only a decentralized, urbanized state like the Dutch Republic could grab and fully exploit the new opportunities offered by warfare.

This is not to say that individuals did not matter. On the contrary, the previous chapters have shown the crucial importance of the decisive leadership and imaginative insights of statesmen like Orange, Van Oldenbarnevelt, Maurice, William-Louis, Frederick Henry, John de Witt and William III. But their actions were magnificently supported by the precocious administrative developments in Holland, developments that dated from the late fifteenth century and must have been furthered at all points by numerous anonymous but rather skilful administrators, secretaries, receivers and clerks. By the start of the Revolt the densely populated province of Holland already held the trump card of efficient fiscal-financial cooperation between the towns, the true carriers of wealth in this province, giving the provincial rulers (including their stadholders) a kind of natural leadership within the Union. The step towards an efficient military structure was a relatively small one. As a result, the province of Holland was the solid foundation that helped the Republic time and again through times of crises. The United Provinces had a federal constitution, but in practice command and control was centred in Holland. It was to Holland's advantage, moreover, that up to the mid-century the other belligerents were caught up in widespread revolts and civil warfare, while the province itself was virtually free from the presence of enemy troops after the 1580s.

Had there been no war, the northern Netherlands might well have experienced some sort of Golden Age. But that Golden Age would have been quite different. Holland would never have been in a position to attract such a concentration of manpower and resources to its territory. To begin with, the Golden Age would have started later because of the regional dominance of Flanders and Brabant, which suffered extensively from the fighting. The war made Holland a region full of promise, one that gained in economic importance, outdoing the other rebellious provinces and reducing them to second-rate participants. Physical destruction due to pillaging, strategic flooding and scorched earth campaigns was experienced by the countryside and more peripheral areas, such as Northern Brabant. The Golden Age of the Dutch Wars of Independence was thus very much a Holland phenomenon; other provinces of the Dutch Republic only participated to a much smaller extent.[6]

War had for Holland the advantageous effect of directing enormous tax revenues into the coffers of the provincial government, furthering the tapping of old and new credit resources that were extremely useful not only for warfare but also for other purposes – for instance, the protection of trade routes and support of colonial companies. Loans enabled pressing war expenses to be spread over a longer period, while war expenditure once again served the commercialization of the economy, for example through the housing of soldiers and the management of the public debt, which permitted numerous households in Holland to benefit from regular transfers from the state in the form of compensation and interest payments. The regulation of the public debt allowed substantial capital accumulation for a large number of the wealthier households, capital accumulation protected by a military buffer zone and not threatened by unruly garrison soldiers. No mutinies menaced the property of the Holland bourgeoisie. As a result, the Dutch Wars of Independence stimulated the rise of capitalism in an emerging national setting, at a time when capitalists in other states were suffering from war-related damage and persistent insecurity. A generation later, the English were the first to copy a number of Dutch institutions and practices that fostered domestic capital accumulation in times of warfare.[7]

Not all groups, however, profited equally from the new opportunities to accumulate capital. A shift of wealth from the countryside to urban communities took place, especially during the early decades of the Revolt, since the defence of towns was given priority. Rural areas suffered disproportionally from the violence that accompanied the passage and operations of armies, alongside the scorched earth campaigns and strategic flooding ordered by Dutch commanders. Towns, and in particular Holland's towns, grew rapidly throughout the war. Fortifications and garrisons strengthened Dutch urban communities, a critical element being the peaceful co-existence of soldiers with citizens and cooperation between regular troops and militiamen. New ramparts heightened a town's prestige. But the war also had different effects within the towns. The higher war-related loans necessitated higher taxes to fund the greater interest charges, and since most taxes came from excises on necessities, the lower and middle classes paid disproportionately. Only a proportion of these social groups received compensation from billeting soldiers, labouring at the fortifications or in armament workshops, interest payments on loans, or new employment at wharves. The war also affected the prospects of merchants in different ways; traders orientated towards the inland trade saw a contracting of their opportunities, while those with sea-borne links had a chance to expand.

The growth of colonial trade was a new war-related development, characterized above all by the 'logic of capital accumulation' and stimulating the changes that made the Dutch Republic the 'core' of a world-wide capitalist network.[8] The colonial connection in the East Indies endured due to efficient state formation and a firm economic base at home. The navy and also the West India Company performed their tasks of defending Dutch traders much better than is usually acknowledged. As a result, the Dutch Republic played a prominent part in the process of early modern globalization, not least because of its advanced skills – including those of modern logistics – in military matters. Governance during wartime was regularly constrained by urban elites who had a major say in political decision-making. Large commercial centres like Amsterdam dominated, of course, but smaller towns also had substantial leverage in politics and enjoyed *quid pro quo* possibilities in exchange for casting their votes in a particular way. Meanwhile, authorities in garrison towns noted the rising yields of local taxes and the beneficial economic consequences of the presence of soldiers.[9] Warfare, politics and economic interests similarly interacted closely in Dutch expansion overseas – thus advancing the expansion of Europe.

A buffer zone kept most of the war-related destruction outside the core territory of Holland after the 1580s.[10] Although the province paid the bulk of the war costs, it was not a problem since it also profited disproportionately from the newly won independence. The distributional effects of war expenditure benefitted above all Holland's urbanized economy; in turn, the urban communities of this province were able to bear the increasing burden of the Eighty Years War because the yield of excise taxes in particular was so profitable in this commercialized economic setting. This answers the question posed at the beginning of this book, how 'funds extracted from the common people seemed to return by other ways again, like the waters which are transported by the rivers into the sea and which are returned by nature to its resources in a way unknown to us', in the quotation from the Council of State:[11] within the borders of the Dutch Republic there developed a genuine system of commercialized warfare.

This self-enriching process seemed to slow down after the signing of peace in 1648; there was less willingness to pay taxes, while military efficiency and discipline slackened in the absence of an on-going threat of war. This was the reason why the wars of the early 1670s seriously endangered Dutch independence. The disastrous situation did not last long, however. The institutions that favoured the commercialization of warfare had not disappeared and Dutch state authorities remained reliable employers and customers; when the military threat was suddenly renewed, Holland continued to be the principal resource. The general prosperity of the country remained high; growth rates slowed after 1670 but per capita income remained one of the highest in Europe.[12]

While the Dutch Republic was still a major player in international rivalries, its competitive edge as a military state disappeared. Dutch rulers became adept at diplomacy; actual involvement in wars was brief or indirect – for example, its long-lasting alliance with England (1688/9–1780) in effect eliminated the need for any thorough reform of army or navy. In contrast to the first decades of the Revolt, military innovations became piecemeal instead of revolutionary and Dutch military commanders became followers rather than initiators of change. Moreover, international conditions were transformed. Since the mid-seventeenth century England had developed into a substantial naval power; not much later, France's military potential began to be realized and it acquired a more formidable army. The contrast with the situation earlier in the seventeenth century – when both England and France had been preoccupied with devastating civil wars – was striking.

In two respects, moreover, the northern Netherlands also experienced difficulties in the commercialization of warfare after 1650. First, the Dutch Wars of Independence had advanced the expansion of their position in international trade; war had fed trade and trade had fed war, not least because of the favourable decentralized position of the admiralty boards, which served so well to protect their seaborne merchant communities. Yet this growth was increasingly hampered as emerging nation states gradually closed their borders to Dutch merchants or raised their custom duties on the Republic's exports, partly because of mercantilist views and partly because their traders no longer needed Dutch entrepreneurship to the same degree. Second, the positive distributive effects of war expenditure diminished. Payments for housing soldiers and the upkeep of fortifications halved after 1650, making such activities less profitable and so of less interest to urban dwellers. At the same time the growth of the public debt was halted, reducing the number of households profiting from interest payments. Thereafter, necessary additions to the public debt were increasingly subscribed by the financial elite, furthering the accumulation of capital among a smaller number of households than previously. Commercialization of warfare was still possible after 1650, but the dynamics of the Dutch Wars of Independence, which had pumped so much war expenditure back into broader sections of the domestic social economy, were now much weaker.

Notes

1 Descartes, *Discourse on Method*, p. 20. On Descartes and his praise of Dutch military organization and discipline, see also Borel, *Summary or Compendium*, pp. 7–8, and Gaukroger, *Descartes*, p. 65.
2 De Vries and Van der Woude, *First Modern Economy*, p. 672.
3 See quotation at head of chapter.
4 Parrott, *Business of War*, pp. 227–8, 241.
5 Following here the definition by James Wheeler, who defined the Military Revolution as an 'interrelated succession of developments in tactics, strategy, technology, and government which changed warfare and the participating states'. Wheeler, *Making of a World Power*, p. 9.
6 Prak, *Dutch Republic*, Chapter 3.
7 Dickson, *Financial Revolution*; Brewer, *Sinews of Power*.
8 Arrighi, *Long Twentieth Century*, p. 33.
9 Resulting in the aggregation of local business interests with those of the central state, not least because of the high 'protection-selling capacity' of the Dutch military institutions, convincing local elites to contribute to the Dutch war effort. See Mann, *Sources of Social Power*, p. 477; Glete, *War and the State*, pp. 52–4; Lane, *Profits*.
10 It has been argued by John Nef that this was the reason that Holland experienced a Golden Age in the middle of war. This is only partly true. Spain hardly experienced any warfare in its core territory (Castile), neither did France (*pays d'élections*), yet their economies languished under the massive load of war expenditure, just like so many other early modern states of the seventeenth century. Nef, *War and Human Progress*, p. 109.
11 See introduction, p. 1 of this book.
12 Van Zanden and Van Leeuwen, 'Persistent'; De Vries and Van der Woude, *First Modern Economy*, p. 707.

Bibliography

Abel, Wilhelm, *Agricultural Fluctuations in Europe: From the Thirteenth to the Twentieth Centuries* (London, 1980)

Abrahamsson, Bengt, *Military Professionalization and Political Power* (Beverly Hills CA, 1972)

Adams, Julia, 'Trading states, trading places: the role of patrimonialism in early modern Dutch development', *Comparative Studies in Society and History*, 36–2 (1994), pp. 319–55

Adams, Simon, 'Tactics or politics? "The military revolution" and the Hapsburg hegemony, 1525–1648', in: John A. Lynn (ed.), *Tools of War: Instruments, Ideas, and Institutions of Warfare, 1445–1871* (Urbana and Chicago, 1990), pp. 28–52

Adriaenssen, L.F.W., 'De Amsterdamse geschutgieterij: Over het oorlogsindustriële ondernemerschap van de stedelijke overheid', *Jaarboek Amstelodamum* 94 (2002), pp. 44–89

——, 'Hoe Tilburg in de Opstand goed garen spon: De opkomst van Tilburg als lakencentrum', *Bijdragen tot de Geschiedenis* 85 (2002), pp. 5–34

——, *Staatsvormend geweld. Overleven aan de frontlinies in de meierij van Den Bosch, 1572–1629* (Tilburg, 2007)

Aelianus, *The Tactiks of AElian or Art of Embattailing an Army after ye Grecian Manner* (London, 1616)

Aglionby, William, *The Present State of the United Provinces of the Low-Countries as to the Government, Laws, Forces, Riches, Manners, Customes, Revenue, and Territory of the Dutch* (London, 1669)

Ágoston, Gábor, 'Empires and warfare in east-central Europe, 1550–1750: the Ottoman-Habsburg rivalry and military transformation', in: Frank Tallett and D.J.B. Trim (eds), *European Warfare, 1350–1750* (Cambridge, 2010), pp. 110–34

Aitzema, Lion, *Notable Revolutions Beeing a True Relation of What Hap'ned in the United Provinces of the Netherlands in the Years MDCL and MDCLI* (London, 1653)

Anderson, M.S., *War and Society in Europe of the Old Regime, 1618–1789* (Leicester, 1988)

Anon., *Ordonnanties op gemene middelen Wedde en Westerwolde 1603–53* (Groningen, 1653; orig. Rijksarchief Groningen, Staten van Stad en Lande, no. 527)

Anon., *The Dutch Drawn to Life* (London, 1664)

Appel, Michael, *Werner Sombart: Historiker und Theoretiker des modernen Kapitalismus* (Marburg, 1992)

Arentz, B., 'Schadevergoeding bij militaire inundaties: Van het Ontzet van Leiden tot de Tweede Wereldoorlog', *Tijdschrift voor Waterstaatsgeschiedenis* 9 (2000), pp. 67–76

Arnade, Peter, *Beggars, Iconoclasts, and Civic Patriots: The Political Culture of the Dutch Revolt* (Ithaca and London, 2008)

Arnold, Thomas F., 'Fortifications and the military revolution: the Gonzaga experience, 1530–1630', in: Clifford J. Rogers (ed.), *The Military Revolution Debate: Readings on the Military Transformation of Early Modern Europe* (Boulder CO, 1995), pp. 201–26

Arrighi, Giovanni, *The Long Twentieth Century: Money, Power, and the Origins of Our Time* (London, 1994)

Asch, Ronald G., 'War and state-building', in: Frank Tallett and D.J.B. Trim (eds), *European Warfare, 1350–1750* (Cambridge, 2010), pp. 322–38

Ashton, Robert, 'Deficit finance in the reign of James I', *Economic History Review* 10 (1957), pp. 15–29

Aten, Diederik, *Als het gewelt komt: Politiek en economie in Holland benoorden het IJ 1500–1800* (Hilversum, 1995)

Badalo-Dulong, Claude, *Banquier du Roi. Bartélemy Hervart 1606–1676* (Paris, 1951)

Baetens, R. 'Organisatie en resultaten van de Vlaamse kaapvaart in de 17e eeuw', *Mededelingen van de Marine Academie van België* 21 (1969–71), pp. 89–125

Bannerman, Gordon E., *Merchants and the Military in Eighteenth-Century Britain* (London, 2008)

Barbera, Henry, *Rich Nations and Poor in Peace and War* (Lexington MA, 1973)

Barbour, Violet, *Capitalism in Amsterdam in the 17th Century* (Ann Arbor MI, 1963)

Barnekamp, Josef, 'Sie hausen uebell, schlagen die leuth und schatzen über die massen. Velen und Ramsdorf 1580–1650', in: Timothy Sodmann (ed.), *1568–1648. Zu den Auswirkungen des Achtzigjährigen Krieges auf die östlichen Niederlande und das Westmünsterland* (Vreden, 2002), 29–64

Bartstra, J.S., *Vlootherstel en legeraugmentatie 1770–1780* (Assen, 1952)

Baumann, Reinhard, *Landsknechte. Ihre Geschichte und Kultur vom Späten Mittelalter bis zum Dreissigjährigen Krieg* (Munich, 1994)

Becht, H.E., *Statistische gegevens betreffende den handelsomzet van de Republiek der Verenigde Nederlanden gedurende de 17e eeuw (1579–1715)* (The Hague, 1908)

Beguin, Katia, 'La circulation des rentes constituées dans la France du XVIIe siècle. Une approche de l' incertitude économique', *Annales* 60 (2005), pp. 1229–44

Bennett, Matthew, 'Legality and legitimacy in war and its conduct, 1350–1650', in: Frank Tallett and D.J.B. Trim (eds), *European Warfare, 1350–1750* (Cambridge, 2010), pp. 264–77

Bentivoglio, Guido, *The Compleat History of the Warrs of Flanders* (London, 1654; orig. 1635)

Bérenger, Jean, *Finances et absolutisme autrichien dans la seconde moitié du XVIIeme siècle* (Paris, 1970)

Bernstein, Michael A. and Mark R. Wilson, 'New perspectives on the history of the military-industrial complex', *Enterprise & Society* 12 (2011), pp. 1–9

Bieleman, Jan, *Boeren op het Drentse Zand (1600–1910). Een nieuwe visie op de 'oude' landbouw* (Wageningen, 1987)

Black, Jeremy, *A Military Revolution? Military Change and European Society 1500–1800* (London, 1991)

——, *European Warfare 1660–1815* (London, 1994)

——, 'A military revolution? A 1660–1792 perspective', in: Clifford J. Rogers (ed.), *The Military Revolution Debate: Readings on the Military Transformation of Early Modern Europe* (Boulder CO, 1995), pp. 95–114

——, 'Introduction', in: Jeremy Black (ed.), *War in the Early Modern World* (London, 1999), pp. 1–24

Blockmans, Wim P., 'Voracious states and obstructing cities', in: Charles Tilly and Wim P. Blockmans (eds), *Cities and the Rise of States in Europe, AD 1000 to 1800* (New York, 1994), pp. 218–50

Blockmans, Wim, *Metropolen aan de Noordzee: De geschiedenis van Nederland 1100–1560* (Amsterdam, 2010)

Bonke, A.H., 'Het eiland Onrust. Van scheepswerf van de VOC tot bedreigd historisch-archeologisch monument', in: M.H. Bartels, E.H.P. Cordfunke and H. Sarfatij (eds), *Hollanders uit en thuis: Archeologie, geschiedenis en bouwhistorie gedurende de VOC-tijd in de Oost, de West en thuis: Cultuurhistorie van de Nederlandse expansie* (Hilversum, 2002), pp. 45–60

Bonney, Richard (ed.), *Economic Systems and State Finance* (Oxford, 1995)

Boogman, J.C., 'De overgang van Gouda, Dordrecht, Leiden en Delft in de zomer van het jaar 1572', *Tijdschrift voor Geschiedenis* 57 (1942), pp. 81–112

Borel, Pierre, *A Summary or Compendium of the Life of the Most Famous Philosopher Renatus Descartes* (London, 1670)

Bos-Rops, J.A.M.Y., *Graven op zoek naar geld: De inkomsten van de graven van Holland en Zeeland, 1389–1433* (Hilversum, 1993)

Braddick, Michael, *God's Fury, England's Fire: A New History of the English Civil Wars* (London, 2008)

Brandon, Pepijn, 'Marxism and the Dutch miracle: the Dutch Republic and the transition-debate', *Historical Materialism* 19:2 (2011), pp. 90–130

——, *Masters of War: State, Capital, and Military Enterprise in the Dutch Cycle of Accumulation (1600–1795)* (Leiden, forthcoming 2014)

Braudel, Fernand, *Civilisation matérielle, économie et capitalisme, XVe-XVIIe siècle. Tome III: Le temps du monde* (Paris, 1979)

Braunius, S.W.P.C., 'Oorlogsvloot', in: L. M. Akveld, S. Hart and W.J. van Hoboken (eds), *Maritieme geschiedenis der Nederlanden* II (Bussum, 1977), pp. 316–56

Brewer, John, *The Sinews of Power: War, Money, and the English State (1688–1783)* (Cambridge, 1989)

Browning, Andrew (ed.), *English Historical Documents 1660–1714* (London, 1953)

Bruijn, J.R. (ed.), *De oorlogvoering ter zee in 1673 in journalen en andere stukken* (Groningen, 1966)

Bruijn, J.R., *De admiraliteit van Amsterdam in rustige jaren 1713–1751* (Amsterdam and Haarlem, 1970)

——, 'Dutch Privateering during the Second and Third Anglo-Dutch Wars', *The Low Countries History Yearbook* 12 (1978), pp. 79–93

——, 'Mercurius en Mars uiteen. De uitrusting van de oorlogsvloot in de zeventiende eeuw', in: S. Groenveld, M.E.H.N. Mout and I. Schöffer (eds), *Bestuurders en Geleerden: Opstellen over onderwerpen uit de Nederlandse geschiedenis van de zestiende, zeventiende en achttiende eeuw* (Amsterdam and Dieren, 1985), pp. 97–106.

——, *The Dutch Navy of the Seventeenth and Eighteenth Centuries* (Columbia SC, 1993)

——, 'States and their navies from the late sixteenth to the end of the eighteenth centuries', in: Philippe Contamine (ed.), *War and Competition between States* (Oxford, 2000), pp. 69–98

Brulez, Wilfried, 'Het gewicht van de oorlog in de nieuwe tijden', *Tijdschrift voor Geschiedenis* 91 (1978), pp. 386–406

Burschel, Peter, *Söldner im Nordwestdeutschland des 16. und 17. Jahrhunderts. Sozialgeschichtliche Studien* (Göttingen, 1994)

Caferro, William P. 'Warfare and economy in Renaissance Italy, 1350–1450', *Journal of Interdisciplinary History* 39 (2008), pp. 167–209

Caldecott-Baird, Duncan, *The Expedition in Holland 1572–1574. The Revolt of the Netherlands: The Early Struggle for Independence: From the Manuscript by Walter Morgan* (London, 1976)

Chase, Kenneth, *Firearms: A Global History to 1700* (Cambridge, 2003)

Chase-Dunn, Christopher, *Global Formation: Structures of the World Economy* (Cambridge MA, 1989)

Chaudhuri, K.N., *Trade and Civilisation in the Indian Ocean: An Economic History from the Rise of Islam to 1750* (Cambridge, 1985)

Childs, John, *Armies and Warfare in Europe 1648–1789* (New York, 1982)

Cipolla, Carlo M., *Guns, Sails and Empires: Technological Innovation and the Early Phases of European Expansion 1400–1700* (New York, 1965)

——, *Before the Industrial Revolution: European Society and Economy, 1000–1700* (New York, 1976)

Clark, Peter, *English Provincial Society from the Reformation to the Revolution: Religion, Politics and Society in Kent 1500–1640* (Hassocks, 1977)

Collins Baker, C.H. *The Life and Circumstances of James Brydges, First Duke of Chandos* (Oxford, 1949)

Corvisier, André, *Armies and Societies in Europe 1494–1789* (Bloomington and London, 1979)

Coulomb, Fanny and Jacques Fontanel, 'Disarmamanent: a century of economic thought', *Defence and Peace Economics* 14 (2003), pp. 193–208

Croxton, Derek, 'A territorial imperative? The military revolution, strategy and peacemaking in the Thirty Years War', *War in History* 5 (1998), pp. 253–79

Dambruyne, Johan, *Mensen en centen: Het 16de-eeuwse Gent in demografisch en economisch perspectief* (Ghent, 2001)

Darley, Gillian, *John Evelyn: Living for Ingenuity* (New Haven CT, 2006)

Davids, Karel, *The Rise and Decline of Dutch Technological Leadership: Technology, Economy and Culture in the Netherlands, 1350–1800* (Leiden, 2008)

Davids, Karel and Jan Lucassen (eds), *A Miracle Mirrored: The Dutch Republic in an European Perspective* (Cambridge, 1995)

Davies, C.S.L., 'Provisions for armies, 1509–50: a study in the effectiveness of early Tudor government', *Economic History Review* 17 (1964), pp. 234–48

De Cauwer, Peter, *Tranen van bloed: Het beleg van 's-Hertogenbosch en de oorlog in de Nederlanden, 1629* (Amsterdam, 2008)

De Graaf, Ronald, *Oorlog, mijn arme schapen: Een andere kijk op de Tachtigjarige Oorlog, 1565–1648* (Franeker, 2004)

De Jong, J.J., *Met goed fatsoen: De elite in een Hollandse stad: Gouda* (Amsterdam, 1985)

De Jong, Michiel, *Staat van Oorlog: Wapenbedrijf en militaire hervorming in de Republiek der Verenigde Nederlanden, 1585–1621* (Hilversum, 2005)

De Korte, J.P., *De jaarlijkse financiële verantwoording in de Verenigde Oostindische Compagnie* (The Hague, 1983)

De Kraker, Adriaan M.J., *Landschap uit balans: De invloed van de natuur, de economie en de politiek op de ontwikkeling van het landschap in de Vier Ambachten en het Land van Saeftinghe tussen 1488 en 1609* (Utrecht, 1997)

De Swaan, Abram, 'Widening circles of social identification: emotional concerns in sociogenetic perspective', *Theory, Culture and Society* 12 (1995), pp. 25–39

De Vries, Jan, *The Economy of Europe in an Age of Crisis 1600–1750* (New York, 1976)

——, 'The political economy of bread in the Dutch Republic', in: Oscar Gelderblom (ed.), *The Political Economy of the Dutch Republic* (Surrey, 2009), pp. 85–114

De Vries, Jan and Ad van der Woude, *The First Modern Economy: Success, Failure, and Perseverance of the Dutch Economy, 1500–1815* (Cambridge, 1995)

Deane, Phyllis, 'War and industrialisation', in: J.M. Winter (ed.), *War and Economic Development: Essays in Memory of David Joslin* (Cambridge, 1975), pp. 91–102

Decavele, Johan, 'Willem van Oranje, de vader van een verscheurd vaderland (1577–84)', *Handelingen der Maatschappij voor Geschiedenis en Oudheidkunde te Gent* 38 (1984), pp. 69–85

Dekker, Rudolf, *Holland in beroering. Oproeren in de 17de en 18de eeuw* (Baarn, 1982)

Dekker, Rudolf and Lotte van der Pol, *The Tradition of Female Transvestism in Early Modern Europe* (London, 1989)

Den Heijer, Henk, *Goud, ivoor en slaven. Scheepvaart en handel van de Tweede Westindische Compagnie op Afrika, 1674–1740* (Zutphen, 1997)

——, *De geschiedenis van de WIC* (Zutphen, 2002)

Descartes, René, (David Weissman, ed.), *Discourse on the Method and Meditations on First Philosophy* (New Haven and London, 1996; orig. Amsterdam, 1637)

Despretz, A., 'Stadsversterkingen en burgerwacht tijdens de instauratiejaren der Gentse Calvinistische Republiek (1577–79)', *Maatschappij voor Geschiedenis en Oudheidkunde te Gent* 20 (1966), pp. 3–18

Diamond, Jared, *Guns, Germs, and Steel: A Short History of Everybody for the Last 13,000 Years* (New York, 1997)

Dickson, P.G.M., *The Financial Revolution in England: A Study in the Development of Public Credit, 1688–1756* (London, 1967)

Diekerhoff, F.L., *De oorlogsvloot in de zeventiende eeuw* (Bussum, 1967)

Dormans, E.H.M., *Het tekort: Staatsschuld in de tijd der Republiek* (Amsterdam, 1991)

Downing, Brian M., *The Military Revolution and Political Change: Origins of Democracy and Autocracy in Early Modern Europe* (Princeton, 1992)

Drake, Michael S., *Problematics of Military Power: Government, Discipline and the Subject of Violence* (Portland OR, 2001)

Drelichman, Mauricio, and Hans-Joachim Voth, 'The sustainable debts of Philip II: a reconstruction of Castile's fiscal position, 1566–96', *The Journal of Economic History* 70 (2010), pp. 813–42

——, 'Serial defaults, serial profits: returns to sovereign lending in Habsburg Spain, 1566–1600', *Explorations in Economic History* 48 (2011), pp. 1–19

Duerloo, Luc, *Dynasty and Piety: Archduke Albert (1598–1621) and Habsburg Political Culture in an Age of Religious Wars* (Surrey, 2012)

Duffy, C., *Siege Warfare: the Fortress in the Early Modern World 1494–1660* (London, 1979)

Duffy, Michael, 'Introduction: the military revolution and the state 1500–1800', in: Michael Duffy (ed.), *The Military Revolution and the State 1500–1800* (Exeter, 1980), pp. 1–9

——, 'The foundations of British naval power', in: Michael Duffy (ed.), *The Military Revolution and the State 1500–1800* (Exeter, 1980), pp. 49–85

Duindam, Jeroen, 'Geschiedschrijving en oorlogvoering: de metamorfose van een klassiek thema', *Bijdragen en Mededelingen betreffende de Geschiedenis der Nederlanden* 118 (2003), pp. 455–66

Ebben, Maurits A., *Zilver, brood en kogels voor de koning: Kredietverlening door Portugese bankiers aan de Spaanse kroon 1621–1665* (Leiden, 1996)

Edwards, P., 'The Low Countries, the arms trade and the British Civil War', *The Journal of European Economic History* 32 (2002), pp. 141–68

Elias, Joh. E., *De vlootbouw in Nederland in de eerste helft der 17e eeuw 1596–1655* (Amsterdam, 1933)

Ellemers, J.E., 'The revolt of the Netherlands: the part played by religion in the process of nation-building', *Social Compass* 14:2 (1967), pp. 93–103

Elliott, John, *Richelieu and Olivares* (Cambridge, 1984)

Engel, Jeffrey A., 'Not yet a garrison state: reconsidering Eisenhower's military-industrial complex', *Enterprise & Society* 12 (2011), pp. 175–99

Enthoven, Victor, 'De oorlog wordt duur betaald: Een vergelijking van de financiering van de zeeoorlog in Spanje en de Republiek naar aanleiding van de slag bij Duins, 1639', in: W. Fritschy, J.K.T. Postma and J. Roelevink (eds), *Doel en middel: Aspecten van financieel overheidsbeleid in de Nederlanden van de zestiende eeuw tot heden* (Amsterdam, 1995), pp. 59–73

——, *Zeeland en de opkomst van de Republiek: Handel en strijd in de Scheldedelta, c. 1550–1621* (Leiden, 1996)

——, 'Mars en Mercurius bijeen: De smalle marges van het Nederlandse maritieme veiligheidsbeleid rond 1650', in: Leo Akveld a.o. (eds), *In het kielzog: Maritiem-historische studies aangeboden aan Jaap R. Bruijn* (Amsterdam, 2003), pp. 40–60

Ergang, Robert, *The Myth of the All-Destructive Fury of the Thirty Years' War* (Pocono Pines PA, 1956)

Ernstberger, Anton, *Hans de Witte: Finanzmann Wallensteins* (Wiesbaden, 1954)

Faber, J.A., *Drie eeuwen Friesland: Economische en sociale ontwikkelingen van 1500 tot 1800* (Leeuwarden, 1973)

Feitsma, W.A., *Delft en haar krijgsgeschiedenis* (Delft, 1987)

Feld, M.D., 'Middle-class society and the rise of military professionalism: the Dutch army 1589–1609', *Armed Forces and Society* 1 (1975), pp. 419–42

Feltham, Owen, *A Brief Character of the Low-Countries under the States: Being Three Weeks Observation of the Vices and Vertues of the Inhabitants* (London, 1652)

Fishman, Jane Susannah, *Boerenverdriet: Violence between Peasants and Soldiers in Early Modern Netherlands Art* (Ann Arbor MI, 1979)

Fissel, Mark C., *English Warfare 1511–1642* (London and New York, 2001)

Fletcher, Anthony, *A County Community in Peace and War: Sussex 1600–1660* (London and New York, 1975)

Floore, Pieter, 'Bouw en onderhoud van VOC-forten in de 17e eeuw', in: M.H. Bartels, E.H.P. Cordfunke and H. Sarfatij (eds), *Hollanders uit en thuis: Archeologie, geschiedenis en bouwhistorie gedurende de VOC-tijd in de Oost, de West en thuis. Cultuurhistorie van de Nederlandse expansie* (Hilversum, 2002), pp. 161–84

Formsma, W.J., *Geschiedenis tussen Eems en Lauwers* (Assen and Maastricht, 1988)

Friedrichs, C.R., *Urban Society in an Age of War: Nördlingen, 1580–1720* (Princeton, 1979)

——, 'The war and German society', in: Geoffrey Parker (ed.), *The Thirty Years War* (London and New York, 1997), pp. 186–92

Frijhoff, Willem and Marijke Spies, *1650: Hard-Won Unity* (Assen and Basingstoke, 2004)

Fritschy, Wantje, *Gewestelijke financiën ten tijde van de Republiek der Verenigde Nederlanden: Overijssel (1604–1795)* (The Hague, 1995)

——, 'A financial revolution reconsidered: public finance in Holland during the Dutch revolt, 1568–1648', *Economic History Review* 56 (2003), pp. 57–89

——, 'Holland's public debt and Amsterdam's capital market (1585–1609)', in: C.S. Ayá and B.J. García García (eds), *Banca, crédito y capital: La Monarquía Hispánica y los antiguos Países Bajos (1505–1700)* (Madrid, 2006), pp. 39–59

——, 'The efficiency of taxation in Holland', in: Oscar Gelderblom (ed.), *The Political Economy of the Dutch Republic* (Surrey, 2009), pp. 55–84

Frost, Robert I., *The Northern Wars: War, State and Society in Northeastern Europe, 1558–1721* (Harlow, 2000)

Fruin, R. *Tien jaren uit den Tachtigjarigen Oorlog, 1588–1598* (The Hague, 1941)

Fynn-Paul, Jeff (ed.), *War, Entrepreneurs, and the State in Europe and the Mediterranean, 1300–1800* (Leiden, forthcoming 2014)

Gaastra, F.S., 'Arbeid op Oostenburg: Het personeel van de kamer Amsterdam van de VOC', in: J.B. Kist a.o. (eds), *Van VOC tot Werkspoor: Het Amsterdamse Industrieterrein Oostenburg* (Utrecht, 1986), pp. 63–80

——, *De Geschiedenis van de VOC* (Zutphen, 2002)

——, 'Sware continuerende lasten en groten ommeslagh: Kosten van de oorlogsvoering van de Verenigde Oost-Indische Compagnie', in: Gerrit Knaap en Ger Teitler (eds), *De Verenigde Oost-Indische Compagnie tussen oorlog en diplomatie* (Leiden, 2002), pp. 81–104

Gaastra, F.S. and J.R. Bruijn, 'The Dutch East India Company's shipping, 1602–1795, in a comparative perspective', in: Jaap R. Bruijn and Femme S. Gaastra (eds), *Ships, Sailors, and Spices: East India Companies and Their Shipping in the 16th, 17th and 18th Centuries* (Amsterdam, 1993), pp. 177–208

Gaukroger, Stephen, *Descartes: An Intellectual Biography* (Oxford, 1995)

Gaunt, Peter, 'One of the goodliest and strongest places that I ever looked upon: Montgomery and the Civil War', in: Diana Dunn (ed.) *War and Society in Medieval and Early Modern Britain* (Liverpool, 2000), 180–203

Gelderblom, Oscar, *Zuid-Nederlandse kooplieden en de opkomst van de Amsterdamse stapelmarkt (1578–1630)* (Hilversum, 2000)

——, 'From Antwerp to Amsterdam: the contribution of merchants from the Southern Netherlands to the commercial expansion of Amsterdam c. 1540–1609', *Review* 26 (2003), pp. 247–82

——, 'The governance of early modern trade: the case of Hans Thijs, 1556–1611', *Enterprise and Society* 4 (2003), pp. 606–39

——, 'The organization of long-distance trade in England and the Dutch republic, 1550–1650', in: Oscar Gelderblom (ed.), *The Political Economy of the Dutch Republic* (Surrey, 2009), pp. 223–54

Gelderblom, Oscar and Joost Jonker, 'Completing a financial revolution: the finance of the Dutch East India trade and the rise of the Amsterdam capital market, 1595–1612', *Journal of Economic History* 64 (2004), pp. 641–72

——, 'Public finance and economic growth: the case of Holland in the seventeenth century', *The Journal of Economic History* 71 (2011), pp. 1–39

Geyl, Pieter, *The Revolt of the Netherlands (1555–1609)* (London, 1932)

Gijsbers, Wilma, *Kapitale ossen: De internationale handel in slachtvee in Noordwest-Europa (1300–1750)* (Hilversum, 1999)

Glamann, Kristof, *Dutch-Asiatic Trade 1620–1740* (The Hague, 1981)

Glete, Jan, *Navies and Nations: Warships, Navies and State Building in Europe and America, 1500–1800* (Stockholm, 1993)

——, *War and the State in Early Modern Europe: Spain, the Dutch Republic and Sweden as Fiscal-Military States, 1500–1660* (London, 2002)

González de León, Fernando, 'Doctors of military discipline: technical expertise and the paradigm of the Spanish soldier in the early modern period', *Sixteenth Century Journal* 27 (1996), 61–85

——, *The Road to Rocroi. Class, Culture and Command in the Spanish Army of Flanders, 1567–1659* (Leiden, 2009)

Goodman, David, *Spanish Naval Power, 1589–1665: Reconstruction and Defeat* (Cambridge, 1997)

——, 'Armadas in an age of scarce resources: struggling to maintain the fleet in seventeenth-century Spain', *The Journal of European Economic History* 28 (1999), pp. 49–76

Goossens, Thomas, *Staat, leger en ondernemers in de Oostenrijkse Nederlanden: De centralisering van de militaire organisatie en het beheer van de militaire bevoorradingscontracten* (unpublished PhD, Vrije Universiteit Brussel, 2012)

Gorski, Philip S., *The Disciplinary Revolution: Calvinism and the Rise of the State in Early Modern Europe* (Chicago, 2003)

Göse, Frank, 'Landstände und Militär: Die Haltung der kur und neumärkischen Ständerepräsentanten zum brandenburg-preussischen Militärsystem im ausgehenden 17. und 18. Jahrhundert', in: Stefan Kroll and Kersten Krüger (eds), *Militär und ländliche Gesellschaft in der frühen Neuzeit* (Hamburg, 2000), pp. 191–222

Grapperhaus, F.H.M., *Alva en de tiende penning* (Deventer, 1982)

Greif, Avner, *Institutions and the Path to Modern Economy: Lessons from Medieval Trade* (Cambridge, 2006)

Griffiths, Gordon, 'The revolutionary character of the revolt of the Netherlands', *Comparative Studies in Society and History* 2 (1960), pp. 452–72

Groenveld, S., *Van vyanden und vrienden bedroevet: De gevolgen van het beleg van Leiden voor de omgeving van de stad* (The Hague, 2001)

——, *De Winterkoning: Balling aan het Haagse hof* (The Hague, 2003)

Gunn, Steven, 'War and the emergence of the state: Western Europe, 1350–1600', in: Frank Tallett and D.J.B. Trim (eds), *European Warfare, 1350–1750* (Cambridge, 2010), pp. 50–73

Gunn, Steven, David Grummit, and Hans Cools, *War, State, and Society in England and the Netherlands 1477–1559* (Oxford, 2007)

Gutmann, Myron P., 'Why they stayed: the problem of wartime population loss', *Tijdschrift voor Geschiedenis* 91 (1978), pp. 407–28

——, *War and Rural Life in the Early Modern Low Countries* (Assen, 1980)

Haan, Heinrich, 'Prosperität und Dreißigjähriger Krieg', *Geschichte und Gesellschaft* 7 (1981), pp. 91–118

Hacker, Barton C., 'Military institutions, weapons, and social change: toward a new history of military technology', *Technology and Culture* 35 (1994), pp. 768–834

Hahlweg, Werner, *Die Heeresreform der Oranier und die Antike: Studien zur Geschichte des Kriegswesens der Niederlande, Deutschlands, Frankreichs, Englands, Italiens, Spaniens und der Schweiz vom Jahre 1589 bis zum Dreissigjährigen Kriege* (Osnabrück, 1987)

Hahn, Peter-Michael, 'Kriegserfahrungen von Kindern und Jugendlichen im Zeitalter des Dreißigjährigen Krieges', in: Dittmar Dahlmann (ed.), *Kinder und Jugendliche in Krieg und Revolution: Vom Dreissigjärigen Krieg bis zu den Kindersoldaten Afrikas* (Paderborn, 2000) pp. 1–15

Hale, J.R., 'Armies, navies and the art of war', in: G.R. Elton (ed.), *New Cambridge Modern History* Vol. 2 (Cambridge, 1958), pp. 481–509

——, *War and Society in Renaissance Europe 1450–1620* (London, 1985)

Hale, J.R. and M.E. Mallett, *The Military Organization of a Renaissance State: Venice c. 1400 to 1617* (Cambridge, 1984)

Halkos, George E. and Nickolas C. Kyriazis, 'A naval revolution and institutional change: the case of the united provinces', *European Journal of Law and Economics* 19 (2005), pp. 41–68

Hall, Bert S. and Kelly R. DeVries, 'Essay review – the "military revolution" revisited', *Technology and Culture* 31 (1990), pp. 500–507

Harding, Richard, *Seapower and Naval Warfare 1650–1830* (London, 1999)

Hart, Simon, 'Scheepsbouw', in: L.M. Akveld, S. Hart and W.J. van Hoboken (eds), *Maritieme Geschiedenis der Nederlanden* Vol. 2 (Bussum, 1977), pp. 72–7

Harvey, David, *Spaces of Global Capitalism* (London, 2006)

Hemann, Friedrich-Wilhelm, 'Die Beziehungen zwischen dem Münsterland und des östlichen Niederlandem im Mittelalter', in: Jenny Sarrazin (ed.), *Kaufmann, Kram und Karrrenspur: Handel zwischen IJssel und Berkel* (Lüdinghausen, 2001), pp. 115–57

Hibben, C.C., *Gouda in Revolt: Particularism and Pacifism in the Revolt of the Netherlands 1572–1588* (Utrecht, 1983)

Hintze, Otto, *Staat und Verfassung. Gesammelte Abhandlungen zur allgemeinen Verfassungsgeschichte* (Göttingen, 1962)

Hoffman, Philip T., 'Prices, the military revolution, and western Europe's comparative advantage in violence', *Economic History Review* 64:S1 (2011), pp. 39–59

Hoffman, Philip and Jean-Laurent Rosenthal, 'The political economy of warfare and taxation in early modern Europe: historical lessons for economic development', in: John Drobak and John Nye (eds), *The Frontiers of the New Institutional Economics* (San Diego, London and Toronto, 1997), pp. 31–55

Holthuis, Paul, *Frontierstad bij het scheiden van de markt: Deventer, militair, demografisch, economisch, 1578–1648* (Deventer, 1993)

Hoppenbrouwers, Peter, 'The use and management of commons in the Netherlands: an overview', in: Martina de Moor, Leigh Shaw-Taylor and Paul Warde (eds), *The Management of Common Land in North West Europe c. 1500–1850* (Turnhout, 2002), pp. 87–112

Howard, Michael, 'Tools of war: concepts and technology', in: John A. Lynn (ed.), *Tools of War: Instruments, Ideas, and Institutions of Warfare, 1445–1871* (Urbana and Chicago, 1990), pp. 238–46

——, *War in European History* (London, 1984)

Huizing, J.S.A., 'Inkomsten en uitgaven van de familie Lewe 1586–89 uit hun Wester-wolds bezit', *Tijdschrift Westerwolde* 18 (1997), pp. 7–14

Inghenthron, Maximiliam, 'Einleitung', in: Erich Kuttner, *Das Hungerjahr 1566: Eine Studie zur Geschichte des niederländsichen Frühproletariats und seiner Revolution* (Mannheim, 1997), pp. 16–104.

Israel, Jonathan, *Dutch Primacy in World Trade, 1585–1740* (Oxford, 1989)

——, *The Dutch Republic: Its Rise, Greatness, and Fall* (Oxford, 1995)

Jacobsen Jensen, J.N., 'Moryson's reis en zijn karakteristiek van de Nederlanden', *Bijdragen en Mededeelingen van het Historisch Genootschap* 39 (1918), pp. 214–305

Jahn, Peter-Michael, 'Kriegserfahrungen von Kindern und Jugendlichen im Zeitalter des Dreissigjährigen Krieges', in: Dittmar Dahlmann (ed.), *Kinder und Jugendliche in Krieg und Revolution: Vom Dreissigjährigen Krieg bis zu den Kindersoldaten Afrikas* (Paderborn, 2000), pp. 1–15

Jayasena, Ranjith M., 'Katuwana. Archeologisch onderzoek van een VOC-fort in Sri-Lanka', in: M.H. Bartels, E.H.P. Cordfunke and H. Sarfatij (eds), *Hollanders uit en thuis: Archeologie, geschiedenis en bouwhistorie gedurende de VOC-tijd in de Oost, de West en thuis. Cultuurhistorie van de Nederlandse expansie* (Hilversum, 2002), pp. 141–60

Jespersen, Knud J.V., 'Social change and military revolution in early modern Europe: some Danish evidence', *Historical Journal* 26 (1983), pp. 1–13

Joas, Hans, 'The modernity of war: modernization theory and the problem of violence', *International Sociology* 14 (1999), pp. 457–72

John, A.H., 'War and the English economy, 1700–1763', *Economic History Review* 7 (1955), pp. 329–44

Johnson, Joan, *Princely Chandos: James Brydges 1674–1744* (Gloucester, 1984)

Jones, Colin, 'The Military Revolution and the professionalisation of the French Army under the Ancien Régime', in: Clifford J. Rogers (ed.), *The Military Revolution Debate: Readings on the Military Transformation of Early Modern Europe* (Boulder CO, 1995), pp. 149–67

Jones, Eric, *The European Miracle: Environments, Economies and Geopolitics in the History of Europe and Asia* (Cambridge, 1982)

Jones, J.R., *The Anglo-Dutch Wars of the Seventeenth Century* (London and New York, 1996)

Joosting, J.G.C., *De Marken van Drente, Groningen, Overijssel en Gelderland* Vol. I (The Hague, 1920)

Judges, A.V., 'Philip Burlamachi: a financier of the Thirty Years' War', *Economica* 6 (1926), pp. 285–300

Kamen, Henry, 'The economic and social consequences of the Thirty Years' War', *Past and Present* 39 (1968), pp. 44–61

Kang, Seonjou and James Meernik, 'Civil war destruction and the prospects for economic growth', *Journal of Politics* 67:1 (2005), pp. 88–109

Kaptein, Herman, *De Hollandse textielnijverheid 1350–1600: Conjunctuur en continuïteit* (Hilversum, 1998)

Kennedy, Paul, *The Rise and Fall of Great Powers: Economic Change and Military Conflict from 1500 to 2000* (New York, 1987)

Kernkamp, J.H., *De handel op den vijand 1572–1609* (Utrecht, 1931)

Kingra, Mahinder S., 'The trace italienne and the military revolution during the Eighty Years' War', *Journal of Military History* 57 (1993), pp. 431–46

Kist, J.B., 'De VOC op Oostenburg. Gebouwen en terreinen', in: J.B. Kist a.o. (eds), *Van VOC tot Werkspoor. Het Amsterdamse industrieterrein Oostenburg* (Utrecht, 1986), pp. 11–34

Kleij, P., 'De scheepsbouw en scheepswerven aan de Hogendijk in Zaansdam', in: M.H. Bartels, E.H.P. Cordfunke and H. Sarfatij (eds), *Hollanders uit en thuis: Archeologie, geschiedenis en bouwhistorie gedurende de VOC-tijd in de Oost, de West en thuis. Cultuurhistorie van de Nederlandse expansie* (Hilversum, 2002), pp. 9–26

Klein, P.W., *De Trippen in de 17e eeuw: Een studie over het ondernemersgedrag op de Hollandse stapelmarkt* (Assen, 1965)

——, 'De Nederlandse handelspolitiek in de tijd van het mercantilisme: een nieuwe kijk op een oude kwestie', *Tijdschrift voor geschiedenis* 102 (1989), pp. 189–212

Kleinehagenbrock, Frank, 'Einquartierung als Last für Einheimische und Fremde: Ein Beispiel aus einem hohenlohischen Amt während des Dreissigjärigen Krieges', in: Matthias Asche a.o. (eds), *Krieg, Militär und Migration in der Frühen Neuzeit* (Berlin, 2008), pp. 167–85

Klinkert, Wim, 'Water in oorlog: De rol van het water in de militaire geschiedenis', in: Eelco Beukers (ed.), *Hollanders en het water* Vol.2 (Hilversum, 2007), pp. 451–504

Knevel, Paul, *Burgers in het geweer: De schutterijen in Holland, 1550–1700* (Hilversum, 1994)

Koenen, H.J., *Voorlezingen over de geschiedenis der finantiën van Amsterdam* (Amsterdam, 1855)

Koenigsberger, H.G., 'The organization of revolutionary parties in France and the Netherlands during the sixteenth century', *Journal of Modern History* 27 (1955), pp. 335–51

Kooijmans, Luc, *Onder regenten: De elite in een Hollandse stad: Hoorn* (Amsterdam, 1985)

Koopmans, J.W., *De Staten van Holland en de Opstand: De ontwikkeling van hun functies en organisatie in de periode 1544–1588* (The Hague, 1990)

Kroener, Bernhard R., 'Soldat oder Soldateska? Programmatischer Aufriss einer Sozialgeschichte militärischer Unterschichten in der ersten Hälfte des 17. Jahrhunderts', in: Manfred Messerschmidt a.o. (eds), *Militärgeschichte: Probleme – Thesen – Wege* (Stuttgart, 1982), pp. 100–23

——, 'The modern state and military society in the eighteenth century', in: Philippe Contamine (ed.), *War and Competition between States* (Oxford, 2000), pp. 195–220

Kroener, Bernhard R. and Ralf Pröve (eds), *Krieg und Frieden: Militär und Gesellschaft in der Frühen Neuzeit* (Paderborn, 1996)

Kroll, Stefan, *Stadtgesellschaft und Krieg: Sozialstruktur, Bevolkerung und Wirtschaft in Stralsund und Stade 1700 bis 1715* (Göttingen, 1997)

Krüger, Kersten, 'Dänische und schwedische Kriegsfinanzierung im Dreissigjährigen Krieg bis 1635', in: Konrad Repgen (ed.), *Krieg und Politik 1618–1648* (München, 1988), pp. 275–98

Kuttner, Erich (Maximiliam Inghenthron, ed.), *Das Hungerjahr 1566: Eine Studie zur geschichte des niederländsichen Frühproletariats und seiner Revolution* (Mannheim, 1997)

Kuznets, Simon S., *Postwar Economic Growth: Four Lectures* (Cambridge MA, 1964)

Kyriazis, Nicholas, 'Seapower and socioeconomic change', *Theory and Society* 30 (2006), pp. 71–108

Lammers, Cornelis J., 'Strikes and mutinies: a comparative study of organizational conflicts between rulers and ruled', *Administrative Science Quarterly* 14 (1969), pp. 558–72

——, 'Mutiny in comparative perspective', *International Review of Social History* 48 (2003), pp. 473–82

Landers, John, *The Field and the Forge: Population, Production, and Power in the Pre-industrial West* (Oxford, 2003)

Lane, Frederick C., 'Family partnerships and joint ventures in the Venetian Republic', *Journal of Economic History* 4 (1944), pp. 178–96

——, 'The role of governments in economic growth in early modern times', *Journal of Economic History* 35 (1975), pp. 8–17

——, *Profits from Power. Readings in Protection Rent and Violence-Controlling Enterprises* (Albany NY, 1979)

Lemmink, Fredericus H.J., *Het ontstaan van de Staten van Zeeland en hun geschiedenis tot het jaar 1555* (Roosendaal, 1951)

Lepage, Jean-Denis, *Vestingen en schansen in Groningen: Eeuwenlang de hoeksteen van de Nederlandse defensie* (Utrecht, 1994)

Leper, J., *Kunstmatige inundaties in maritiem Vlaanderen 1316–1945* (Tongeren, 1957)

Lesger, Clé, *Handel in Amsterdam ten tijde van de Opstand: Kooplieden, commerciële expansie en verandering in de ruimtelijke economie van de Nederlanden c.1550–c.1630* (Hilversum, 2001)

Leuftink, A.E., *De geneeskunde bij 's lands oorlogsvloot in de 17e eeuw* (Assen, 1953)

Liesker, Ruud and Wantje Fritschy, *Gewestelijke financiën ten tijde van de Republiek der Verenigde Nederlanden: Holland (1572–1795)* (The Hague, 2004)

Limm, Peter, *The Thirty Years War* (London and New York, 1984)

Lindegren, Jan, 'Men, money, and means', in: Philippe Contamine (ed.), *War and Competition between States* (Oxford, 2000), pp. 129–62

Lorge, Peter, *War, Politics and Society in Early Modern China, 900–1795* (London and New York, 2005)

Lynn, John A., 'Tactical evolution in the French army. 1560–1660', *French Historical Studies* 14 (1985), pp. 176–91

——, 'The trace italienne and the growth of armies: the French case', *The Journal of Military History* 55 (1991), pp. 297–330

——'The history of logistics and supplying war', in: John A. Lynn (ed.), *Feeding Mars: Logistics in Warfare from the Middle Ages to the Present* (New York, 1993), pp. 9–27

——, 'The evolution of army style in the modern west', *International History Review* 18 (1996), pp. 505–45

——, *Giant of the Grand Siècle: The French Army, 1610–1715* (Cambridge, 1997)

——, 'Forging the Western army in seventeenth-century France', in: MacGregor Knox and Williamson Murray (eds), *The Dynamics of Military Revolution 1300–2050* (Cambridge, 2001), pp. 35–56

Mann, Michael, *The Sources of Social Power: A History of Power from the Beginning to AD 1760* (Cambridge, 1986)

——, *States, War and Capitalism: Studies in Political Sociology* (Oxford, 1988)

Manning, Roger B., *An Apprenticeship in Arms: The Origins of the British Army 1585–1702* (Oxford, 2006)

Martens, P., *Militaire architectuur en vestingbouw in de Nederlanden tijdens het regentschap van Maria van Hongarije (1531–1555): De ontwikkeling van een gebastioneerde vestingbouw* (Louvain, 2009)

McNeill, William, *Plagues and Peoples* (Garden City NY, 1976)

McNeill, William H., *The Pursuit of Power: Technology, Armed Force, and Society since AD 1000* (Chicago, 1982)

——, *Keeping Together in Time: Dance and Drill in Human History* (Cambridge MA, 1995)

Merriman, R.B., *Six Contemporaneous Revolutions* (Glasgow, 1937)

Millar, Gilbert John, 'The landsknecht: his recruitment and organization', *Military Affairs* 35 (1971), pp. 95–9

Milward, Alan S., *War, Economy and Society 1939–1945* (Berkeley and Los Angeles, 1979)

Modelski, George, 'The long cycle of global politics and the nation-state', *Comparative Studies in Society and History* 20 (1978), pp. 214–35

Modelski, George and William R. Thompson, ' Long cycles and global war', in: Manus I. Midlarski (ed.), *Handbook of War Studies* (London, 1989), pp. 23–54

Mokyr, Joel, *Industrialization in the Low Countries, 1795–1850* (New Haven, 1976)

Möller, Hans Michael, *Das Regiment der Landsknechte* (Wiesbaden, 1976)

Murphy, Rhoads, 'Ottoman military organisation in south-eastern Europe, *c.*1420–1720', in: Frank Tallett and D.J.B. Trim (eds), *European Warfare, 1350–1750* (Cambridge, 2010), pp. 135–58

Murray, Williamson and MacGregor Knox, 'Thinking about revolutions in warfare', in: MacGregor Knox and Williamson Murray (eds), *The Dynamics of Military Revolution 1300–2050* (Cambridge, 2001), pp. 1–14

Nadel, George, 'The logic of the anatomy of revolution, with reference to the Netherlands' Revolt', *Comparative Studies in Society and History* 2 (1960), pp. 473–84

Neal, Larry, 'How it all began: the monetary and financial architecture of Europe during the first global capital markets, 1648–1815', *Financial History Review* 7 (2000), pp. 117–40

Nef, John U., 'A comparison of industrial growth in France and England from 1540 to 1640', *Journal of Political Economy* 44 (1936), pp. 289–317

——, *War and Human Progress* (London, 1950)

Nickle, B.H., *The Military Reforms of Prince Maurice of Nassau* (Newark DE, 1975)

Nolan, John S., *Sir John Norreys and the Elizabethan Military World* (Exeter, 1997)

Noordegraaf, Leo, *Hollands welvaren: Levensstandaard in Holland 1450–1600* (Bergen, 1985)

——, 'Dutch industry in the Golden Age', *Economic and Social History in the Netherlands* 4 (1992), pp. 131–58

——, 'Economie en Opstand. Oorzaak en gevolg? Of gevolg en oorzaak?', *Spiegel Historiael* 19 (1994), pp. 488–93

North, Douglass, *Structure and Change in Economic History* (New York, 1981)

——, 'Transaction costs, institutions, and economic history', *Zeitschrift für die gesamte Staatswissenschaft* 140 (1984), pp. 7–17

O'Brien, Patrick Karl, 'Fiscal exceptionalism: Great Britain and its European rivals from Civil War to triumph at Trafalgar and Waterloo', in: David Winch and Patrick K. O'Brien (eds), *The Political Economy of British Historical Experience* (Oxford, 2002), pp. 245–65

——, *Fiscal and Financial Preconditions for the Rise of British Naval Hegemony 1485–1815* (London, 2005)

——, 'The nature and historical evolution of an exceptional fiscal state and its possible significance for the precocious commercialization and industrialization of the British economy from Cromwell to Nelson', *The Economic History Review*, 64:2 (2011), pp. 408–46

Oosterhoff, F.G., *Leicester and the Netherlands 1586–1587* (Utrecht, 1988)

Organski, A.F.K. and Jacek Kugler, *The War Ledger* (Chicago, 1980)

Otte, Arjan, 'Zeeuwse zeezaken: Een admiraliteit rond de Eerste Engelse Oorlog, 1651–55',*Tijdschrift voor Zeegeschiedenis* 23 (2004), pp. 142–57

Pagès, G., *The Thirty Years War, 1618–1648* (London, 1970)

Parker, Geoffrey, *Spain and the Netherlands. Ten Studies* (London, 1979)

——, *The Dutch Revolt* (London, 1985)

——, *The Military Revolution: Military Innovation and the Rise of the West, 1500–1800* (Cambridge, 1988)

——, 'In defense of the military revolution', in: Clifford J. Rogers (ed.), *The Military Revolution Debate: Readings on the Military Transformation of Early Modern Europe* (Boulder CO, 1995), pp. 337–65

——, 'The military revolution, 1560–1660 – a myth?', in: Clifford J. Rogers (ed.), *The Military Revolution Debate: Readings on the Military Transformation of Early Modern Europe* (Boulder CO, 1995), pp. 37–54

——, *The Thirty Years War* (London and New York, 1997)

——, *The Grand Strategy of Philip II* (New Haven CT, 1998)

——, 'From the House of Orange to the House of Bush: 400 years of revolutions in military affairs', *Militaire Spectator* 172 (2003), pp. 177–93

——, *The Army of Flanders and the Spanish Road, 1567–1659: The Logistics of Spanish Victory and Defeat in the Low Countries' Wars* (2nd ed., Cambridge, 2004)

Parrott, David A., 'Strategy and tactics in the Thirty Years' War: the military revolution', in: Clifford J. Rogers (ed.), *The Military Revolution Debate: Readings on the Military Transformation of Early Modern Europe* (Boulder CO, 1995), pp. 227–51

——, 'The utility of fortifications in early modern Europe: Italian princes and their citadels, 1540–1640', *War in History* 7 (2000), pp. 127–53

——, *Richelieu's Army: War, Government and Society in France, 1624–1642* (Cambridge, 2001)

——, 'From military enterprise to standing armies: war, state, and society in western Europe, 1600–1700', in: Frank Tallett and D.J.B. Trim (eds), *European Warfare, 1350–1750* (Cambridge, 2010), pp. 74–95

——, *The Business of War: Military Enterprise and the Military Revolution in Early Modern Europe* (Cambridge, 2012)

Pelus, Marie-Louise, 'A Lübeck et Hambourg au XVIIe siècle: crise financière, conjoncture économique, potentiel économique, progrès économique: Une série de questions', in: Neithard Bulst and Jean-Philippe Genet (eds), *La ville, la bourgeoisie et la genese de l'état moderne* (Paris, 1988), pp. 243–62

Pepper, Simon, 'Aspects of operational art: communications, cannon, and small war', in: Frank Tallett and D.J.B. Trim (eds), *European Warfare, 1350–1750* (Cambridge, 2010), 181–202

Perjés, G., 'Army provisioning, logistics and strategy in the second half of the 17th century', *Acta Historica Academicae Scientiarum Hungaricae* 16 (1970), pp. 1–52

Poelwijk, Arjan, *In dienste vant suyckerbacken: De Amsterdamse suikernijverheid en haar ondernemers, 1580–1630* (Hilversum, 2003)

Polišenský, J.V., *War and Society in Europe 1618–1648* (Cambridge, 1978)

Pollmann, Judith, 'Countering the Reformation in France and the Netherlands: clerical leadership and Catholic violence 1560–85', *Past and Present* 190 (2006), pp. 83–120

——, 'Internationalisering en de Nederlandse Opstand', *Bijdragen en Mededelingen betreffende de Geschiedenis der Nederlanden* 124 (2009), pp. 515–35

Post, F. and A.C. van Oorschot, *De middelen van bestaan: De geschiedenis van Westerwolde* (Groningen, 1993)

Postema, Jan, *Johan van den Corput (1542–1611): Kaartmaker, Vestingbouwer, Krijgsman* (Kampen, 1993)

Potter, Mark, 'War finance and absolutist state development in early modern Europe: an examination of French venality in the seventeenth century', *Journal of Early Modern History* 7 (2003), pp. 138–47

Potter, Mark and Jean-Laurent Rosenthal, 'Politics and public finance in France: the estates of Burgundy, 1660–1790', *Journal of Interdisciplinary History* 27 (1997), pp. 577–612

——, 'The development of intermediation in French credit markets: evidence from the estates of Burgundy', *The Journal of Economic History* 62 (2002), pp. 1024–49

Prak, Maarten, *Gezeten burgers: De elite in een Hollandse stad: Leiden* (Amsterdam, 1985)

——, *The Dutch Republic in the Seventeenth Century: The Golden Age* (Cambridge, 2005)

Prak, Maarten and Jan Luiten van Zanden, 'Tax morale and citizenship in the Dutch Republic', in: Oscar Gelderblom (ed.), *The Political Economy of the Dutch Republic* (Surrey, 2009), pp. 143–65

Price, J.L., *Holland and the Dutch Republic in the Seventeenth Century: The Politics of Particularism* (Oxford, 1994)

——, 'A state dedicated to war? The Dutch Republic in the seventeenth century', in: A. Ayton and J.L. Price (eds), *The Medieval Military Revolution: State, Society and Military Change in Medieval and Early Modern Europe* (London, 1995), pp. 183–200

Rabb, Theodore K., 'The effects of the Thirty Years' War on the German economy', *The Journal of Modern History* 34 (1962), pp. 40–51

Rasler, Karen A. and William R. Thompson, *War and State Making: The Shaping of Global Powers* (Boston, 1989)

Raven, G.J.A., 'Naval organization', *Revue Internationale d'Histoire Militaire* 58 (1984), pp. 155–66

——, 'That expensive asset: a short history of Netherlands naval personnel', *Revue Internationale d'Histoire Militaire* 58 (1984), pp. 167–86

Redlich, Fritz, 'Contributions in the Thirty Years' War', *Economic History Review* 12 (1959–60), pp. 247–54

——, *The German Military Enterpriser and his Work Force: A Study in European Economic and Social History*, Vols 1–2 (Wiesbaden, 1964–65)

Reitsma, R. *Centrifugal and Centripetal Forces in the early Dutch Republic: The States of Overijssel 1566–1600* (Amsterdam, 1982)

——, 'Dutch finance and the English taxes in the seventeenth century', in: S. Groenveld, M.E.H.N. Mout and I. Schöffer, *Bestuurders en Geleerden: Opstellen over onderwerpen uit de Nederlandse geschiedenis* (Amsterdam and Dieren, 1985), pp. 107–12

Richards, John F., *Unending Frontier: An Environmental History of the Early Modern World* (Berkeley and London, 2003)

Roberts, Michael, *Essays in Swedish History* (London, 1967)

——, *The Swedish Imperial Experience, 1560–1718* (Cambridge, 1979)

——, 'The military revolution, 1560–1660', in: Clifford J. Rogers (ed.), *The Military Revolution Debate: Readings on the Military Transformation of Early Modern Europe* (Boulder CO, 1995), pp. 13–35

Robiseaux, Thomas, *Rural Society and the Search for Order in Early Modern Germany* (Cambridge, 1989)

Rodger, Nicolas, 'The military revolution at sea', *Social Science Tribune* 37 (2003), pp. 59–76

Rogers, Clifford J. (ed.) *Military Revolution Debate: Readings on the Military Transformation of Early Modern Europe* (Boulder CO, 1995), 169–99

——, 'The military revolutions of the Hundred Years War', in: Clifford J. Rogers (ed.), *The Military Revolution Debate: Readings on the Military Transformation of Early Modern Europe* (Boulder CO, 1995), pp. 55–93

——, 'Tactics and the face of battle', in: Frank Tallett and D.J.B. Trim (eds), *European Warfare, 1350–1750* (Cambridge, 2010), pp. 203–35

Rommelse, Gijs, 'English privateering against the Dutch Republic during the Second Anglo-Dutch War (1664–67)', *Tijdschrift voor Zeegeschiedenis* 22 (2003), pp. 17–31

——, *The Second Anglo-Dutch War (1665–1667): Raison d'Etat, Mercantilism and Maritime Strife* (Hilversum, 2006)

——, 'The role of mercantilism in Anglo-Dutch political relations, 1650–74', *The Economic History Review* 63:3 (2010), pp. 591–611

Roodhuyzen, Thea, *De admiraliteit van Friesland* (Franeker, 2003)

Rooms, Etienne, *De organisatie van de troepen van de Spaans-Habsburgse monarchie in de Zuidelijke Nederlanden (1659–1700)* (Brussels, 2003)

——, 'Bezoldiging, bevoorrading en inkwartiering in de Spaanse Nederlanden', *Bijdragen en Mededelingen betreffende de Geschiedenis der Nederlanden* 118 (2003), pp. 519–44

Rooze-Stouthamer, C., *De opmaat tot de Opstand: Zeeland en het centraal gezag (1566–1572)* (Hilversum, 2009)

Rose, Elihu, 'The anatomy of mutiny', *Armed Forces and Society* 8 (1982), pp. 561–74

Rothenberg, Gunther E., 'Maurice of Nassau, Gustavus Adolphus, Raimondo Montecuccoli, and the military revolution of the seventeenth century', in: Peter Paret (ed.), *Makers of Modern Strategy: From Machiavelli to the Nuclear Age* (Oxford, 1986), pp. 32–63

Rowlands, Guy, *The Dynastic State and the Army under Louis XIV: Royal Service and Private Interest, 1661–1701* (Cambridge, 2002)

Roy, Kaushik, 'The hybrid military establishment of the East India Company in South Asia: 1750–1849', *Journal of Global History* 6 (2011), pp. 195–218

Schennach, Martin, 'Der Soldat sich nit mit den Baurn, auch der Baur nit mit den Soldaten betragt: Das Verhältnis zwischen Tiroler Landbevölkerung und Militär von 1600 bis 1650', in: Stefan Kroll and Kersten Krüger (eds), *Militär und ländliche Gesellschaft in der frühen Neuzeit* (Hamburg 2000), pp. 41–78

Schlögl, Rudolf, *Bauern, Krieg und Staat: Overbayerische Bauernwirtschaft und frühmoderner Staat im 17. Jahrhundert* (Göttingen, 1988)

Schnee, Heinrich, *Die Hoffinanz und der moderne Staat. Geschichte und System der Hoffaktoren an deutschen Fürstenhöfen im Zeitalter des Absolutismus*, Vols 1–3 (Berlin, 1953–55)

Schöffer, I., 'The Dutch Revolt anatomized. Some comments', *Comparative Studies in Society and History* 3 (1961), pp. 470–77

Schulten, C.M. and J.W.M. Schulten, *Het leger in de zeventiende eeuw* (Bussum, 1969)

Schulten, Kees, 'Ontstaan van de Republiek en het Staatse leger', in: Jaap R. Bruijn and Cees B. Wels, *Met man en macht: De militaire geschiedenis van Nederland 1550–2000* (Amsterdam, 2003), pp. 13–43

Showalter, Dennis E., 'Caste, skill, and training: the evolution of cohesion in European armies from the Middle Ages to the sixteenth century', *The Journal of Military History* 57 (1993), pp. 407–30

Sicking, Louis, 'Naval warfare in Europe, *c*.1330-*c*.1680', in: Frank Tallett and D.J.B. Trim (eds), *European Warfare, 1350–1750* (Cambridge, 2010), pp. 236–63

Sikora, Michael, 'Söldner – historische Annäherung an einen Kriegertypus', *Geschichte und Gesellschaft* 29 (2003), pp. 210–38

Slack, Paul, 'Material progress and the challenge of affluence in seventeenth-century England', *Economic History Review* 62 (2009), pp. 576–603

Smith, R.P., 'Military expenditure and capitalism', *Cambridge Journal of Economics* 1 (1977), pp. 61–76

Snapper, Frits, *Oorlogsinvloeden op de overzeese handel van Holland 1551–1719* (Amsterdam, 1959)

Soly, Hugo, 'Een Antwerpse Compagnie voor de levensmiddelenbevoorrading van het leger in de Nederlanden in de zestiende eeuw', *Bijdragen en Mededelingen betreffende de Geschiedenis der Nederlanden* 86 (1971), pp. 350–62

——, *Urbanisme en kapitalisme te Antwerpen in de 16e eeuw: De stedebouwkundige en industriële ondernemingen van Gilbert van Schoonebeke* (Brussels, 1977)

Sombart, Werner, *Krieg und Kapitalismus* (München, 1913)

——, *Der moderne Kapitalismus: Historisch-systematischer Darstellung des gesamteuropäirischen Wirtschaftslebens von seinen Anfängen bis zur gegenwart* (München and Leipzig, 1928)

Sonnino, Paul, *Louis XIV and the Origins of the Dutch War* (Cambridge, 1988)

——, *Mazarin's Quest: The Congress of Westphalia and the Coming of the Fronde* (Cambridge MA, 2008)

Starkey, Armstrong, *War in the Age of Enlightenment, 1700–1789* (Westport, 2003)

Stasavage, David, *States of Credit: Size, Power, and the Development of European Polities* (Princeton, 2011)

Steegen, Erwin, *Kleinhandel en stedelijke ontwikkeling: Het kramersambacht te Maastricht in de vroegmoderne tijd* (Hilversum, 2006)

Steensgaard, Niels, *The Asian Trade Revolution of the Seventeenth Century: the East India Companies and the Decline of the Caravan Trade* (Chicago and London, 1974)

Stol, T., 'Schaalvergroting in de polders in Amstelland in de 17e en 18e eeuw', *Tijdschrift voor Waterstaatgeschiedenis* 3 (1994), pp. 13–21

Stols, Eddy, *De Spaanse Brabanders of de handelsbetrekkingen der Zuidelijke Nederlanden met de Iberische Wereld 1598–1648*, Vols 1–2 (Brussels, 1971)

Storrs, Christopher, 'The army of Lombardy and the resilience of Spanish power in the reign of Carlos II (1665–1700), Part I', *War in History* 4 (1997), pp. 371–97

Stradling, R.A., 'The Spanish Dunkirkers, 1621–48: a record of plunder and destruction', *Tijdschrift voor Geschiedenis* 93 (1980), pp. 541–59

——, *The Armada of Flanders: Spanish Military Policy and European War, 1568–1668* (Cambridge, 1992)

Strubbe, Benoit, *Oorlogsscheepsbouw en werven in Zeeland tijdens de Engels-Staatse Oorlogen (1650–1674)* (unpublished MA thesis, Ghent, 2007)

Swart, Erik, *Krijgsvolk. Militaire professionalisering en het ontstaan van het Staatse leger, 1568–1590* (Amsterdam, 2006)

——, 'From landsknecht to soldier: the low German foot soldiers of the Low Countries in the second half of the sixteenth century', *International Review of Social History* 51 (2006), pp. 75–92

——, 'The field of finance: war and taxation in Holland, Flanders and Brabant, ca. 1572–85', *Sixteenth Century Journal* 42 (2011), pp. 1051–71

——, 'De mythe van Maurits en de moderniteit? Militair professionalisme en adelscultuur in de Noordelijke en Zuidelijke Nederlanden, circa 1590–1625', in: Luc Duerloo and Liesbeth De Frenne (eds), *Het verdeelde huis: De Nederlandse adel tussen opstand en reconciliatie* (Maastricht 2011), pp. 101–18

Tallett, Frank, *War and Society in Early Modern Europe, 1495–1715* (London and New York, 1992)

Tallett, Frank, and D.J.B. Trim (eds), *European Warfare, 1350–1750* (Cambridge, 2009)

Tamaki, Toshiaki, 'The formation of the fiscal military state and the network of merchants', *KSU Economic and Business Review* 25 (1998), pp. 73–87

Tawney, R.H., *Business and Politics under James I: Lionel Cranfield as Merchant and Minister* (Cambridge, 1958)

Te Brake, Wayne, *Shaping History, Ordinary People in European Politics, 1500–1700* (Berkeley and Los Angeles, 1998)

Temple, William, *Observations upon the United Provinces of the Netherlands* (London, 1673)

Ten Raa, F.J.G. and F. De Bas, *Het Staatsche Leger, 1568–1795* (Breda and The Hague, 1911–50) 't Hart, G., 'Rijnlands bestuur en waterstaat rondom het beleg en ontzet van Leiden (1570–80),' *Jaarboekje voor de Geschiedenis en Oudheidkunde van Leiden en Omstreken* 66 (1974), pp. 13–33

't Hart, Marjolein, *In Quest for Funds: Warfare and State Formation in the Netherlands, 1620–1650* (Leiden, 1989)

——, 'Cities and statemaking in the Dutch Republic, 1580–1680', *Theory and Society* 18 (1989), pp. 663–89

——, 'Public loans and lenders in the seventeenth century Netherlands', *Economic and Social History in the Netherlands* 1 (1989), pp. 119–40

——, *The Making of a Bourgeois State: War, Politics and Finance during the Dutch Revolt* (Manchester, 1993)

——, 'The Dutch Republic: the urban impact upon politics', in: Karel Davids and Jan Lucassen (eds), *A Miracle Mirrored: The Dutch Republic in an European Perspective* (Cambridge, 1995), pp. 57–98

——, 'The Dutch Revolt 1566–81: A national revolution?', in: David Parker (ed.), *Revolutions and the Revolutionary Tradition* (London and New York, 2000), pp. 15–33

——, 'The common soldier in rebel armies: an introduction', *International Review of Social History* 51 (2006), pp. 71–4

——, 'Mutual advantages: state bankers as brokers between the city of Amsterdam and the Dutch Republic', Oscar Gelderblom (ed.), *The Political Economy of the Dutch Republic* (Surrey, 2009), pp. 115–42

——, 'De democratische paradox en de Opstand in Vlaanderen, Brabant en Holland', in: Mario Damen and Louis Sicking (eds.), *Bourgondië voorbij: de Nederlanden 1250-1650: liber alumnorum Wim Blockmans* (Hilversum, 2010), pp. 375–88

't Hart, Marjolein and Michael Limberger, 'Staatsmacht en stedelijke autonomie: Het geld van Antwerpen en Amsterdam (1500–1700)', *Tijdschrift voor Sociale en Economische Geschiedenis* 3 (2006), pp. 36–72

Theibault, John, *German Villages in Crisis. Rural Life in Hesse-Hassel and the Thirty Years' War, 1580–1720* (Atlantic Highways NJ, 1995)

Thijs, Alfons K., *Van 'werkwinkel' tot 'fabriek': De textielnijverheid te Antwerpen (einde 15de-begin 19de eeuw)* (Brussel, 1987)

Thoen, Erik, 'Oorlogen en platteland: Sociale en ekonomische aspekten van militaire destruktie in Vlaanderen tijdens de late middeleeuwen en de vroege moderne tijden', *Tijdschrift voor Geschiedenis* 91 (1978), pp. 363–78

Thompson, I.A.A., *War and Government in Habsburg Spain 1560–1620* (London, 1976)

——, *War and Society in Habsburg Spain* (Aldershot, 1992)

——, 'Money, money, and yet more money! Finance, the fiscal state, and the military revolution: Spain 1500–1650', in: Clifford J. Rogers (ed.), *The Military Revolution Debate: Readings on the Military Transformation of Early Modern Europe* (Boulder CO, 1995), pp. 273–98

Thompson, William R., *On Global War: Historical-Structural Approaches to World Politics* (Columbia SC, 1988)

——, 'The military superiority thesis and the ascendancy of Western Eurasia in the world system', *Journal of World History* 10 (1999), pp. 143–78

Tilly, Charles, 'War making and state making as organized crime', in: Peter B. Evans, Dietrich Rueschemeyer and Theda Skocpol (eds), *Bringing the State Back In* (Cambridge MA, 1985), pp. 169–91

——, *The Contentious French* (Cambridge MA, 1986)

——, *Coercion, Capital, and European States*, AD 1990–1990 (Cambridge MA and Oxford, 1990)

——, *European Revolutions, 1492–1992* (Oxford and Cambridge MA, 1993)

Tops, N.J., 'De heffing der Spaanse contributiën tot 1635 in het oosten der Republiek of the "landbederfelijke" rol van Grol, Oldenzaal en Lingen', *Bijdragen en Mededelingen Gelre* 78 (1987), pp. 34–64

Tracy, James D., *A Financial Revolution in the Habsburg Netherlands: Renten and Renteniers in the County of Holland, 1515–1565* (Berkeley, 1985)

——, *The Founding of the Dutch Republic: War, Finance, and Politics in Holland, 1572–1588* (Oxford, 2008)

——, 'Holland's new fiscal Regime, 1572–76', in: Oscar Gelderblom (ed.), *The Political Economy of the Dutch Republic* (Surrey, 2009), pp. 41–54

Trim, D.J.B., 'Army, society and military professionalism in the Netherlands during the Eighty Years' War', in: David Trim (ed.), *The Chivalric Ethos and the Development of Military Professionalism* (Leiden, 2003), pp. 269–89

——, 'Introduction', in: David Trim (ed.), *The Chivalric Ethos and the Development of Military Professionalism* (Leiden, 2003), pp. 1–38

Trompetter, Cor, *Leven aan de rand van de Republiek: Stad en gericht Almelo 1580–1700* (Hilversum, 2006)

——, *Gewestelijke financiën ten tijde van de Republiek der Verenigde Nederlanden: Friesland (1587–1795)* (The Hague, 2007)

Troost, Wout, *William III, the Stadholder-King: A Political Biography* (Aldershot, 2005)

Turnbull, Stephen, *The Art of Renaissance Warfare: From the Fall of Constantinople to the Thirty Years War* (London, 2006)

Ulrich, Bernd, 'Militärgeschichte von unten. Anmerkungen zu ihren Ursprüngen, Quellen und Perspektiven im 20. Jahrhundert', *Geschichte und Gesellschaft* 22 (1996), pp. 473–503

Valkenier, Petrus, *'t Verwerd Europa, ofte Politijke en Historische Beschryving* (Amsterdam, 1675)

Van Aitzema, Lieuwe, *Historie of Verhael van Saken van Staet en Oorlogh in, ende omtrent de Vereenigde Nederlanden*, Vols 1–4 (The Hague, 1667)

Van Bavel, Bas, 'Rural development and landownership in Holland, c.1400–1650', in: Oscar Gelderblom (ed.), *The Political Economy of the Dutch Republic* (Surrey, 2009), pp. 167–96

——, *Manors and Markets: Economy and Society in the Low Countries, 500–1600* (Oxford, 2010)

Van Bavel, Bas and Jan Luiten Van Zanden, 'The jump-start of the Holland economy during the late medieval crisis, c. 1350-c.1500', *Economic History Review* 57 (2004), pp. 503–32

Van Beek, B.L., 'Zout uit het Caribisch gebied: Archeologische verkenningen nabij het fort Araya en op het eiland La Tortuga, Venezuela', in: M.H. Bartels, E.H.P. Cordfunke and H. Sarfatij (eds), *Hollanders uit en thuis: Archeologie, geschiedenis en bouwhistorie gedurende de VOC-tijd in de Oost, de West en thuis. Cultuurhistorie van de Nederlandse expansie* (Hilversum, 2002), pp. 71–84

Van Beylen, J., *Schepen van de Nederlanden: Van de late middeleeuwen tot het einde van de 17e eeuw* (Amsterdam, 1970)

Van Bochove, Christiaan, 'De Hollandse haringvisserij tijdens de vroegmoderne tijd', *Tijdschrift voor Sociale en Economische Geschiedenis* 1 (2004), pp. 3–27

Van Dam, Petra, 'Fuzzy boundaries and three-legged tables: A comment on ecological and spatial dynamics in Bas van Bavel's *Manors and Markets*', *Tijdschrift voor Sociale en Economische Geschiedenis* 8:2 (2011), pp. 103–13

Van den Heuvel, Charles, *'Papiere Bolwercken': De introductie van de Italiaanse stede en vestingbouw in de Nederlanden (1540–1609) en het gebruik van tekeningen* (Alphen aan den Rijn, 1991)

Van der Burg, Martijn, 'Rotterdamse stadsfinanciën in de tweede helft van de zeventiende eeuw', *Rotterdams Jaarboekje Rotterdams* (2003), pp. 106–30

Van der Burg, Martijn and Marjolein 't Hart, 'Renteniers and the recovery of Amsterdam's credit (1578–1605)', in: M. Boone, K. Davids and P. Janssens (eds), *Urban Public Debts: Urban Government and the Market for Annuities in Western Europe (14th-18th centuries)* (Turnhout, 2003), pp. 197–218

Van der Ent, L., 'Oostersche contributiën: Contributie aan de vijand in Drenthe, 1621–33', in: W. Fritschy, J.K.T. Postma and J. Roelevink (eds), *Doel en middel: Aspecten van financieel overheidsbeleid in de Nederlanden van de zestiende eeuw tot heden* (Amsterdam, 1995)

Van der Ent, L. and V. Enthoven, *Gewestelijke financiën ten tijde van de Republiek der Verenigde Nederlanden: Groningen (1594–1795)* (The Hague, 2001)

Van der Heijden, Manon, *Geldschieters van de stad: Financiële relaties tussen stad, burgers en overheden 1550–1650* (Amsterdam, 2006)

Van der Heijden, Manon, Elise van Nederveen Meerkerk, Griet Vermeesch and Martijn van der Burg (eds), *Serving the Urban Community: The Rise of Public Facilities in the Low Countries* (Amsterdam, 2009)

Van der Linden, Marcel, 'Marx und Engels, der niederländische Marxismus und die kapitalistische Musternation des 17. Jahrhunderts', in: Marcel van der Linden (ed.), *Die Rezeption der Marxschen Theorie in den Niederlanden* (Trier, 1992), pp. 9–46

Van der Wee, Herman, *The Growth of the Antwerp Market and the European Economy* (The Hague, 1963)

——, 'De stedelijke economie in de Zuidelijke Nederlanden en het prinsbisdom Luik in de 16de en de 17de eeuw', in: Jean-Marie Duvosquel and Ignace Vandevivere (eds), *Luister van Spanje en de Belgische steden, 1500–1700*, Vol. 1 (Brussels, 1985), pp. 107–22

——, *The Low Countries in the Early Modern World* (Aldershot, 1993)

Van der Woude, A.M., *Het Noorderkwartier: Een regionaal historisch onderzoek in de demografische en economische geschiedenis van westelijk Nederland van de late middeleeuwen tot het begin van de negentiende eeuw* (Utrecht, 1983)

——, 'De vrede van Munster en de economische ontwikkelingen in de Republiek', *De zeventiende eeuw* 13 (1997), pp. 99–120

Van Deursen, A.Th., 'Holland's experience of war during the Revolt of the Netherlands', in: A.C. Duke and C.A. Tamse (eds), *Britain and the Netherlands. Vol. 4, War and Society* (The Hague, 1977), pp. 19–53

——, *Het kopergeld van de Gouden Eeuw: Volk en overheid* (Assen, 1979)

——, 'De Raad van State onder de Republiek van 1588–1795', *Raad van State 450 Jaar* (The Hague, 1981), pp. 47–92

——, *Maurits van Nassau: De winnaar die faalde* (Amsterdam, 2000)

Van Dillen, J.G, *Van Rijkdom en regenten: Handboek tot de economische en sociale geschiedenis van Nederland tijdens de Republiek* (The Hague, 1970)

Van Gelder, H.A. Enno, *Revolutionnaire Reformatie: De vestiging van de gereformeerde kerk in de Nederlandse gewesten, gedurende de eerste jaren van de Opstand tegen Filips I, 1575–1585* (Amsterdam, 1943)

——, *De Nederlandse munten* (Utrecht and Antwerpen, 1965)

Van Gelder, Roelof, *Sailing Letters: Verslag van een inventariserend onderzoek* (The Hague, 2006)

Van Hoof, J.P.C.M., 'Met een vijand als bondgenoot', *Bijdragen en Mededelingen betreffende de Geschiedenis der Nederlanden* 103 (1988), pp. 622–51

——, 'Nieuwe manieren, sterke frontieren: Het bouwconcept van Menno van Coehoorn en zijn aandeel in de verbetering van het verdedigingsstelsel', *Bijdragen en Mededelingen betreffende de Geschiedenis der Nederlanden* 118 (2003), pp. 545–66

Van Houtte, J.A., 'Onze zeventiende eeuw, ongelukseeuw?', *Mededelingen van de Koninklijke Vlaamse Academie voor Wetenschappen, Letteren en Schone Kunsten van België* 15:8 (1953), pp. 3–32

Van Loo, Ivo, 'For freedom and fortune: the rise of Dutch privateering in the first half of the Revolt, 1568–1609', in: Marco van der Hoeven (ed.), *Exercise of Arms: Warfare in the Netherlands 1568–1648* (Leiden 1988), pp. 173–96

Van Nierop, H.F.K., 'De troon van Alva: Over de interpretatie van de Nederlandse Opstand', *Bijdragen en Mededelingen betreffende de Geschiedenis der Nederlanden* 110 (1995), pp. 205–23

——, *Het verraad van het Noorderkwartier: Oorlog, terreur en recht in de Nederlandse Opstand* (Amsterdam, 1999)

Van Nimwegen, Olaf, *De subsistentie van het leger: Logistiek en strategie van het geallieerde en met name het Staatse leger tijdens de Spaanse Successieoorlog in de Nederlanden en het Heilige Roomse Rijk (1701–1712)* (The Hague, 1995)

——, 'Het Staatse leger en de militaire revolutie van de vroegmoderne tijd', *Bijdragen en Mededelingen betreffende de Geschiedenis der Nederlanden* 118 (2003), pp. 494–518

——, *Deser landen crijchsvolck: Het Staatse leger en de militaire revoluties 1588–1688* (Amsterdam, 2006)

——, 'The transformation of army organisation in early-modern western Europe, c. 1500–1789', in: Frank Tallett and D.J.B. Trim (eds), *European Warfare, 1350–1750* (Cambridge, 2010), pp. 159–80

Van Peteghem, P., 'Vlaanderen in 1576: revolutionair of reactionair?', *Tijdschrift voor Geschiedenis* 89 (1976), pp. 335–57

Van Slingelandt, Simon, *Staatkundige geschriften* (Amsterdam, 1784–85; orig. 1722)

Van Strien, Cornelis D., *British Travellers in Holland during the Stuart Period: Edward Browne and John Locke as Tourists in the United Provinces* (Amsterdam, 1989)

Van Tielhof, Milja, *The Mother of All Trades: The Baltic Grain Trade in Amsterdam from the Late 16th to the Early 19th Century* (Leiden, 2002)

——, 'Turfwinning en proletarisering in Rijnland 1530–1670', *Tijdschrift voor Sociale en Economische Geschiedenis* 2:4 (2005), pp. 95–121

——, 'Financing water management in Rijnland, 1500–1800', in: Oscar Gelderblom (ed.), *The Political Economy of the Dutch Republic* (Surrey, 2009), pp. 197–222

Van Vliet, A.P., 'Foundation, organization and effects of the Dutch Navy (1568–1648)', in: Marco van der Hoeven (ed.), *Exercise of Arms: Warfare in the Netherlands 1568–1648* (Leiden, 1988), pp. 153–72

——, *Vissers en kapers: De zeevisserij vanuit het Maasmondgebied en de Duinkerker kapers (ca. 1580–1648)* (The Hague, 1994)

——, 'De Staatse vloot in de Tachtigjarige Oorlog', in: Jaap R. Bruijn and Cees B. Wels (eds), *Met man en macht: De militaire geschiedenis van Nederland 1550–2000* (Amsterdam, 2003), pp. 44–64

Van Winter, P.J., *Westerwolde generaliteitsland* (Assen, 1948)

Van Zanden, Jan Luiten, 'De economie van Holland in de periode 1650–1805: groei of achteruitgang? Een overzicht van bronnen, problemen en resultaten', *Bijdragen en Mededelingen betreffende de Geschiedenis der Nederlanden* 102 (1987), pp. 562–609

——, 'Een fraaie synthese op een wankele basis', *Bijdragen en Mededelingen betreffende de Geschiedenis der Nederlanden* 106 (1991), pp. 451–7

——, 'Economic growth in the Golden Age: the development of the economy of Holland, 1500–1650', *Economic and Social History of the Netherlands* 4 (1993), pp. 5–26

Van Zanden, Jan Luiten, *The Rise and Decline of Holland's Economy: Merchant Capitalism and the Labour Market* (Manchester, 1993)

Van Zanden, Jan Luiten and Arthur van Riel, *The Strictures of Inheritance: The Dutch Economy in the Nineteenth Century* (Princeton, 2004)

Van Zanden, Jan Luiten and Maarten Prak, 'Towards an economic interpretation of citizenship: the Dutch Republic between medieval communes and modern nation states', *European Review of Economic History* 10 (2006), pp. 111–45

Van Zanden, Jan Luiten and Bas van Leeuwen, 'Persistent but not consistent: the growth of national income in Holland 1347–1807', *Explorations in Economic History* 49 (2012), pp. 119–30

Van Zwet, Han, *Lofwaerdighe dijckagies en miserabele polders: Een financiële analyse van landaanwinningsprojecten in Hollands Noorderkwartier, 1597–1643* (Hilversum, 2009)

Veenstra, Wietse, *Gewestelijke financiën ten tijde van de Republiek der Verenigde Nederlanden: Zeeland (1573–1795)*(The Hague, 2009)

Verlinden, Charles, 'En Flandre sous Philippe II: durée de la crise économique', *Annales. Économies, Sociétés, Civilisations* 7 (1952), pp. 21–30

Vermeesch, Griet, *Oorlog, steden en staatsvorming: De grenssteden Gorinchem en Doesburg tijdens de geboorte-eeuw van de Republiek (1570–1680)* (Amsterdam, 2006)

——, 'Organisation stratégique et bénéfices économiques: Les garnisons à Gorinchem et Doesburg pendant la révolte des Pays-Bas (1572–1648)', in: Philippe Bragard a.o. (eds), *L'armée et la ville dans l'Europe du nord et du Nord-Ouest: Du XVe siècle à nos jours* (Louvain, 2006), pp. 275–89

——, 'War and garrison towns in the Dutch Republic: the cases of Gorinchem and Doesburg (c. 1570-c. 1660)', *Urban History* 36 (2009), pp. 3–23

Vermeir, René, *In staat van oorlog: Filips IV en de Zuidelijke Nederlanden, 1629–1648* (Maastricht, 2001)

Vogel, Hans, 'Arms production and exports in the Dutch Republic, 1600–1650', in: Marco van der Hoeven (ed.), *Exercise of Arms: Warfare in the Netherlands 1568–1648* (Leiden 1988), pp. 197–210

——, 'De republiek als wapenexporteur 1600–1650', in: J.P. Puype and M. van der Hoeven (eds), *Het arsenaal van de wereld: De Nederlandse wapenhandel in de Gouden eeuw* (Amsterdam, 1993), pp. 13–21

Von Grimmelshausen, Johann Jakob Christoffel (translated by Monte Aclair), *Simplicius Simplicissimus* (New York and London, 1986)

Vorsters, S.A., *Het beleg en de overgave van Breda*, Vol. 1 (Breda, 1993)

Vries, Peer, 'Governing growth: a comparative analysis of the role of the state in the rise of the West', *Journal of World History* 13 (2002), pp. 67–138

Wagenaar, Pieter, 'De waardgelders of Den Haag', in: van der Hoeven (ed.), *Exercise of Arms: Warfare in the Netherlands 1568–1648* (Leiden, 1988), pp. 211–30

Wallerstein, Immanuel, *The Modern World-System. Vol. II: Mercantilism and the Consolidation of the European World-Economy, 1600–1750* (New York, 1980)

Wätjen, Hermann, *Das holländische Kolonialreich in Brasilien: Ein Kapitel aus der Kolonialgeschichte des 17. Jahrhunderts* (Gotha, 1921)

Watson, Ian Bruce, 'Fortifications and the "idea" of force in early English East India Company relations with India', *Past and Present* 88 (1980), pp. 70–87

Weber, Max (H.H. Gerth and C. Wright Mills, ed.), *From Max Weber: Essays in Sociology* (New York, 1946)

Wegman, C.J. and R.M.A. Wegman, *Westerwolders en hun woningbezit van 1568 tot 1829*, Vols. I-VI (Wierden, 1991–2004)

——, *Het kerspel Wedde* (Wierden, 2004)

Weir, William R., *Turning Points in Military History* (New York, 2005)

Westera, L.D., 'De geschutsgieterij in de Republiek', in: Clé Lesger and Leo Noordegraaf (eds), *Ondernemers en bestuurders: Economie en politiek in de Noordelijke Nederlanden in de late middeleeuwen en vroegmoderne tijd* (Amsterdam, 1999), pp. 575–602

Westra, Frans, *Nederlandse ingenieurs en de fortificatiewerken in het eerste tijdperk van de Tachtigjarige Oorlog, 1573–1604* (Groningen, 1992)

Wheeler, James Scott, *The Making of a World Power: War and the Military Revolution in Seventeenth-Century England* (Stroud, 1999)

White, Lorraine, 'The experience of Spain's early modern soldiers: combat, welfare and violence', *War in History* 9 (2002), pp. 1–38

Wijffels, Alan and Ivo van Loo, 'Zealand privateering and the Anglo-Spanish peace treaty of 1630: the admiralty proceedings in the case Le Clercq c. Lopez Fernandez', in: B.C.M. Jacobs and E.C. Coppens (eds), *Een rijk gerecht: Opstellen aangeboden aan Prof. Mr. P.L. Nève* (Nijmegen, 1998), pp. 635–74

Wijn, J.W., *Het krijgswezen in den tijd van Prins Maurits* (Utrecht, 1934)

——, 'Military forces and warfare, 1610–48', in: J.P. Cooper (ed.), *The New Cambridge Modern History*, Vol. 4 (Cambridge, 1970), pp. 202–25

Willemsen, R., *Enkhuizen tijdens de Republiek: Een economisch-historisch onderzoek naar stad en samenleving van de 16e tot de 19e eeuw* (Hilversum, 1988)

Wilson, Charles, *England's Apprenticeship 1603–1763* (London, 1965)

——, *Economic History and the Historian* (New York, 1969)

Wilson, Peter H., *War, State and Society in Württemberg, 1677–1793* (Cambridge, 1995)

——, 'German women and war, 1500–1800', *War in History* 3 (1996), pp. 127–60

——, *The Thirty Years War: Europe's Tragedy* (Cambridge, Mass., 2009)

Wolf, Eric, *Europe and the People Without History* (Berkeley CA, 1982)

Woltjer, J.J., *Tussen vrijheidsstrijd en burgeroorlog: over de Nederlandse Opstand 1555–1580* (Amsterdam, 1994)

Wood, John B., *The King's Army: Warfare, Soldiers and Society during the Wars of Religion in France, 1562–1576* (Cambridge, 2000)

Yntema, Richard, 'Entrepreneurship and technological change in Holland's brewing industry, 1500–1580', in: L. Noordegraaf and C. Lesger (eds), *Entrepreneurs and Entrepreneurship in Early Modern times: Merchants and Industrialists within the Orbit of the Dutch Staple Market* (The Hague, 1995), pp. 185–201

Zagorin, Perez, *Rebels and Rulers, 1500–1660. Volume II. Provincial Rebellion: Revolutionary civil wars, 1560–1660* (Cambridge, 1982)

Zandvliet, Kees, *Mapping for Money: Maps, Plans and Topographic Paintings and their Role in Dutch Overseas Expansion during the 16th and 17th Centuries* (Amsterdam, 1998)

Zuijderduijn, Jaco, *Medieval Capital Markets: Markets for Renten, State Formation and Private Investment in Holland (1300–1550)* (Leiden, 2009)

Zwitzer, H.L., *De militie van den staat: Het leger van de Republiek der Verenigde Nederlanden* (Amsterdam, 1991)

——, 'De soldaat', in: H.M. Beliën, A.Th. van Deursen and G.J. van Setten (eds), *Gestalten van de Gouden Eeuw: Een Hollands groepsportret* (Amsterdam, 1995)

Index